MW01169832

Experience Sampling Method

Experience Sampling Method

Measuring the Quality of Everyday Life

Joel M. Hektner
North Dakota State University

Jennifer A. Schmidt
Northern Illinois University

Mihaly Csikszentmihalyi
Claremont Graduate University

SAGE Publications
Thousand Oaks ▪ London ▪ New Delhi

Copyright © 2007 by Sage Publications, Inc.

All rights reserved. No part of this book may be reproduced or utilized in any form or by any means, electronic or mechanical, including photocopying, recording, or by any information storage and retrieval system, without permission in writing from the publisher.

For information:

Sage Publications, Inc.
2455 Teller Road
Thousand Oaks, California 91320
E-mail: order@sagepub.com

Sage Publications Ltd.
1 Oliver's Yard
55 City Road
London EC1Y 1SP
United Kingdom

Sage Publications India Pvt. Ltd.
B-42, Panchsheel Enclave
Post Box 4109
New Delhi 110 017 India

Printed in the United States of America.

Library of Congress Cataloging-in-Publication Data

Hektner, Joel M.
Experience sampling method: measuring the quality of everyday life / Joel M. Hektner, Jennifer A. Schmidt, Mihaly Csikszentmihalyi.
    p. cm.
Includes bibliographical references (p.) and index.
    ISBN 1-4129-4923-8 (cloth) — ISBN 1-4129-2557-6 (pbk.) 1. Experiential research. 2. Psychology—Research—Methodology. I. Schmidt, Jennifer A. II. Csikszentmihalyi, Mihaly. III. Title.
    BF76.6.E94H45 2007
    150.72'3—dc22   2006004829

This book is printed on acid-free paper.

06   07   08   09   10   10   9   8   7   6   5   4   3   2   1

Acquisitions Editor:	Lisa Cuevas Shaw
Editorial Assistant:	Karen Greene
Project Editor:	Tracy Alpern
Associate Editor:	Margo Crouppen
Copy Editor:	Amy Freitag, Four Lakes Colorgraphics
Proofreader:	Sue Irwin
Typesetter:	C&M Digitals (P) Ltd.
Indexer:	Maria Sosnowski
Cover Designer:	Candice Harman

Contents

List of Tables and Figures

Acknowledgments

We would like to extend our gratitude to Barbara Schneider at Michigan State University, University of Chicago, and NORC for her enthusiastic encouragement for us to write this book and for her generosity in allowing us to include instruments and coding schemes from her studies in this volume. We thank Lisa Feldman Barrett at Boston College for her extraordinarily helpful comments on an earlier draft of this book; her comments vastly improved the manuscript. We thank Antonella Delle Fave from the University of Milan for contributing Chapter 2 of this volume. Many thanks to our student assistants for their countless hours spent tracking down original sources, organizing references, and proofreading text: Lisa Johnson at Northern Illinois and Susan Ostby, Daniel Moen, Jess Bartelt, Victoria Hogen, and Caroline Homan at North Dakota State University. Finally, a special thanks to our families—Tony and Zoe (J. S.); Kristin, Ben and Owen (J. H.); and Isabella (M.C.) for their patience in this long process.

PART I

The Origins of ESM

1

Epistemological Foundations for the Measurement of Experience

This volume is intended as a guide for social scientists who are interested in doing research about the quality of people's everyday lives—of what they do and how they feel about it. In some respects it is a textbook that provides step-by-step instructions on how to proceed; but it is also an exciting journey into intellectual territory unfamiliar to most readers.

The technology on which this research method is based has changed extensively over the past 30 years, moving from pagers to programmable watches, to two-way "personal assistants" to solicit respondents' answers at random moments of the day. However, the basic features of the method have remained essentially the same since its inception in the 1970s and, with appropriate changes dictated by technological advances, are likely to remain the same in the future as well.

The information presented in these pages gives an intimate and exhaustive account of how people go about their daily existence. Thus it can serve as an introduction to this fascinating and understudied topic, even for those who do not intend to research it themselves or for those who are not professionally involved in the study of human behavior. More specifically, Part I deals with the importance of experience in human psychology and should be of interest to social scientists in general. Part II provides the psychometric information necessary to evaluate the reliability and validity of the measurements and is addressed primarily to investigators interested in applying the method to their own research. Part III presents a sampler of findings as an indication of the kind of questions that such studies can answer, and it should intrigue anyone interested in how people live and in how they feel about it.

What is common to the approaches described in this book is that they study *experience* in the naturally occurring contexts of everyday life. By experience we mean any of the contents of consciousness: thoughts, feelings, sensations. Whatever I become aware of as I drive from home to work will constitute my experience of commuting—an experience that in some ways will be different each day, yet have some common characteristics that are distinctly different from other aspects of my life, such as having breakfast or working at the office. How people feel about their lives is an important datum for many of the social and behavioral sciences: It has been studied by epidemiologists; by clinicians concerned with addictions and depression; and by researchers interested in work, education, and family relations. Although of interest to all of the social sciences, the quality of experience is fundamentally a problem for psychologists, so we should start by considering what this one discipline may have to say about the study of experiences.

A Systematic Phenomenology

Psychology has sometimes been described as a hybrid offspring of philosophy and natural science (Leahey, 1997). The outcome of this mixed ancestry has been a continuing tension between subjective and objective approaches to the study of psychological phenomena. On the one hand we have clinical and humanistic psychology, which privileges subjective experience and personal meaning; on the other are the more rigorous approaches of behavioral, biological, cognitive, and social psychology, which tend to recognize as valid data only results of controlled experiments. What normal people typically do and feel in their natural environments has been largely ignored by both approaches. Yet psychology will not become a complete science unless it provides an accurate mapping of everyday life in all its complexity, drawing equally on subjective and objective approaches.

One attempt in this direction has been the *systematic phenomenology* developed at the University of Chicago in the past 30 years (Csikszentmihalyi, 2000, pp. ix–xxviii). This line of research was in part inspired by the "pure" phenomenology advocated by the German philosopher Edmund Husserl, who reminded us that the only things we can really know are the events represented in our individual stream of consciousness. Although he did not go as far as doubting the existence of objects outside the mind, Husserl advocated the radical methodological step of "bracketing" the existence of material entities such as stars, molecules, bodily processes, or anything else. By bracketing he meant not worrying about their existence but instead focusing on how they are perceived and represented in consciousness. Therefore, pure phenomenology is the mirror image of radical behaviorism. The behaviorist concerns himself only with overt actions and consigns all mental processes to a "black box"; whereas the phenomenologist is concerned only with mental processes and places everything else inside brackets that are the equivalent of a black box.

For example, a biochemist may understand hunger as a physiological process dependent on a shortage of sugar in the blood and consequent neurological responses. But a phenomenologist does not need to know what is happening at this level—he can bracket the physiological processes and be concerned only with how a person *experiences* hunger—how he describes its effects to himself and to others. We generally use both of these perspectives in everyday life, shifting moment-by-moment from one to the other. When we look at other people we tend to be behaviorists, paying attention to what they *do* and largely ignoring what might be going on in their consciousness. But when we turn attention inward we become phenomenologists, concerned primarily with how we feel rather than with what we do.

Of course, like all methods, phenomenology has its limitations. The way we represent events in consciousness is based on cognitive schemata that are partly inherited and partly learned and based on linguistic conventions and idiosyncratic modes of expression. Consequently what we think or feel about events can easily change as the filters we use to interpret them change. And we can never hope to get at the real events in someone else's consciousness, only at their pictures mediated by the accounts of the experiencing individual. Nevertheless, Husserl's foregrounding of the stream of consciousness as the subject matter of philosophy has been a welcome breakthrough, one that is also extremely relevant to psychology.

If one takes this approach, attentional processes acquire a fundamental importance. What we pay attention to, for how long, and how intensely will determine the content of consciousness and, hence, our experience of the world. Here phenomenology connects with the pragmatism of William James, who held that the paramount question of psychology is how a person's attention is allocated. The content of a person's life can be seen as the sum of billions of *experiences*—bits of information he or she has processed across the span of years (James, 1890).

But attention is an extremely scarce resource. Out of potentially thousands of things to notice, we cannot be aware of more than a few at a time. Yet every conscious act requires attention: Even everyday routines such as showering, dressing, having breakfast, and driving to work require that we allocate attentional resources to it. Therefore we may think of attention as the *psychic energy* required to do the "work" of living. At the same time, it is through this psychic energy that we experience what living consists of. If such is the case, the main methodological challenge is to develop a reliable measure of the events occurring in the stream of consciousness over time (Csikszentmihalyi, 1978; Csikszentmihalyi & Csikszentmihalyi, 1988). It is as a response to this challenge that the Experience Sampling Method (ESM) was devised.

The measurement of experience made possible by ESM can be called a *systematic phenomenology* in that it departs from pure phenomenology by combining a focus on lived experience with an attempt to use the tools of empirical investigation—including available technologies, research designs, and statistical analyses. Were Husserl still alive, he would probably recoil at such a nomothetic contamination of his ideographic approach. Yet knowledge evolves, and by standing on the shoulders of giants one might see views that the giants themselves could not perceive.

The Experience Sampling Method

ESM is a means for collecting information about both the context and content of the daily life of individuals. This purpose is shared by other methods, but the unique advantage of ESM is its ability to capture daily life as it is directly perceived from one moment to the next, affording an opportunity to examine fluctuations in the stream of consciousness and the links between the external context and the contents of the mind. The method achieves this degree of immediacy by asking individuals to provide written responses to both open- and closed-ended questions at several random points throughout each day of a normal week, whenever a signaling device—a pager or a Palm Pilot—prompts them to respond. The questions can be fully tailored to the interests and goals of the researcher but generally include queries focused on physical context (location, time of day), social context (number and description of others sharing the moment), activities, thoughts, feelings, and cognitive and motivational self-appraisals.

A more thorough understanding of the ESM can be derived from comparisons of the method to other means of data collection. In a naturalistic behavioral observation, information is obtained about the activities of people and the contexts within which these activities occur, but no information is gained on how people are actually experiencing those activities and contexts. The cognitive and affective dimensions of experience are lost. Further, observers either are limited to studying only public activities or, when studying more private behavior, must consider how their presence is influencing the behavior they are observing.

Asking individuals to complete diaries of their experiences removes both of these problems and potentially allows for the gathering of perceptions, thoughts, and feelings, as well as respondents' behavior and contexts. However, diaries have rarely been used to provide reports of the subjective dimensions of experience. Major diary studies have typically focused on activity and time use (Hochschild, 1989; Robinson, 1977; Wheeler & Reis, 1991). Even for this limited purpose, diaries may not be the most accurate method of data collection. How individuals reconstruct episodic memories calls into question the accuracy of recollected reports of experiences (Yarmey, 1979).

ESM combines the ecological validity of naturalistic behavioral observation with the nonintrusive nature of diaries and the precision of scaled questionnaire measures. By sampling experience the moment it occurs, it avoids the potential distortions associated with the use of daily or weekly retrospective diaries. Of course, the method is not without its limitations. One major drawback is the demands it imposes on respondents, a burden that contributes to self-selection bias and selective nonresponse (Mulligan, Schneider, & Wolfe, 2000; Zuzanek, 1999). Another consideration is its high cost of implementation. Nevertheless, these drawbacks are well worth the richness of the data obtained. For more extensive discussions of the strengths and limitations of ESM, see Alliger and Williams (1993) and Csikszentmihalyi and Larson (1987), as well as the next few chapters.

A Brief History

The first studies using pagers activated by electronic signals transmitted at random times from a central radio station were conducted in the laboratory of coauthor Mihaly Csikszentmihalyi at the Committee on Human Development of the University of Chicago in the early 1970s. The original intent was to study "flow" experiences in everyday life. At first we asked informants to write down into diaries what they had done during the day and what the most enjoyable moments had been. However, we were soon disillusioned by the dry and generalized nature of such reports. It was obvious that people summarized the events of the day without much discrimination, according to predictable scripts. How could one obtain fresh accounts of cross sections from the stream of consciousness, short of following respondents throughout the day, which would be extremely intrusive and expensive? At the time we asked this question, certain categories of workers—physicians, plumbers, policemen—began to use electronic pagers as a way of staying connected with their dispatchers. One afternoon, as we were discussing the problems of getting timely reports of everyday experience, Suzanne Prescott—then a graduate student in Human Development—and Mihaly Csikszentmihalyi began to talk about the possibility of using such pagers to trigger self-reports. We drafted a response sheet (similar to the ones still in use), rented two pagers, and tried out the method on ourselves for a week. The experience, while somewhat obtrusive at first, turned out to be quite fun—and the data produced, even from a single person, was unbelievably rich.

The method quickly acquired a life of its own. It soon became apparent that it provided a means of answering a whole range of questions about human behavior that were previously beyond the reach of researchers, and so for the next few decades, ESM studies were mainly method driven or problem driven, rather than theoretically inspired. The very first published report of ESM data was a study of adolescents conducted with Reed Larson and Suzanne Prescott, both graduate students at Chicago (Csikszentmihalyi, Larson, & Prescott, 1977). The first doctoral dissertations using the method were those of Reed Larson (1977), Patrick Mayers (1978), and Ronald Graef (1978). Since then the number of theses and publications has grown beyond reckoning; the most salient landmarks are reported in the chapters that follow.

At the time we were developing ESM in Chicago, other investigators had the idea of using the emerging beeper technology to stimulate responses. The main difference between these other attempts and the stream of ESM studies coming out of Chicago was that our competitors used the technique to answer specific questions rather than provide a full map of everyday activities and experiences. For instance John Robinson, a leading survey researcher at the University of Michigan, wanted to validate the diary responses he was getting from his subjects, and to do this he used pagers to see if the types of activities and the length of interaction reported in diary entries matched the responses to the pagers (which they did). About the same time Mark Klinger, who was interested in sexual imagery among adolescents, used pagers to ascertain how often young people thought about sex during the day. It is perfectly appropriate to use ESM in such a focused way, but as we will argue in the following paragraphs, the really unique contribution of the method is when it is used to obtain a random selection of everything a person does and experiences in everyday life.

A few years later, researchers in Germany also began to use electronic signaling and reporting devices to study behavior (Hormuth, 1986; Pawlik & Buse, 1982), and this tradition continues. A great impetus to ESM studies came when Professor Fausto Massimini of the University of Milan, Italy, and his students established close connections with our lab. During the 1980s and up to the present, a great number of collaborative cross-national ESM studies were published. Massimini's influence was important both theoretically and methodologically. He perceived ESM as a means of documenting the process of *psychological selection,* or the steps by which individuals, as they allocate attention selectively to certain activities and stimuli, collaborate in actualizing cultural evolution (see, e.g., Inghilleri, 1999).

The ESM tradition continues at the Claremont Graduate University, where our original lab moved in 1999, and at the University of Chicago under the direction of colleague Barbara Schneider. Schneider's vision and organizational ability should guarantee that this approach will not die out in the place it originally started. In the meantime, however, a great many other centers have begun to use research designs that—sometimes explicitly, sometimes not—resemble ESM. In this volume we are trying to include all studies that use electronic signals to focus on the stream of consciousness, whether they count ESM in their intellectual ancestry or not. However, given the proliferation of such studies, we are regretfully aware that some important references might be left out.

How Trustworthy Are Subjective Self-Reports?

Social scientists whose aim is to achieve objectivity are justifiably leery of putting too much credence in what people say about themselves, especially when they describe their thoughts and feelings. After all, it is well known that we tend to be biased and forgetful, that we deny and repress, that we edit our responses according to social desirability. What does it really mean when I score myself 6 on a scale where 1 corresponds to "very unhappy" and 7 to "very happy"? It could mean I actually felt the way that I think people who are "quite happy" feel according to the definition of my culture. But it could also mean that I am wrong in my assessment—what I felt is not what most people would call "happy." Or I might have been really miserable but didn't want anyone to know about it. Or I might have been just fed up with the study and circled the number at random. Unfortunately none of these possibilities can be ruled out when we try to measure a person's experience. So if that is the case, what's the point of studying something so ephemeral and elusive?

In some of the chapters that follow (especially Chapter 6), we will present ample evidence to the effect that despite the many distortions and contaminations that can mar self-reports, the data provided by ESM are surprisingly reliable and valid. For example, people rate themselves as much happier when they eat or have sex than when they clean the house or are stuck in traffic. People who at age 12 are relatively happier than other 12-year-olds are still happier at 17 than other 17-year-olds. All these psychometric issues will be discussed in detail later. At this point, it may be useful to consider three issues of a more general nature.

In the first place, a phenomenological approach assumes that subjective experience is the most objective datum we have access to and trying to reduce it to a more objective standard only decreases its objectivity. In other words, if I say I am happy—and I am not trying to deceive myself or others—then this is a fact that cannot be denied, even if a host of physiological, social, or other indicators external to my consciousness suggest otherwise. If I believe I am happy, I *am* happy—case closed. Accustomed as we are to the impressive machinery of science, it is difficult to accept the idea that nothing is as real as one's subjective experience. What we know about physics or chemistry, history or biology, we accept on faith from the experience of others—but whether we are angry or happy or hungry we know directly as incontrovertible fact.

This does not mean that ESM will always give a truthful account of a person's inner reality. It is always possible for the respondent to lie or subtly distort the account he or she gives. The argument applies to the reasonably accurate responses that most people give most of the time, as evidenced by the validity and reliability of the data. When the responses are reasonably accurate—as they usually appear to be—they give the best access we have to the inner reality of people's existence.

The second general argument for the appropriateness of ESM as a tool for assessing experience is based on the fact that a typical respondent will give between 15 and 50 "snapshots" of his or her life during a week. Thus the method allows *intra*personal as well as *inter*personal comparisons. For example, what does it mean if my average happiness score while in math classes was 5.65? It could mean either that I was generally happy doing math, or its opposite—depending on my scores in other parts of my life. For example, if I scored 6.25 in music class and 5.12 in history, we would know that I felt happier when doing math than when studying history, but less happy than when involved with music.

This feature of the ESM is so important because while there is no stable and shared metric for assessing happiness (or concentration, creativity, self-esteem, and so on) *across* persons, it is sensible to assume that there is a reasonable stable metric *within* persons. In other words, my score of 5 on happiness may express the same intensity of that emotion as your score of 4, or someone else's score of 6. But it is likely that when I scored my happiness at 5, I was less happy than when I scored it 6, and more happy than when I scored it 4. Therefore many ESM analyses use Z-scores, where raw scores are transformed so that a person's mean score on a given variable becomes 0 and scores that are one standard deviation above are 1.0, and one standard deviation below −1.0. This transformation equalizes different uses of the response scale and makes it possible to compare how different individuals deviate from their own average set-point on a given variable in different circumstances. Outside ESM there is no other method that allows such intrapersonal study of psychological variables.

A third characteristic of ESM that should be kept in mind is that it samples experiences randomly. It is easy to underestimate this feature. In fact, if one wants to use the method for a very specific purpose—such as the experience of driving on freeways, for instance—targeted rather than random responses are more appropriate. But for most purposes, random responses are more preferable. In the first place, they make it possible to estimate how much time people spend doing various activities during their waking hours. They give a relatively complete and undistorted picture of daily life, and often provide unexpected glimpses into it that one would have never anticipated. Most importantly, by using a random schedule, researchers with different questions and divergent interests can use the same data, or the same investigator can use the same data again at a later time for a different purpose. None of this would be possible if one only sampled responses at the workplace, for instance, or only when watching television or only on weekends.

What Can We Learn From ESM?

In the last analysis, even the severest critic must agree that, at the very least, ESM responses measure what the person decides to communicate about his or her inner states. When I rate my happiness at 6 on a 7-point scale, I am saying that at this moment I am willing to state that I am quite happy. Does this mean that I am *really* quite happy? We will probably never know. In real life, however, we take such verbal accounts quite seriously. We are often willing to share life and property with someone who says, "I love you," even though we really don't quite know what this other person means by "love." If your boss says "I am not happy with your work" often enough, you will get ready to start looking for a different job, even though you don't know whether the boss is really unhappy with the work you did, or she just says so out of envy or plain meanness. We could not function in a social world if we did not take seriously what others say. Of course we always have to take such communications with a healthy dose of skepticism, but by and large verbal accounts are the currency of social life.

Purists may still object that when we claim to measure concepts such as self-esteem, creativity, or happiness with ESM, we only assess pale verbal signs of the underlying complex reality. My inclination in responding to such objections is to invoke a variation on the old saying, *If something is worth doing, it's worth doing well*. Abraham Maslow once pointed out that it was equally true that *If something is not worth doing, it's not worth doing well*. Both of these sayings make sense, and we would add a third one that is also true: *If something is worth doing, it's worth doing not well*. In other words, if there is no better way of doing something that needs to be done, it's preferable to do it as well as possible—even if it isn't perfect (here another old saying comes in handy: *Perfection is the enemy of the good*). At this point, ESM, while far from perfect, is the best method for getting information on two important topics: (1) what people do all day, where, and with whom; and (2) how people report experiencing different moments in their lives, along a great variety of dimensions.

These two sources of data in turn can be used to answer an almost endless chain of further questions. For example, here are a few that have been answered by ESM studies: Do Asian American students experience studying differently from Caucasian Americans (Asakawa & Csikszentmihalyi, 1998)? Do Himalayan mountain climbers buried in their tent by an avalanche for 72 hours enjoy themselves (Bassi, 2002)? Can the frequency of physical pain in young adults be predicted by how they had experienced their middle school years (Patton, 1998)? Does the amount of material energy (e.g., electricity) we use contribute to how happy we feel (Graef, McManama, & Csikszentmihalyi, 1981)?

As these examples suggest, the range of possible applications of the method is rather extensive. Thus far, most studies have been concerned with one of the following nine major themes: (1) the psychology of adolescence, especially in educational settings; (2) the experience of work, work stress, and work satisfaction; (3) family dynamics and marital satisfaction; (4) the experience of psychopathology (e.g., eating disorders, depression, substance abuse); (5) the experience of media, especially television viewing; (6) cross-cultural comparisons of time use and quality of experience; (7) gender differences in activities and in the quality of experience; (8) solitude, friendship, and affiliation; (9) the optimal experience of flow. These and other applications of ESM will be reviewed in detail in the chapters that follow.

In fact, there are few important questions in psychology that cannot benefit from the systematic sampling of experiences. The method is not easy to use, so it should not be adopted lightly. But after one tries it once, it can become addictive. For one thing, it gives such an enormously rich and intimate perspective on people's lives. Second, the data it provides are almost infinitely generative: They suggest new ideas about new questions that can be tested with the data at hand, without needing to go into the field again. Finally, a solid sample of 100 or so respondents can generate about 4,000 responses in a week, and this database need not become obsolete. It is possible to return to it again and again with new questions in mind, and the old data can be used to test new hypotheses. A good ESM database is like a virtual laboratory that yields unique results for many years to come.

Having said this much, we are now ready to flesh out the rough sketch outlined so far. It is our hope that some who read this book will catch our excitement about ESM and perhaps be tempted to use it as a tool for pursuing their own interests. In any case, the glimpses into the human experience that the following pages afford should be intriguing to anyone curious about what it means to be alive.

2

Theoretical Foundations of ESM

This chapter will briefly describe the main theoretical frameworks underlying the study of subjective experience in the context of daily life. We will outline the basic constructs comprising these frameworks and then discuss the contributions of ESM research to the exploration of these issues. The impetus for studying the quality of subjective experience as it unfolds during real life has emerged as a result of a shift in social science research toward exploration of the *interaction* of the individual with the environment. Among the broad theoretical questions that have arisen from this perspective are the following:

- What is the impact of biological and cultural inheritance on human behavior?
- What is the relationship between psychological processes and cognitive or brain functions?
- What is the role of individuals in their interaction with their natural and cultural environment?

The following pages will offer an overview of these three broad questions and a discussion of the potential of ESM to be a source of information relevant to each of them. In each section of this chapter the theoretical constructs will be first outlined, and the contribution of ESM to their empirical investigation will subsequently be discussed. We do not intend to suggest

Authors' Note: This chapter was contributed by Antonella Delle Fave, University of Milan.

that as an investigative tool ESM is sufficient to provide definitive answers to any of the questions. Issues as complex as these require investigation using multiple perspectives and methods. In this chapter we simply wish to orient the reader to the broader theoretical issues underlying the development of ESM itself and the empirical studies that employ it.

Biology, Culture, and Daily Behavior

During the second half of the twentieth century, theoretical and empirical advances in the natural and social sciences have prompted an interdisciplinary debate about the influence of biology and culture on human behavior. Research studies have increasingly focused on either the relationship between psychological functioning and behavior or on the genetic and environmental influences on human action.

Cross-Cultural Studies

For decades, research in psychology could be characterized by the study of a universal *Homo Psychologicus,* built in European and North American laboratories, showing strictly Western behavioral features. More recent evidence in a variety of domains has led to the development of a psychology that seeks to take cultural influences into account. One such attempt is the development of cross-cultural psychology. A goal of cross-cultural psychology is to investigate the influence of culture-specific norms, habits, and beliefs on psychological functioning and development. Only after having assessed the extent and quality of this influence, cross-cultural psychology aims at identifying universal features that most individuals share, beyond or notwithstanding cultural differences, and that are most likely related to our common biological inheritance (Berry et al., 1997). From a different perspective, cultural psychology (Cole, 1996; Stigler, Schweder, & Herdt, 1990) and indigenous psychologies (Kim & Berry, 1993) investigate the interaction between individuals and context within each culture, considered on its own, thus avoiding cross-cultural comparisons and the search for universals. Individual behavior is analyzed only within the context of the philosophical, religious, historical, and psychological knowledge and beliefs developed within the culture to which participants belong.

The Evolutionary Perspective

Other research approaches have been investigating the biological and cultural roots of individual and group behavior within an evolutionary framework. Like every other living species, humans show adaptive biological features that result from natural selection and that are genetically transmitted across generations because they enhance individual fitness (i.e., the ability to survive and to reproduce in a given natural environment). More specifically, three emergent traits have been crucial for our survival and adaptation: (1) the upright standing position, which frees upper limbs from having to support movement; (2) the opposable thumb, which improves the quality and precision of hand movements; and (3) the increase in size and complexity of cortical areas, which support refined and flexible patterns of information processing. The joint contribution of these traits enables human beings to observe and describe themselves and the world and to facilitate the development of their own culture. Humans began creating artifacts, social norms, and cultural rules that increased our species' flexibility and ability to cope with the demands of the environment. Several theories have been developed to explain the impact of such evolutionary shifts on human behavior.

Sociobiology and evolutionary psychology emphasize the prominent role of biological fitness in directing human actions: behavior has the ultimate function of ensuring genes' survival and transmission. Within this approach, the development of culture provided individuals with epigenetic rules, strategies, and instruments that enhanced adaptation in our ancestral natural environment. The mind itself emerged as an adapted organ, a flexible learning machine that increased the chances of human survival and reproduction during evolutionary history (Barkow, Cosmides, & Tooby, 1992; Buss, 1994; Changeux & Chavaillon, 1995; Nicholson, 1997; Wilson, 1975).

Other evolutionary approaches highlight the inextricable interplay of biology and culture in human behavior and development. This assumption gave impulse to theories and models based on the concept of coevolution: biology and culture are two different but mutually interacting inheritance systems (Boyd & Richerson, 1985, 1990; Durham, 1991; Laland, Kumm, & Feldman, 1995). Cultural information units, defined as *memes* (Dawkins, 1976), are stored in the human central nervous system as the result of social learning and direct interaction with the environment as well as in material and symbolic artifacts. Cultures change in time according to evolution patterns: some memes are selectively transmitted across generations, some others become extinct in that they prove to be unfit for survival in that environment (Delle Fave & Massimini, 1999; Richerson & Boyd, 1978). Culture as an evolving system shows a higher flexibility in comparison with biology (Mundinger, 1980). Artifacts allow memes to survive their human carriers. Memes are memorized and transmitted through various coding systems: natural languages, mathematical formulas, arts, rituals, and material tools. Individuals create, reproduce, and spread memes throughout their life span;

memes are spread much faster than genes and in a potentially unlimited amount. Finally, cultural variation does not occur through random mutations and passive change in memes' frequency under adaptive pressures. Rather, cultural changes are often intentionally developed and spread through innovation and social transmission (Laland, Odling-Smee, & Feldman, 2000). Thanks to our ability to build mental representations of the world, to modify the environment, to plan, to solve complex problems, and to store information in artifacts, humans survived in every ecological niche (Diamond, 1997). Ultimately, human communities are much more influenced by our cultural inheritance than by our biological one. Cultural norms, values, beliefs, and artifacts substantially contribute to shape individual and group behaviors (Massimini, 1982; Rokeach, 1974; Schwartz & Bilsky, 1987).

ESM and the Online Analysis of Individual-Environment Interaction

Not surprisingly, the biological and cultural influences on human behavior specified by the cross-cultural and evolutionary domains are extremely different to address empirically. It has become clear, however, that researchers in psychology cannot ignore these factors in their investigations: individual daily behavior is strongly shaped by biological and cultural factors. ESM offers a new perspective in the analysis of these issues. The online and repeated assessment of individual behavior and experience in the daily context provides glimpses into the real-life habits of a human community that are otherwise difficult to detect in retrospective studies or through single administration research instruments. Participants describe themselves while interacting with their environment, be it social, material, or natural. They report their experience during activities strictly related to biology, such as eating and resting, or to culture, such as driving a car, watching TV, or reading a book.

Researchers can select participants for ESM studies according to biological traits. They can investigate how peculiar physical constraints, such as spinal injuries, visual or hearing impairments, chronic diseases, or acute disorders influence daily experience, behavior, and social relations. They can construct experimental settings where ESM is used to monitor the effects of sleep modifications or drug administration on the quality of experience and behavior. In Chapter 13 we review the many ways ESM has been used to capture the quality of daily experience among people with psychiatric diagnoses, eating disorders, drug addictions, and physical impairments. Implications for clinical and psychosocial intervention will be also highlighted.

Researchers can also focus on cultural factors. They can decide to analyze the amount of time people devote to specific activities in the domains of work, education, leisure, or religion. They can explore the quality and frequency of daily interactions, according to social roles, hierarchical versus peer relations, face-to-face versus artifact-mediated communication, and their influence on participants' life and experience. One can explore the impact of technology and tool use on daily experience and can examine links between the allocation of attention and psychic resources and the types of artifacts produced by a particular culture. As described in Chapters 10, 11, and 12, these issues have been explored through ESM in single-culture investigations and in cross-cultural comparisons as well.

Finally, researchers can use ESM to investigate the interplay between biological and cultural influences at the individual level. For example, studies can be conducted on gender differences in the perceived quality of daily experience. Gender is a typical biocultural issue. In every society it deeply influences individuals' identity building, as well as individuals' access to social roles and to opportunities for development and skill cultivation. Even in egalitarian Western societies, women and men often differ in daily time budget and preferentially selected activities and interests. A peculiar domain where gender differences in daily life and subjective experience most clearly emerge is represented by parenthood, child rearing, and family relationships. Chapters 8 and 9 will discuss findings from ESM studies aimed at investigating gender-related issues, the daily experience of parents and children, as well as the impact of pregnancy and parenthood on fathers and mothers from a longitudinal perspective.

Subjective Experience in Context: The Interplay of Psychological Processes and Cognitive Functions

Most current researchers investigating human behavior, regardless of their theoretical approach, recognize that individuals play an active role in their interaction with the environment. Individuals grow within a developmental niche (Super & Harkness, 1986) that includes the natural environment, the psychology of the caregivers, and the broader cultural set of memes and social interaction rules. Through direct experience, socialization, and cultural learning they acquire new information. As a result, they can develop adaptive behaviors and engage in meaningful goal-directed activities reflecting their culture's values (Gauvain, 1995). But they can also modify their environment, contributing to *niche construction* (Laland et al., 2000); they can create new memes by introducing innovation in their culture (Simonton, 1999).

Several biocultural models assume that biological heritage, culture, and individuals represent three distinct and interacting systems: they are interconnected through mutual influences, but none of them is entirely determined by the others (Massimini, 1982; Richerson & Boyd, 1978). Culture basically originates in the minds of people, as new ideas or solutions to problems. Anthropological studies show that dyads and groups of individuals co-construct their culture through learning and mutual interaction (King, 2000).

Attention and Psychological Selection

Day by day and throughout their life span, individuals reproduce a limited number of information units within their inheritance systems. At the biological level, they can intentionally restrict their potential for biological reproduction, fix the number of children they desire, and select their mating partners. At the cultural level, they differentially reproduce and transmit a subset of the memes available in the environment, in terms of activities, interests, and political and moral beliefs. Selection of memes can be more or less strictly controlled by culture itself. For example, in highly stratified groups, access to knowledge and social roles depends on the hierarchy status of the individuals; gender stratification restrains women from getting involved in activities that are considered men's domain. However, in most cultures each person is provided with a relatively wide range of meme alternatives. Therefore, a third selection process can be described at the individual level: it has been labeled *psychological selection* (Csikszentmihalyi & Massimini, 1985; Massimini, Inghilleri, & Delle Fave, 1996). Individuals represent the living selectors of biological and cultural information. Through active learning and experience they differentially acquire, elaborate, and transmit genes and memes.

Psychological selection unfolds from a single core function: attention (Csikszentmihalyi, 1978). Being a limited resource, attention compels individuals to focus on a restricted number of environmental or internal stimuli per time unit. Therefore, each person effectively perceives only a small part of the available information, subsequently processing and organizing it for future use and transmission.

Psychological Selection and Subjective Experience

Psychological selection is guided by the quality of experience *subjectively* perceived in the interaction with the environment. Individuals evaluate their own experience from a subjective perspective: we can observe ourselves through an endopsychical perceptual system (Shaffer, 1968) that allows us to assess our internal states and to describe them. We do this from a unique point of view, moving from our own experience of what an emotion or a thought is (Gomes, 1995).

A procedure such as ESM, based on the repeated sampling of subjective experience, can provide information on these processes. It allows researchers to calculate for each participant a "mean subjective evaluation" of each emotional, motivational, and cognitive component of the experience and to analyze the fluctuations of each variable's values around this subjective mean. We can examine how a person's experience of an ordinary activity (e.g., housework) varies depending on her companionship at the time (e.g., being alone vs. with a spouse or children). We can explore fluctuations in experience as they relate to other contextual factors like time of day or content of thoughts. This fine-tuned analysis takes us into the microlevel dynamics of the psychological processes underlying the integration of internal and external information and the subjective construction of self and world representations.

Kunnen and Bosma (1996) argue that subjective experience should be taken as the starting point in the investigation of individual development and goals as well. Kegan (1994) pointed out that, in time, individuals can attribute different meanings to the same situation according to progressively more complex principles in organizing experience. The longitudinal use of ESM can shed light on the dynamics of psychological selection in the long run and on the meaning-making process—that is, the way in which people actively organize their own experience in time (Kunnen & Bosma, 2000). As a complement to in-depth interviews and questionnaires exploring life histories, personality traits, and attitudes, longitudinal ESM sampling can shed light on the mechanisms and contents of the individual *life theme*, which comprises the overall goals and lifelong targets each person uniquely selects for preferential cultivation throughout life (Csikszentmihalyi & Beattie, 1979). The moment-by-moment building of a life theme through preferential activity selection can be detected. The quality of experience associated with life-theme related activities can be analyzed and compared with the experience reported during other daily situations.

Finally, individuals differ from one another in their experience of similar situations. ESM can help detect such differences through the comparison of individuals' daily experience fluctuations as a whole, as well as through more analytic comparative analysis of social contexts, activities, and emotional and motivational patterns. Of course, the interplay between biocultural background and individual features has to be taken into account in all these investigations. Examples of such investigations are presented in Chapter 8, where men's and women's experiences of family life are examined.

Complexity and Information Processing

A growing number of research studies analyze human beings as open living systems, exchanging information with the environment throughout their lives. As living systems, humans show two peculiar traits: a far-from-equilibrium (or negentropic) energetic pattern (Prigogine, 1980; Prigogine & Stengers, 1984) and autopoiesis, or self-organization ability (Maturana, 1975; Maturana & Varela, 1986). These traits promote complexity that is progressively increasing levels of order and integration in the systems' internal information. Both at the biological and psychological levels, the individual attains higher levels of complexity through information exchange with the environment. Complexity and related concepts have proven to be heuristically relevant in the analysis of human communities and social organizations as well (Eldredge & Grene, 1992; Khalil & Boulding, 1996).

Neuroscience Perspectives on Complexity

Complexity is a central concept in current neuroscience studies investigating the relations between brain and mind functions. From the perspective of neurophysiology, Tononi and Edelman (1998) describe consciousness as a process emerging from *dynamic cores,* functional clusters of neurons characterized by integration and differentiation at the same time. Each conscious experience results from the moment-by-moment integration of specific groups of neurons that selectively interact through "a rich and diverse repertoire of neural activity patterns" (p. 1848). The specific state of consciousness thus arising is one among billions of others, and in this sense it represents a specific piece of information, a peculiar configuration of neural activities that reduces uncertainty and that therefore can be considered an ordered and negentropic entity.

From a neurobiological point of view, Joseph LeDoux (2002) stresses the necessity of considering experience as a unitary complex, emerging from the interplay between emotions, motivations, and cognitions (not necessarily arising from sensorial inputs). Experience biologically consists of networks of neural connections modulated by chemical transmitters. It does not exactly correspond to the external world; rather, it is a subjective representation and reconstruction of the world, based on memories and information whose original acquisition was—in its turn—influenced by the ongoing emotional, motivational, and cognitive state of the individual.

However, complexity is not a recent concept in the study of conscious experience and its biological correlates. William James stated that evolution turned the brain into an "instrument of possibilities, characterized by plasticity, dynamic structure, and a lower dependence from environmental stimuli" (1890, vol. 1, p. 689). James identified two different forms of consciousness: the first is the sensational, or reproductive, consciousness (Shapiro, 1997), common to all mammalians and related to *empirical knowledge.* The learning process promotes the stabilization of reactions to environmental stimuli that repeatedly occur, and the individual acquires new behavioral patterns in this way that can be carried out when the same or similar stimuli arise. The second form, the relating or productive consciousness (Shapiro, 1997), implies the emergence of new knowledge from inside the individual, through new patterns of integration and connection between information units previously acquired. Productive consciousness generates *relational knowledge* about the world. It promotes world reconstruction and interpretation through new configurations of information that can be used to solve new problems, build new artifacts, and develop new ideas.

ESM and the Exploration of the Dynamic Complexity of Experience

Recent discoveries in the various fields of neurosciences lead us as psychologists to agree with Chalmers that "experience may arise from the physical, but it is not entailed by the physical" (1995, p. 208). Although different disciplines focus on different levels of analysis in their investigation of consciousness, research studies within the complexity framework emphasize a basic outcome of conscious experience: transformation (Pribram, 1996). Environmental stimuli provide individuals with sensorial information, which is transformed into neural activity and later on into connections between cerebral areas through the development of new synapses. These connections promote the functional configuration of dynamic cores, which represent the physiological correlates of consciousness. Neither connections nor dynamic cores are stable entities: they change with time and with the integration of new information (be it empirical or relational knowledge). Starting from these premises, psychologists who investigate conscious experience have to take into account two factors: experience is idiosyncratic, in that it is related to the specific biological configuration of each individual, and it undergoes ceaseless changes according to the progressive increase in individual's complexity.

From this perspective, the repeated assessments of the quality of experience gathered through ESM can help investigate the structurally dynamic nature of experience itself. This cannot be obtained through single measurements. The importance of gathering online data on the quality of experience is that such a method tries to circumscribe one of the most well-known errors of our information processing: distortion of memories. James already stated that recall is imprecise because it is partial and often lacking the emotional components of the past experience. After more than one century, advances in psychology and neurobiology show that we memorize only parts of the experience, we interpret them and we associate them with previous similar situations. This is one of the major problems of recalling, especially when the memory should be as precise as possible, as it happens for testimonies of eyewitnesses in trials (LeDoux, 2002).

Capturing the Interplay of Experience Components

Emotions, motivations, and cognitive processes coexist and contribute to experience in every moment of our life. However, the systematic storage of this whole set of information and the activation of the corresponding neuronal circuits would be useless and energy-consuming when performed for routine daily activities and situations. On the other hand, analytical data on moment-by-moment fluctuations of the experience and on the interplay of its various components are useful to better understand the psychological aspects of mind-brain functioning. We cannot rely on retrospective reports because of the previously mentioned distortions toward an "average" experience. The only way to capture emotions, motivations, and cognitive processes is by asking people to describe them at the moment they occur. Most parts of daily life consist of apparently irrelevant episodes and experiences, but psychological selection operates on them, and its long-term outcomes are built on this microlevel information.

Interaction of Individuals and Environments

In the field of motivation studies, the traditional approaches centered on material rewards and incentive-based models have been gradually supplanted by putting greater emphasis on the active and creative role of the individual. Abraham Maslow (1968) introduced the concept of self-actualization, a need that stems from the person's subjective perception of her own potentials and meanings. Maslow stressed the human capability to set goals that foster the implementation of complexity at the psychological and behavioral levels. More recently, Deci and Ryan (1985) developed the theory of self-determination, centered on the tendency to pursue intrinsically motivated needs: competence, autonomy, and relatedness. These needs do not necessarily provide individuals with extrinsic or material rewards. Rather, they promote the refinement of skills and competence in specific domains, the expansion of the interpersonal network, a creative and autonomous interaction with the environment, and well-being (Ryan & Deci, 2000). Moreover, several studies in this field have pointed out that extrinsic rewards undermine the quality of performance in otherwise intrinsically motivated activities (Deci, Koestner, & Ryan, 1999). These studies highlight the relevance of self-selected goals and meanings in supporting development and personal growth. Moreover, they identify autonomy, creativity, and potential for innovation as structural components of human autopoiesis.

Other researchers have recently explored motivation from a more cognitive perspective. Intentional goal setting and its influence on identity development have been investigated in adolescents and young adults (Nurmi, 1993; Salmela-Aro & Nurmi, 1997). The facilitating role of implementation intentions in goal-directed behavior and the influence of mindset, self-efficacy, and self-esteem on setting and implementing goals have been explored in various life domains (Gollwitzer, 1999; Taylor & Gollwitzer, 1995).

ESM and the Online Study of Motivations

As concerns the study of motivation, ESM allows researchers to analyze its moment-by-moment typology and intensity. In each ESM form, participants are invited to report how much they feel free, involved, and willing to do the present activity. They can also provide qualitative descriptions of short- and long-term goals associated with the current situation. This information sheds light on the meanings that each person subjectively attributes to daily activities and events. It also enables researchers to explore the interplay between motivation and other components of experience.

ESM allows researchers to dynamically investigate motivation's daily fluctuations, detecting the stability or variation of motivational patterns in specific daily tasks. For example, an activity that is most often reported as intrinsically rewarding can be sometimes described as compulsory or boring, depending on the external setting, the specific task, other events occurring in the day, or the emotional and cognitive components of the experience. (See Chapter 10 for examples of this pattern as seen in work and leisure activities.)

These fluctuations, especially when analyzed in longitudinal studies, provide information on the meaning individuals attach to their major daily activities. The pursuit of self-actualization and self-determined goals can be followed in its day-by-day progression, and the influence of extrinsic rewards on the quality of performance can be assessed online. The relationship between perceived motivation and the overall quality of experience can shed light on the impact of short- and long-term goals and meanings on the subjective perception of daily life.

Experience Fluctuations, Well-Being, and Development

Psychological selection is a ceaseless process that shapes an individual's life. Its consequences, however, are not limited to the person herself: as previously reported, individuals learn and transmit information to others. Therefore each person, through the replication and transmission of a specific subset of memes, and through the intentional regulation of genetic reproduction patterns, will contribute to the long-term selection of biocultural information. Daily life is the best condition for analyzing psychological selection at work, and the quality of experience people associate with daily situations represents the key information for investigating this process and its moment-by-moment outcomes.

The various theories that have flourished throughout the history of psychology, regardless of their interpretative framework, agree that individuals look for pleasure and avoid pain. Of course, we do not expect that individuals can always choose to do what they find most enjoyable. However, because attention and psychic resources are limited, we expect that during daily life people will preferentially spend their time in activities and social relations they associate with a positive experience, trying to avoid those perceived as negative.

The Investigation of Optimal Experience

Researchers started to look for the basic features of positive and negative experiences a long time before the introduction of experience sampling procedures. In particular, by means of interviews with people who devoted themselves to complex and involving activities, such as surgery or rock climbing, Csikszentmihalyi (1975) identified *Optimal Experience,* or *Flow.* Participants described it as a positive and gratifying state of consciousness. They associated it with the perception of high challenges in the task at hand and personal skills high enough to face those challenges. Participants also described flow as a situation of high concentration, involvement, enjoyment, absorption in the task, unselfconsciousness, control, and clear-cut feedback on the course of the activity. They reported getting involved in the task for its own sake, regardless of extrinsic rewards or social approval—in other words, on the basis of intrinsic motivation.

Since the first assessments of optimal experience, a large number of research studies have shown its occurrence in the life of people belonging to the most varied age groups, cultures, socioeconomic status (SES) levels, and occupational categories (Csikszentmihalyi & Csikszentmihalyi, 1988; Massimini & Delle Fave, 2000). People associate flow with various contexts: work, family, and leisure. Most daily activities potentially foster the onset of this experience. However, the situation has to be challenging enough to require an active engagement and to promote satisfaction in the use of personal skills. Data gathered among over 4,500 participants highlighted that repetitive, easy, and low-information tasks are never associated with flow, while complex activities requiring specific competencies, autonomous initiative, and focused attention are widely reported (Massimini et al., 1996).

Flow experience shows an intrinsically dynamic structure, which is embedded in the perceived match between high environmental challenges and adequate personal skills. This match is not stable: while first engaging in a new activity, for example playing music, people perceive challenges as much higher than their abilities. The cultivation of the activity progressively promotes the increase of related skills, and the person will subsequently look for more difficult challenges. This process gives rise to a sort of virtuous cycle fostering individual development and a ceaseless acquisition of new and increasingly complex information. The association of specific activities with optimal experience leads to the preferential cultivation of individual skills in those activities. Thus, flow can be considered the psychic "compass" directing psychological selection and supporting the developmental trajectory each individual constructs and follows throughout life (Delle Fave & Bassi, 2000). In this sense, it contributes to the identification and pursuit of the individual life theme. ESM can provide online information on the experiential features of flow as people experience it during their real life, thus allowing researchers to draw comparisons with retrospective descriptions of this state of consciousness. Details on the investigation of flow experience through ESM will be provided in the subsequent chapters of this volume.

ESM and Person-Centered Intervention

Several studies show that psychological selection does not automatically lead to personal growth. The ultimate result depends upon the type of activities an individual preferentially reproduces. True development means increase in complexity at the psychological level: its outcome is a creative, socially integrated, and satisfied person.

ESM can be fruitfully used to identify the typologies of experience arising during the day, their motivational, emotional, and cognitive structure, and the frequency of their daily occurrence. It can help detect recurrent associations between specific experiences and specific activities (Delle Fave & Bassi, 2000). Moreover, as previously discussed, researchers can use ESM to investigate which activities are prominently associated with optimal experience, their features and complexity, and their potential for fostering individual development in order to better understand both the optimal and the deviant anatomy of behavior (Csikszentmihalyi & Larson, 1987).

From this perspective, ESM data can be used not only for research purposes, but also for designing intervention programs in the domains of education (Csikszentmihalyi & Larson, 1984; Csikszentmihalyi, Rathunde, & Whalen, 1993), mental health (deVries, 1992; Inghilleri, 1999), rehabilitation and social maladjustment (Delle Fave & Massimini, 2000a, 2003). Some key findings obtained from these studies will be discussed throughout Part III of this volume.

A Theoretical Compass for Exploring Experience

The following chapters will describe in detail the applications of ESM in the various domains of daily life, the related methodological problems, and the strategies adopted to solve them. This chapter was developed to provide a general overview of the theoretical framework this procedure is built on. Of course, this is only one of the possible approaches to the study of experience. Some may wonder whether a "psychological truth" does exist (Smith, Harré, & Van Langenhove, 1995). We may also wonder whether it is possible to overcome cultural boundaries in order to find the "universal human being." Such a search is as old as our effort to understand reality, through philosophies, religions, and scientific constructs. As a representative of the many thinkers who—throughout the millennia—strived to achieve a comprehensive vision of human nature and destiny, we can mention Diogenes, a Greek philosopher who lived in the fourth century BC. He was described as wandering in Athens with a lamp to "search for the Man." He did not succeed in his search: he was looking for an ideal human being, free from weaknesses, cultural constraints and prejudices, and he could never find it in his environment.

Today, the availability of instruments like ESM offers the opportunity to start from the opposite side, namely the individual, and to work on a qualitative and quantitative data set based on the idiosyncratic features of each person and her subjective description of reality. ESM findings can support the implementation of models of individual optimal functioning, their application in clinical, educational, and organizational domains, the evaluation of both the objective and perceived role of environment in fostering individual autonomy, and integration. ESM studies can highlight the effectiveness of the social context in providing its members with daily opportunities for optimal experience. This can help researchers identify cultural features and trends that promote both individual development and cultural complexity. Moving from the subjective perspective, this process could lead to a better understanding of the person-environment interplay and to the design of environmental, social, and individual interventions striving for an optimal match between the needs of the person, the society, and the natural environment.

PART II

How to Measure the Quality of Everyday Life

3

Collecting the Data

The following four chapters will be of greatest interest to those readers who are considering or planning to field their own ESM study. In the pages that follow, we provide a step-by-step guide to designing, fielding, coding, and analyzing an ESM study. Readers not planning to conduct their own research may wish to skip to Chapter 7, where we begin our review of the uses of ESM research to date.

Before you begin signaling subjects, and even before you start designing questionnaires, there are a number of decisions to be made about the types of research questions to ask, the population to study, the contexts and experiences you are interested in learning about, the equipment to use, and the constraints that a particular sample population or research question might place on the study's design. In this chapter we review some of the decisions that must be made when designing an ESM study. Some of these issues are unique to experience sampling methodology, while others are more general issues in social science research that often arise in our discussions with novice ESM researchers. This chapter essentially presents, in chronological order, the different stages of designing and implementing an ESM study. This how-to begins with identifying research problems and study populations and moves on to the choice of signaling equipment and signaling schedules. We then discuss common issues that arise when designing the Experience Sampling Form (ESF). Finally, we make some practical suggestions based on our experience about procedures involved in fielding an ESM study—from recruitment and orientation to subject retention and retrieval of the data.

Designing a Study Using ESM

Of course, one of the first decisions to be made concerns whether or not ESM is an appropriate method for addressing one's research question. ESM research requires a substantial investment of time and resources on the part of researchers and participants, and we urge those considering the method to carefully determine the utility of the method for your particular research question. ESM is designed to capture individuals' representation of experience as it occurs, within the context of everyday life. It is best suited to measure dimensions of experience that are likely to be context-dependent (i.e., "How do you feel about yourself right now?") and/or are likely to fluctuate over the course of a day or week. Researchers interested in more global or retrospective perceptions (e.g., "How do you generally feel about yourself?" "How did you feel about yourself last week?") are advised to use more traditional survey methods, as ESM is not particularly well suited to provide this type of information (Conner Christensen, Feldman Barrett, Bliss-Moreau, Lebo, & Kaschub, 2003). While it is likely that momentary and global representations are related to one another, they can be distinguished from one another both conceptually and empirically (Klein, 2001). Both types of information provide important insights into human experience, but it is important that researchers understand that the strength of ESM lies in its ability to capture one's momentary, or episodic, representations rather than more global perceptions.

Type of Appropriate Problems

Assuming that ESM is the right tool for your research question, collecting data using ESM yields a tremendous amount of information about study participants. Because the method gathers data at multiple time points from multiple individuals, researchers have the ability to do both detailed studies of individual cases as well as more general analyses by aggregating across cases. ESM is designed to study simultaneously both *persons* and *situations* (Hormuth, 1983; Larson & Delespaul, 1992). In the design phases of research, it is important to keep in mind which of these types of questions you are interested in asking. In a book chapter titled "Analyzing Experience Sampling Data: A Guidebook for the Perplexed," Reed Larson and Philippe Delespaul (1992) provide a cogent discussion of research questions involving individuals, situations, and those issues that are "apt to create confusion" (p. 61) about what one intends to study.

Questions about groups of persons have the purpose of making comparisons between groups—for example, people with different traits, who come from different backgrounds, who spend their time in dramatically different ways, or who have different clinical diagnoses. Examples of "person-centered" questions that have been addressed in ESM research include: "Do adolescents have more severe mood swings than adults?" (Csikszentmihalyi & Larson, 1984); "Do Asian American students experience schoolwork differently from their European American peers?" (Asakawa & Csikszentmihalyi, 2000b); "Do individuals who work a lot experience their work differently from those who work less?" (Schmidt, Rich, & Makris, 2000); and "Are there differences between chronic mental patients and normal groups in time allocation in daily life?" (Delespaul & deVries, 1992).

Questions about situations, on the other hand, do not involve comparisons of groups of people, but rather are focused on comparisons made within individuals that examine different moments in time or different situations. In most ESM research the term *situation* can be broadly defined. These situations can refer to activities (e.g., work vs. leisure), companionship (e.g., being with friends vs. being alone), physical location (e.g., English class vs. math class), day of the week, or time of day. Previous ESM research has asked the following questions about situations: "How do different types of classroom activities affect the daily experiences of high school students?" (Shernoff, Knauth, & Makris, 2000); "How do spouses feel when they are together compared with when they are apart?" (Larson & Richards, 1994a); "How do adolescents' moods change across the day?" (Csikszentmihalyi & Larson, 1984). All of these questions compare the same individuals across different situations.

As Larson and Delespaul (1992) point out, researchers often get into trouble by specifying research questions in which it is not clear whether the inquiry is focused on persons or situations. An example they provide about a confusing research question is "Is TV viewing correlated with depression?" This confusing question can be clarified into a question about persons ("Is the amount of TV a person watches associated with the severity of that person's depression?") or into a question about situations ("Are persons more depressed when watching TV?") (p. 61). Defining one's research goal is important because it enables the design of an ESF that most effectively addresses it. Whether the research question is focused on persons or situations will, of course, also have ramifications for how the data are analyzed once they are collected. This issue will be taken up in Chapter 5.

ESM can also be used to assess the effect of experimental treatments. Although in most cases a treatment (e.g., a therapeutic intervention to alleviate tobacco addiction) would fall under the rubric of "situations," the method allows the study of interactions between person-level traits and experimental conditions. For example, one might find that therapy A alleviates dependence on tobacco for people who usually smoke alone, whereas therapy B is more effective for social smokers.

Type of Appropriate Samples

ESM has been used in studies involving diverse samples. Participants have ranged in age from 10 to 95 years old. Studies have involved physically and mentally healthy individuals, as well as schizophrenics, bulimics, substance abusers, the physically disabled, and the clinically depressed. The method has been used to study the experience of the rich and the poor. ESM research has been conducted in cultures throughout the world and has involved business people, factory workers, mountain climbers, first-time parents, and talented teenagers.

Because of the considerable effort that must be expended in an ESM study, most sample sizes are modest by social science research standards. Because of the richness of the data however, even studies with as few as 5 or 10 participants can produce enough data to be used reliably in simple statistical analyses. ESM samples are usually purposive and are not typically designed to be nationally representative. Rather, they are targeted at understanding the experience of a specific group or groups. One notable exception is the Sloan Study of Youth and Social Development, a longitudinal ESM study of approximately 1,200 teenagers across the United States who were selected to be racially and ethnically representative of the U.S. population aged 12–18 (Csikszentmihalyi & Schneider, 2000).

There are, of course, certain populations for which ESM is simply not appropriate. For example, respondents who are not comfortable with reading and writing will provide poor responses. This rules out most children below about 7 years of age and functionally illiterate adults. Persons who are hard of hearing may also have difficulty with ESM studies because they may not hear the signals prompting them to complete a questionnaire, though a few types of signaling devices can be set to vibrator mode (Scollon, Kim-Prieto & Diener, 2003). There are certain types of adult occupations for which research using ESM may be impractical, at least as a means for learning about one's professional experiences. For example, it would be unrealistic to expect full participation from a surgeon who performs medical procedures all day or from a construction worker assigned to the task of flagging traffic on a busy freeway. In many instances, simple modifications in procedure or equipment can be made to accommodate the needs of the population being studied. For instance, in a study of business executives it was found that in order to prevent disruptions, respondents turned off the signaling device when they entered a sensitive meeting with clients or engaged in an important business negotiation. Thus the method selectively missed the most interesting aspects of the respondents' work life. In such situations, it is important to devise back-up procedures; for instance, by providing respondents with silent, vibrating units, and instructing them to fill out the ESF as soon after the signal as possible. A more problematic restriction to collecting useable ESM data concerns the relationship of the sample to the investigator. If the respondents feel that their answers can be used by the researcher to adversely affect their well-being, it is likely that the answers will be biased in the direction of social desirability. Thus it would be impossible to get veridical responses from delinquents on probation if the states attorney's office conducted the study or from workers at a factory if management ran the study.

Equipment and Signaling Schedules

Computerized or Paper-and-Pencil Methods?

When it comes to the equipment used to conduct an ESM study, researchers have several choices. At the most basic level, one must decide whether to use computerized methods of data collection or to rely on paper-and-pencil methods. Within each of these general types of approaches there are several distinct equipment options. Even in cases where the ESF is completed using paper and pencil, some type of signaling equipment is necessary. There is a good deal of variety in the way participants can be signaled, and any device will have some limitations. In this section we review the options that have been used to date. Unfortunately, technological advances tend to outpace the book publishing industry, so it is likely that there will be further advances in the equipment available for ESM studies by the time this book is available to the public. The best we can do here is to offer descriptions of the equipment-related options available at the time this book went to print and encourage future researchers to consult with experienced ESM researchers for more state-of-the-art options.

In some of the earliest ESM studies, Csikszentmihalyi and others (Csikszentmihalyi & Larson, 1984; deVries, Delespaul, & Theunissen, 1984) used pagers that beeped or vibrated in response to a radio signal. Participants would then respond to ESFs in paper-and-pencil format. The drawback of this method is that most pagers can only pick up the signals in a limited geographical range (at the time of these early studies the range was approximately 30 miles) and buildings or hills may obstruct transmission of the signals. This method also requires that all research participants be on the same signaling schedule, as only one set of signals is transmitted to all paging devices. While only a few researchers use pagers these days, an advantage to using this method is that pagers are relatively inexpensive to rent and do not need to be programmed individually, as is the case with most of the other signaling devices discussed here.

Because having a self-contained signaling device is desirable, data bank watches that had the capability to store enough signals for the research design became attractive for use with paper-and-pencil ESFs. Today, most data bank watches have the capacity to store several hundred, or even several thousand, preprogrammed signals. Watches are desirable because they make it possible to tailor individualized schedules for each participant and because they feel more "natural" to subjects and are often more easily portable than pagers. Further, because such watches are commercially available, equipment tends to be even less expensive than renting pagers. At the time of the printing of this book, watches of this sort can be purchased for about US$40 each. The downside is that data bank watches take considerably longer to program than pagers (each of the 56-plus signaling times has to be programmed by hand into each watch), and there is a greater margin of error with inputting the scheduled times into the watches. Also, most watches today do not have a "vibrator mode," so the audible signal cannot be turned off in situations where a beeping watch might be inappropriate. Nonetheless, data bank watches continue to be a popular choice among researchers choosing to use paper-and-pencil methods.

While the equipment used for paper-and-pencil methods tends to be relatively inexpensive and convenient for participants to carry, there are several drawbacks to these methods as well. Participants must keep track of the signaling device, the booklet in which they record their responses, and a pencil or pen, whereas participants using computerized methods need only remember to carry the signaling device. The biggest drawback of paper-and-pencil methods concerns getting the data into a useable electronic format. Paper questionnaires must be coded and entered into electronic format by hand, introducing considerable cost, time delay, and risk of human error. Several researchers have eliminated many of these concerns by collecting their data electronically using a device that allows participants to enter their responses directly into the signaling device. These methods, of course, have their own set of advantages and limitations. We turn now to a discussion of available options for electronic collection of ESM data.

As early as 1982, researchers designed a study using a "pocket microcomputer" in which participants typed their coded responses to questions displayed on a screen (Pawlik & Buse, 1982). Stefan Hormuth and his colleagues (Hormuth, 1983) have developed and refined a self-contained signaling device that can be easily programmed via computer. These devices are not commercially available, however. Ellwood (2002) developed a device called the TimeCorder, which is a small computer used to study time use. Each time participants change from one activity to another, they are required to press a button to select the new activity they have begun. Participants make their selection from a list of up to 26 activities. The TimeCorder device has the ability to record exactly how much time participants spend in activities, which gives the device an advantage over more traditional time-diary studies in which participants estimate their time use at the end of a day. However, this method would be too burdensome to participants if used for more than 24 hours. Also, the device is limited to tracking time use and is not capable of recording the more affective aspects of human experience. Conti (2001) has used electronic planners in research. They tend to be more expensive than wristwatches or pagers and are more difficult for participants to keep with them at all times. Chen, Wigand, and Nilan (1999, 2000) developed a Web-based computer application called "Auto Ask," which is designed to signal individuals using pop-up windows as they are navigating the World Wide Web. While this approach is probably the least expensive of all the methods reviewed here, and would enable data collection from large numbers of people, it is severely limited in that it can only provide in situ reports of participants' experiences while using the World Wide Web. This particular method is probably best suited to studies of computer use or more retrospective studies where subjects are being asked to recall their experiences in the last day or two.

Perhaps the most promising and widely used technological advance in ESM research involves the use of Personal Data Assistants (PDAs). With the growing technology in this area, researchers are using palmtop computers or PDAs to signal participants and to input their responses (Feldman Barrett, 2004; Feldman Barrett & Barrett, 2001; Oishi, 2002; Perrez, Schoebi, & Wilhelm, 2000; Shiffman, 2000). Lisa Feldman Barrett has used palmtop computers and PDAs to signal college students about ten times a day, prompting them to answer scaled questions about their emotions at the time of the signal. Along with Daniel Barrett, a computer scientist, Feldman Barrett designed an Experience Sampling Program (ESP) that is available to the public. This program is available to download for free at Barrett's Web site (http://www2.bc.edu/~barretli/esp). The images that appear on the palmtop computer are also viewable at this Web site or in Hoyle, Harris, and Judd (2002). This and similar methods are in many ways ideal because not only do researchers have a self-contained signaling device that can be easily programmed via a computer, participants' responses can be entered directly into the PDAs, thus eliminating the step of entering (and in most cases, coding) the data. This is a considerable advantage over paper-and-pencil methods, where coding and data entry can be extremely time consuming, costly, and susceptible to human error. Another advantage of computerized methods is that researchers have better control over the timing of participants' responses, as the computer records exactly how much time elapses between the signal and response. In paper-and-pencil methods it is possible for participants to falsify information about when they actually responded to signals. Computerized methods can also be programmed to give participants feedback about their response rates, which may help boost participation throughout the entire course of the study. There is some empirical evidence documenting higher compliance rates with computerized methods compared to paper-and-pencil methods, at least among samples of medical patients (Stone, Shiffman, Schwartz, Broderick, & Hufford, 2002). Computerized methods also allow for greater flexibility in item presentation order, allowing for a variety of fixed or random presentation orders.

As with all design choices, the choice of computerized procedures does not come without considerable tradeoffs. So far, most ESM studies that utilize PDAs are restricted in the specificity of participants' responses about their physical location, their thoughts, and their actions. Rather than having respondents write responses in their own words to questions about their location, thoughts, and actions, participants have been asked to choose from a fixed number of responses, if they are asked at all. Having fixed responses saves the step of coding these items, but a degree of specificity is lost, and researchers are forced to rely on participants to self-code. The difficulty in using PDAs for an open-ended question format has been a major factor in our decision to continue using paper-and-pencil methods for the time being. Obviously as the technology improves for writing by hand in PDAs and as individuals get more accustomed to this rapidly expanding technology, it will become easier to have respondents simply write responses to open-ended questions into the PDA, though this will likely reintroduce the necessity to code data. Because most PDAs have a relatively small display screen, questions asked using this method must be fairly short. The soft-touch screen on PDAs introduces a different type of human error, where respondents will inadvertently tap a response more than once, thus recording the same response for multiple questions (Conner Christensen et al., 2003). Another drawback to using PDAs is cost. The equipment costs of doing research with these devices are considerably higher than using watches or pagers (at the time of publication a single device cost anywhere between US$100 and US$600). Because PDAs are somewhat fragile, most researchers choose to invest in protective carrying cases and insurance for the equipment, which introduces additional cost (Conner Christensen et al., 2003). Further, if the ESM instrument you design contains features that are not available for free download, you will have to hire a programmer to modify the software or purchase commercially available software that will support the features you need. Of course, using PDAs eliminates the cost of coding and entering data, so over the course of many studies this data collection method may not be that much more expensive than paper-and-pencil methods. PDAs can present some logistical challenges because most cannot be worn as accessibly as a watch or pager. It may be more difficult for participants to hear the signals when the device is buried in a purse, backpack, or briefcase than if they were wearing a watch on their wrist or a pager on their belt. This could result in missing data because the signal couldn't be heard. Another concern with PDAs is the risk of theft or loss. With extensive experience in this area, Lisa Feldman Barrett and her colleagues (Conner Christensen et al., 2003) have several suggestions for avoiding damage and theft and recommend purchasing several more devices than you will actually need at the outset of the study. Because technology changes so rapidly, you may not be able to find a model that is compatible with your software if you delay purchasing backups until the need arises. These researchers note that while they experience regular damage to their devices due to heavy usage, they have experienced minimal loss or theft. However, most of their research has involved undergraduate students at their home university. It is likely that these risks might be higher with other populations. Also, when using PDAs, the risk of damage, loss, or theft is greater than the cost of replacing the equipment—if the device is lost, stolen, or damaged, so is the data. This is less of a concern with paper-and-pencil methods because while a watch or pager may be an attractive target to a thief, the paper diary typically is not. Another data loss risk concerns power. If the batteries run out on a portable sampling device, all of the data stored in that device is lost. It is necessary then for researchers to meet with study participants regularly to download the data and change the batteries in the signaling device. Scheduling these meetings may be more practical with some populations than others. While battery life will depend on the model being used and the usage pattern specified by the study design, researchers at Feldman Barrett's lab report that top of the line batteries (which they strongly recommend) will last about one week with palmtop computers and about two weeks with PDAs (Conner Christensen et al., 2003). In contrast, the batteries for watches used in paper-and-pencil studies can last two to three months with regular usage, and there is a much lower risk of data loss if the battery dies.

There are advantages and drawbacks to both the paper-and-pencil methods and the electronic methods of data collection. For further information about conducting studies electronically, the reader is referred to Conner

Christensen and colleagues (2003). A researcher's decision about which method to use will depend on the research question, the population studied, the available budget, and other design needs. As technology advances there will continue to be advances in the way ESM research is conducted. As participants' familiarity with PDAs continues to grow and the cost of the devices comes down, these devices will likely replace the use of watches and pagers in ESM research.

The Signaling Schedule

If we consider experience sampling studies most broadly, three general classes of signaling schedules exist (Reis & Gable, 2000; Scollon et al., 2003). *Interval-contingent sampling* refers to a signaling schedule where participants complete self-reports at the same time every day or at regular intervals (e.g., hourly reports). In *event-contingent sampling,* participants are simply instructed to complete a self-report following a particular event of interest (e.g., a social interaction). Because the timing of events in such studies are unpredictable, a signaling schedule is not used to prompt a response per se, though some researchers have found it beneficial to signal participants in such studies at regular intervals throughout the day to simply remind them that they are participating in the study so they will not forget to respond following an event of interest (Côté & Moskowitz, 1998). The most typical type of ESM studies involve *signal-contingent sampling,* where participants are signaled at random times over the course of several days or weeks. A majority of the studies reviewed in this book are signal-contingent studies, thus our discussion of signaling schedules deals primarily with signal-contingent methods.

When designing an ESM study, researchers must decide how many days participants will be asked to report on their experiences and how many times per day they will be signaled to provide these reports. Both the duration of the signaling period and the frequency of signals can be fully tailored to the purposes of the researcher. These decisions depend on the frequency of occurrence of the phenomena being studied, the anticipated compliance of potential respondents, the types of statistical analyses to be applied to the resulting data, and the degree of burden of filling out the ESF for participants. A period of one week (seven days) is the time frame we personally have used most often, though published studies have lasted as few as three days (Hurlburt, 1979) or as many as several weeks or even months (Feldman Barrett, 1998; LeFevre, Hendricks, Church, & McClintock, 1992). In a study by Massimini and Delle Fave, one respondent, a noted poet, became so interested in the pattern of her answers that she requested to be signaled for a week each month over two years. The same investigators studied a team of mountain climbers for a week before leaving for India, then for six weeks while climbing in the Himalayas, and then for a week after they returned to Europe (Bassi, 2002). In our experience, signaling participants for a full week is desirable in most cases because seven days are likely to yield a fairly representative sample of the various activities individuals engage in and to elicit multiple responses from many of these activities. Sampling for more than seven days may place excessive burden on some participants, though for certain types of research questions (particularly those involving phenomena that occur relatively rarely) longer signaling periods may be desirable.

The key is striking a balance between getting a representative sampling of daily experience and overburdening respondents. Delespaul (1992) suggests that longer signaling periods (lasting three weeks or more) are most feasible only if the reporting forms used are short (taking less than two minutes to complete) and/or if the number of signals per day is low (under six). In a review of signal-contingent methods of data collection like ESM, Reis and Gable (2000) estimate that the average number of signals is somewhere between 56 and 168, with studies running between 1 and 2 weeks, averaging 8–12 signals per day. Beal and Weiss (2003) report measurable deterioration in the quality of the data for studies lasting longer than three weeks. Most signaling schedules are designed to be random, while providing a sampling of experience across the entire day. Researchers must first identify parameters for the beeping schedule—usually defined as those hours during which participants are most likely to be awake. For example, in Csikszentmihalyi and Schneider's (2000) study of adolescents, signaling began as early as 7:30 a.m. and ended by 10:30 p.m. In a study of working families, Schneider and Waite (2005) created more personalized schedules, asking participants to specify their own waking hours, and then constructing individual signaling schedules accordingly. Participants' waking hours are typically divided into blocks of time, most often ranging from 90 to 120 minutes. Within each time block, an exact time is randomly selected, often with the added condition that signals must be at least 10 or 20 minutes apart. The exact time chosen within each time block varies from day to day, so that respondents do not come to anticipate the signal. These randomized schedules can be generated fairly easily using statistical software programs such as SPSS. The distribution of signals need not be uniform across the day. For example, Larson and Richards (1994a) signaled parents and adolescents every 120 minutes during the workday and every 90 minutes during the evening hours because their research was focused on family interactions.

Some studies are designed to sample only certain activities or certain times of day (such as leisure activities or school hours). Studies interested in understanding children's experiences in schools, for example, have signaled students only during class time and only for a few weekdays (Turner, Cox, DiCintio, Meyer, Logan, & Thomas, 1998; Uekawa, Borman, & Lee, 2005). Such studies may be event-contingent (where participants provide reports only after a particular event of interest to the researcher has occurred) or interval-contingent (where participants provide reports at the same time each day). These studies differ from signal-contingent studies in which participants are signaled at random times throughout the day. While such studies have the advantage of being less burdensome to respondents and more focused on the particular context of interest, they are limited in that researchers are not able to compare subjective experience across contexts. While we may know that person A is happier in school than person B, for example, we are unable to determine whether person A is simply always happier than person B or whether this difference is observed only in school. If one is not able to compare experience in one situation (or in one day) with an individual's other experiences, it is difficult to make sense of the findings.

In designing a signaling schedule, researchers must consider how compliant their study participants are likely to be. If participants are likely to respond to only 70 percent of the signals, a longer signaling period might be necessary in order to obtain the desired number of responses. While response rates for studies signaling respondents 1–2 times per day tend to be relatively high (around 95 percent), more typical ESM studies in which participants are signaled 8 or more times a day over the course of 1–2 weeks tend to be much lower, ranging from 50–80 percent (Conner Christensen et al., 2003; see also Chapter 6 of this volume for a more thorough discussion of response rates).

The duration and intensity of the signaling schedule may also be influenced by researchers' plans for analyses. For example, a large number of cases for each person may be necessary if data are to be analyzed using multilevel modeling procedures (e.g., Goldstein, 1995; Raudenbush & Bryk, 2002; see also Chapter 5 of this volume). Prior to the design of the signaling schedule, researchers can run a multilevel power analysis to compute the number of cases necessary to estimate within-subjects variance components (for more information on this issue see Snijders & Bosker, 1999; Snijders, Bosker, & Guldemond, 1999).

The signaling schedule must also be designed with the length of the ESF in mind. Both of these elements factor into the level of burden placed on participants. In a study where the form takes more than two or three minutes to fill out, the frequency and/or duration of signaling may need to be curtailed to fewer than six signals per day and/or fewer than seven days. Studies involving shorter forms (from 30 seconds to 2 minutes) can signal respondents many times per day (up to 10) for several days or weeks without becoming overly burdensome.

Designing the Form

One question that we are most frequently asked by researchers planning their first ESM study is "What is the standard ESM form?" While there are a number of features of the ESF that are uniform across studies, the number and content of items varies widely from study to study depending on the research question being addressed. One advantage of ESM is that it is flexible and can be applied in a variety of research settings. Rather than being tailored to measure one dimension of reality, as IQ tests ostensibly measure intelligence, ESM has been left unstructured to encourage researchers to use it for their own purposes (Kubey, Larson, & Csikszentmihalyi, 1996). Studies of adolescent career development contain a number of questions about the importance of activities to one's future and living up to expectations (cf. Csikszentmihalyi & Schneider, 2000), while studies of families ask adults about their interactions with spouses and children (cf. Larson & Richards, 1994a). Studies with more clinical implications ask questions aimed to measure depression, feelings of control, or drug use (cf. Kraan, Meertens, Hilwig, Volovics, Dijkman-Caes, & Portegijs, 1992). Sample ESFs from two different studies are presented in Appendix A.

ESM was originally designed to capture both the *external* and *internal* coordinates (or dimensions) of experience (Csikszentmihalyi & Larson, 1984). External dimensions include the date and time of day, physical location, activities, and companions. All of these elements paint the backdrop against which one's daily experience is lived out. Internal dimensions of experience refer to thoughts and feelings as respondents interact with other people and perform the activities that make up their daily life.

Measuring the External Coordinates of Experience

The external dimensions of experience are measured on the ESF using a series of several standard questions. First, respondents are asked to record the date and time that they were signaled (or beeped) and the time that they responded to the signal (recall that this information is recorded automatically in computerized methods). Knowing the date and time of day are important aspects of external experience, and this information allows us to examine, for example, whether people feel differently at night than they do in the morning, or whether workers' feelings about their jobs are different on Mondays as compared to Fridays. The second component of external experience is the respondent's location, as indicated by answers to the question "As you were beeped, where were you?" In answer to this question respondents record, either in open- or closed-ended format, a description of their physical location. Common responses include "in the kitchen," "at a friend's house," "at the movie theater," or "at my desk at work." Coding of these and other items on the ESF will be discussed in Chapter 4.

The third external coordinate is a person's activity. Respondents are asked, "As you were beeped what was the main thing you were doing?" Here respondents record, in open- or closed-ended format, their descriptions of the activity that was taking up the bulk of their attention just before they were signaled. Typical answers to this item include "studying for a math test," "waiting to catch a bus," and "talking with my boss."

Different individuals will describe the same activity in greater or lesser detail. For instance, a person sitting in her office may write, "I was working," whereas another in the exact same situation may write, "I was writing a memo," or "I was writing the plans for our new acquisition," or "I was implementing the board's decision." In most ESM studies, all of these answers would be coded as *working* without further distinction. But if the research was focused on more specific elements of one's work life, then researchers might want to encourage respondents to give more nuanced descriptions of their job-related activities. Researchers must keep their coding plans in mind when considering the level of specificity in their questions.

Because we are in the age of multitasking, many ESFs give respondents the opportunity to report that they are doing more than one activity simultaneously. Typically, they will be asked the question "What else were you doing at the same time?" Here respondents can indicate activities that may not be taking up as much of their attention, like "listening to the radio," "watching my daughter play in the backyard," or "peeling potatoes." It is up to the respondent to determine which activities are primary and which are secondary.

The fourth and final component of external experience captured by the ESF is companionship. Respondents are typically asked to indicate, "Who were you with" on a fixed checklist of possibilities such as "parents," "friends," "coworkers," and "alone," checking all categories that apply.

These four components of external experience tend to be relatively consistent across ESM studies, though there is obvious variation in the specificity of information that will be obtained if the items used to gather this information are open- or closed-ended. In some cases, simply knowing whether one is at home, at work, or in public might be sufficient to address the question at hand, while in other cases more detailed information might be necessary.

Measuring the Internal Coordinates of Experience

There is considerable variation across ESM studies in both the dimensions of internal experience that are recorded and the structure used to elicit these reports. In a few studies, researchers have asked respondents simply to take notes describing their thoughts and feelings, and these notes were later coded by the researcher (Hulburt, 1979) or the respondents (Brandstätter, 1983). Many studies have taken a combined approach to the structure of self-report, asking subjects to describe the external dimensions of their experience using an open-ended format while relying on rating scales to record internal dimensions of experience.

Such rating scale items are often designed to measure concentration or attention, one's assessments about the activity itself (in terms of its importance, difficulty, or challenge), one's feelings about oneself and/or others, and one's general mood. You may refer to Appendix A to get some idea of the variation in these items. Often, rating scale items are combined in analyses to form composite measures of constructs such as self-esteem, mood, or motivation. Several commonly used composite measures are discussed and presented in Chapter 6. It is important to identify desired composite measures ahead of time in order to include all the necessary items on the ESF. After data have been collected, the measures themselves can be established through factor analysis.

Filling In the Gaps

Some ESFs contain items that ask participants to provide information about activities or experiences that occurred since the last time they were signaled. These types of items can refer to either internal or external dimensions of experience. The purpose of such items is to get a better sense of what has been "missed" when respondents were not being signaled and also to provide a better understanding of situations or emotional states that could have an impact on the way participants are experiencing the current situation. Examples of these types of questions geared toward external experience include "Since the last report, how much time have you spent: Watching television? Doing homework? Doing paid work?" (Csikszentmihalyi & Schneider, 2000). Items aimed at filling in the gaps of one's internal experience include "Did you feel a strong emotion since the last report? What did you feel and what made you feel that way?" (Schneider & Waite, 2005). If the signals in a study are indeed random within each time period, researchers should obtain a representative sampling of the activities participants engage in throughout the week, so knowing about these in-between times may not be of particular interest. In some cases, however, one may want a more comprehensive account.

Measuring Flow

Because ESM studies are often conducted with the express purpose of studying optimal experience or "flow," a few words about designing an ESF to measure flow are warranted (for more comprehensive discussions of flow see Csikszentmihalyi, 1990; Csikszentmihalyi & Csikszentmihalyi, 1988; and Chapter 5 of this volume). Flow has most often been operationalized using two items on the ESF. One item asks individuals to rate the "challenges of the activity" and the other asks the respondent to rate "your skills in the activity." A flow variable is typically operationalized by identifying those moments when an individual rates both the challenges of the activity and his or her skills in the activity as relatively high and in balance. These two indicators define the conditions in which the flow experience is most likely to occur.

A balance of high challenge and high skill defines the *conditions* where optimal experience is most likely to occur, but does not necessarily describe the *experience* of flow. Experientially, flow is characterized not only by a balance of challenges and skills but also by deep concentration, loss of self-consciousness, and deep engagement. Many of these aspects of the experience of flow can be captured by the ESF, and recently researchers have used this more experiential operationalization of flow in their research (cf. Schmidt, Shernoff, & Csikszentmihalyi, 2006). The benefit of using this more comprehensive definition of flow is that one can be more confident that one is actually capturing the flow *experience* rather than the *conditions* under which flow tends to occur. The drawback of this method is that as more items are included to define the independent variable, fewer are left to measure its effects. So one must decide whether the research question would be better addressed using indicators of the conditions for flow or the experience of flow. In Chapter 5 we provide a detailed discussion of the various ways to construct measures of flow using the scaled items described here.

Other Design Decisions

In addition to the decisions already discussed, there are a number of other choices to be made when designing an ESF. If you are using a paper-and-pencil method, how will the ESFs be "packaged" for easy use by participants? For electronic or paper-and-pencil methods, how will scaled items be presented? How many questions can reasonably be asked on one ESF? There are benefits and drawbacks to each decision you will make. The most common issues to consider when designing an ESF follow, and when appropriate, references are provided to representative implementations of these different choices.

One Book per Day or One per Week?

In a study that follows a typical signaling schedule (8 beeps a day for 7 days), each participant could potentially produce 56 completed ESFs. Given that participants will be providing so much information, it is important to package the brief questionnaires they fill out in a way that is easy to carry, easy to remember, and will cause the least harm to the study if lost. Most paper-and-pencil ESM studies employ some type of bound booklet, usually small enough to fit in a purse or a back pocket if folded in half (common dimensions are 8½ by 5½ inches). Some sort of identifying information other than a name (typically an ID number) is printed on the front of the booklet. It is important to make sure that these booklets are bound in a way so that individual pages are not likely to fall out when participants shove them carelessly into a book bag, briefcase, or pocket.

Some researchers choose to bind together the entire week's worth of ESFs in one booklet or spiral-bound notebook (Hormuth, 1986; Larson & Richards, 1994a), while others choose to create separate booklets for each day respondents are signaled (Csikszentmihalyi & Larson, 1984; Csikszentmihalyi & Schneider, 2000). The benefit of having a single booklet for the entire week is that participants have to remember only to carry around and keep track of the one booklet rather than switching them each day and keeping track of seven different booklets. On the other hand, a drawback of using a single booklet is that any booklet with 56 or more pages tends to be bulky and is difficult to carry around in one's pocket or purse. A second drawback of using a single booklet is that if a participant loses the booklet, all of the data for that participant is lost forever, whereas when researchers use separate booklets for each day, they are only likely to lose one day's worth of responses if a booklet gets lost or stolen. Using one booklet per day also makes it possible for researchers to retrieve data daily, enabling early detection of nonresponse. Whichever method you chose, it is important to include a few more pages in the ESM booklets than you expect participants to complete—participants will often use the extra pages if they make mistakes in filling out one of the forms. The use of extra pages becomes particularly important when the study uses separate booklets for each day of the week—this way if a participant realizes she is carrying around yesterday's booklet, she'll have a few extra pages to use to respond to today's signals. In our recent research, we have tended to use one booklet per day, and we include ten ESFs in each booklet (leaving two "extra" ESFs per day). Of course this issue is not of concern with computerized ESM procedures, where all responses are stored within the signaling device.

Unipolar or Bipolar Items?

Once you decide which items to use in the ESF, there are a number of decisions about how the scaled items are to be presented. These issues are not unique to ESM but rather are of concern to survey construction more generally. We briefly raise a few of these issues here because they are common concerns of researchers when designing an ESF. We encourage readers interested in this topic to consult the literature on survey item construction and the consequences of different scale designs (cf. Krosnick & Fabrigar, 2005; Schaeffer & Presser, 2003; Schwarz, Grayson, & Knauper, 1998; Schwarz & Hippler, 1995; Sudman & Bradburn, 1982). The first of these concerns has to do with unipolar versus bipolar (or semantic differential) scales. Moods can be assessed using single dimensions or by pairs of "opposites," asking participants to indicate how they feel on the continuum from one pole to the other. For example, an ESF could ask a participant "How happy do you feel?" on a scale of 1 to 7, with 1 meaning not at all happy and 7 being very happy. Similarly, the same question could be asked about sadness, with 1 meaning not at all sad and 7 meaning very sad. On the other hand, the items could be presented as a continuum from happiness to sadness, with 1 signifying very happy and 7 signifying very sad. In this case, a score of 4 indicates that a respondent is not particularly happy or sad. Presenting moods or emotions as opposites sometimes helps respondents think about their feelings by giving them a reference point. The downside to bipolar items is that even when there are easily identifiable pairs of opposites (as in the case of happy and sad), sometimes people can feel simultaneously happy and sad, and this is impossible to indicate on a bipolar scale (Schwarz, 2000). Respondents' preferences for unipolar versus bipolar scales may vary by age. In pilot studies in which ESF formats were discussed in detail, we have found that children and adolescents tend to prefer a bipolar format (it helps them to have the anchors), while adults tend to prefer unipolar scales. Many ESFs contain some combination of unipolar and bipolar items.

What Should the Scale Range Be?

This is also a commonly asked question that is not unique to the design of an ESF. For decades social scientists have debated about how many meaningful distinctions can be made on a scale, and researchers who use ESM have not resolved this debate. We again refer readers to the survey design literature previously cited. In our review of the research using ESM, we have noticed several trends in scale use. Most items that are presented as bipolar scales tend to have seven different response categories (see Csikszentmihalyi & Schneider, 2000; Larson & Richards, 1994a). There is greater variation, however, in the scale range of unipolar items. Most studies we have reviewed employ either 10-point scales (e.g., Csikszentmihalyi, Rathunde, & Whalen, 1993; Csikszentmihalyi & Schneider, 2000), 7-point scales (e.g., Feldman

Barrett, 1998; Scollon, Diener, Oishi, & Biswas-Diener, 2005), or 4-point scales (e.g., Larson & Richards, 1994a; Schneider & Waite, 2005). The argument for using 10-point scales is that the researcher will end up with greater variation on the items. Proponents of fewer response categories cite research showing that most people are not able to reliably distinguish between more than 7 scale points, as indicated by low retest reliability on such items (Krosnick & Fabrigar, 2005; Schwarz, 2000). In pilot testing, respondents often report that shorter scales are less burdensome. Regardless of which type of scale you chose to use, it is important to pilot test the items to make sure that the population you intend to study actually varies in their responses to these questions.

How Many Items Can Be Included on an ESF?

Because ESM involves asking respondents to stop what they are doing several times a day for several days, it is desirable to try to make these frequent interruptions as brief and nonintrusive as possible. As with the signaling schedule, one must walk a fine line between getting enough information to reliably answer one's research question and overburdening the respondents to the point where they stop participating in the study. Based on our experience, we recommend designing a form that will take respondents about one to two minutes to complete once they become accustomed to the routine. Of course, as we discussed earlier, longer forms will create less burden if they are used with a signaling schedule that only lasts a few days or one that signals participants infrequently throughout the day. The number of questions that can be answered in one to two minutes will depend on the population and the nature and format of questions. Our survey of ESFs from a variety of studies indicates that in addition to the standard questions about external experience (day and time, location, activities, companionship), they tend to include about 35 additional items tapping thoughts and other dimensions of internal experience. There is, of course wide variation across studies. We advise researchers to pilot test ESFs to determine if the number and complexity of questions is appropriate for the population of interest. If it is essential to ask a large number of questions on the ESF and a large enough sample is available, the sample can be divided into several groups, with each group receiving a slightly different, but overlapping set of questions (cf. Larson & Richards, 1994a).

Another issue to consider in the design of the ESF is the presentation order of the questions. This is another survey design issue that is not unique to ESM research, and it is widely known that the order in which questions are presented does influences participants' responses. A full discussion of the merits of various fixed or random presentation orders is beyond the scope of this chapter, and we again direct readers interested in exploring the complexities of this topic to the resources on survey design issues referenced earlier in this chapter. In our recent studies we tend to first present items related to the external dimensions of experience (e.g., date, time, location, activities) and then follow with a series of questions about the internal dimensions of experience (e.g., concentration, affect, etc.). We have chosen this order because questions about the external dimensions of experience tend to feel less threatening and may require less reflection than items asking about participants' affective and cognitive states. However, we do acknowledge that for many types of research questions other item orders are desirable. An advantage of using any of the computerized ESM procedures (palmtop computers, PDAs, or Web-based platforms) is that researchers are allowed much more flexibility in presentation order. In order to minimize the effect of item order on responses, computerized procedures can be programmed to present respondents with one of several fixed presentation formats or to present items in random order (see Conner Christensen et al., 2003; Feldman Barrett & Barrett, 2001).

Implementing the Study

So you have designed a study and developed an ESF that will address your research question and is appropriate for the population of interest. Now what? Because ESM is so labor intensive for participants and because the "beeping" typically takes place in naturalistic settings beyond the careful eye of the researcher, it is important to recruit and interact with subjects in a way that will maximize participation levels and data quality.

Recruitment of Participants

Recruiting subjects to participate in an ESM study can be difficult because you are asking participants to share their daily lives with you. We find that the most effective strategy for recruiting participants into this deeply personal experience is to develop what Offer and Sabshin (1967) have called a *research alliance*—a mutual understanding between researcher and participant about the procedures, goals, and plans for the study. Researchers and research assistants must work hard to develop a sense of trust and collaboration with potential participants. In previous studies, a few potential participants have voiced concern that our signaling devices contained hidden cameras, microphones, or global positioning systems. It is important to put to rest any concerns like these at the outset of the study and to be open and honest about your intentions.

On the whole, most participants are cooperative and find that the procedure is rewarding in some way, particularly when researchers offer to make information about the study available to them in the future. The promise of sharing results with participants is one of the more successful recruiting tools. Success in recruiting will depend on your ability to gain participants' trust and communicate that the research is worthwhile. This means that deception—so prevalent in social psychological experiments—should be avoided, and the respondents should be encouraged to be honest and precise in their answers because that will allow their voices to be heard and their experiences to be counted. People in general will be willing to go to some lengths to help you if they feel that what they say will be taken seriously and used for worthwhile purposes.

The actual logistics of how participants are recruited varies depending on the population being studied and on human subjects' guidelines from the host institution. Some researchers recruit undergraduate subjects at their home institution, either through courses or advertisements posted on campus. Other studies have sought to recruit a stratified random sample from the population of a high school or a community. Still others employ more purposive samples and draw participants through the use of advertisements in newspapers or recruitment through places of employment. What typically happens is that some initial contact is made through a letter or a personal appearance in which the purpose and methods of the study are described. We tell participants that we are interested in learning about daily experience. In many cases, a more personal plea is effective—explaining that we are interested in *your* experience. Appealing to potential participants' more altruistic side works as well. Parents who participated in a recent ESM study of families were interested in providing us with information about their struggles to balance work and family so that action could be taken to ease the strain of future generations.

Incentives

Beyond the more altruistic incentives of providing greater understanding for humankind, some studies build in other types of more tangible incentives for participation. In our research, we typically do not provide monetary compensation. We may present participants with thank-you gifts such as certificates to a local store or restaurant, T-shirts, or coffee mugs with the logo of our university or research center, but these are not offered in exchange for participation. We find that more than money or gifts, one of the best returns one can give is information. We suggest building into the research plans the production of a newsletter that can be mailed when results become available or a Web site that participants can access to check up on what is happening with the study. Other researchers using ESM find monetary and material incentives to be highly effective recruiting and retention tools. For example, Conner Christensen and colleagues (2003) report using a complex incentive process in their research. Undergraduate participants are paid for their participation (typically $20 per week). In addition, they receive smaller tokens (e.g., candy, movie passes) throughout the course of their participation. For studies lasting more than one week, the researchers hold weekly drawings for smaller prizes such as restaurant gift certificates or university sweatshirts and then hold a drawing at the end of the study for a "grand prize," where participants are eligible to win a PDA like the one they have been using for the study.

The Orientation Meeting

Participants will need some training in the procedures. Once they agree to participate in the study, it is necessary to meet with respondents in person not only to provide instruction about the procedures but also to strengthen the research alliance by providing further explanation of the study's goals and answering any questions (though presumably these issues have been discussed prior to the participants' consent). These orientation meetings typically last 45 minutes to an hour, depending on the size of the meeting. It is ideal to meet with five to ten participants at a time, but the nature of your study population will be the major determinant of the size of meetings. In studies of families, for example, orientation meetings are held in participant's homes and only involve the two or three family members who are participating in the study (cf. Larson & Richards, 1994a; Schneider & Waite, 2005). Studies that take place in the context of schools (cf. Csikszentmihalyi & Schneider, 2000) may have only limited access to classrooms, and students and may be forced to meet in groups as large as 20 or 25. In cases like these it is important to have several research assistants present to provide instruction and feedback.

The orientation meeting typically begins with a description of the study's goals, reassurance to the participant about confidentiality, signing of any consent forms (if not previously done), and a question-and-answer session. After all questions have been answered, participants must be trained in all study procedures including how to use the signaling device and how to answer the ESF. A demonstration of the signal is given, and participants are shown how to turn off the signaling device and how to turn the device to vibrator mode (if applicable). Respondents are reminded of when the signaling period will begin (typically within 24 hours of the orientation meeting), how many times the device will signal each day, and which hours of the day will mark the beginning and end of the signaling period.

Participants should be reminded to fill out the ESF as soon as possible after the signal. Some researchers instruct participants *not* to complete the ESF if more than 15 minutes has passed since the time of the beep. Others ask participants to respond regardless of the delay. Because the signal time and response time are both recorded (either by the participant or by the computerized device), it is possible to retain in analyses only those responses that occurred within a given time range of the signal, even if participants were not instructed to avoid making late responses. Note that some programs used on PDAs do not allow participants to delay answering the signal: if participants are not able to respond immediately, they cannot delay their response to a more convenient time. It is important to give explicit instructions about what to do when signals cannot be answered right away or are missed entirely. Participants need to know what to do in situations where answering the signal (or even carrying the signaling device) is impossible. For example, participants will need to know what to do with their research equipment when they are participating in swim meets, attending religious services, or listening to an opera. If a signaling device can be set to vibrator mode, signals can still be answered in situations where an audio pager would be intrusive. In cases like swim meets, participants are usually told to give the signaling device to a coach, teammate, or fan who could let them know if they were signaled during the meet. If this is not possible, participants are simply asked to store the signaling device somewhere where it will not be lost or stolen and to retrieve it as soon as possible.

During the orientation meeting, the entire ESF should be reviewed, providing explanation about any items that may be confusing and answering questions along the way. In some cases it may be necessary to make participants aware of certain locations, activities, or companions that are of interest to the study. For example, in their study of how middle-class couples balance the demands of work and family, Schneider and Waite (2005) instructed participants to be explicit about exactly where they were completing work for their job because many worked at home. Participants were asked to avoid saying that they were "in my office" but were instead to specify if they were in an office in their home or an office in another location. As illustrated by this example, it is critical to specify relevant coding categories before the data are collected so that, if necessary, participants can be properly instructed about how to respond to open-ended questions. Coding issues will be discussed in detail in Chapter 4.

When procedures for completing the ESF have been reviewed, each participant should fill out at least one practice page so they can get used to the method. The practice page often brings up new questions or tips the researcher off to any misunderstandings participants may have about the form. If computerized data collection methods are being used, several practice signals may be necessary for participants to become accustomed to the process of providing responses on a PDA or palmtop computer.

Once participants are comfortable filling out ESFs, it is important to make them aware of any special measures that must be taken with the signaling device (e.g., don't bring it in the shower, don't leave it in places where it could be stolen). In addition to covering these "ground rules," participants should be left with information about how to contact the study staff in case a question or a problem arises during the week (e.g., "How do I answer this question?" "My watch is malfunctioning." "The battery on my PDA ran out."). It is important that the contact information given puts respondents in touch with a person (not a voicemail system) who can help them right away (cellular phones are good for this purpose). In our experience most questions have to do with malfunctioning equipment, which could result in substantial data loss, so it is imperative to address these issues as soon as possible. Some researchers also give participants troubleshooting information sheets that they can consult during the course of the study if they have questions about how to operate their signaling device (Conner Christensen et al., 2003). It is also generally a good idea to provide participants with a letter stating that they are participating in an experience sampling study. This letter can be shown to teachers, professors, or employers who may be disturbed by the signals. This letter should be signed by the study's principal investigator and by any other appropriate persons who have approved the study (e.g., school principal, superintendent) and should include the principal investigator's telephone number. Over the years, in our research involving thousands of adolescents and adults, we have only been contacted a handful of times from a teacher or employer who was bothered by the signal. At the end of the orientation meeting you can make plans for any future meetings with participants (for example, interviews, retrieval of data).

Retention

Providing a thorough and honest explanation of the study and establishing a relationship of trust in the orientation meeting are two important first steps in ensuring that participants remain in the study through the signaling period. But inevitably some subjects will stop participating before the study is complete, either because they become annoyed or bored or because they lose the signaling device and/or the ESF booklets. In our research, we typically make telephone calls to participants about midway through the signaling period to ask them how they are doing and to answer questions or provide encouragement as needed. The phone conversations are typically brief, but they show participants your interest in their participation and are effective in preventing dropouts and solving technical or logistical problems before it is too late. If a participant is feeling particularly frustrated with the study and is considering dropping out, one effective strategy is to suggest that they "take a short break" from the study and come back to it the next day. You can suggest that the participant put the research equipment in a safe place where it will not disturb him and try returning to it the next day. After this break you can follow up with a phone call to see how things are going. In cases where the sample is located in a single physical space (e.g., a school or an office building), it is a good idea for staff to be present from time to time in these locations during the period of the study. This way, participants will see you in the hallways or in the cafeteria, will know that you are available if there are questions or concerns, and may feel a more personal obligation to complete the study. In studies involving college undergraduates, Feldman Barrett and colleagues make regular appointments to check in with participants at her campus lab to monitor their progress and download data from their PDAs (Conner Christensen et al., 2003). One particularly effective practice used by a number of researchers is to assign specific participants to each researcher so that the same researcher is working with a given participant throughout the study period. This way, participants feel accountable to a specific individual, and this personal connection enhances participation.

Retrieving the Data

Data should be retrieved as soon as possible after the signaling period has ended. Often, retrieval meetings (of about the same size as orientation meetings) are held the day after the end of signaling. At this time the ESM booklets and/or signaling devices are returned, as well as any other materials that may be part of the study (e.g., other questionnaires). The staff checks in all materials, and arrangements are made with participants who have not returned all study materials. In studies where the sample is centrally located, we have often made use of a confidential drop box to return completed ESM books on a daily basis. In the orientation meeting, participants are instructed to bring their completed daily ESM books to a predetermined location and put them in a drop box similar to a ballot box, where others cannot access the contents. Each day, respondents return their completed booklet from the previous day. This strategy makes it possible to identify subjects who may not be fully participating early on in the study and allows for the identification of any participants who may not be following the procedure as it was described in the orientation. Identifying these cases early on in the study allows the researcher to solve problems before it is too late and save data that might otherwise have been unusable. Another advantage to the daily drop box is that it may reduce the likelihood that participants will complete the booklets from memory rather than at the time of each signal. In studies where a drop box is used, there is little or no need to retrieve ESM booklets at a final retrieval meeting, but the signaling devices and any other materials must be returned. Similarly, in studies involving computerized methods, data are typically retrieved at regular intervals throughout the study period, so this final meeting may involve the downloading of minimal data and retrieval of the equipment.

Upon retrieval of the data, participants are often administered a brief questionnaire asking whether or not they felt that the period of signaling represented a "normal week" in their lives and whether there had been any specific activities or situations that caused them to fail to answer the signal. It is possible to use this debriefing period at the end for more extensive interviews or testing of participants. The debriefing interview has also been used as a way to focus on the ESF reports, for instance by choosing the most "happy" or most "sad" responses and asking about why these experiences were so extreme, or by choosing a person's ESF when at work, or with friends, or with family, and then asking if this kind of experience is typical, thus initiating an interview that is specifically focused on actual life events (Csikszentmihalyi & Schneider, 2000).

Other options for retrieval are possible as well. For example, in a national study of families in which field travel budgets did not allow for staff to be physically present in every family's home for orientation *and* retrieval, all study materials were returned to researchers via prepaid shipping envelopes (Schneider & Waite, 2005). Face-to-face retrieval is always desirable, but there are other workable options if this is impossible. When retrieval by mail is the only option, we strongly urge researchers to use shipping methods that are traceable, guaranteed, and insured, and to provide packaging materials that will ensure the signaling devices don't get destroyed.

The Importance of Pilot Testing

This chapter has outlined, from start to finish, many of the important issues to consider in designing and carrying out an ESM study. As was mentioned repeatedly, there are a number of decisions that must be made in the design and implementation of a study, and some choices will work better than others, depending on the population one wants to study. What works well with one sample may be impractical or even impossible with another. It would be difficult to overstate the importance of pilot testing when doing an ESM study. Before actually going into the field, a researcher should be confident not only about the content of the ESF itself, but also about the signaling schedule, the signaling equipment, the protocol for the orientation meeting, and the procedures for retrieving, coding, entering, and cleaning the data. If any of these factors are ineffective, the quality of the data will suffer. We recommend pilot testing first on the researchers and research assistants involved in the study. Not only does this process identify elements of the study that may need modification (e.g., question wording, form length, signaling tone), but it gives researchers a valuable connection to their participants. As researchers, it is important to understand exactly what you are asking your participants to do. While at first it may *sound* relatively unobtrusive to signal participants 12 times a day ("If it takes only 30 seconds to answer we're only asking for 6 minutes a day, right?"), you tend to look at things a bit differently when *you* are the one who has to provide those 6 minutes by taking unexpected breaks from your classes, your writing time, your tennis match, and your dinner with your family. This experience also gives us much more credibility with our participants. We are able to say to them, "I have done exactly what I am asking you to do: I understand the challenges it presents and have found them to be manageable." We have found this to be extraordinarily valuable in the recruitment and retention of participants.

After the initial test with the research team, it is important to select a small number of subjects who resemble the intended study population and to pilot-test the study using all of the parameters of the intended study. The number of pilot subjects depends on the size of the full-scale study and the extent to which you are familiar with the population being studied. Our recent studies have involved pilot samples of 10–20 individuals, but in many cases smaller pilot samples would be acceptable as well. Pilot participants should be exposed to all study procedures and should be encouraged to provide feedback about any aspect of the study. We typically ask for feedback about our instructional procedures after the initial orientation meeting, and then encourage participants to write comments about particular questionnaire items in the margins of their ESM booklets. At the end of the signaling period we have a debriefing meeting with participants in which we discuss elements of the study (e.g., Which items seemed confusing, irrelevant, or redundant? Did the response options make sense to you? How long did it typically take you to complete the form? Did it seem too long or cumbersome? Could you hear the signals made by the signaling device? In which situations was it difficult to answer? Was there a point during the week where you were particularly frustrated with the study? What did you do when you had to miss a signal?). It is also helpful to pilot test a number of different situations you are likely to encounter in the full-scale study. Ask participants to intentionally miss a response occasion, to intentionally produce false data, or to try to answer the form in a situation that you anticipate will be difficult. For example, we had participants wear our watches on the windy streets of Chicago with their winter coats on to make sure watch signals were audible under these conditions.

The pilot process does not stop after the last debriefing meeting. Once the data are collected, the research team should code and enter or upload the data to make sure these processes go smoothly. Then the data should be cleaned and simple descriptive statistics should be examined. Often these postcollection procedures can identify problems with the questionnaire that were not evident during administration. You may discover that certain questions are difficult to code due to the instruction that was given, or that a particular response category was not specified correctly in the computer program, or that certain items are likely to be skipped due to the question layout, or that a particular item has no variance and does not effectively demonstrate any individual or situational difference in experience. Given the considerable investment required to conduct an ESM study, it is well worth the effort of thorough pilot testing to ensure that the data are useable. In some cases, multiple pilot tests may be necessary. In their national study of families, Schneider and Waite (2005) pilot tested three successive revisions of the ESM form before arriving at the version that was ultimately used in the full-scale study.

Documentation

We and others (Conner Christensen et al., 2003) have found it absolutely necessary to provide extensive documentation when designing an ESM study. This practice is, of course, advisable in any type of research, but due to the complexity in design, programming, instruction, and often coding in ESM studies, it is particularly crucial in this case. We have found it best to create documents for the field procedures, for coding the data, and for managing, manipulating, and analyzing the data. Even in a small-scale study, details will be lost if they are not written down. As the study is being designed, it is a good idea to create a field manual that documents procedures to be adhered to in the administration of the study. This manual contains information about programming the signaling schedule and troubleshooting problems with the signaling devices. It includes an outline or an actual script to be followed in the orientation meeting so that all participants will be instructed in the same manner. It includes information about the goals of the study that can be shared with interested parties, as well as extra copies of necessary consent forms. When our research has involved travel to other cities, the manual also includes necessary documents regarding university insurance and tax-exempt numbers. In this manual, those administering the study can take notes about any special circumstances or modifications in standard procedure that took place. The manual should also contain any checklists that will help field researchers keep track of the administration and collection of equipment and data. For studies that require coding of data, a coding manual is a must. It is also necessary to document the procedures of uploading data (if collected in electronic format) and for the management of files. These issues are taken up in detail in Chapter 4.

All of this advice may seem daunting to someone familiar with simple paper-and-pencil testing in a safe and convenient college classroom situation. One should remember, however, that the initial investment of time and energy in an ESM study will produce data that are difficult to envision in terms of both quantity and quality. With imagination and perseverance, a single study of a few dozen participants can yield enough information for years of productive analysis and writing.

4

Dealing With the Data

Coding, Entry, Cleaning, and Data Management

Once ESM data are collected, responses to each question on the ESF must be assigned a numeric value so that the information can be entered into an electronic database and analyzed using software designed for quantitative analysis. For those using computerized data collection techniques this process is simple: The researcher simply uploads the data following the procedures for the particular electronic device being used. It is recommended to upload data at regular intervals, following procedures that are well-documented in a manual, using a dedicated computer that is not used for other purposes (for more information see Conner Christensen, Feldman Barrett, Bliss-Moreau, Lebo, & Kaschub, 2003). There is no need for coding or hand entry, and once data are uploaded, they are ready for cleaning. Much of this chapter, then, pertains only to research in which paper-and-pencil methods are being used. Readers planning to use electronic formats may wish to skip to the section in this chapter titled Setup, Cleaning, and Manipulation of Data Files, which pertains to ESM studies of any kind.

For researchers using paper-and-pencil methods, the process of getting the data into an electronic format is straightforward in many cases: participants will circle a number on a scale indicating their degree of concentration, happiness, or skill, and this number is simply entered by hand into a database.

In other cases, coders must evaluate respondents' descriptions of their locations, thoughts, and activities, and make a decision to place these responses into one of several predetermined, mutually exclusive categories. While the process of physically coding the data cannot begin until after the data have been collected, the coding procedures and criteria must be carefully considered and established prior to fielding the study. In this chapter we discuss coding issues that should be considered prior to fielding an ESM study and offer suggestions from our own experience about developing codebooks, as well as establishing and implementing coding procedures. We also discuss issues relevant to constructing a user-friendly electronic database (whether from paper data or computerized data), including file structure and data manipulation and reduction. Discussion of these topics will focus as much as possible on issues that are unique to ESM research, but out of necessity our comments are also peppered with more general practices used in sound quantitative research, regardless of the methodology being employed.

The complexity and labor intensity of the coding process will vary greatly, depending on the research questions to be addressed, the design of the ESF itself, and the particular signaling methodology used. Studies that rely exclusively on multiple choice and Likert scale items (and those employing PDAs, of course) require little or no coding at all; while studies that include free-response items can necessitate elaborate coding schemes. Minimal coding will save time and money and removes much of the decision-making burden from the researcher. On the other hand, such studies may fail to tap into the full richness of information that is possible to obtain with this methodology and may suffer from inconsistencies among participants in their ability to self-code the information they provide. Studies that employ more open-ended questions and are thus more coding intensive have the advantage of providing incredibly rich information about participants' thoughts and activities, may allow for more flexibility for future analyses, and provide the researcher, rather than the participant, with greater control over how responses are coded. The downside of this approach, however, is that coding can be extremely costly in terms of time and money, and interrater reliability and coder accuracy is of greater concern. Regardless of the complexity of coding required by a study, it is a good practice to develop a well-defined codebook that coders can use to accurately and consistently assign numeric values to participants' written responses.

Developing a Codebook

The first step in the coding process is developing a codebook. In this document, the researcher specifies every piece of information on the ESF that will be entered into the database and defines the numeric codes that will be applied to each piece of information. The layout and format of the codebook itself will vary depending on the particular ESF that is used. As an example, text from the codebook used in the Sloan Study of Youth and Social Development (Csikszentmihalyi & Schneider, 2000) is included in Appendix B. To organize our discussion of the types of coding schemes that are typically generated and applied, we refer back to the distinction introduced in Chapter 3 between the external and internal coordinates of experience.

Coding the External Coordinates of Experience

It is the so-called external dimensions of experience—one's location and activities—that are most often recorded in open-ended formats that require coding. Regardless of whether these external dimensions are recorded in an open- or closed-ended format, however, the relevant coding categories and the level of coding specificity for each variable must be indicated. It is necessary, for example, to specify what categories of the "location" variable will be required in order to answer the research questions. A study focused on the quality of students' experience in high school classrooms may require a great deal of specificity in coding various school locations (e.g., algebra class vs. art class vs. cafeteria), while a study of family processes may not require such detailed coding of school locations. Obviously in studies where location and the other external dimensions of experience are recorded using multiple-choice formats, as is typically the case when computerized data collection methods are used, these categories must be severely limited in number (to however many will fit on the screen of the signaling device), and must be determined before the ESF is designed. It is no less important to make these important decisions about coding categories and level of specificity when using open-ended response formats. It is crucial to have clearly defined coding categories before collecting data so that in the orientation to the study, participants can be directed about the level of specificity with which to respond to the open-ended questions (see Chapter 3). There are a number of issues to consider when developing and implementing procedures to code the external coordinates of experience on the ESF. We discuss special considerations for each of these dimensions of experience in the following sections.

Coding Date and Time of Day

The first information recorded on the ESF is the date and time of day. While this item is extremely straightforward, a few words about coding are still necessary. Even if all of the data were collected within the span of a single month or a single year, we advise coding the date to represent the month, day, and year in which data were collected. The reason for this is that most statistical software programs can use this information to generate the day of the week. It is often useful to compare responses on weekdays with those that occurred on weekends or compare subjective experience on different days of the week (Mondays vs. Fridays, for example). Before coding information about the date of the signal, it is advisable to refer to the specific software that will be used in the analysis to make sure that the data are coded in such a way that performing these or similar functions will be possible.

In addition to the date, participants also record the time they were signaled and the time they responded to the signal. Typically, these two "time" variables are coded in military time. For example, a response that occurred at 3:42 p.m. is coded as 1542. As with the coding of the date, this requires little forethought or training. There are two considerations about coding the "time" variables, however, which deserve mention here. The first is relevant in studies where participants are likely to be signaled or to respond to a signal after midnight, as might be the case in research involving night-shift workers. In such instances, one must devise a system for connecting a given signal to the correct date. For example, if a person is signaled at 11:57 p.m. on December 12 and responds to the signal at 12:02 a.m., it is important to know that this response occurred on December 13, not December 12. These distinctions become particularly important when analysis is focused on only those responses that occurred within a given time from the signal (say 15 minutes). If care is not taken to make this distinction, cases like the previous example will be unnecessarily excluded from analyses because it will appear that the signal was answered nearly 24 hours *before* it occurred. Such confusion can be avoided either by designing studies where signaling stops well before midnight (as is most often the case), by taking care to record the date when one is signaled and the date when one answers as two separate fields, or by otherwise flagging responses that occurred after midnight.

The second caveat when coding the time variable is relevant only in studies where data from different participants will ultimately be matched to one another according to the date and time of the signal. This is most often a consideration in studies of families where researchers are interested in examining different family members' perspectives at the same moment in time (see, e.g., Larson & Richards, 1994a; Schneider & Waite, 2005). In such cases, the time-signaled variable might require some force coding so that responses can be matched. Respondents are not always entirely accurate in their reports of the time they were signaled—often they misreport this information by a minute or two. In order for the data to be properly matched it is necessary for the *time-signaled* variable to be identical for all family members. The way this is typically done is that as the time variables are being coded, the coder refers to the master signaling schedule that was used to program the signaling device and makes sure that the *time-signaled* variable is identical to the time specified on the master schedule. For example, if a respondent reported being signaled at 10:43 a.m., and the master schedule indicates that he was to be signaled at 10:42 a.m., the *time-signaled* variable gets coded as 10:42 a.m. When we have used force coding on our studies, we typically specify that a reported time that falls within 10 minutes (plus or minus) of the scheduled time gets force coded to the scheduled time. Any responses that are more than 10 minutes apart from the scheduled signaling time must be examined to determine the cause of the discrepancy. We recommend doing this force coding by hand as we have just described rather than manipulating the data after it has been entered because often there are "extra" responses that don't appear to follow the intended signaling schedule. Physically looking at the ESF can reveal whether the reason for this discrepancy was a programming error in the schedule, misreporting of the date by the respondent (this is often the case), or a respondent who seems to be falsifying data.

Coding Locations

The second external dimension of experience concerns physical location. At the time of the signal, was the respondent at home in her kitchen, at work in her office, or on a bus? Typically, location is determined by the answer to an open-ended question "When signaled, where were you?" In an orientation meeting (see Chapter 3), participants are given instruction about how to respond to this question, and these responses are later reviewed by trained coders who place each response into one of several mutually exclusive coding categories. The substance and specificity of these coding categories depends on the type of research question being used. Studies have employed as few as 15 or 25 location categories (Csikszentmihalyi & Larson, 1984; Perrez, Schoebi, & Wilhelm, 2000) or as many as 150 (Schneider & Waite, 2005). Regardless of how many discrete categories are used, locations in most studies can usually be placed into the broader categories "school or work" (depending on whether it is a study of children or adults), "home," and "public." The degree of specificity within each of these domains is what tends to vary from study to study. For example, in their study of adolescents conducted in the late 1970s, Csikszentmihalyi and Larson (1984) specified eight location categories pertaining to the general domain of "school": classroom, gym and locker room, library, cafeteria, halls and bathrooms, student center, school grounds, and other. By contrast, in a later study of adolescents, Csikszentmihalyi and Schneider (2000) developed 47 discrete location categories in the school domain in order to obtain a more fine-grained picture of what adolescent experience is like inside particular classrooms. Examples of these location categories include mathematics class, biology class, history class, fine art class, as well as codes for being on the sports field, in the locker room, or in the hallway.

Analysis is easiest when specific location codes are organized in numerically sequential order according to broader categories. For example, codes 10 through 63 might refer to various school locations, 70 through 77 to home locations, and public place codes would be represented by location codes 80 through 130. If a study requires that location codes be very specific, further subgroups can be created (academic classes, nonacademic classes, etc.), and codes can be ordered in numerically sequential order according to these subcategories as well. As an illustration of this practice, we refer the reader to the location codes displayed in the codebook from the Sloan Study of Youth and Social Development in Appendix B. Organizing the codebook in this way makes coding easier, as coders will be able to more quickly find the appropriate code for a given response. Such organization makes analysis simpler as well, because often the detailed location categories are collapsed into more general categories (e.g., home, work, public). When codes are arranged in sequential order according to subcategories, recoding into more general categories is simpler. For example, analysts can simply recode the values 10–63 of the location variable into the value 1, which would represent all school locations. If codes are not arranged in numerically sequential order, such recoding is much more tedious.

The careful reader will note that in the examples previously given and in Appendix B there are numeric values in the sequential order of codes that are unoccupied by specific coding categories. For example, in the coding scheme previously described the values 63–69 have not been assigned to any specific location—they fall in between the "school" and "home" location codes. When developing the coding scheme, it is a good idea to leave a number of "free" codes in between major coding categories in order to allow for the possible addition of new codes during the coding process without interrupting the organization of the scheme. It is not advisable to add new coding categories once coding has begun, as this may require some recoding of previously coded data. However, in certain instances it may be necessary to do so, and this process is made a bit simpler by developing a scheme that will accommodate such additions should the need arise.

In some instances, it may be necessary to rely on supplementary information to accurately code participants' location. Respondents do not always describe where they are in a way that is informative to the researcher, but often their location can be ascertained by looking at other information on the ESF. For example, a child might respond that she is "in the library." It is not clear from this item alone whether she is in a public library, her school library, or even a library in her home. A quick glance at the rest of the ESF, however, indicates that this response occurred at 11:22 a.m. on a school day, and that the respondent was with classmates at the time of the signal. Further, the previous signal (recorded on the previous page in the book) occurred in gym class, and the next signal occurred in language arts. One can conclude with relative certainty that the location for this response should be coded using the "school" codes rather than a "public place" or "home" code. Some respondents will refer to names of local establishments when describing their location. For example, a respondent may report that he was "at the Mill" when he was signaled. It might not be obvious to the coder what "the Mill" is, particularly if the coder does not live in the same town as the respondent. However, in response to the question "What were you doing?" the respondent replies, "Ordering dinner and talking to the waiter." Looking at this supplementary information helps to conclude that the respondent's location should be coded as "restaurant."

There will inevitably be some responses that remain unclear, or do not fit neatly into any of the specified categories. We recommend establishing several location codes labeled "unspecified" or "other." It is advisable, for example, to have an "unspecified/other school (or work)" code, an "unspecified/other home" code, and an "unspecified/other public" code. "Unspecified" refers to those locations where respondents indicate only a general place, while "other" refers to more specific locations that are not explicitly defined in the coding scheme. For example, though advised not to do this, participants will often write "school" in response to the question "Where were you when signaled?" It is not clear from this if the respondent is in class, in the gym locker room, or in the cafeteria, and sometimes other information on the ESF does not help to clarify this. Responses of this type are coded as unspecified school locations. An example of an "other" home location might be when a respondent indicates that she is in "the exercise room" in her home. There is no code for home exercise room, and it does not fit well into any of the other home location categories. It is unlikely that many other respondents in the sample will have exercise rooms in their homes, and personal exercise is not of particular interest to the study, so developing a new location category for this response is not necessary. This response, then, is coded as an "other" home location. If during the coding process it becomes evident that a particular location coded as "other" is being mentioned by multiple respondents, and that this location might be of interest, one may want to consider creating a new code so that responses in that particular location can be examined separately.

Coding Activities

The coding of activities is similar to the coding of locations, though activity-coding schemes tend to be more complex and less clear-cut. A numeric code is typically assigned to participants' answers to the question "What was the main thing you were doing when signaled?" Many studies also include a question about secondary activities as well ("What else were you doing at the same time?"). The primary and secondary activities are coded using identical coding schemes. If a respondent lists more than two distinct activities (which in our experience is rare), only the first two activities listed are coded. As with location, it is easiest if the activity codes are organized by subcategory and assigned numeric codes in sequential order within each subcategory, taking care to leave "free codes" to develop new categories if absolutely necessary. As with the location codes, it is also advisable to designate "unspecified/other" codes for each relevant subcategory. An example of the activity codes used in the codebook for the Sloan Study of Youth and Social Development appears in Appendix B.

Just as many researchers, in their analyses, collapse more specific location codes into the more general categories of home, school (or work), and public, they also collapse activity codes to form more general categories, though there is not as much uniformity across studies regarding what these more general categories are. One distinction used frequently by Csikszentmihalyi and his colleagues in studies of adolescents (Csikszentmihalyi & Larson, 1984; Csikszentmihalyi, Rathunde, & Whalen, 1993) is to divide activities into the categories: productive activity, maintenance activity, and leisure. Productive activity includes class work, studying, and paid employment. Maintenance activities include eating, personal care, transportation, chores, and rest and napping. Leisure includes socializing, watching television, sports and games, music, art, hobbies, reading, thinking, and daydreaming. Oftentimes, the leisure category is further broken down into active leisure (sports, music, art, hobbies, socializing) and passive leisure (watching TV, reading, thinking, daydreaming, etc.).

Again as with location, it is sometimes necessary to rely on supplementary information to accurately code activity. For instance, a woman may respond that the main thing she was doing is "talking with Chuck." It is not clear simply by looking at the response to the activity question who Chuck is. Looking at the respondent's report of where she is and whom she is with, however, reveals that she is in the kitchen with her husband, enabling the researcher to code the activity as "talking with family." Referring to the respondent's location and companions often enables more accurate and specific coding of activity.

Although many ESFs include a question that asks respondents to record their thoughts at the time of the signal, occasionally respondents will report that "thinking" is their primary or secondary activity. Participants may report that the main thing they are doing is "wondering when my son will come home" or "thinking about the future." In order to facilitate the coding of these and similar responses, it is necessary to include one or more activity codes in the coding scheme that refer specifically to thinking. For example, in the activity codes listed in Appendix B, codes 350–356 refer to topics that adolescents were often thinking about, such as oneself, friends, family, and romantic interests. Coding a thought process as a primary or secondary activity is not to be confused with coding a participants' response to the question "What was on your mind?" which is described in the following section on coding the internal coordinates of experience.

The coding of participants' activities is not nearly as tidy as the coding of their location. For this reason it is extremely important to keep a running list of coding decisions to maintain consistent coding (e.g., "shopping for groceries" is considered a chore/errand, while "shopping at the mall with friends" is coded as socializing). In order to maintain the highest possible level of interrater reliability, it is necessary to have well-trained coders who meet regularly to discuss decisions and potential problems.

Coding Companionship

The final external dimension concerns who one was with at the time of the signal. This is usually assessed using a checklist on which participants indicate whether they were alone or with several other categories of people. The simplest way to code these data is to treat each category on the list as a separate variable to be dummy coded, for example, *alone, mother, father, sibling(s), friend(s), coworker(s),* and so on. Each category of person is assigned a value of 1 if the respondent was with this person at the time of the signal and is assigned a value of 0 if he was not. The same principle applies to the category "alone"—it is equal to 1 if the person was alone and 0 if the person was not. In analysis, these individually coded variables can later be used in conjunction with one another to construct mutually exclusive indicators of companionship.

Coding the Internal Coordinates of Experience

In most ESM studies, the internal coordinates of experience tend to be assessed primarily using semantic differential or Likert-type rating scales that require little or no coding.[1] For example, responses to numeric rating scales designed to measure levels of concentration, happiness, or attention can simply be entered into the database, without any coding or processing. One aspect of internal experience that is commonly assessed using an open-ended format is the participant's thoughts at the time of the signal. Typically, respondents are asked, "What was on your mind as you were signaled?" As one might imagine, responses to this type of question run the gamut, and coding of these responses is often tricky. Children and adolescents often think about hanging out with their friends, playing sports, doing their homework, or about the fight they had last night with their parents. Adults' minds may be occupied with concerns about the job, housework, their children, or an upcoming vacation. To code a person's thoughts, it works well to rely on the same list of categories used to code activities. Because the question being coded refers to thoughts and not actions, it is understood for example, when the response "hanging out with friends" gets coded as "socializing," that the respondent is *thinking about socializing,* but not necessarily doing it. Because respondents occasionally refer to general thoughts rather than thoughts about specific activities, it is important to develop a series of "thinking about" activities as discussed earlier. For example, in response to the question "What was on your mind?" many parents will respond, "My kids." Obviously "my kids" does not suggest any particular activity, so it is necessary to designate a category that represents "thinking about family" or even "thinking about children," depending on how specific the coding scheme is. You may refer again to the activity codes in Appendix B for examples of "thinking about" codes used in the Sloan Study of Youth and Social Development.

Coding one's thoughts and activities with the same coding scheme has several advantages. First, it significantly minimizes the already extensive list of codes that researchers must be familiar with in order to code the data. Coding ESM data is an extremely time-intensive process because of the complexity of the coding schemes and the sheer volume of data that is generated by each participant. Streamlining the coding in this way not only speeds up the process but also probably increases the accuracy with which these codes are applied. A second advantage to having identical coding schemes for thoughts and actions is that these two variables can be directly compared in analysis. It might be of interest, for example, to know whether participants are thinking about the activity in which they are engaged or whether their thoughts are focused elsewhere. Such convergence of thoughts and actions may indicate more focused attention and may be related to qualitatively different subjective experience (Delespaul & deVries, 1987; deVries & Delespaul, 1989; Schmidt, Shernoff, & Csikszentmihalyi, 2005).

Thus far we have described how to develop a coding scheme and how to apply it most effectively when making coding decisions. In the sections that follow, we discuss issues pertaining to the next steps in the process—physically coding and entering the data.

What to Do With the Codes Once They Are Developed: Physically Coding and Entering the Data

Researchers using paper-and-pencil methods often have questions about the best way to physically get the information from the written page into an electronic database. Because of the sheer volume of data that is generated in an ESM study, we have found it easiest in our research to physically code the data in the ESM booklets themselves (an alternative would be to record codes on a separate coding sheet, which would then be used for data entry). Typically, coders use pens with red ink, or some other color that is clearly discernable from participants' writing, and record the appropriate codes in the left-hand or right-hand margin of the ESF, alongside the item that is being coded. It is recommended that coders also be provided with an ample supply of correction fluid so that any inaccurate codes can be removed from sight to avoid confusion during data entry. Coding the open-ended items goes rather slowly at first, but as coders become more familiar with the codebook the process moves along much more quickly. We have found that after just a few days, research assistants become so familiar with the frequently used codes that they are able to entertain themselves by speaking to one another in ESM code. For example, a student might say, "I'm going to go the 61, then I'm off to the 52 to 431" (translation: "I'm going to go to the restroom, then I'm off to the cafeteria to eat lunch"). The time it takes to code the data for a single person will depend on the format of the ESF, the number of times respondents were signaled, the response rate, and the familiarity of the coder with the codebook. In studies involving ESFs like the ones shown in Appendix A (which involved fairly substantial coding), we estimate that it took experienced coders just over an hour on average to code the data for a single person (each person was signaled 56 times). In order to budget the appropriate amount of time and financial resources to coding, we recommend keeping careful track of the time it takes to code the data in the pilot study and use this as a guide for planning for the full-scale study.

All coding should be randomly checked throughout the process. Early on, some portion of the data should be coded by at least two persons to determine interrater reliability, and changes should be made in the procedures if the reliability does not meet acceptable levels. We typically expect our coders to agree on codes at least 85 percent of the time—usually interrater reliability in our studies falls in the 85–90 percent range (see Chapter 6 for more information on interrater reliability across several different types of studies). We can offer no hard-and-fast rules about how much of the data should be checked for interrater reliability: this depends on the size of the sample and how many different people are coding the data. In a study involving only 30 participants whose data are being coded by 2 researchers, double-coding 10 percent of the data (or 3 persons' worth) seems adequate (recall that 3 persons' worth of data can be a lot of data, with 56 or more responses per person). However, in very large studies where 15 or 20 research assistants are coding the data, it may be necessary to devise a more complex system for checking reliability, where different coders are paired with one another to check reliability among several combinations of coders.

An advantage to hand coding the data is that it may enable researchers to more readily identify participants who did not take the study seriously. As one is coding the ESF, it is easy to spot those cases where a respondent marked the same answer for every response on a given page, seemed to be responding randomly, or ordered his or her responses to make recognizable patterns on the page. Because coders are looking at each individual's entire set of responses, it is also easier to identify respondents who may have falsified their data. For example, you may run across a day's worth of reports where at 9:20 a.m. the respondent reports being at home napping, and at 10:05 a.m. he says he is in the exercise room at an out-of-state hotel (on a business trip), and at 11:37 a.m. he is sitting in his backyard reading a newspaper. As this series of activities is logistically impossible, the coder should investigate whether the data appear to be falsified or whether the respondent made some error in recording the date and/or time. This and other types of data falsification does happen from time to time and is more difficult to detect using computerized data collection methods because researchers are not physically looking at the data as a whole. We discuss several ways to identify questionable data electronically in the section below on data file setup, cleaning, and manipulation. Questionable entries can either be entered and flagged as questionable or excluded from the electronic data file.

Once the data have been coded and interrater reliability checked, the data must be entered (by research assistants or a data entry service) into an electronic database. We highly recommend the use of a data-entry service if at all possible. In our experience, a service will complete the data entry task much more quickly than even the most motivated research assistants. Also, most services operate on a per-keystroke fee schedule and can estimate fairly accurately how much a job will cost and how long it will take, so you will know exactly how much time and money to budget. Further, services typically provide accuracy guarantees, double entering a certain percentage of the data, checking for agreement, and re-entering the data if the error rate is higher than a certain percentage.

Setup, Cleaning, and Manipulation of Data Files

The topics covered in the remainder of this chapter pertain to both computerized and paper-and-pencil ESM studies. The data must be either uploaded or entered by hand into a file. Here we discuss the structure and manipulation of typical ESM files. The structure of an ESM file differs from standard surveys in that data are recorded at the level of the response, not the person. Each person, then, contributes multiple cases to the file. The number of cases per person is usually not uniform but varies according to the number of signals each person responded to.[2] Because in ESM data sets a "case" refers to a response and not a person, even in studies with small samples the number of cases is very large. For example, an ESM study of 50 people is likely to generate a data file with more than 2,000 cases.

In data sets created from most standard surveys, cases are uniquely identified by an ID number: This is not the case with ESM data. Here cases are uniquely identified by the combination of an ID number, the date (month, day, and year), and the time of signal. Such files are typically referred to as *response-level* or *beep-level* data files (as compared to *person-level* data files, described in the following paragraphs). Occasionally researchers also record the ESM booklet number (if multiple booklets are used by a single person in a paper-and-pencil study) and the page number in the booklet in order to find specific responses more efficiently in the paper data, should the need arise. This type of cataloging is not necessary in order to uniquely identify cases, but is often helpful in the process of data cleaning and in cases where one wishes to return to the original data source. Table 4.1 provides an illustration of what nine responses from two hypothetical teenage participants (ID#101 and #102) might look like when stored as a data file using a program like SPSS or Excel. If these data were from an actual study, each participant would likely have more than four or five responses, and each case would contain more than the 18 variables listed. This table is simply intended to give the reader a sense of the general structure of a response-level data file.

Referring to the codes displayed in Appendix B, one can see how a person's responses are quantified and stored in electronic format. For example, the first entry in Table 4.1 came from respondent #101 on September 25, 2002. He was signaled at 5:26 p.m. (1726 in military time) and responded

Table 4.1   Illustration of Hypothetical ESM Data

	Month	Day	Year	Time Signaled	Time Responded	Location	Main Activity	Secondary Activity	Thoughts	Was Alone	Was w/Mother	Was w/Father	Was w/Friends	Was w/Classmates	Concentration	Enjoyment	Etc.
101	09	25	02	1726	1726	72	232	401	232	1	0	0	0	0	8	3	⋮
101	09	25	02	2007	2019	72	401	434	351	1	0	0	0	0	5	2	⋮
101	09	26	02	0811	0812	53	334	435	231	0	0	0	1	0	3	7	⋮
101	09	26	02	0956	1002	26	214	212	246	0	0	0	1	1	9	7	⋮
102	09	25	02	0742	0748	71	431	331	200	0	1	1	0	0	5	6	⋮
102	09	25	02	1007	1007	60	231	451	231	0	0	0	1	1	8	4	⋮
102	09	25	02	1114	1128	52	334	431	356	0	0	0	1	0	5	9	⋮
102	09	25	02	1401	1401	15	215	333	215	0	0	0	0	1	9	7	⋮

immediately. When he was signaled he was in his bedroom (location code 72), and the main thing he was doing was English homework (activity code 232). He was also listening to the radio at the same time (activity code 401), but his thoughts were focused on the homework he was doing (thought code 232). He was alone, and while his concentration was high (8 on a 9-point scale), he was not particularly enjoying himself at this moment (3 on a 9-point scale) and did not feel particularly skilled (4 on a 9-point scale). Once all of the raw scores are stored in the database, one can format the data for use by any statistical software package, specifying variable names and adding variable labels, value labels, and defining missing value codes as needed.

The sheer volume of data and the various steps involved in getting them into useable format essentially guarantees that some errors, either in coding, data entry, or data file specification will occur. Of course the potential for many of these errors is reduced significantly with computerized formats, though there is still a small risk of error in reading the data or properly specifying the file. As with all new data sets, it is necessary to do careful checking and appropriate cleaning of the data file by closely examining frequency distributions for unexpected patterns or out-of-range values, cross-tabulating key variables with one another, and comparing random cases in the electronic file to the original paper data (if applicable). One method we have found useful for identifying respondents who may not have taken the ESM seriously is to compute and examine within-person correlations between variables one might expect to be related to one another in some way. For example, if a respondent has a within-person correlation between happiness and enjoyment that is near 0 or is negative, this might indicate that she was filling out her responses randomly. Similarly, someone with a within-person correlation between happiness and sadness that is near 1 might be marking the same response (e.g., all 7s) for all scaled questions without considering his true feelings. If paper-and-pencil methods are being used, coders will be able to identify many of the respondents not taking the process seriously simply by looking at the ESFs (this was discussed in the previous section on coding). This type of electronic data checking will likely yield a few more suspect cases in paper-and-pencil methods and is the primary tool for identifying questionable cases when using computerized methods.

Response-Level Data and Person-Level Data

The beauty and strength of ESM lies in the fact that it produces multiple assessments of a single individual, allowing for the observation of within-person changes in subjective experience across the many contexts of life.

There are some pieces of information that we may want to know—like one's gender, age, ethnicity, or annual income—that are not likely to change at all over the course of the study and thus don't need to be asked each time a person is signaled. To deal with the fact that most questions addressed by ESM research also require the collection of some person-level data, participants are typically asked to respond to a more traditional survey in addition to completing the ESM. These surveys can provide a variety of information ranging from demographic characteristics to general descriptions of one's work or family life, to more global assessments of cognitive, affective, or personality variables. Once these person-level data are available electronically they can be matched, either temporarily or permanently, to the response-level ESM file using the respondents' ID numbers. Often very basic descriptive information like gender, age, or race/ethnicity is permanently added to the ESM file, while other person-level data are stored in a separate data file that can be temporarily matched to the ESM file as the need arises.

Person-level and response-level data can be matched using two different methods. First, as was previously suggested, person-level data can simply be matched to the response-level ESM file. In other words, survey data from one case (representing one person, who is uniquely identified in the file by an ID number) will be matched to multiple cases in the ESM file (representing multiple responses from that same person, which are *not* uniquely identified in the file by the ID number). An alternative method that sometimes is used is that ESM data are aggregated to the level of the person, such that a case now represents a person rather than a single response. In this aggregated file, measures of happiness, concentration, enjoyment and the like represent the *average* of a given person's responses across the entire study rather than one's rating at a single moment in time. An example of what aggregated data for the two individuals presented in Table 4.1 might look like is presented in Table 4.2. Note that when data are aggregated, all of the context-specific information in the response-level data file is lost. Only variables that can be meaningfully consolidated (by computing a mean, sum, or percentage, for example) can be retained in an aggregated file. Our sample aggregated data set no longer includes variables representing the date or time signaled or one's activities or thoughts. The data file now contains variables representing the mean levels of concentration, enjoyment, and skill across all responses. Additionally, there are variables indicating the percentage of responses in which respondents indicated that they were alone, and the percentage of responses in which they indicated they were with classmates or friends. One could similarly construct variables to represent the percentage of responses in which participants reported being in a certain location or engaging in a particular type of activity.

Table 4.2   Illustration of Aggregation of Hypothetical ESM Data From Table 4.1

ID	% Time Alone	% Time With Classmates/ Friends	Concentration	Enjoyment	Skill	Etc.
101	.50	.50	6.25	3.80	6.25	...
102	0	.80	5.80	7.00	5.00	...

One can also construct person-level data sets based on only a subset of all ESM responses. For example, one could select only those cases where respondents reported being alone and aggregate only these responses to the person level. The resulting data set would represent respondents' average ratings of their experience when they were alone. Once the ESM data have been aggregated to the person level, they can easily be matched to the person-level survey data using respondents' ID (which serves as a unique identifier in both files, enabling a one-to-one match). The process of data aggregation and the implications of person-level versus response-level analysis are discussed in greater detail in Chapter 5.

Postentry Data Manipulation

Once the data have been entered, formatted for one's software of choice, and cleaned, the fun of exploring the data and testing hypotheses can begin. Because ESM data sets tend to be very complex, prior to conducting detailed analyses most ESM researchers use statistical analysis software to recode and otherwise manipulate the data in order to make it more user-friendly or to construct new variables. Such data manipulation (e.g., reverse-scoring negatively worded items, computing factor scores) is standard in quantitative research, and it is beyond the scope of this chapter to describe the many ways this can be done. We do think it is necessary, however, to mention a few modifications that may be somewhat unique to ESM studies. As was just mentioned, person-level information such as gender, race and ethnicity, or age is often permanently added to the ESM data file so that group comparisons can be made easily without having to match response-level ESM data to person-level survey data. Second, information about the month, day, and year of each response is typically used to generate information about the day of the week. This simple operation is a standard function in most statistical analysis software and can be achieved through issuing the appropriate syntax or using pull-down menus.

There are also a variety of data-reduction techniques that are commonly used among ESM researchers. As is the case in any analytical project, it is important for the analyst to look carefully at descriptive statistics for each variable before taking steps to consolidate the data. Combining multiple variables could make it more difficult to detect both interesting patterns and errors in the data. As was previously mentioned, it is common to construct more general categories to represent locations, activities, and thoughts—essentially collapsing the more specific codes that were originally assigned. This can be done either by recoding the existing entry or by computing a new variable to represent the more general categories (the latter procedure keeps the original coding intact, which is usually desirable). For example, one might collapse the location codes listed in Appendix B into three general location codes. One could create a new variable (called *generalplace*) that would take on a value of "1" when the original place code fell between 10 and 63, "2" when place was between 70 and 77, and "3" when place was between 80 and 130. Here the original location codes have been reduced from 80 categories to three, representing school locations (*generalplace* = 1), home locations (*generalplace* = 2), and public locations (*generalplace* = 3).

The data regarding one's companions is often used to construct a variety of more complex representations of whom the respondent was with at the time of the signal. For each occasion that respondents are not alone, they have the potential to be with any combination of others (e.g., alone with their spouse, with their spouse and children, with coworkers and strangers). One can use the dummy-coded companion variables to construct a single indicator that represents every possible combination of companions. If one is interested in studying experience with specific companions (say, spouses vs. friends), decisions must be made about how to construct mutually exclusive companion categories (i.e., how does one categorize situations where one is with one's spouse *and* one's friends?). Let's say we want to be able to compare situations where one is with one's spouse to when one is with friends. For the sake of this example, we will exclude all cases where children are present and assume that it is not important whether or not additional others (strangers, coworkers, for example) are present as well. We can decide that situations where both one's spouse and one's friends are present will be coded as "spouse" occasions rather than "friend" occasions (alternatively, we could have constructed three categories—spouse only, friend only, and spouse and friend). To do this we simply create a new variable (called *whowith*) that is equal to "1" when respondents are with their spouse and not with their children (regardless of whether or not they were with friends). The variable *whowith* equals "2" when respondents are with friends and not with their spouses or children. A value of "0" indicates either that children were present at the same time as spouses or friends, or that neither spouses nor friends were present.

ESF variables are often used in combination with one another to construct composite indicators of internal states like general mood, activation, or motivation. As in traditional survey research, composite measures may emerge as a result of factor analysis or may be designed to be consistent with previous research. Composite measures can be constructed in a variety of ways—by computing means, sums, factor scores, or a variety of other methods. Composite measures that have become common in ESM research and their psychometric properties are discussed in Chapter 6.

For rating scale data, often a standardized metric is easier to interpret than raw scores and offers the advantage of controlling for individual differences in scale usage (favoring extremes versus middling responses, for example). Taking each variable separately, response-level data are standardized (Z-scored) by subtracting the individual's overall mean on that variable and then dividing by the individual's standard deviation on that variable. (In SPSS, this procedure is easily accomplished by splitting the file by a variable distinguishing unique individuals, such as ID number, and then performing a "descriptives" analysis and selecting the option to "save standardized values as variables.") The result is a variable in which the value 0 represents an average score for a given person, whether that rating is 5.7 for one individual or 3.2 for another, on the same 10-point raw scale. Further, the value of 1 indicates a score one standard deviation above the individual's mean, and −1 indicates one standard deviation below the individual's mean. Applications for the use and interpretation of person-level Z-scores are described in detail in Chapter 5.

Data File Management and Documentation

Once again, we must remind the reader of the importance of establishing and documenting clear procedures for the storage and manipulation of electronic data. Because ESM research is so labor intensive, there are often multiple researchers and research assistants handling the data. Multiple data handlers means greater risk that the data will be saved or stored incorrectly, that important files will be unintentionally overwritten, or that analysts will be using files that are outdated. No matter what procedures you develop to avoid these often catastrophic mishaps, it is important that everyone working with the data has been trained in these procedures, and that there is a manual that anyone involved can refer to for any question. There are a few data management issues that are unique to data collected via PDAs or palmtop computers. In order to minimize the risk of data loss due to dying batteries, machine damage, loss or theft, participants in such studies are often required to meet with researchers multiple times during the signaling period to upload their data to a computer. It is important to make sure that uploaded data are saved in the proper directory, using the proper filenames, making sure that previously saved data are not being duplicated or over-written. As we mentioned previously, it is advisable to have a single computer with an easy-to-follow directory structure whose only use is uploading and housing data (Conner Christensen et al., 2003).

In our lab we have found it useful to designate a single data manager: This person is responsible for handling the data file until it is ready to be distributed to multiple analysts. This person makes sure all appropriate labels are put on the variables in the file and oversees the cleaning and checking of the file. He or she handles all of the "postentry data manipulation" we described previously and constructs any composite variables that may be of interest to multiple users of the data. The data manager then constructs a document detailing names and descriptions of each variable in the file, as well as any special issues users of the data should be aware of. A well-documented data set will minimize the misuse of data in analyses. If multiple versions of the data file are to be released, the data manager is responsible for notifying all users when a new version is ready for release. The data manager is also the point person for analysts who find abnormalities in the data: when analysts find previously unidentified errors in the data (and they will), they inform the data manager, who is then responsible for correcting the problem and redistributing the (now cleaner) data. The data file manager is also responsible for maintaining backup copies of all data files in the event that the computer on which data are stored gets corrupted or damaged.

The aforementioned procedures and documentation are all intended to facilitate productive analysis of the data. Once the initial investment has been made in collecting and setting up a data set, the payoff is a wide range of analytical possibilities. In the chapters that follow, we offer specific details about the types of analyses that are possible with these data and will provide many illustrations of work that has been done using this methodology.

Notes

1. Notable exceptions include studies by Hulburt (1979) and Brandstätter (1983), in which respondents simply took notes in an open-ended format that were later coded.

2. Alternatively, one could construct a data file that contains the same number of cases for each person: cases representing missed signals would simply indicate the date and time of the signal, but all other data in the case would be missing. This file structure is desirable if you plan to do extensive analyses of response rates at specific times of day.

5

Types of Analyses

A s psychological research has been expanding it has become increasingly specialized, carving out ever more narrow topic areas with the result that findings are often decontextualized from each other and from lived experience. The particular research design, the experimental condition and instrumentation used, may generate interesting results but without much "ecological validity"—in other words, they often only apply within the conditions of the study and not beyond.

One of the unfortunate consequences of this trend is that specialization extends to research methodologies. At the most basic level, most researchers would recognize the "qualitative" versus "quantitative" distinction and would readily place themselves within one or the other research paradigm. Many could go much further and name specific qualitative or quantitative methodologies they routinely employ in their studies. Those with this sharp distinction in mind will then develop a first impression that ESM is not just another quantitative method, it is a quantitative researcher's dream. After all, the sheer volume of numbers produced by an ESM study lends itself well to some complex statistical analyses. Aspects of personality manifested in daily life, such as self-esteem, can be measured by multiple items over multiple time points across multiple contexts. Thus the utility of ESM for quantitative research on human lives and conditions can hardly be overstated.

Yet ESM can also be a valuable qualitative research tool, letting us know, in the participants' own voices, what they are doing, thinking, and feeling, and how they are perceiving their social and physical environment. The questions asked on each ESM form can be fully tailored by the researcher and can be made more or less open ended as the researcher sees fit. For example, the question "How do different classroom activities affect the engagement of high school students in the curricular content?" could be addressed with a purely qualitative approach. This would involve analyzing responses students provided during classes to the question "As you were beeped, what were you thinking?" for narrative content to reveal connections (or disconnections) between the thoughts of students and the topic of the class. On the other hand, the same question could be addressed through purely quantitative means by comparing the average ratings students gave during different classroom activities on scales measuring "interest," "enjoyment," or "concentration."

This two-pronged example is not meant to imply that qualitative researchers should design their own qualitative ESM and quantitative researchers should focus only on numeric rating scales and percentages. In fact, ESM is best used when both the qualitative and quantitative information it provides is brought to bear on a broad question. By linking together quantitative and qualitative approaches in one instrument, ESM transcends the dichotomy between the two and encourages researchers to break the habit of addressing research problems with only one narrow methodology. ESM research can also be combined with lab studies to address both qualitative and quantitative questions, as Feldman Barrett (e.g., Feldman Barrett, Gross, Christensen, & Benvenuto, 2001) has done.

In this chapter, types of analyses that can be useful with ESM data will be described and examples in past research of specific applications of each analysis will be provided. The order of presentation will follow the continuum from qualitative to quantitative. The choice of which analyses to perform is obviously dependent on the kind of question one is interested in. However, for any given purpose, even if it involves a precisely worded question about persons or about situations (see Chapter 3 and Larson & Delespaul, 1992), there will be multiple analytical options, as evidenced by the previous example. Although performing more analyses and more complex analyses of different types is likely to produce the richest picture of the contents and contexts of human lives, there is also something powerful about a simple graph of one participant's mood changes over one week, denoted with her concurrent thoughts and activities.

Qualitative Approaches

One of the most widely used qualitative functions of ESM data is to illustrate a particular experiential pattern through the use of the detailed description of a single case. Three books, each describing a different ESM study, provide the best examples of the use of this approach (Csikszentmihalyi &

Larson, 1984; Csikszentmihalyi, Rathunde, & Whalen, 1993; Larson & Richards, 1994a). In each book a description of a single individual (or family) is presented within the first five pages. The descriptions focus in on a precise moment in time and provide details on what the respondents were doing, thinking, and feeling, as well as where they were and who they were with. From there, the discussion broadens to consider the participant's entire week, and how this pattern of experience is both illustrative of a wider pattern and unique to a particular individual. This qualitative technique serves not only as a means of capturing the reader's interest by giving life to the data in a way that a numerical table could not. It also reminds both the reader and the researcher that the actual lives behind the data are much more complex, messy, and nuanced than even the most sophisticated statistical analyses could show. Finally, the process of doing this qualitative work may lead the researcher to discover trends or patterns that had not previously been considered. Recognizing the power of single-case studies, Valsiner and Molenaar (2005) recently launched a journal dedicated to the analysis of single cases. Of course, reading through individual ESM forms, unlike split-second statistical computations, requires a tremendous amount of time. But the advantages of doing so usually make the effort worthwhile.

Another qualitative approach is to focus on a single situation, rather than a single person. Csikszentmihalyi and Larson (1984), for example, focused on one world history class over four days in the lives of eight members of their high school sample. They described the activation level, thoughts, actions, and comments of each of the students during this class period. This approach is not as frequently used as person descriptions, perhaps because it is difficult to find well-defined situations shared by several members of a sample over several days. One way to gather more information about specific situations and issues is to supplement ESM with individual semistructured interviews. If the interviews are conducted at the end of the ESM signaling period, the interviewer can read through the participant's responses, asking for elaboration on particularly interesting moments in order to stimulate a conversation about specific issues. Csikszentmihalyi and Schneider (2000) used this technique to bring both ESM and interview data to shed light on the tension between what students enjoy in school and what they believe will be important for their future.

Often a week of ESM responses will include unexpected, unique situations that could not be studied any other way. For instance while Ann Wells (1985) was collecting data for her dissertation, a couple decided to get divorced in the middle of the week; this made it possible to compare in detail the changes in mood and emotion the two partners underwent before and after the event. In a study of high school math students by Rick Robinson (1986), one of the teenage boys who had been depressed for several days made a serious suicide attempt that fortunately was foiled by his sister noticing an empty bottle of pills near his bed. Following this boy's activities, thoughts, and feelings for the several days preceding the event gives a powerful insight into the dynamics of suicidal behavior. Two Himalayan climbers, members of an expedition studied by colleagues at the University of Milan, were buried in their tents by an avalanche for two days—their ESM reports provide a unique window into extremely stressful situations (Delle Fave, Bassi, & Massimini, 2003). Such unexpected opportunities may not interest those who want only a "yes-or-no" answer to a specific question, but they can be illuminating to anyone who cares to understand the complexity of human experience in all its facets.

Graphic and Numeric Descriptive Information

To supplement their qualitative analysis of the world history class, Csikszentmihalyi and Larson (1984) provided a simple graphic depicting each person's self-rated level of activation in the class, as well as the average activation level for the class as a whole. Elsewhere in the book, they plotted one student's mood ratings over the course of 36 moments in 1 week and recorded her thoughts and activities corresponding to each point on the graph. These graphs are reproduced here as Figures 5.1 and 5.2. Graphs such as these bridge the gap between qualitative and quantitative approaches. Numbers from ESM are tabled or graphed to make the qualitative description of the person or situation more complete. These numbers are derived from the rating scales and from percentages of moments spent in different categories of thought, activity, location, or companionship.

Response-Level Data

In addition to describing a single case, numbers and graphs can also be used descriptively to summarize characteristics of a sample. Before discussing these approaches further, we need first to consider what the "sample" is. At one level (what some have called the "beep" or "response-level"), the sample is comprised of a collection of moments in time in the lives of several individuals. When data are initially entered, the structure of the database is usually designed as a response-level file, wherein one "case," or row of data, represents one self-report form completed by one person in response to one ESM signal. A summary of these moments can be created in tables or graphs of mean ratings of continuous scales and relative frequencies (percentages) of categorical variables. This strategy was used by Csikszentmihalyi and Larson (1984), who used pie charts to depict how adolescents allocated their time among different activities and locations (see Figure 5.3).

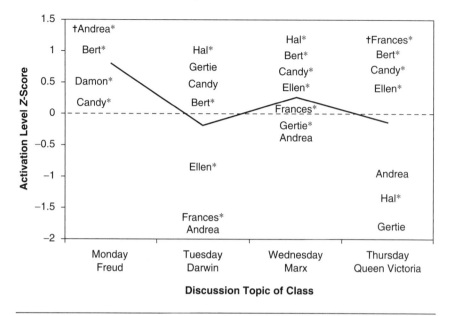

Figure 5.1   A Profile of Activation Levels in One History Class Over Four Days

SOURCE: From *Being Adolescent: Conflict and Growth in the Teenage Years* by Mihaly Csikszentmihalyi. Copyright © 1984 by Basic Books, Inc. Reprinted by permission of Basic Books, a member of Perseus Books, L.L.C.

NOTES: The dark line shows the average for each class session. †Indicates student who is giving the presentation. *Students who report paying attention.

Using Z-Scores

As was described in Chapter 4, it is often desirable to apply a standardized metric to rating scale data. Standardized scores offer the advantage of controlling for individual differences in scale usage (favoring extremes versus middling responses, for example). Z-scored variables are not useful in examining the overall means of a sample because those means will be zero by definition. Where Z-scored variables can offer an advantage is in more fine-grained examinations of experience in different contexts. To see how this works, consider the ratings of happiness recorded by two hypothetical participants in an ESM study. In Figure 5.4, we plot their raw scores and corresponding Z-scores over ten ESM responses. Heather uses a smaller range of the response scale than Michael and favors more positive responses overall. If we are interested in the context of "TV watching," and both participants were watching TV during response 6, we would reach different conclusions depending on which measurement scale we used. When raw scores are used, it appears that TV is a neutral event for Heather, who rated

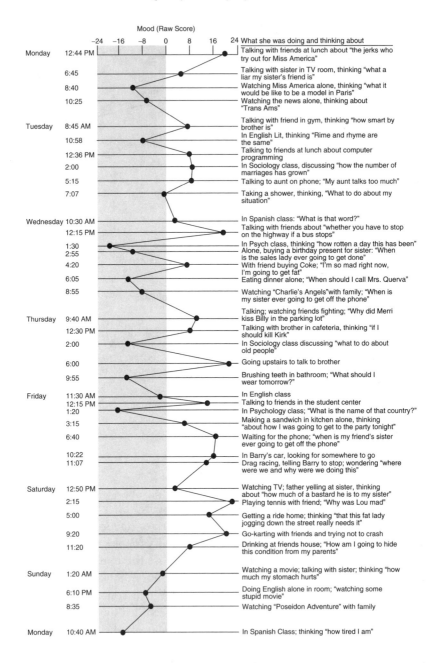

Figure 5.2   The Week of Lorraine Monawski

SOURCE: From *Being Adolescent: Conflict and Growth in the Teenage Years* by Mihaly Csikszentmihalyi. Copyright © 1984 by Basic Books, Inc. Reprinted by permission of Basic Books, a member of Perseus Books, L.L.C.

NOTE: Chart shows Lorraine's mood score for each of her self-reports.

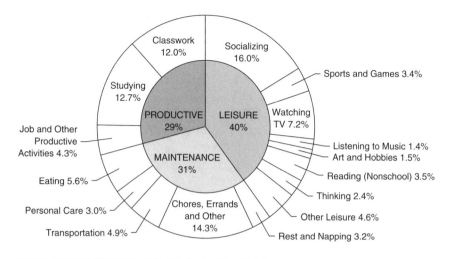

Figure 5.3   The External Landscape: What Adolescents Spend Their Time Doing

SOURCE: From *Being Adolescent: Conflict and Growth in the Teenage Years* by Mihaly Csikszentmihalyi. Copyright © 1984 by Basic Books, Inc. Reprinted by permission of Basic Books, a member of Perseus Books, L.L.C.

it a 4, the midpoint of the 7-point scale. Michael appears to be slightly unhappier during TV watching, as indicated by the 3 he recorded. We could stop with this interpretation and conclude that Heather is objectively happier than Michael. On the other hand, relative to Heather's other experiences, TV watching appears to be a pretty negative experience (Z-score of −1.2), whereas it is much less negative (−0.5) within the realm of Michael's experiences. Thus if we are interested in levels of happiness during different contexts as it is perceived within each person's own frame of reference, we would do well to use Z-scores. In a real-life example of this approach, Larson and Richards (1994a) plotted the Z-scored emotion ratings of working mothers and fathers at seven different times of the day, documenting the "six o'clock crash" of negative emotions experienced by mothers (but not fathers) when they return home from work.

Person-Level Data

In considering the research question underlying such a graph, one may have difficulty determining whether the relevant sample is the response-level sample of moments or the smaller sample of individuals. For analyses employing inferential statistics, it is usually best to focus on the sample of individuals, as we will explain shortly. For descriptive purposes, either sampling level can be used, depending on the research questions. To construct a

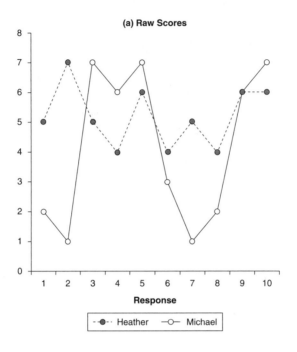

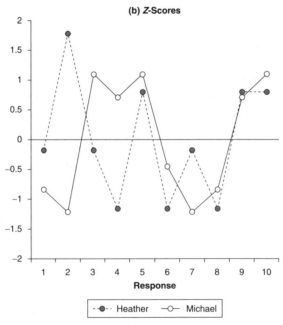

Figure 5.4   Comparison of Raw and Z-Scores Over Ten Responses of Two Hypothetical Participants

NOTE: (a) shows the raw scores, and (b) shows how the same scores would look when transformed into Z-scores.

person-level data file, that is, a dataset in which the individual person is the fundamental unit, data are aggregated within each person by taking the mean of each rating scale across all observations and by calculating the percentage of the person's observations in each of several relevant categories of location, activity, and thought content (see Chapter 4 for further discussion). The person-level data file can also contain mean (raw and/or Z-scored) ratings of scale variables while the person is in specific contexts (e.g., with friends, at work, at 6 p.m., or while watching television). For more details on creating these files, see also Larson and Delespaul's (1992) excellent guidebook.

Planning for Statistical Analyses

Given the complexity of ESM data, researchers may develop the impression that only complex statistical analyses are appropriate in ESM research. Although complex multivariate strategies show much promise for particular applications, we would advise against relying on any one technique to make sense of ESM data. Instead, researchers would do well to pursue several qualitative and quantitative approaches to address a set of related questions.

As a way of organizing the multiple statistical procedures that should be considered in any analysis plan, we have arranged our discussion from the most basic and traditional strategies to the newer and more complex analyses. A useful way of categorizing these strategies would divide them into those based on the ordinary least squares (OLS) linear model, such as analysis of variance (ANOVA) and OLS regression, and those based on multilevel modeling or hierarchical linear modeling. One of the major decisions necessary when using OLS strategies, which is whether to analyze the data using the response-level or person-level approach, becomes irrelevant in a multilevel approach that considers responses and persons simultaneously. For this reason, ESM researchers are increasingly turning to multilevel strategies. Nevertheless, a basic grounding in issues and techniques surrounding the use of OLS strategies with ESM data is essential.

Choosing the Response or Person-Level Approach in OLS Strategies

Whether the research question is one about situations or about persons, analyses appropriate to the question can be conducted at the response level or person level. In most cases, the person-level approach is to be preferred if p-values are going to be examined. One of the problems of response-level analysis is that it violates the assumption of independence of observations, an assumption required in order to validly infer from a sample to a population. Observations within each person are not independent, and observations that are adjacent in time are likely to be interrelated even more. It should be noted, however, that although response-level data are not independent because many responses come from the same person, they are independent in another sense: they come from different situations and different points in time. Traditional testing involves placing many subjects (who are independent from each other) in one large hall or laboratory at one time (negating the possible effects of different times and places). Thus both ways of gathering data have their advantages and disadvantages.

One feature of response-level analysis, the large N, might be seen as an advantage to researchers bent on achieving statistical significance, but can actually be a problem if trivial effects are given too much credence. P-values are partly dependent on sample size, so that with, say, 3,000 total responses, the tiniest of differences will turn out to be statistically significant. Therefore if results from response-level analyses are reported, they should be accompanied by effect-size information so the reader can judge the "meaningful" or "clinical" significance of the result alongside the statistical significance. A further problem of response-level analysis is that some individuals contribute more data than others to the dataset, and the individuals who complete the most self-reports may not be representative of the whole sample.

Person-level analysis avoids these problems because each person is "counted" in the data just once. Inferential statistics are based on the number of persons and are consequently more conservative, making a Type I error less likely. However, person-level analysis is often more complex. The tricky part is in setting up the data to be analyzed, specifically in determining how to create a single aggregated variable that measures what it is intended to measure. For example, to measure (at the person-level) alertness while watching television, one would compute an aggregate alertness value for each person by averaging across only those self-reports on which the person reported watching television. This process does not entirely remove the problem of unequal weighting because the aggregated alertness ratings of some people will be based on many TV-watching moments, while others may have only one or none at all. Indeed, to conduct analyses of experience during rare contexts (such as during illegal drug use), researchers may be forced to use response-level data, as most respondents would have no data to aggregate.

OLS Statistical Techniques

Comparing Groups of People

One of the most basic types of analyses is to compare groups of people, such as females to males, adolescents to parents, and clinical to normative

Table 5.1   Mean Level of Moods Over the Course of a Week

Mood	Talented (N = 208)	Average (N = 41)
Affect		
Happy	4.87	5.15**
Cheerful	4.51	4.89***
Sociable	4.59	5.06***
Potency		
Alert	4.68	5.04**
Active	4.25	4.46
Strong	4.41	4.69**
Excited	4.10	4.43**
Concentration		
(How much were you concentrating)	4.39	4.82**
Motivation		
(Wish to be doing activity)	4.29	5.26***

SOURCE: Csikszentmihalyi, Rathunde, and Whalen. Copyright © 1993 Cambridge University Press. Reprinted with the permission of Cambridge University Press.

NOTES: The figures above are group-means based on individual means. The actual number of observations that contributed to them was over 7,000 for the talented group and over 1,500 for the average group.

Significance of t-tests between the two groups: $*p < .05$. $**p < .01$. $***p < .001$.

samples. Groups can be compared on how much time they spend in various locations, with various types of companions, or doing different kinds of activities. The aggregate variables in these types of analyses are usually expressed as a percentage of the individual's total self-reports. Thus if a given individual submitted 30 self-reports and reported daydreaming on 3 of them, a researcher creating a "percent time daydreaming" variable would compute 10 percent for this person. Rating scales are another dimension on which groups can be compared. Csikszentmihalyi and colleagues (1993) compared talented to average adolescents on nine dimensions of experience by simply computing a person-level average rating across all self-reports for each individual on each dimension (see Table 5.1). They used t-tests to test for statistical significance, but if more than two groups are being compared, ANOVAs could be used instead. Analysis of covariance (ANCOVA) could also be used if the researcher wanted to control for a covariate.

Groups of individuals can also be compared on their ratings of experience within specific contexts, as in the previous example of alertness during TV viewing. In these cases, either raw scores or Z-scores can be used to create within-context aggregated variables. Which type of scores to use depends on the aims of the research and the assumptions underlying response scale usage. If all participants are assumed to map their internal states onto the raw scales in the same way, and the goal is to test for group differences using a common "objective" scale, then raw scores should be used. If the goal is to treat every individual's experience in a context relative to his or her own internal frame of reference, then Z-scores would be preferred. Whichever method is chosen, the process for computing within-context aggregated variables is the same. From a response-level file, compute individual averages of the desired variables using only those self-reports matching the desired context. Continuing with the comparison of their talented and average adolescent samples, Csikszentmihalyi and colleagues (1993) compared mean Z-scores of nine dimensions of experience during several different contexts (alone, with friends, while working on productive activities, etc.). Their analyses revealed interesting and theoretically meaningful differences, not only between the two samples, but also between overall (raw-scored) experience and relative quality of experience in the different contexts.

If Z-scores are used in the creation of within-context aggregated variables, one additional caveat must be noted. Because of the properties of Z-scores, the closer the context comes to encompassing all of an individual's responses, the closer the average Z-scored response within that context will come to zero. In a concrete example, if 90 percent of a student's responses were during school, and we aggregate across the school responses, the resulting average of Z-scores will necessarily be close to the average of Z-scores across all responses, which is by definition zero. When comparing groups of people within a context, this issue becomes a problem only if one group has a large majority of responses within the context while the other group does not. When comparing situations, as we discuss next, this issue must be considered if a very frequent context is compared to an infrequent one. In either case, a simple solution is to use sufficiently specific contextual categories so that participants do not have large proportions of responses within any one category.

Comparing Situations

Although it may sound confusing, person-level analyses also can (and should) be used to assess differences between situations. Before proceeding with an example, it will be helpful first to consider a response-level analysis. To compare mood at home versus at work one could use a response-level file and simply conduct a *t*-test, comparing all "at home" beeps to all "at work" beeps. This same comparison could be done at the person level with a few additional steps. First, two person-level aggregated variables would need to be created, one for mood during reports at home and one for mood during work. For reasons given previously, *Z*-scores should be used, either alone or in addition to another set of raw-scored mood variables. Then using the person-level data file, a matched pair *t*-test is conducted. To compare multiple situations at the person level, a repeated measures multivariate analysis of variance (MANOVA) can be conducted with context as a within-subjects variable. A covariate could also be included by using a MANCOVA. Finally, more complex statistical interactions between person-level grouping variables (say, gender) and situational variables can be tested by using a MANOVA or MANCOVA with context as a within-subjects variable and the grouping variable as a between-subjects variable.

This family of repeated-measures techniques has been used to analyze how differences in experience are related to different activities, companions, and locations. One of the more creative uses of these analyses was by Larson and Richards (1994a), who compared the emotional experience of spouses during times they were together to the responses just before. Both spouses experienced an emotional boost from togetherness. Larson and Richards also used this type of sequential analysis to show that fathers are usually in a positive mood before they start child-care activities. A similar set of analyses was done by Kubey and Csikszentmihalyi (1990) to see the effects of television viewing. As shown in Figure 5.5, the moods of a person while watching television were compared to the moods just before and just after viewing. The pattern obtained was then compared to the before-during-after sequence of moods while doing other leisure activities—such as sports and reading books—at the same time on other days of the week.

Measuring Flow

One of the "situations" that researchers frequently attempt to capture with ESM is the experience of flow. As first mentioned in Chapter 3, ESM can be useful for measuring both the conditions necessary for flow and the experience of flow. The most commonly measured conditions of flow are individuals' perceptions of their challenges and skills during the moment they were signaled. Several different ways of combining these two measures into an overall "flow conditions" variable have been used. Each method represents one solution for satisfying two criteria central to the theory of flow (Csikszentmihalyi, 1988, 1990, 1997): that perceived challenges and skills are in balance and that they are high (Massimini & Carli, 1988).

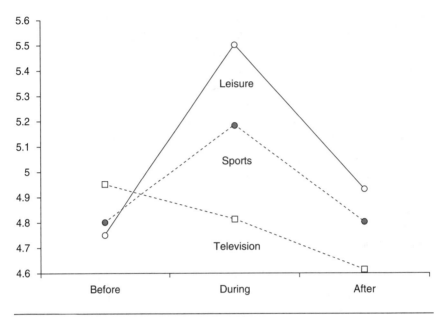

Figure 5.5   Mean Responses on Affect Before, During, and After Television, Sports, and Leisure

SOURCE: Copyright © Kubey, R., and Csikszentmihalyi, M. (1990). *Television and the quality of life: How viewing shapes everyday experience.* Hillsdale, NJ: Erlbaum. Reprinted with permission of Lawrence Erlbaum Associates.

The computation of several different categorical measures begins by first standardizing challenge and skill within the individual. In the most commonly used categorical approach, responses are then divided into one of four categories, or "quadrants," depending on whether challenge and skill are above the individual's average (i.e., have positive Z-scores) or not. The flow condition is defined as perceptions of challenge and skill that are above average. The condition when both challenge and skill are below average has been called apathy or boredom. Relaxation is the condition characterized by high skills and low challenges, while the anxiety condition is defined as low skills and high challenges. This four-channel measurement model has been used in several studies (e.g., Csikszentmihalyi & LeFevre, 1989; Nakamura, 1988). The model treats flow as a relatively common experience accessible to all individuals. More restrictive cutoff values (e.g., Z-scored challenge and skill both above 0.5 instead of 0) can be used if one wishes to treat flow as a more uncommon, distinctive experience. Other narrower variations have included models that divide the Cartesian space formed by the intersection of the challenge and skill axes into 8 or 16 channels instead of 4 quadrants (Massimini & Carli, 1988).

In models based on Z-scored challenge and skill, almost all individuals will have at least one response during conditions of flow. Definitions of the flow condition can also be based on raw-scored challenge and skill. When this is done, it is more probable that some individuals will have no responses in the flow condition, whereas others may have almost all in flow. One way to choose raw-score cutoff values for challenge and skill is to use the sample averages (Csikszentmihalyi et al., 1993). Another method, employing a stricter definition of "balance," designates as flow all responses in which raw-scored challenge and skill exactly match and are greater than 5 on a 9-point scale (Ellis, Voelkl, & Morris, 1994).

Whichever categorical measure of the flow condition is used, two different types of person-level analyses are possible. The flow condition can be treated as a context and responses on other variables can be aggregated within that context and then compared to their aggregated values within other contexts. For example, one can compare happiness and concentration while "in flow" to happiness and concentration during conditions of apathy (challenge and skill both below average). Or percentage of flow time that is spent alone can be compared to the percentage of nonflow time that is spent alone. The second type of analysis starts by aggregating the categorical flow variable itself so that an overall percentage of time in flow is computed for each individual. Within-context percentages of time in flow can also be computed for any number of contexts of interest. Thus we could flip our last example around and compare the percentage of alone time spent in flow to the percentage of nonalone time spent in flow.

Whereas the percentage-of-time measure is based on a fundamentally categorical definition of flow, other continuous measures of the strength of the flow condition have been derived directly from various mathematical combinations of challenge and skill. Ellis and colleagues (1994) multiplied raw-scored challenge and skill to create an interaction term that they tested along with the separate challenge and skill variables. Modifying this approach, Hektner (1996) computed the geometric mean (i.e., square root of the product) of raw-scored challenge and skill to create a continuous flow variable with the same scaling as the original challenge and skill variables. This measure gave greater weight to the intensity of challenge and skill than to their balance; an alternative approach that places sole emphasis on the balance of challenge and skill is to use the absolute value of their difference (Moneta & Csikszentmihalyi, 1996). Finally, Moneta and Csikszentmihalyi (1999) found some utility in using trigonometric formulas to produce a "rotated model," which essentially combines a quadratic weighted difference and weighted sum of challenges and skills.

While the conditions of flow (high challenge, high skill) reliably predict a better quality of experience typical of flow, it is occasionally possible for a person to be anxious or bored while in such a condition, while someone else may have the experience of flow in conditions that would predict boredom or anxiety. Therefore one can separately measure the experience of flow. Unlike measures of the conditions for flow, there is not a long history or proliferation of single ESM measures of the experience of flow. This is because the initial empirical focus of ESM-based flow research was on testing how the conditions of flow (and the various categories of nonflow) related to several different qualities of experience (see Csikszentmihalyi & Csikszentmihalyi, 1988). Now that the link between the conditions of flow and a set of experiential variables has been amply documented, some researchers have attempted to use this set of cognitive and affective variables to construct a single measure of the experience of flow. Because flow involves so many dimensions of experience (e.g., concentration, control, a distorted sense of time, lack of self-consciousness, enjoyment), completely capturing it on a short-answer form is difficult. And measuring only a few dimensions of it may be misleading because we may miss some important ingredient.

Nevertheless, because it is such an important construct, we have typically operationalized flow as a continuum based on the sum of three variables. Two of the three are "Concentration" and "Enjoyment." The third can be either "Interest" or "Wish to be doing the activity" or "Excitement," depending on whether one wants to privilege, respectively, the cognitive, conative, or emotional components of the experience (Hunter, 2002; Schmidt, Shernoff, & Csikszentmihalyi, 2005; Shernoff, 2001). However, there are no strict rules, and, depending on the interest of the researcher, other combinations may be appropriate.

Testing and Modeling Relationships Among Variables

Rather than testing for differences between situations or between groups of people, researchers are often interested in testing the multivariate relationships among a set of continuous variables. In the most basic analysis, a correlation coefficient would indicate the direction and strength of the relationship between two variables, such as between percentage of time watching television and overall average ratings of affect. To statistically control for a third group of variables, or to model the relationships between a set of variables and a single dependent one, OLS multiple regression analyses can be used. As an alternative to using Z-scored variables at the beep level to control for individual differences, Ellis and colleagues (1994) used the method of criterion scaling in their regression models, in which the individual's mean on the dependent variable was included among the set of independent variables (this value would be a constant for every response within each individual, but would vary among individuals).

Although regression analyses have been used in many different ESM studies, one specialized application deserves mention. Larson and Richards (1994a) employed multiple regression to study the transmission of emotions between spouses and between parents and adolescents. In the spouse models, for example, they tested whether the wives' emotion at one time point could be predicted by the husbands' emotion at the preceding time point, while controlling for the wives' activities and emotions at the preceding time point (see Figure 5.6). They included in the analysis only those responses in which the spouses were together during at least one of the time points. This analysis not only illustrates how regression can be used to make sense of the complex interrelationships between people and their social context, it also serves as an example of an effective use of response-level analysis. For this particular question, analysis at the person level would not be desired or feasible.

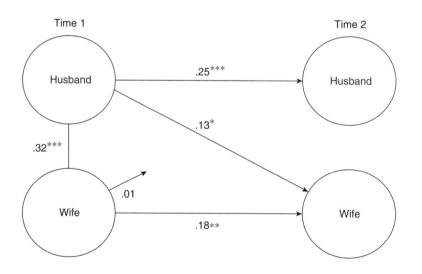

Figure 5.6   Emotional Transmission Between Husband and Wife

SOURCE: From *Divergent Realities* by Reed Larson. Copyright © 1994 by Reed Larson and Maryse Richards. Reprinted by permission of Basic Books, a member of Perseus Books, L.L.C.

NOTES: Figure displays beta weights for predicting Time 2 emotions, based on times that both say they are together at Time 1 or Time 2; N = 253. Regressions were computed on values of emotion with activity controlled. Only occasions when reports occurred within four hours of each other are included (median time difference = 1.67 hours).

The relationship between two experiential variables can also be thought of and analyzed as a personality characteristic unique to each individual. For example, for one person, the correlation between ratings of challenge and enjoyment might be high and positive, whereas for another it might be low and near zero. Using a standard formula, an intraindividual correlation coefficient can be computed, thus becoming another person-level variable. Asakawa and Csikszentmihalyi (2000b) employed this correlation-coefficient-as-variable strategy and found that compared to Caucasian American adolescents, Asian American teens experience a stronger and more positive connection between perceived future importance of an activity and happiness, enjoyment, and self-esteem. In another study, correlations among four positive emotion terms were normalized with Fisher's r-to-z transformation and then averaged for each person to create an index of positive emotion differentiation (Feldman Barrett et al., 2001). An alternative to these types of analyses that may provide more flexibility would be to use multilevel modeling with analysis of variance components.

Multilevel and Other Complex Statistical Techniques

Two features of ESM data have been a source of consistent concern among those who use inferential statistics to draw conclusions from it. First, as in any other one-time questionnaire, there is the question of how best to measure complex constructs such as self-esteem, affect, motivation, or flow. No matter how such constructs are measured, measurement error is impossible to eliminate; in ESM these errors become even more worrisome because they can be compounded as one aggregates the multiple responses. Second, the hierarchical structure of ESM data, with varying numbers of responses nested within persons, is not compatible with the assumptions underlying many traditional statistical procedures. Aggregating the data in order to satisfy those assumptions often results in a loss of important nuances, such as intraindividual variation. In the sections that follow we describe the approaches that are being used to address each of these issues.

Structural Equation Modeling

Several researchers have performed exploratory factor analyses to determine the best way to group ESM items into a smaller set of composite factors. These items are then summed or averaged to arrive at a composite score for each factor. Using such multi-item factors to measure psychological constructs is in accord with principles of measurement theory. A list of commonly used composite variables and their constituent ESM items is provided in Chapter 6. Although these variables have acceptable reliability, they still bring measurement error into every analyses. The use of structural equation modeling (SEM) to create latent variables from several measured ESM items allows the researcher to separate the unique variation in those items from the shared variation. The variance that the items share in common then defines a latent variable that is free from measurement error. The process of testing how well proposed latent factors fit the data has been called "confirmatory factor analysis" or testing the "measurement model." In one application of this method, Eid and Diener (1999) created confirmatory models of intraindividual variability in emotion factors such as love, anger, fear, shame, sadness, and joy; each factor was measured by the intraindividual standard deviations of four items.

In a typical SEM analysis, the measurement model is joined with a structural model in which hypothesized paths between constructs are tested, analogous to conducting several multiple regressions simultaneously. This ability to model a pattern of relationships in which not just one but several variables are "dependent" is another advantage of SEM. One ESM study making use of SEM was conducted by Hektner (2001), who created a latent construct for "growth conducive experience" using the ESM items "intrinsic motivation," "importance to future goals," and "concentration."

Multilevel Modeling

Nested data structures are found in many non-ESM datasets, including all longitudinal data (time points nested within persons) and many educational datasets (children nested within classrooms nested within schools). To address this complex structure, researchers in many fields are increasingly turning to hierarchical linear modeling (HLM; Bryk & Raudenbush, 1992), or variations of HLM called multilevel modeling (Goldstein, 1987, 1995), or mixed-effects random regression analysis (Gibbons et al., 1993). HLM can handle nested data with unequal numbers of observations across individuals and unequally spaced time intervals between observations. It improves upon traditional person-level analyses by taking into account the underlying response-level variability. These features lead Walls, Jung, and Schwartz (2006) to conclude that multilevel modeling is ideally suited to "intensive longitudinal data" (i.e., data derived from multiple measurements closely spaced in time, such as that from ESM). The new volume by Walls and Schafer (2006) includes several instructive examples on the use of multilevel models with ESM-type data. Other excellent resources on this topic include reviews by Bolger, Davis, and Rafaeli (2003); Kenny, Kashy, and Bolger (1998); and Reis and Gable (2000).

The analysis can be thought of as a nested set of multiple regression equations. At the first level, coefficients are estimated for an equation within each person that expresses a dependent variable (the person's affect, for example) as a function of a one or more other response-level variables. These individual parameter estimates then become the dependent variables in the Level 2 equations, in which estimates of effects for the population are produced. Effects of person-level variables, such as gender or SES, can also be estimated in these Level 2 equations. Finally, HLM also provides a way to obtain estimates of intraindividual and interindividual variability. Computation of estimates in HLM can be accomplished via OLS methods, but maximum likelihood estimation is recommended for its greater efficiency and precision (Reis & Gable, 2000). Several statistical programs are now available to conduct HLM analyses (e.g., HLM, SAS PROC MIXED).

Several researchers have used multilevel models to study flow, testing how well various combinations of momentary perceptions of challenge and skill predict momentary quality of experience (Moneta & Csikszentmihalyi, 1996, 1999; Moneta, Schneider, & Csikszentmihalyi, 2001; Schmidt et al., 2005). Another good example of this analytical strategy is the event-sampling study by Laurenceau, Feldman Barrett, and Pietromonaco (1998), in which participants completed reports of each of their interactions with other people. Multiple reports were nested within each person. The analyses showed that perceptions of intimacy during any given interpersonal interaction were related to the degree of self-disclosure from each partner, particularly if that disclosure was based on emotions rather than facts or information. Recently, Adam (2005) used multilevel modeling to predict momentary levels of cortisol (a stress hormone measured in saliva) from both observation level (e.g., time of day, mood state) and person-level factors (e.g., gender, health status). The commonality underlying this diverse range of studies is their use of multilevel analytical techniques to understand how factors in both the person and the situation influence momentary experiences.

Future Possibilities

New statistical procedures that combine the strengths of HLM and SEM are emerging. Recent volumes by Moskowitz and Hershberger (2002) and Walls and Schafer (2006) provide detailed explanations on the use of these techniques with ESM-type data. Papers on the use of dynamic factor analysis to model multivariate time-series reflecting intraindividual variability may also have some relevance to ESM applications (e.g., Molenaar, 1985; Wood & Brown, 1994). Ideally, these analyses will allow for multiple variables to be modeled across multiple waves of multilevel data, such as would be produced by the use of ESM in a longitudinal study. In another promising approach, Kimberly Maier (2001, 2002) developed hierarchical measurement models of ESM data using Rasch Item Response Theory (IRT) and partial credit IRT models. She used these models to measure a latent mood variable and to assess the effects of gender and different classroom activities on that variable.

As a final note, we emphasize that there is no single standard approach for analyzing ESM data. The same research question can and should be addressed through many different types of analyses. In this regard, we wholeheartedly echo Larson and Delespaul's admonition:

> We advise investigators to start with . . . basic descriptive statistic techniques, because their robustness is well known and findings closer to the original data are more easily understood. Most ESM questions can be translated into a set of alternative operationalizations, sometimes leading to divergent results. Our advice is to select multiple approaches when possible and look for results that converge upon the same conclusion. Nothing can replace the basic process, supported with elementary statistics, of looking at the data and getting a feel for it. Writing out and submitting case studies should also not be neglected. After doing these simpler steps it may be possible to explore the new horizons of the sophisticated statistical techniques. Remember though that statistical procedures, after all, are a means not an end. (1992, p. 74)

6

Psychometrics of ESM Data

E very measurement is subject to error, and thus researchers have always attempted to both limit and measure the discrepancy between reality and its measure. This concern is reflected in the development of methods to assess the validity and reliability of research instruments. Questions of validity and reliability speak directly to issues of usefulness and accuracy: How closely does the measurement reflect what it was intended to measure? How consistent is it? How generalizable are the findings derived from it? Numerous ways of answering these questions exist for traditional experimental methods, naturalistic observations, and questionnaires. However, not all of them make sense when applied to ESM.

For example, test-retest reliability checks for stability in the measurement of a construct across a specified time interval, typically several weeks. Yet ESM respondents are expected to experience variations in their levels of affect, concentration, and behavior from one signal to the next, just as these variations occur in daily life. The measurement of momentary states of experience is not inherently unreliable, but because the underlying experience (the construct being measured) changes, reliability cannot be assessed through comparison of one measurement to the next. On the other hand, as explained in sections that follow, a person's traits (as measured by aggregated data across many ESM reports) might be expected to show stability over time.

In this chapter, we will first consider the validity of ESM as a method—how meaningful and defensible are conclusions drawn from it. Then we will turn more specifically to the validity of the measurements typically included in an ESM study, asking how closely they represent the underlying reality they are intended to assess. Finally, we will examine several different approaches to measuring the reliability of ESM measures.

Validity of Method

Two fundamental questions must be addressed in any research study. First, are confounding variables controlled so that the conclusions are warranted by the data? Second, can generalizations be made beyond the specific individuals and moments sampled? These are questions of internal and external validity, respectively.

Internal Validity

A major goal of research is to identify and isolate cause-effect relationships. Traditionally, experimental psychologists maintained high internal validity by adhering to a strictly standardized protocol carried out with human or animal subjects in a research laboratory. The rationale for insisting on high levels of experimental control is to eliminate all possible alternate explanations (variables other than those under study), lest they confound the experimental variables. Unfortunately, the rigorous pursuit of high internal validity often results in low external validity—the participants are immersed in a situation that is so contrived as to lose relevance to the world outside the lab.

With its focus on everyday life, ESM clearly avoids this problem. The method emphasizes external or "ecological" validity over internal validity. Many internal validity issues are factors of experimental research designs, and although ESM can be employed in experiments, it is more often seen in nonexperimental studies. Because ESM is a methodological tool and not a research design, validity issues specific to experiments will not be discussed here. Instead we focus on the question, relevant in any design, of whether explanations other than the participants' natural experience could account for their ESM responses.

There are many indications that internal validity is stronger in ESM than in one-time questionnaires. Zuzanek (1999) suggested that the immediacy of the questions reduces the potential for failure of recall and the tendency to choose responses on the basis of social desirability. The randomness of the signals diminishes the reflexivity bias, attempts of the respondents to discern the purpose of the research and tailor their responses accordingly (Kubey, Larson, & Csikszentmihalyi, 1996; Zuzanek, 1999). The sheer number of signals leads participants to habituate to the recording of their personal behavior, somewhat like how interviewees in other studies eventually forget that they are being monitored by a tape recorder or video camera.

Overreporting and underreporting certain behaviors and activities is easier and more tempting for respondents completing a one-time questionnaire than for those reporting repeatedly and randomly on their momentary experiences and activities (see, for example, the comparison of ESM and survey responses on hours of housework reported by Lee, 2005). Time-budget and diary studies often do not even have a category for "idling" (doing nothing, daydreaming, etc.) because participants either forget those moments or deem them too unimportant to mention. ESM studies, by contrast, show that the amount of time people spend doing "nothing" is not insignificant (Csikszentmihalyi & Larson, 1987). ESM may also be able to reduce the potential for cultural norms to confound individual experience. Oishi (2002) showed that European Americans and Asians reported no differences in emotional well-being in ESM reports, but European Americans gave a rosier picture in retrospective questionnaires. In contrast to global responses on questionnaires, Canadian ESM participants reported enjoying moments of paid work more and moments of cooking less, which suggests that their questionnaire responses may have been influenced by a cultural climate that denigrates work and glamorizes cooking (Zuzanek, 1999).

Larson and Richards (1994a) used a direct way of obtaining evidence on the accuracy of ESM responses. At the end of the ESM week, participants were asked whether there were times they "did not tell the truth or changed what was going on." "Never" was the response of 78 percent of the sample, with an additional 16 percent admitting "just once." Contrary to Hormuth's (1986) belief that the primary methodological weakness of ESM is in the responsibility it places on the participant to accurately report the objective features of each moment, these participants admitted to disguising their subjective thoughts and feelings much more than their activities. If a researcher is concerned that participants might fill in responses long after a signal has occurred, Feldman Barrett and Barrett (2001) point out that palmtop computers automatically time-stamp each response and can be programmed to prevent a participant from responding after a certain amount of time has elapsed since the signal.

Another piece of evidence for the veridicality of ESM responses comes from the internal logic of the responses themselves. In every ESM study, emotional states that one would expect to be experienced together in fact are reported to occur at the same time, and those that are opposite are not. For instance, in one study the correlation between being "happy" and "sociable" was .52, but the correlation between "happy" and being "unselfconscious" was −.09 (N = 2734; Csikszentmihalyi & Larson, 1984); the correlation between an ESM measure of "flow" and "concentration" was .48, but between "flow" and "relaxation," only .01 (N = 9141; Hektner, 1996). Respondents who were misrepresenting their experiences, intentionally or not, would not be able to produce a pattern so consistent with universally experienced linkages among different but related states.

Although reporting accuracy is a goal, it is not sufficient for internal validity—there is also reactivity to consider. Reactivity is a methodological confound that occurs when respondents report accurately but change their behavior or internal experiences as a direct result of their participation in a method. For example, do ESM participants alter their activities for the week or during the course of a day in anticipation of being signaled? One slightly humorous artifact shows the potential of the method to alter experience: respondents awoken from a nap by their ESM signal report negative moods, presumably not due to the experience of napping but due to the artificial intrusion on their sleep. Other instances of reactivity have occurred when participants report playing with or using their signaling device for other purposes. Watches that can store a schedule of 50 or more signals typically also have a calculator, memo function, and other capabilities. Palmtop computers could be potentially even more enticing, but they can be programmed to shut out all uses other than the ESM functions (Feldman Barrett & Barrett, 2001).

Nevertheless, analyses from several studies of debriefing questionnaires completed at the end of the sampling week show that the vast majority of respondents (80% to 90%) report having a "normal" week and that the ESM captured their week well (Csikszentmihalyi & Larson, 1987). In a sample of German adults, only 14 percent indicated that the signal bothered them in public and 22 percent said it disrupted their daily routine (Hormuth, 1986). Larson and Richards (1994a) asked families participating in the ESM, "Do you think the family's week was different because of the study?" Over half (54%) responded "not at all"; 8 percent said "quite a bit," and no one said "very much" (pp. 267–268). Undergraduate problem drinkers maintained a consistent level of drinking behaviors and motivation before, during, and after two weeks of ESM participation (Hufford, Shields, Shiffman, Paty, & Balabanis, 2002). The vast range of activities that have been reported in ESM studies also attests to the fact that people do not refrain from engaging in or reporting on activities that may be inconvenient to interrupt (working on a roof), embarrassing (talking to oneself), intensely private (attempting suicide), or all of the above (having sex).

Besides reports of activities, reports of internal experiences also appear not to be affected significantly by the process of recording them. For example, prior to a major Tae Kwon Do competition, participants in an

ESM study showed no differences in levels and temporal patterns of emotions from competitors who reported emotions less frequently or retrospectively (Cerin, Szabo, & Williams, 2001). One might also wonder whether participants become more self-reflective as a result of being asked to report their experiences several times a day. Early investigations into the degree of self-consciousness reported by ESM participants show that self-focused attention is dominant in only a fraction of moments (Csikszentmihalyi & Figurski, 1982; Hormuth, 1986) and that general self-consciousness was not higher after a sampling period than before (Franzoi & Brewer, 1984). On the other hand, as Hurlburt (1997) noted and we will document in Chapter 13, some participants find participation in an ESM study to be therapeutic. Typically, though, significant changes in these participants' inner experiences would not occur until after their sampling period.

External Validity

Researchers typically want to make inferences about some larger population from which their sample was taken. In ESM research, the "population" of interest can be thought of in two senses: as a collection of people or of moments of experience. In assessing the validity of inferences made about either of these populations, ESM shares with many traditional methods a concern about how well the sample represents that population. Sampling methodologies and their relationship to external validity are covered extensively in standard research methodology texts, and the same principles apply to ESM studies. Regarding populations of people, Zuzanek (1999) noted that a serious challenge for ESM researchers would be to move from the purposive sampling that has been dominant (e.g., sampling from a very specific local population) to more representative sampling techniques.

We will not discuss the logistics of choosing and implementing a sampling method but will concern ourselves with the proportion of targeted participants for an ESM study who are actually enrolled and kept in the study until its end. Although the term *response rate* is used in regard to one-time questionnaires, the complexity of ESM requires a distinction between the volunteer rate, which is the proportion of recruits for the study sample who actually agree to participate, and the signal response rate, the proportion of signals for which responses are completed. The latter is sometimes expressed in terms of the proportion of enrolled participants who responded to at least a minimum number of signals, typically 15. When ESM is used in longitudinal studies, a third type of data loss also becomes important: the attrition rate, or the proportion of participants who do not complete subsequent waves of data collection.

For mail surveys, volunteer rates of 30 percent to 50 percent are considered quite good, whereas other studies using an interested captive audience and incentives (such as a college class) may be able to achieve volunteer rates over 90 percent. In ESM studies, volunteer rates are similarly quite variable and depend on the recruitment methods used. Rates have been reported as low as 12 percent for unskilled, blue-collar workers and as high as 91 percent for fifth and eighth graders (Csikszentmihalyi & Larson, 1987). Signal response rates among those who do enroll in ESM studies seem to fall in a narrower range, with rates from 70 percent to 80 percent typically reported (e.g., Csikszentmihalyi & Larson, 1987; Hormuth, 1986; Larson, Moneta, Richards, & Wilson, 2002; Zuzanek, 1999). In line with recent trends in survey response rates, ESM signal response rates in recent years appear to be declining. Mulligan and colleagues (2000) reported a signal response rate of 58 percent in a recent national study of adolescents. Recent rates for college students completing computerized ESM range from 50 percent to 75 percent depending on the hardware and whether or not a follow-up beep is provided if the person misses the first beep (Feldman Barrett, 2004, personal communication).

Besides shrinking the sample size, rates of data loss through refusal, non-response, or attrition are a problem for external validity to the extent that the remaining data are less representative of the intended population. The sharpest criticisms of ESM have focused on this problem. Maintaining the representativeness of a random sample requires obtaining a high volunteer rate and signal response rate, but this is an especially difficult goal to reach in ESM research due to the intrusive and burdensome nature of the task (Lawton, 1999). In ESM studies, self-selection bias must be examined at both the person and signal level. At the person level, there is some evidence that those who volunteer and complete an ESM study differ somewhat from those who do not. For example, females are usually overrepresented among ESM completers (Csikszentmihalyi & Larson, 1987; Larson et al., 2002; Mulligan, Schneider, & Wolfe, 2000; Waite, Claffey, & Hillbrand, 1998). This reflects both a greater tendency of females to volunteer for ESM studies and to complete more signals than males do.

Critics also point to other evidence that organized, diligent, conscientious, and psychologically healthy people volunteer for ESM studies at greater rates than others do, thus rendering study samples nonrepresentative of the full range of people. In a recent adolescent sample, high school seniors had a slightly lower response rate than sixth graders, and students who responded to at least 15 signals had higher grades than those who did not (Mulligan et al., 2000). Besides gender and grades, attrition in another longitudinal study of adolescents was also related to lower affect and self-esteem and more behavior problems (Larson et al., 2002). Similarly, college students who volunteered for an ESM study were less anxious, less likely to employ pathological defensive styles, and more well-adjusted over-all than those who refused to do the ESM (Waite et al., 1998). Researchers designing a new study should take these trends into account when selecting a sample and should document if and how the final study sample differs from the original intended sample.

At the signal level, the relevant question is how well the signal responses that were completed represent the population of moments of lived experience. In comparison to a one-time survey that might ask questions such as "How many hours a week do you watch TV?" ESM data clearly have the potential for a more accurate representation of a person's experience. Whether that potential is realized depends on the diligence of the participants. As might be expected, adolescent participants are not as conscientious about responding to each signal as adults; adults who agree to participate in an ESM study generally respond to more signals than adolescents. There is a possibility of self-selection here too, for instance if participants decide not to respond during certain activities or situations.

An early comparison of ESM and daily diary approaches to measuring time use led Robinson (1985) to conclude that "the beeper approach is more likely than the diary approach to suffer from a lack of validity" (p. 37). Respondents in this study sometimes forgot or chose not to carry their beeper with them outside the home, and thus their diaries showed more time spent on activities inside the home. However, these participants were beeped 40 times in one day! Given such frequent signals, it is not surprising that participants would want to be free of their beeper while in public. As we report in the next section, participants beeped on a more reasonable (and more commonly used) schedule do not show this tendency to the same degree. Moreover, Robinson acknowledged that the ESM approach revealed more time spent on the telephone than respondents recalled in their diaries.

Robinson's (1985) questionable conclusion notwithstanding, there are some justifiable concerns and criticisms of ESM regarding self-selection of moments. In the recent Sloan study of adolescents, weekends, school nights, and work hours were underrepresented and school days were overrepresented (Mulligan et al., 2000). Perhaps because this sample was introduced to ESM in the school context, they were more comfortable responding to signals there than in places where their peers were not also participating. To compensate for such imbalances, weights can be calculated and used in analyses requiring proportional representation of each segment of the day. When weighted for nonresponse, Sloan ESM estimates of time spent by teens on the job are nearly identical to estimates from nationally representative questionnaire studies. Another source of nonrepresentativeness may be designed into an ESM study itself in the form of the signaling schedule. When researchers set the earliest and latest possible times for a signal to occur, respecting the participant's need to sleep without interruption, they also inevitably miss the early morning and late night activities of some of their participants. Mulligan and his colleagues concluded, for example, that ESM underestimated TV watching among Sloan study participants because signaling stopped soon after 10 p.m. Larson and Richards (1994a) also surmised that they missed some alone time between spouses for the same reason. To avoid this problem, signaling schedules could be tailored to each participant's self-reported waking hours or participants could be given the control to turn the signaling device on upon waking and off upon retiring. Both of these approaches have drawbacks, however. Individually tailored schedules may still miss some waking moments that the participant did not anticipate, whereas participants who are allowed to turn the device off when they fall asleep may not remember to turn it on again when they wake.

To insure that all activities are captured in the data, researchers conducting time use studies may find value in supplementing ESM with nightly and/or weekly retrospective diaries. Zuzanek (1999) and Hormuth (1986) stress that the strongest research uses a multimethod approach in which ESM is one important complementary strategy. In many cases, documenting how individuals spend their time is secondary to examining the relationships among activities, social context, and inner psychological states. For this purpose, perfect representative sampling of all of an individual's waking moments is not necessary.

Representativeness, and thus external validity, implies more than just proportionality between the mix of contexts, activities, and states in the population of moments and the mix portrayed in the sample of signal responses. At least as important is the accuracy of each response in representing a moment of natural (uncontrived) experience. In other words, any assessment of external validity must also ask whether the data reflect everyday thoughts and feelings accurately. In this respect, mundane realism suggests that ESM provides unsurpassed ecological validity. Eschewing artifice or deception, ESM allows respondents to go about daily life, capturing their experience before it has a chance to be filtered by memory or altered through subsequent self-reflection.

Validity of ESM Measurements

Assessment of validity includes the degree that the items included on the ESM form are appropriate to measure what they are intended to measure.

Of the many different forms of validity devised to assess this question, the most basic is face (or content) validity. Although ESM can be used to measure a wide variety of phenomena, we will discuss the validity of measurement within three commonly used domains: context and activities, internal states, and individual traits.

Context and Activities

ESM responses to questions asking participants to note what they were doing, where they were, and who they were with can be compared with estimates based on non-ESM measures. Csikszentmihalyi and Graef (1980) found a rank-order correlation of .93 between similarly coded ESM and diary-based measures of time spent in different activities. Robinson (1985), despite the exception noted previously, also found a high degree of correspondence between diary and ESM estimates of time use patterns. The discrepancies that do appear between ESM and diary measures of time use suggest that ESM captures moments that are otherwise deemed insignificant to remember or report. Such moments include reports of idling or doing nothing, mentioned earlier, which do not appear in time-budget or diary studies (Csikszentmihalyi & Larson, 1987). Zuzanek (1999) adds that talking on the telephone and in person to family members were other activities mentioned more frequently on ESM forms than in recall questionnaires.

Hoover (1983) found evidence of convergent validity between ESM reports of physical activity and readings from heart rate and activity monitors that participants were wearing during the study. The correlation of the self-ratings on the item "active" with simultaneous heart rate was .41 and with wrist and ankle activity readings .36. Heart rate also differed significantly between times when participants reported lying down, sitting, standing, and walking. When external confirmation of a participant's responses via a monitoring device or other means is not available, researchers use some ESM items to cross-validate other items. An indication of what has been called "situational validity" can be derived from examining the internal logic of a reported situation, the convergence of time, context, and activities in expected ways. Participants report talking or conversation as their main activity when there are other people present and not when they are alone. They report personal grooming activities at predictable times of day (morning) and TV watching in predictable places (home).

By collecting reports from members of the same family who were signaled simultaneously, Larson and Richards (1994a) obtained data that are instructive from a validity standpoint. On some self-reports, one spouse reported being "with" the other spouse, whereas the other spouse reported being "alone." At first, this "unmutual togetherness," as Larson and Richards called the phenomenon, may seem to indicate a lack of convergent validity. If social context is thought of merely in terms of physical proximity to others, then this lack of agreement can certainly be considered an error in measurement, for the distance from the wife to the husband is surely the same as from the husband to the wife. However, the goal of ESM studies is usually to measure reality from the participant's point of view. Given this goal, the divergent responses are not evidence of poor validity but rather of the ability of ESM to capture internal perceptions that an observer could not. These moments of unmutual togetherness reflect times when spouses may have been within talking or seeing distance of one another, but were sufficiently disengaged with each other so that one of them felt alone. When taken as an indication of psychological distance between spouses, unmutual togetherness along with time spent apart did show convergent validity with other non-ESM measures of overall lack of warmth in the marriage.

Internal States

The inherent methodological challenges in assessing the validity of social context responses apply even more strongly to ESM measures of internal psychological states, such as thoughts, emotions, and motivations. Ultimately, only the individual respondent can know whether her response is an accurate representation of her internal state at the moment of the signal. Yet, there are enough commonalities in human experience to enable us to compare the overall patterns of responses to expectations derived from our common experiences and observations.

To assess the validity of reports of internal states, researchers once again primarily examine situational validity, asking whether participants' reports of their internal experiences make logical sense given the activities and context they report. For example, one would expect people to report being most relaxed while watching television, and this is what has been found repeatedly (Kubey & Csikszentmihalyi, 1990, 2002). Csikszentmihalyi and Larson (1987) reported that productive activities such as work are seen as obligatory 80 percent of the time, whereas watching TV is hardly ever experienced as obligatory (3%). Wells (1985) found that the self-esteem of working mothers was lower when they were involved in housework or child-care activities than when they were at their jobs or engaged in leisure. For adolescents, time alone is associated with more loneliness and the most negative moods (Csikszentmihalyi & Larson, 1984). As one would expect, students in school experience the highest levels of concentration when they are taking tests and quizzes (Csikszentmihalyi & Larson, 1984; Csikszentmihalyi &

Schneider, 2000). Their motivation is highest and affect is the most positive when they are engaged in leisure activities with friends (Csikszentmihalyi & Larson, 1984). If these findings do not seem earth-shattering, that is precisely the point. The obviousness of the results may lead one to forget the fact that they didn't necessarily have to be this way. The fact that the results do present an organized, coherent representation of the world that is so readily recognized as "normal" or "obvious" speaks well for the validity of the method.

In a rare examination of convergent validity between an ESM measure of momentary internal states and a non-ESM measurement instrument, Klinger, Barta, and Maxeiner (1980) asked participants to complete a questionnaire on which they listed the topics of their most prevalent thoughts over the past two days. These responses were compared to the participants' responses on a "thought-sampling" instrument that collected reports of thoughts roughly every 40 minutes over 24 hours. For each participant, a correlation coefficient was generated to indicate the strength of association between the lists of thoughts generated from the two methods; the median correlation was significant at .34.

Individual Traits or Characteristics

A more common use of non-ESM instruments in validating ESM measures occurs when the measurement in question is an aggregated person-level characteristic or trait. Signal-level ESM responses to items assessing emotions, motivation, and cognitive states are often aggregated to produce a single person-level variable. These variables are then validated by assessing their convergence with one-time questionnaire measures of similar constructs. Using this method, Wong and Csikszentmihalyi (1991) found convergence between the frequency of adolescents' ESM reports of wishing to be with friends and their scores on a standard scale of affiliation motivation. Adolescents scoring high on this scale also reported on the ESM wishing to be alone less often than those scoring low. In another study, a one-time questionnaire measure of optimism was associated with ESM reports of being happy, sociable, and involved as well as experiencing higher levels of self-esteem, concentration, and perceptions of personal skill (Csikszentmihalyi & Schneider, 2000). At the other end of the emotional spectrum, clinical scales of depression and anxiety have been shown to have positive correlations with ESM reports of feeling empty and lonely and negative correlations with the ESM variables energetic, cheerful, satisfied, and self-assured (Kraan, Meertens, Hilwig, Volovics, Dijkman-Caes, & Portegijs, 1992). Other convergences have enabled researchers to provide evidence for the validity of aggregated ESM measures of affect and work involvement (Giannino, Graef, & Csikszentmihalyi, 1979), thoughts about people and relationships (McAdams & Constantian, 1983), and motivation and concentration (Hamilton, Haier, & Buchsbaum, 1984).

It is important to note here that an aggregated person-level variable derived from ESM does not measure the same thing as a one-time questionnaire measure of the "same" construct. For example, a person's response to a questionnaire item asking about his typical level of happiness measures his beliefs about himself, which are accessed via semantic memory (Robinson & Clore, 2002). By contrast, his ESM reports of happiness, even when aggregated, measure his experiences of happiness, which are stored in episodic memory. The point is not that ESM is an inherently better method of measuring emotion-related personality traits, such as general happiness, than one-time questionnaires, but that it measures something a bit different. Aggregated ESM reports and one-time questionnaire reports of emotional experience may well be correlated, but this says as much about the associations among identity, memory, and experience as it does about their measurement validity. Robinson and Clore (2002) provide a comprehensive profile of the many different ways of measuring emotions via self-report, detailing how the method of measurement determines what, exactly, is being measured.

Consistent with this theme, when ESM and questionnaires diverge it may be more an indication of their different purposes than of a lack of validity. Wells's (1985) data on the self-esteem of working mothers illustrate this point. ESM measures of self-esteem aggregated across all contexts were significantly correlated with a one-time assessment of self-esteem, $r = .42$. A more fine-grained analysis revealed that this correlation was strongest when the aggregated ESM measure was taken from only those contexts in which other adults were present and weakest in those contexts when the participants were alone. The self-esteem people indicate on a one-time assessment appears to be their public self-esteem, rather than a perfect average of their self-esteem across all of the contexts of their lives.

Another approach to demonstrating validity is to show that groups of people who share a particular characteristic provide responses on ESM consistent with the characteristic and different from groups without it. Delespaul and deVries (1987; deVries & Delespaul, 1989) have conducted ESM studies on the experience of individuals diagnosed with psychopathology. As expected, compared to healthy individuals, psychiatric patients experienced more moments of incongruence between thought and action and differed on tiredness, mood, motivation, and somatic or psychological complaints. Inpatients experienced much less time alone than nonpatients, whereas psychiatric outpatients experienced much more time alone. Johnson and Larson (1982) compared women with bulimia to a matched sample of other adult women and found several differences in the ESM reports of their experiences. Those in the bulimia group reported more negative affect and more moments of food-related behavior. In another study, adolescents with clinical depression, as assessed by standard diagnostic instruments, indicated both a greater frequency and intensity in ESM reports of feeling sad, lonely, and bored compared to nondepressed teens (Merrick, 1992).

The group comparison approach was also used by Csikszentmihalyi, Rathunde, and Whalen (1993), who showed that teenagers identified as highly talented differed from a sample of average adolescents in how they spent their time. In line with expectations, the talented group spent more time alone, more time doing arts and hobbies, and less time in a paid job. Contrary to expectations, they also spent more time watching television. This comparison was never intended as a validity check, but the results illustrate the importance of having prior evidence or other justification for expectations that are used as the standard to which ESM data are compared for assessing validity. In every case where ESM data were compared to other evidence of individual characteristics, convergent validity has been documented.

Reliability of ESM Measurements

One of the necessary, though not sufficient, requirements for establishing the validity of a measure is to show that it produces consistent results. As stated at the beginning of this chapter, expecting consistency in an individual's responses from one ESM signal to the next would not make sense because a person's experience varies over different moments in time. Lack of variation in responses would be a cause for methodological concern. Yet, when several responses are aggregated, individuals are bound to show a pattern of responses that is consistent with future or past patterns. In ESM research, the traditional protocol for assessing test-retest reliability is thus modified so that one set of aggregated responses (typically one-half of a sampling week) is tested against a second set of aggregated responses from the same person (the second half of the sampling week). Other forms of reliability are also relevant to ESM measurements, including interrater reliability on the application of coding systems to open-ended responses, longitudinal stability over longer time intervals, and internal consistency of multiple-item composite scales. In the following sections we review how reliability has been assessed for ESM assessments of activities and psychological states and traits.

Context and Activities

ESM items gathering contextual and activity information from participants are frequently open ended and thus need to be coded into discrete categories (see Chapter 4). Interrater reliability naturally depends on the complexity and level of detail in the coding system and the level of training of the coders. Csikszentmihalyi and Larson (1987) reported a level of agreement of 88 percent between two coders using 154 activity categories; when these were collapsed into 16 superordinate categories, agreement rose to 96 percent. Larson and Richards (1994a) used 110 activity categories and 68 location categories and reported interrater agreements of 94 percent and 99 percent respectively. In a study of depressed and nondepressed individuals, Kraan and colleagues (1992) assessed interrater reliability via Cohen's Kappa, reporting values of .92 for places, .77 for social context, and .69 for activities.

Besides interrater reliability, researchers have also tested the consistency of frequencies of activities that participants report. Csikszentmihalyi and Larson (1987) noted that activities were reported with the same general frequency in the two halves of the reporting period in a sample of 107 adults. This method is, however, susceptible to systematic variations in weekly schedules. When a sample of adolescents started an ESM study toward the end of a week, the first half of their reporting period included the weekend, whereas the second half did not. This discrepancy may have contributed to a significant difference that was found between halves in the frequency distribution of activities. To prevent this potential problem, Kraan and his colleagues (1992) aggregated data from one weekday in the first half of the reporting period and compared it to data from another weekday in the second half of the period.

Reliability in Measuring Internal States

One of the most commonly reported forms of reliability for questionnaire measures of psychological constructs is Cronbach's alpha, a measure of the internal consistency of the items comprising a scale. Because of the unreliability of responses to a single questionnaire item, variables measuring a construct are often computed as the sum or average of the responses to several related items that are shown to be highly intercorrelated (internally consistent). If aggregated across multiple signals, the use of a single item is less of a reliability risk in ESM research because repeated measurement takes the place of multiple items. Still, to insure strong reliability and for analyses where aggregation is not appropriate, many ESM researchers have used multiple-item scales. Several scales have been developed based on exploratory factor analyses and confirmed through examination of internal consistencies. A list of the most commonly used scales and the items that comprise them is provided in Table 6.1. Across several studies, Cronbach's alphas for these scales have consistently been reported in an acceptable range (primarily .70 to .90; e.g., Csikszentmihalyi et al., 1993; Hektner, 1996; Koh, 2005).

Table 6.1   Commonly Used Composite Variables and Their Internal Consistencies

Scale Variable With Items Comprising the Scale	Alpha	Studies Reporting
(Positive) Affect Happy, Cheerful, Sociable (or Friendly), Relaxed	.75–.85	1, 3, 4
Negative Affect Angry, Frustrated, Irritated, Lonely, Nervous, Strained, Stressed, Worried	.90	4
Potency (or Activation) Strong, Active, Alert, Excited	.78–.87	1, 3, 4
Role Salience Caring, Importance of activity, Responsible, Proud	.82	4
Self-Esteem Living up to own expectations, Living up to others' expectations (or ability to deal with situation), Control, Feeling good about self, Succeeding	.79–.90	2, 3, 4
Intrinsic Motivation Wish to be doing something else (reversed), Enjoyment, Interest	.72–.76	2, 4
Love[a] Affection, Love, Caring, Fondness	.93	5
Joy[a] Joy, Happiness, Contentment, Pride	.80	5
Fear[a] Fear, Worry, Anxiety, Nervous	.91	5
Anger[a] Anger, Irritation, Disgust, Rage	.91	5
Shame[a] Shame, Guilt, Regret, Embarrassment	.94	5
Sadness[a] Sadness, Loneliness, Unhappiness, Depression	.93	5

NOTES: Studies from which alphas are reported: 1. Csikszentmihalyi and Larson (1984); 2. Hektner (1996); 3. Csikszentmihalyi, Rathunde, and Whalen (1993); 4. Koh (2005); 5. Diener, Smith, and Fujita (1995).

a. Scale was used on a once-daily self-report in which participants rated how much of the time during the day they felt that emotion.

There are two other ways to examine the reliability of both single items and scales. Both rely on comparing data from the first half of the sampling period to the second half. One test is to examine the stability of means and standard deviations. Across three samples of adolescents and adults no significant changes were found in mean responses on items assessing emotional state (Csikszentmihalyi & Larson, 1987; Larson & Richards, 1994a). On the other hand, participants did decrease in the variability (i.e., standard deviation) of their responses. Follow-up analyses showed that this decline was not due to a gradual failure of respondents to discriminate between different situations, but rather to an increase in the influence of the individual's characteristic response tendencies. In other words, over the course of a sampling period, individuals tend to find a stable anchor around which they vary their responses according to the situation.

The more common reliability analysis of split-week data is to examine the correlation between average ratings from the first and second halves. For ratings of affect, Larson and colleagues (2002) obtained correlations of .55 to .67. The standard deviation of affect was also correlated from one half-week to the next, $r = .53$ to .66. In a sample mostly of clinically depressed adults, Kraan and colleagues (1992) examined correlational stability in positive and negative moods separately and found significant stability in both central tendency ($r = .81$ to .86) and variation ($r = .45$ to .91). Self-esteem has also been reported to have acceptable reliability according to this method ($r = .86$; Wells, 1985). Across eight variables, Csikszentmihalyi and Larson (1987) found a median correlation between the two halves of the week of .60 for adolescents and .74 for adults.

Reliability of Individual Emotional Characteristics

Rather than comparing aggregated reports of internal states to test the reliability of their measurement, Eid and Diener (1999) tested the psychometric properties of the intraindividual variation in internal emotion states to determine whether this variation itself could be a stable personality characteristic. They examined intraindividual standard deviations across 51 once-daily reports of 7 dimensions of affect, each measured by 2 or 4 emotion terms. Using a confirmatory factor analysis framework, they found that these "variability scores" had acceptable reliability (coefficients ranging from .69 to .91) and construct, predictive, convergent, and discriminant validity. Predictive validity of the variability scores was shown through their relation to the residuals produced from regressing affect from a given day on previous mean affect levels. In other words, "people with high variability are less predictable than people with low variability" (p. 670).

Longitudinal Stability of Internal States

Demonstrating the stability of internal states across intervals much longer than a few days is not a test of reliability nor a required step in testing the psychometric soundness of a measure. Nevertheless, measures of stability in internal psychological constructs over periods of a year or more are of interest in their own right, for what they reveal about change and continuity in lives over time. Freeman, Csikszentmihalyi, and Larson (1986) analyzed ESM data on affect and activation from 27 adolescents collected at 2 points in time separated by 2 years. Across 9 independent variables, there were no significant differences over time in individual mean ratings, and stability of relative position was indicated by correlations of each variable from the first time point to the second ranging from .38 to .77. In a national sample of 236 adolescents, Hektner (2001) found 2-year stability correlations of time spent in productive activities and active leisure of .27 and .26 respectively. Concentration, intrinsic motivation, and goal-directedness while engaged in productive activities also showed significant stability, ranging from .40 to .47. Across all contexts, a continuous measure of flow had a 2-year stability coefficient of .55, although half of the sample experienced a change in mean level equal to one-third or more of their standard deviation (Hektner, 1996).

Patton (1998) measured flow differently but obtained similar stability coefficients across 2 years (.50 to .53), with stability dropping to .30 over 4 years. Stability coefficients for several ESM variables across 2- and 4-year intervals were computed by both Patton (1998) and Moneta and colleagues (2001) from the same adolescent sample and are reported in Table 6.2. The most stability is shown by self-esteem and by the percentage of time spent in low-challenge activities (both apathy and relaxation). Happiness shows the least stability, perhaps reflecting a greater influence of momentary environmental factors. Still, all variables show statistically significant stability over four years, attesting to the consistency of the individual in experiencing daily life, even over a period of the life span often deemed to be the most tumultuous.

Besides stability, some change was also evident in data collected by Larson and colleagues (2002), whose participants provided ESM reports in early adolescence and again four years later. Early adolescents experienced a decline in positive affect that leveled out by the tenth grade, while still remaining above the neutral point on the scale. The stability correlation of affect from baseline to year four was .35, with lesser stability shown among younger cohorts (those beginning the study in fifth or sixth grade) and greater stability among older cohorts (those beginning in seventh or eighth grade).

Table 6.2   Two- and Four-Year Stability Coefficients Across Three Waves of Data Collection

	Comparisons of Waves of Data Collection		
	1st vs. 2nd	2nd vs. 3rd	1st vs. 3rd
Time Lag (Years)	2	2	4
Range of N	455–493	189–199	187–194
Affect	.56	.54	.44
Feeling Happy to Sad	.55	.21	.22
Self-Esteem	.60	.69	.55
Living Up to Your Own Expectations	.51	.48	.38
Living Up to the Expectations of Others	.50	.55	.49
Feeling Successful	.54	.53	.48
Feeling in Control	.43	.42	.34
Feeling Good	.60	.50	.51
Intrinsic Motivation	.53	.57	.43
Flow (% of time in high challenge, high skill)	.53	.50	.30
Relaxation (% of time in low challenge, high skill)	.60	.58	.56
Anxiety (% of time in high challenge, low skill)	.41	.38	.47
Apathy (% of time in low challenge, low skill)	.49	.50	.56

SOURCES: Table adapted from Moneta, Schneider, and Csikszentmihalyi (2001) and Patton (1998).

NOTE: Correlation coefficients were computed between person-level means in each wave after pair-wise elimination of missing data.

As with any methodological tool, there are appropriate and inappropriate uses of ESM. Taking the evidence presented here as a whole, one could rightly conclude that when used appropriately, ESM is psychometrically sound. Evidence from multiple sources has shown that ESM self-reports represent individual experiences with reliability and validity ranging from acceptable to surpassingly high. In many cases, the psychometric properties of ESM are superior to alternative methods. Where divergence has been found between ESM and traditional methods, it generally points to the greater ability of ESM to capture the details of momentary experience that would otherwise have been lost. Researchers planning to use ESM are advised to consider the validity of the method for the purposes they intend and to assess the psychometric properties of any measurements not previously tested.

PART III

Uses of ESM in
Social Science Research

7

Samples of Experience

The research questions that have been addressed using ESM center on the contexts of daily life, the experiential content of life, and the links between context and content. A third dimension to these investigations is added by the characteristics of the sample of participants. The cumulative impact of hundreds of ESM studies to date has been to produce a record of the contexts and content of the lives of people of many cultures, occupations, and ages. In this chapter we begin to dig into that record. Subsequent chapters will focus on specific contexts or issues (e.g., work, family, school) that have generated the most extensive ESM research. Our aim in this chapter is to present findings that fill in the gaps between these areas.

The Who, What, Where, When, and How of Daily Experiences

Much like a newspaper reporter would gather information on the who, what, where, and when, ESM provides a record of what Csikszentmihalyi and Larson (1984) called the "external landscape" of daily life. Three different studies, using different samples of adults over a span of two decades, converge remarkably well on a picture of this landscape for contemporary adults in the United States. These studies are detailed in books by Kubey and Csikszentmihalyi (1990), Larson and Richards (1994a), and Schneider and Waite (2005). Table 7.1 shows the percent of time adults spend in different contexts and activities, as determined by one of these studies. In any given week, adults spend roughly equal amounts of waking time at home and at work (40% and 42%, respectively). However, about one-third of their time spent at work is spent not working, but socializing, eating, and engaging in other personal activities. Both Hoogstra (2005; in Schneider & Waite, 2005)

Table 7.1   Adults' Use of Time

Activity by Environment	Percent of Signals
Work	
Working	27.5
Socializing, eating, other	14.8
Total	**42.3**
Home	
Watching television	6.6
Cooking	2.4
Cleaning	3.4
Eating	2.3
Snacking, drinking, smoking	0.9
Reading	2.7
Talking	2.2
Grooming	3.1
Hobbies, repairing, sewing, gardening	3.7
Other chores	3.0
Idling, resting	4.0
Other, miscellaneous	5.8
Total	**40.1**
Public, others' homes	
Leisure and other activities	8.8
Shopping	3.1
Transportation	5.7
Total	**17.6**

SOURCE: Copyright © Kubey, R., and Csikszentmihalyi, M. (1990). *Television and the quality of life: How viewing shapes everyday experience*. Hillsdale, NJ: Erlbaum. Reprinted with permission of Lawrence Erlbaum Associates.

and Kubey and Csikszentmihalyi (1990) reported that roughly 27 percent of adults' total time is spent actually working. Larson and Richards (1994a) gave a slightly lower figure (23%), but their sample included more non-employed mothers. Full-time workers in these studies typically spent about 45 hours per week at work.

At home, work of a different sort occupies the largest proportion of adults' time. Activities such as cooking, cleaning, childcare, personal care, and eating are typically categorized as "maintenance" activities in ESM studies. The distribution of these activities between the man and the woman in a household is not at all balanced and varies considerably across families, as we will see in Chapter 8. Collapsing across the genders, adults spend from 24 to 29 percent of their time doing maintenance activities (Hoogstra, 2005; Kubey & Csikszentmihalyi, 1990; Larson & Richards, 1994a). The balance of adults' time is consumed with driving or other transportation, socializing, and active or passive leisure pursuits, the most common of which is watching television.

Predictably, the amount of time adults spend alone versus with others depends considerably on their life circumstances. Canadian college students in one study reported being alone 42 percent of the time, whereas mothers employed full-time were alone only 12 percent of the time (O'Connor & Rosenblood, 1996; Larson & Richards, 1994a). Parents of adolescents spent about 18 percent of their time with their children and 21 percent of their time with their spouse, with these two contexts overlapping. As noted in the discussion of "unmutual togetherness" in the previous chapter, social context information gathered via ESM may not be identical to what would be recorded by an independent observer. In addition to spouses, parents and their children also disagree as much as 20 percent of the time as to when they are actually together. The concept of being alone also has some ambiguity. The Canadian college students reported being alone but with other people present 12 percent of the time.

Temporal patterns in the contexts and activities reported by adults also show a connection to life circumstances. For full-time workers, there is a clear weekend-weekday dichotomy, with much more variation in activities, company, and motivation on weekends (Zuzanek & Mannell, 1993). Retirees experience greater free time and an even distribution of activities throughout the week compared to workers. Surprisingly however, retirees do not lose the "Monday blues," an experiential day-profile they share with workers. Certain activities, such as watching television, adhere to a fairly strict temporal rhythm (Kubey & Csikszentmihalyi, 1990). Clearly, the television industry is aware of viewing levels across the day, with its aptly named "prime time" attracting the most viewers.

ESM investigations have also gone beyond cataloguing which activities people engage in, where, and with whom, to focus on the psychological states individuals experience in each context. The unique combinations of emotion, motivation, and cognitive efficiency that accompany each moment of life have been called an individual's "internal landscape" or "quality of experience." Figure 7.1 displays how a sample of 107 working adults experienced several common activities in terms of affect, activation, and intrinsic motivation. The activities falling in the most positive octant (simultaneously above average in all three dimensions) reveal the satisfaction adults derive from fulfilling both physical and psychological needs. In order of decreasing frequency, those activities are talking, eating, cooking, shopping, sports,

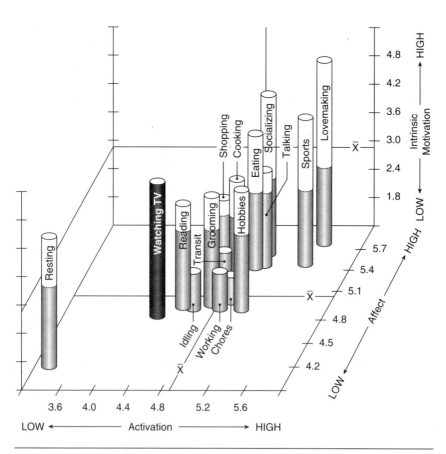

Figure 7.1   The Subjective Landscape of Adult Activities

NOTES: $\overline{X}$ = Mean response for all activities. ----- = Mean intrinsic motivation for all activities.

SOURCE: Copyright © Kubey, R., and Csikszentmihalyi, M. (1990). *Television and the quality of life: How viewing shapes everyday experience.* Hillsdale, NJ: Erlbaum. Reprinted with permission of Lawrence Erlbaum Associates.

socializing, and lovemaking. The only activity to garner below-average ratings on all three dimensions was idling (i.e., waiting, doing nothing, day-dreaming, etc.). Television and resting were accompanied by the lowest levels of affect and activation, but also by above average intrinsic motivation, which was measured in this case as the reversal of the scale "Did you wish you had been doing something else?"

Quality of Experience in Selected Activities

Sleep and Dreams

In a unique application of experience sampling, Stickgold, Malia, Fosse, and Hobson (2001) collected reports throughout the days and nights of 16 college students over a 2-week period. At night, the participants wore a sleep-monitoring system that recorded eyelid and head movements to identify periods of rapid eye movement (REM) and non-REM sleep. On all but four nights, they were awakened either first during REM and then non-REM or vice versa. During each forced and spontaneous awakening and when paged during the daytime, participants dictated a "mentation report" into a handheld tape recorder, describing what was going on in their minds just before the signal. The number of words in these reports differed significantly by sleep state, with reports from REM sleep running twice as long as those from non-REM. Even reports from the waking day were significantly shorter than those from REM sleep, while there were no differences in report length across different portions of the waking day. Further analyses revealed that hallucinations (endogenously generated sensations, felt as realistic) were described in 82 percent of REM reports, 60 percent of non-REM, and less than 1 percent of waking reports (Fosse, Stickgold, & Hobson, 2001).

Wilderness Experiences

ESM has followed Italian mountaineers as they ascended a Himalayan peak, New Zealand students as they rafted down a stream running through a cave, and Georgia canoeists as they navigated the Okefenokee Swamp. The six Italian climbers reported their experiences for 39 days, 26 of which were actually spent on the mountain (Delle Fave & Massimini, 2003). Perhaps surprising to those of us who are not experienced climbers, the majority of their time was spent not climbing, but in basic survival activities (eating, sleeping, cooking, and setting up tents). Other nonclimbing activities included moving from one campsite to another, preparing equipment, planning routes, and leisure (reading, playing cards, conversing). Part of the reason for the abundance of these activities is that the climbers were hindered in their quest by eight days of snowstorms and did not reach the summit. Despite the inherent danger of this situation, the perception of risk played a minor role in these climbers' experiences. Instead, the climbers reported frequent moments of flow, a finding we will explore in more depth later in this chapter. Climbing and camp activities were often seen as things they both wanted to do and had to do. This paradoxical response reflects the combination inherent in their sport of free choice and life-critical demands.

While the climbers by necessity had to focus on their task, less extreme wilderness excursions seem to lead people to focus their attention on nature and on themselves. College students in New Zealand on a three-hour blackwater rafting trip reported an increased focus on nature during their time in the cave (McIntyre & Roggenbuck, 1998). They felt most aroused at a waterfall where they jumped from a ledge into the pool below and most relaxed afterward as they traversed a section lit only by glowworms on the roof of the cave. Although they felt highly sociable throughout the trip, their focus turned to introspection on the drive home. Similarly, canoe paddlers camping one to three days in the Okefenokee Wetlands increased in feelings of humility, primitiveness, oneness with nature, and care for the environment as their time in the wilderness progressed (Borrie & Roggenbuck, 2001). The degree of their focus on others and on social acceptance also dropped during this time.

Listening to Music

Probably no other activity is so rare as a main activity and simultaneously so prevalent as a secondary activity as is listening to music. In a study of nonmusicians, Sloboda, O'Neill, and Ivaldi (2001) found that listening to music was a main activity only 2 percent of the time, but music was being heard during 23 percent of all signals and was heard at some point since the previous signal an additional 21 percent of the time. Music was heard most often in the car, at home, and in shops and entertainment venues. It was not heard at work or outdoors. While listening, people reported socializing, traveling, and doing maintenance and leisure activities. Participants felt more aroused, interested, involved, relaxed, and happy after listening to music than before, with the largest changes in mood occurring if they had a personal choice in hearing the music.

Watching Television

The single most time-consuming activity people engage in at home, occupying 25 percent of all home time, is television viewing. It is also the predominant leisure activity, accounting for 40 percent of all leisure time.

In their extensive study of how people experience television, Kubey and Csikszentmihalyi (1990) found that 10 percent of all ESM signals included TV viewing as either a primary or secondary activity in a group of working adults. This translates to 1.4 hours per day, but does not include any TV viewing that may have occurred before 8 a.m. or after 10 p.m., when no signals were scheduled. Fifteen years later, Dempsey (2005) reported a remarkably similar estimate, 1.3 hours daily, among dual-career parents of teenagers. People are almost always at home when they are watching TV, either with family or alone. While watching, viewers engage in other activities 70 percent of the time (Dempsey, 2005). Whether TV or these other activities are reported as the "main thing" they were doing depends on the time of day and what those activities are. During productive and maintenance activities in the early evening, such as dinnertime, TV is often a background activity. By late evening, TV becomes dominant. Frequent secondary activities—eating, talking, smoking—during this period of viewing often have an oral focus (Kubey & Csikszentmihalyi, 1990).

The subjective experience of watching television appears to be quite similar across diverse groups, including teenagers, adults, elderly persons, Italians, Canadians, and Americans (Kubey & Csikszentmihalyi, 1990). While viewing television, people report feeling relaxation above all else. Generally they say they want to watch and their intrinsic motivation is above average, but they also frequently say they had nothing else to do. TV presents no cognitive or physical demands, as indicated by low levels of concentration, challenge, and skill. Emotionally, TV appears to leave viewers flat or slightly below average. A common finding is that viewers presented with semantic differential scales (e.g., sad to happy) choose the midpoint of the scale, indicating no strong emotions in either direction (Kubey & Csikszentmihalyi, 1990; Larson & Richards, 1994a). Thus rather than facilitating happiness or enjoyment, TV appears to serve the function of draining people of negative emotions, stress, and tension. In support of this conclusion, Kubey and Csikszentmihalyi (1990) found that people tended to watch much more television in the evening if their afternoon was filled with negative affect. Their viewing session did not bring on positive emotions, but rather brought them back up to a neutral point. Similarly, Larson and Richards (1994a) found that fathers who experienced more competitiveness, frustration, and worry at their jobs tended to watch more TV when they got home. The emotional escape that TV provides extends beyond the viewing period in some ways but not in others. After viewing, people remain passive, but they feel less happy and relaxed than they did while viewing (Kubey & Csikszentmihalyi, 1990).

Quality of Experience of Selected Groups of People

Stigmatized Groups

The inner experiences people have depend not only on their momentary activities but also on global personal characteristics and life circumstances. Frable, Platt, and Hoey (1998) focused on the quality of experience of college students with concealable stigmas such as being bisexual, gay, lesbian, bulimic, or poor. This group was compared to students with conspicuous stigmas (e.g., stuttering, being African American or overweight), concealable valued qualities (e.g., Olympic qualifier, wealthy, or child of a celebrity or politician), or conspicuous valued qualities (e.g., physical attractiveness). Over the 11-day signaling period, the group with concealable stigmas reported feeling more anxious and depressed and had lower self-esteem than any other group. They spent more time alone, more time in class, and less time in social settings. They did more academic work and less socializing. These students felt best about themselves when they were with similar others. Surrounded by companions who shared their stigma, their depression and anxiety decreased while their self-esteem increased. Such occasions, however, were more rare than social occasions with dissimilar others, due to the scarcity of others with particular stigmas and the difficulty in identifying them. Students with conspicuous stigmas were more likely to find similar others to socialize with. These findings suggest that organized support groups for those with concealable stigmas may be beneficial for their mental health.

Elderly Persons

Conducting ESM research with elderly persons can present unique challenges. In Hnatiuk's (1991) sample of 29 widows aged 69 or older, over half of them did not take their pager with them on excursions out of their home, feeling it was too loud or intrusive on social activities. Other researchers studying residents of intermediate care facilities used either an in-person approach or a mobile phone to call some participants in lieu of paging them. These residents could provide oral responses to a researcher in person or over the phone but could not respond in writing to a pager (Voelkl & Mathieu, 1993; Voelkl & Nicholson, 1992). Results of these studies showed that residents spent about 30 percent of their time idling or resting, 20 percent in self-care, and 20 percent doing activities. Socializing, eating, and other unstructured activities that offered choice were the most pleasurable activities. Depressed residents spent twice as much time watching TV (26% of their time) as nondepressed residents and they did less self-care.

The social context of elderly persons varies considerably on the basis of their life circumstances. In a study of Canadian retirees, all of whom lived independently, those who were unmarried spent 66 percent of their time alone whereas their married peers were alone 39 percent of the time (Larson, Mannell, & Zuzanek, 1986). These older citizens were most often alone in the morning and less frequently alone in the afternoon and evening. They also tended to feel worse about being alone in the afternoon and evening than in the morning (Larson, Zuzanek, & Mannell, 1985). Unmarried individuals experienced a drop in arousal when alone, in contrast to married individuals, who felt more aroused and challenged when alone. Although time spent with one's spouse (for married persons) was correlated with non-ESM global reports of life satisfaction, the presence of the spouse in any given moment was not related to feelings of positive affect or activation. Instead, for both married and unmarried elderly persons, time spent in the companionship of friends brought on the most positive inner experiences. When with friends, these people tended to engage in active leisure pursuits, whereas maintenance and passive leisure were the predominant activities undertaken with adult children and spouses. Thus both friends and family appear to be instrumental in the well-being of elderly persons, friends for the immediate enjoyment they provide and family for their long-term support and companionship.

Adolescents

No other group has been studied more extensively with ESM than adolescents. Csikszentmihalyi and Larson (1984) began by examining where teenagers spend their time, what they do with their time, and whom they spend time with. At first blush, their findings seem to suggest that teens spend most of their time in contexts that are directly structured and controlled by adults—41 percent of their time is spent at home and 32 percent at school. However, over one-third of their school time is spent outside of class, and the largest chunk of their time at home, roughly 30 percent, is spent in their bedrooms. More than 15 years later, another study of adolescents replicated the school figures nearly perfectly, adding the finding that students in the United States spend only 55 percent of school time in academic classes (Csikszentmihalyi & Schneider, 2000). These data demonstrate the value of using multiple levels of resolution in coding responses, even in addressing a question as seemingly objective as "Where do people spend their time?" Clearly, adolescents occupy physical spaces that are neither wholly their own nor totally constrained by adult structure.

Further evidence that adolescents find ways to avoid adult-structured experiences comes from a look at whom teens spend their time with.

Csikszentmihalyi and Larson (1984) found that adolescents spend just over half of their waking hours with their peers, which breaks down into 23 percent of their time with classmates and 29 percent with friends. They are alone 27 percent of the time and with family members 19 percent, a proportion also reported by Larson and Richards (1994a). As the day progresses, the social context changes for adolescents in predictable ways. Weekday mornings and afternoons are dominated by classmates, with a spike around lunchtime for being with friends. Friends are also the most prevalent companions in the hour or two right after school. In the evening hours, time is distributed fairly evenly on weekdays between being alone, with family, or with friends. On weekends, time with friends accounts for over 50 percent of evening hours (Csikszentmihalyi & Larson, 1984).

In part because of this high degree of peer companionship, weekend evenings are the most emotionally positive times of the week for high schoolers (Larson & Richards, 1998). As adolescents move from the middle school grades into high school, their weekdays develop an increasingly negative emotional profile, while weekends increase in happiness and excitement. In addition to the greater presence of peers and the low degree of adult structure and control, the activities older adolescents engage in on weekends also explain this shift. While their younger counterparts are often at home watching TV, older teens are more often cruising in cars, at parties, with peers of the opposite sex, or engaging in alcohol or drug use. Figure 7.2 shows how the excitement of weekend nights is accompanied by a steep drop in their sense of being in control. Of course, not all teens are out partying every weekend. Older adolescents who happen to be at home alone on a weekend evening experience the worst affect of the week.

Besides companionship (or lack thereof), adolescents' quality of experience is also influenced by how they spend their time. Not surprisingly, socializing is typically accompanied by very positive emotions (Csikszentmihalyi & Hunter, 2003; Csikszentmihalyi & Larson, 1984). However, it is not the most uniformly positive activity across all aspects of internal experience. The loss of control on weekends is one result of the low levels of concentration that teens report when socializing. Activities with the most globally positive ratings are those we would categorize as structured leisure: sports, games, arts, hobbies, and reading. As Figure 7.3 shows, these are the only activities that garner above-average ratings on all major dimensions of inner experience. All other activities offer a mixed bag. Teens concentrate well on classwork and studying, but are unhappy and unmotivated. They are motivated to watch TV, but it doesn't bring them happiness. It appears that the best qualities of inner experience come for these adolescents only when they actively and voluntarily engage their skills. Unfortunately, adolescents spend only about 7 to 8 percent of their time doing these activities, about the same

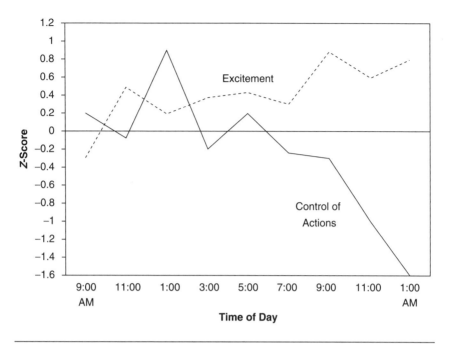

Figure 7.2   Average Excitement and Control of Actions Across the Day on Weekends When Teenagers Were With Friends

SOURCE: From *Being Adolescent: Conflict and Growth in the Teenage Years* by Mihaly Csikszentmihalyi. Copyright © 1984 by Basic Books, Inc. Reprinted by permission of Basic Books, a member of Perseus Books, L.L.C.

amount that they spend watching TV. These findings have been replicated in several studies of U.S. and Italian teens (e.g., Csikszentmihalyi & Larson, 1984; Delle Fave & Bassi, 2000).

One of the sources of variation among teens in how they spend their time is social class. Shernoff and Csikszentmihalyi (2001) found that teens from lower SES neighborhoods spent more time at home and doing passive activities, such as TV watching, whereas their more affluent peers spent more time in school and engaged in hobbies and extracurricular activities. Despite this difference, other findings suggest that teenagers from wealthier communities feel more bored, alienated, and less happy overall than those from less privileged backgrounds (Hunter & Csikszentmihalyi, 2003). Affluent teens enjoy their structured leisure just as much as any other young people, but have less positive experiences in school and at home, perhaps due to greater pressures to achieve and more isolation from adults (Luthar & Becker, 2002). In any case, school appears to be a major source of opportunities for adolescents to engage in productive activities and active leisure, opportunities

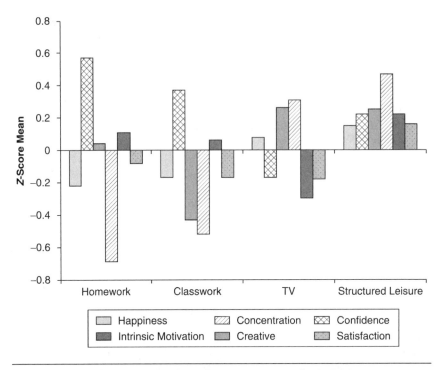

Figure 7.3   Adolescents' Quality of Experience in Daily Activities

SOURCE: Adapted from Delle Fave and Bassi, *Genetic, Social, and General Psychology Monographs, 126,* p. 354, 2000. Reprinted with permission of the Helen Dwight Reid Educational Foundation. Published by Heldref Publications, 1319 Eighteenth St. NW, Washington, DC 20036-1802. Copyright © 2000.

that may have more impact for less privileged youth. Among 36 teenage truants and offenders in Australia, passive leisure was their predominant occupation, taking 49 percent of their time (Farnworth, 2000).

If adolescents experience a sense of autonomy and that opportunities are available for them to exercise their skills in a supportive environment, they will experience growth. In one study, teens who experienced more autonomy during one ESM week also reported more concentration, goal-directedness, and intrinsic motivation during productive activities two years later, compared to their peers with less autonomy (Hektner, 2001). Other longitudinal ESM studies of adolescents have shown a downward slide in affect that is most pronounced in early adolescence and bottoms out around grade 10 (Larson, Moneta, Richards, & Wilson, 2002; Moneta, Schneider, & Csikszentmihalyi, 2001). With age, teens experience less emotional volatility and begin to develop the stability profile common among adults. By the time they reach college age, those who have still not achieved this stability (i.e., those with greater variability in their momentary self-esteem) also experience greater social anxiety, self-consciousness, and social avoidance (Oosterwegel, Field, Hart, & Anderson, 2001). Despite their increasing stability in momentary inner experience, adolescents who answer global questionnaires generally recollect that significant positive changes have occurred (Freeman et al., 1986). This finding once again reflects the different types of information obtained via ESM versus questionnaires.

Emotions, Well-Being, and Flow

Intensity, Frequency, and Structure of Emotions

Among adults, positive emotions are reported with both greater frequency and intensity than negative emotions. Two studies converge on the finding that positive emotions occur 65 to 90 percent of the time, whereas negative feelings are reported 15 to 45 percent of the time (Carstensen, Pasupathi, Mayr, & Nesselroade, 2000; Zelinski & Larsen, 2000). There is a positive correlation between the frequency of pleasant and unpleasant emotions—some people are just more emotional than others, having a greater number of both positive emotional episodes and negative emotional episodes. On the other hand, the amount of time people spend in a pleasant mood is negatively correlated with the amount of time spent in a negative mood (Schimmack, Oishi, Diener, & Suh, 2000). Positive emotions (e.g., excited, interested, enthusiastic, happy) tend to blend together more often than negative emotions, which are experienced as more discrete. When emotions are viewed as person-level traits, they tend to cluster into basic positive or negative affect dimensions that are independent of each other rather than bipolar opposites. In other words, a person who is often happy is also likely to be often excited. However, the correlations among emotions are much lower when they are viewed as momentary states within each person (i.e., the beep-level correlations are lower than the person-level correlations). A sad moment, then, is not necessarily also an angry moment (Zelinski & Larsen, 2000), although there are individual differences in whether emotions tend to cluster together or remain distinct.

Experiencing emotions as discrete rather than as a generalized positive or negative feeling has been called emotional granularity. Tugade and Feldman Barrett (2002) have found that individuals with greater degrees of emotional granularity among the positive emotions also have better coping skills and thus stronger emotion regulation. Emotional granularity among the negative emotions also appears to be healthy. Individuals with more highly differentiated negative emotions more frequently use emotion regulation strategies, especially at higher levels of emotional intensity (Feldman Barrett, Gross, Christensen, & Benvenuto, 2001). This ability to differentiate emotions appears to be a skill that develops throughout adulthood. In a study of 184 adults ranging in age from 18 to 94, Carstensen and associates (2000) computed for each individual the number of factors that accounted for the variance in 19 emotion items on their ESM form. They discovered a positive correlation between emotional differentiation (i.e., number of factors) and age. Besides having a greater number of discrete emotions, older people also were more likely to experience both positive and negative emotions on the same occasion. Emotional differentiation was related to greater emotional control and less intense negative affect. The frequency of negative affect also declined with age across the working years, before leveling off from age 60 on.

Situational factors also play a role in emotional differentiation. Zautra, Berkhof, and Nicolson (2002) showed how the cognitive demands of a stressful event decrease our capacity to differentiate complex emotions. Unsurprisingly, white-collar workers in their study experienced more negative affect and less positive affect during stress than during other times. More interesting is their finding of a stronger negative correlation between positive and negative affect during stress than during nonstressful moments. When under stress, these workers tended to report their emotions in more black and white, undifferentiated terms. The severity of negative mood after stress was moderated to some degree if the worker also perceived some controllability over the event (Van Eck, Nicolson, & Berkhof, 1998).

Role of Cognitive Styles and Strategies

Increasingly, researchers are turning inward to patterns of thought in their attempt to explain emotion variation between persons and contexts. For example, Swendsen (1998) found that French college students experienced more depressed moods after a negative event if they attributed the cause to be pervasive and persistent over time. These pessimistic attributions continued to influence mood up to six hours later. On the other hand, when pessimism is a defensive strategy for thinking about future goals rather than an attributional style for explaining past failures, it may not be as detrimental to quality of experience. Norem and Illingworth (1993) used two different types of ESM self-reports to study both defensive pessimists and optimists. Both groups first completed a preliminary questionnaire in which they listed five personal life tasks or goals they were currently working on. The defensive pessimists who were asked at every beep to rate their progress toward their personal goals felt more in control and had more positive affect than those who were not asked to rate their progress. Optimists in the progress-rating condition felt less positive affect and were less satisfied with their progress toward their goals. Optimists were better off when they did not have to continually reflect and report on their progress.

Another goal-related strategy (or antistrategy, as the case may be) that has been illuminated by ESM is procrastination. Pychyl, Lee, Thibodeau, and Blunt (2000) studied the experience of undergraduates during the five days immediately preceding a major exam or a due date for a paper. The students reported procrastinating 36 percent of the time. In addition to rating what they were doing at the moment, they also rated how they would feel if they were doing the activity they felt they should have been doing instead (usually studying). During procrastination, their actual activity was rated as more pleasant and less confusing, difficult, important, and stressful than their averted activity. Yet, their forecasts of the averted activity were worse than the activity turned out to be. When they were actually studying, they felt more pleasantness and less stress, difficulty, and confusion than they thought they would feel when they rated studying as a "should be doing" activity. In other words, students may justify procrastination by believing that studying is a much more negative experience than it actually is. Students also do not get a boost in positive affect from procrastination; it was not related to either positive or negative affect, but it was positively correlated with guilt.

The opposite of procrastination may not be the healthiest strategy either. Achievement-oriented college women in one study allowed their academic problems to dampen their social satisfaction (Harlow & Cantor, 1994). These women saw academics as a relevant goal even during socializing because they would often get reassurance and encouragement from their companions. However, their persistent orientation toward academics led to less enjoyable social interactions. This finding leads to the conclusion that independent of social context, goal relevance also affects quality of experience (Fleeson & Cantor, 1995). When these students felt their current activity was relevant to the goal of getting along with others, they felt more pleasantness than when their activity was relevant to the goal of doing well academically, regardless of social context.

Trait Explanations for Behavior and Emotional Experience

As we explained in Chapter 5, person-level means can be used as a measurement of a person's cross-situational characteristics. Diener, Suh, and Oishi (1997) concluded that a person-level mean of an ESM well-being variable, such as happiness, yields information different from a one-time questionnaire measure of subjective well-being. The reason is that in reflecting on their experiences to formulate a response to a retrospective questionnaire item, people give more weight to peak moments and they strongly attend to how an episode ended. People also tend to ignore the duration of an emotional episode in formulating a retrospective evaluation of it (Fredrickson & Kahneman, 1993).

Other comparisons of ESM and questionnaire data on personal behavioral characteristics have shown greater convergence. Moskowitz (1994), for example, had participants rate their dominance, submissiveness, agreeableness, and quarrelsomeness on a questionnaire and then included items to monitor the behavioral manifestations of these traits on a three-week ESM protocol. In social situations with friends and acquaintances, the ESM variables measuring the behaviors predicted by the four traits showed moderately strong convergence with their questionnaire counterparts. Dominant people spoke firmly, expressed opinions, and asked others to do things. Submissive people spoke softly, waited for others to speak or act, and kept their feelings to themselves. Agreeable people smiled, laughed, listened, and compromised. Quarrelsome people demanded, criticized, and spoke sarcastically. In interpersonal work situations (e.g., manager-subordinate), there was understandably less convergence between traits and behaviors due to the stronger situational constraints.

This work shows that the usefulness of traits in predicting individual behavior depends on the context. Fleeson (2001) found that there is a high degree of within-person variability in behaviors related to traits such as extraversion and conscientiousness, with considerable overlap between the ranges of relevant behaviors displayed by any two people with different traits. The typical individual has a highly diverse, flexible, and responsive repertoire of behaviors. Yet, when looked at holistically, this repertoire does seem to reflect underlying traits that are stable within individuals but vary across individuals. In Fleeson's study, an individual's mean levels of affect- and trait-related behavior and his or her variability (standard deviation) on these measures were highly stable. Similarly, mood variability emerged in another study as a personality characteristic that is stable across time and across situations (Penner, Shiffman, Paty, & Fritzsche, 1994). Some people experience extreme and frequent mood changes and other people don't, but all people could experience a positive or negative mood at any given moment. This contrast between the broad patterns influenced by personality traits and the momentary states that make up but do not necessarily reflect those patterns is illustrated in Figure 7.4. As shown, a person's level of extraversion during one randomly selected hour is barely related to the same person's extraversion during another randomly selected hour. However, the average level of extraversion across half of a person's reports very strongly predicts the person's average across the other half of reports.

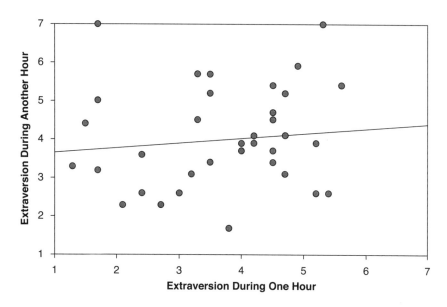

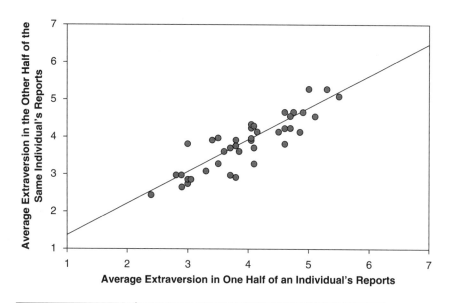

Figure 7.4   Contrasting Consistency in Momentary Extraversion Versus in
Average Extraversion

SOURCE: Fleeson, 2001. *Journal of Personality and Social Psychology, 80*. Copyright © 2001
by the American Psychological Association. Reprinted with permission.

In another example of this phenomenon, trait negative affect, as measured by questionnaire, was a better predictor of daily average negative affect than of momentary negative affect (Marco & Suls, 1993). The mechanism by which the trait affects the state appears to involve how a person reacts to negative events. People with higher levels of trait negative affect report more distress from both current day and prior day problems.

Flow

One of the original purposes of ESM was to capture flow experiences. As we have discussed earlier, variables indicating both the condition for flow and the experience of flow are typically included on ESM forms. Most ESM flow studies have started by defining some relationship between challenges and skills as the condition for flow. A typical approach is illustrated in Figure 7.5. Using an eight-channel model, researchers in Milan have found Italian teenagers to be in the flow condition about 20 percent of the time, a proportion that has not changed in 12 years (Carli, Delle Fave, & Massimini, 1988; Delle Fave & Bassi, 2000). Haworth and Evans (1995) used a slightly modified form of the eight-channel model and found British teens to spend 24 percent of their time in the flow condition. When flow is broadened in the four-channel model to include all instances when challenge and skill are simultaneously above average, findings show both U.S. adults and teens to spend about 33 percent of their time in flow (Adlai-Gail, 1994; LeFevre, 1988).

The key question that gets at the heart of flow theory is whether the flow condition (simultaneously high challenges and skills) actually coincides with the flow experience (positive emotional, motivational, and cognitive experience). On this question, in study after study across wide-ranging samples the results are clear and convincing: the most positive combination of multiple aspects of inner experience occurs in the flow condition. When people are in the flow condition, they have more positive moods, higher self-esteem, stronger intrinsic motivation, more intense concentration, and a greater sense that what they are doing is important (e.g., Hektner, 1996; LeFevre, 1988; Massimini & Carli, 1988). Figure 7.6 illustrates a comparison between the flow condition (denoted as channel 2) and seven other combinations of challenge and skill. There are other channels accompanied by certain positive qualities of experience, but no other channel comes close to matching the overall positive blend of positive affect, cognitive efficiency, and intrinsic motivation that occurs when challenges and skills are simultaneously high. Furthermore, as the intensity of challenges and skills increases, the experience becomes even more positive and complex (Delle Fave & Bassi, 2000).

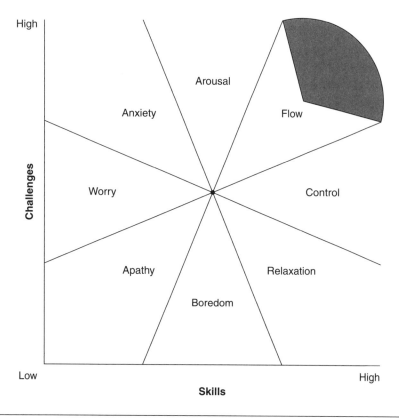

Figure 7.5   The Quality of Experience as a Function of the Relationship
Between Challenges and Skills

SOURCE: From *Finding Flow* by Mihaly Csikszentmihalyi. Copyright © 1997 by Mihaly
Csikszentmihalyi. Reprinted by permission of Basic Books, a member of Perseus Books, L.L.C.

NOTE: Optimal experience, or flow, occurs when both variables are high.

A recent focus of ESM-based flow research has been the attempt to mathematically define the exact relationship between challenges and skills that is most closely associated with the flow experience. (See Chapter 5 for further discussion of the different approaches.) For example, Moneta and Csikszentmihalyi (1996) tested the relationship of challenge, skill, and the difference between challenge and skill, on the one hand, to concentration, involvement, happiness, and wish to be doing the activity. They found the imbalance of challenge and skill (i.e., the absolute value of the difference) to be negatively related to all four experiential variables. The intensity of both

Quality of Experience	Challenge/Skill Channels							
	1	2	3	4	5	6	7	8
Concentration	P	P		N	N	N		P
Ease of concentration						N	N	N
Unselfconsciousness							N	N
Control of situation		P	P	P		N	N	N
Alert-drowsy						N		
Happy-sad		P				N	N	
Strong-weak		P				N	N	
Friendly-angry			P			N		
Active-passive	P	P			N	N	N	
Involved-detached	P	P				N		P
Creative-apathetic		P			N	N	N	
Free-constrained		P				N	N	
Excited-bored	P	P				N		
Open-closed		P				N	N	
Clear-confused		P				N	N	
Relaxed-anxious			P				N	N
Wish doing the activity	P	P				N	N	
Something at stake in activity	P	P		N	N	N		P
Time speed[a]	N							N
Satisfaction	P	P			N	N	N	
W.B.S.E.[b]	N	N				N		

Figure 7.6   Congruence of the Flow Experience and Comparison to Seven Other States

SOURCE: Csikszentmihalyi, M., & Csikszentmihalyi, I. S. (Eds.). (1988). *Optimal experience: Psychological studies of flow in consciousness.* Copyright © 1988. Reprinted with the permission of Cambridge University Press.

NOTES: The table shows the association of positive (P) and negative (N) levels of the variables describing the experience in the 8 different situations defined in terms of challenges/skills ratio.

1 = Arousal. 2 = Flow. 3 = Control. 4 = Relaxation. 5 = Boredom. 6 = Apathy. 7 = Worry. 8 = Anxiety.

a. Time speed: negative values mean that time is perceived to go faster.

b. W.B.S.E.: Wish to be somewhere else: negative values mean the absence of the wish to be somewhere else.

challenge and skill was positively related to concentration and involvement, but high challenge by itself was negatively correlated with happiness and wishing to be doing the activity. In a later article (1999), these authors found that the positive effect of balance was greater at higher levels of challenge and skill than lower levels and that the overall effect of the balance was small relative to the main effects of challenge and skill independently. Among talented adolescents, concentration was optimized when challenges slightly exceeded the teens' perceived skills. Thus, there should not necessarily be a strict definition of "the balance of challenges and skills," but rather a flexible interpretation that recognizes contextual and individual factors.

In another approach, Voelkl and Ellis (1998) asked half of their participants to rate challenges and skills in relation to their activity and half in relation to the focus of their thoughts. When rated on activities, challenge, skill, and the challenge-skill difference all predicted affect and self-affirmation. When rated on thoughts, challenge predicted affect, skill predicted self-affirmation, and the challenge-skill difference did not significantly predict either.

When people are in the flow condition, what are they doing, and what is the context? The Himalayan climbers we introduced earlier were most commonly climbing or doing camp activities while in flow (Delle Fave et al., 2003). For Italian teens, the instances in which their challenges and skills are the highest are those involving structured leisure activities such as hobbies and sports (Delle Fave & Bassi, 2000). Canadian retirees experienced the flow condition most often when they were doing freely chosen activities (Mannell, Zuzanek, & Larson, 1988). The Internet, by its interactive and user-directed nature, can also be a context for flow. As people surf the Internet, Web sites that are well-structured and provide immediate feedback from navigational tools not only entice them to stay longer but also lead to more flow than other sites (Tzanetakis, 2002). Viennese University students experienced the most flow from e-mail, chatrooms, and games; the least amount of flow came from pursuing information related to finding a job. For many adults, working on a job is a primary context for flow, but only if it provides enough challenge. Managers and engineers experience more flow during work than clerical or assembly-line workers (LeFevre, 1988).

Investigators at the University of Zurich have used ESM to investigate the "paradox of work"—namely, that people report higher levels of flow at work than at home, yet they can hardly wait to get home from work most days. Why does momentary flow on the job not add up to a general motivation to enjoy work? Their conclusion is that flow on the job is not an optimal experience for many workers. When not at work, flow measured by high challenges and high skills is associated by positive activation: alert, energetic, motivated. On the job, in addition to positive variables people also report high negative activation: stress, worry, and anger (Pfister, 2002;

Schallberger & Pfister, 2001). These results, which have been replicated with several Swiss samples, suggest some interesting modifications of flow theory.

The paradox of work has a parallel in adolescence. Adolescents often indicate that moments of studying at home or in class involve high levels of challenge and skill, but they give some of their lowest happiness ratings to these moments. When we aggregate responses within the person we find a surprising reversal from the beep-level results: teens who study more are happier overall than teens who study less (Csikszentmihalyi & Hunter, 2003). Perhaps an individual's momentary judgment of happiness is based on superficial cultural meanings that say work and study are not fun. Over time, though, flow appears to have the capacity to transform these experiences into a positive part of life.

If the relationship among challenges, skills, and the flow experience varies across contexts, then it must also be a characteristic that varies across individuals. Some people appear to be better able to derive the cognitive, motivational, and affective benefits from high challenge, high skill situations than other people. Adlai-Gail (1994) studied a group of autotelic adolescents—those who were most often in the flow condition—and compared them to a group on nonautotelic teens. Besides spending more time in high challenge, high skill situations, the autotelic group also had higher levels of concentration, self-esteem, enjoyment, and interest than the nonautotelic group, both while in flow and while not in the flow condition. During productive activities, the autotelic group felt more motivated, potent, and happy in the flow condition than in nonflow. On the other hand, the nonautotelic group felt less motivated, potent, and happy in flow than in nonflow.

A characteristic that is closely related to flow, intrinsic motivation, may also vary across individuals. College students with higher levels of intrinsic motivation check the time less often, experience time as moving more quickly, and lose track of time more often compared to those who have lower intrinsic motivation (Conti, 2001). This mode of experiencing time is one of the hallmarks of the flow experience. Students who let an awareness of time invade their consciousness more often also experience more negative affect.

Upon finding a characteristic such as the ability to maximize flow and intrinsic motivation, the next question is how stable this characteristic is in individuals. In a sample of adolescents who completed ESM twice over 2 years, Hektner (1996) found that 40 percent experienced a significant change in the level of flow they experienced, with half of this group increasing in the flow condition and half decreasing. During the final ESM wave, those who increased also spent more time studying and less time engaged in passive leisure than they did initially. Their levels of concentration, self-esteem, enjoyment, and interest were higher than the levels experienced by those who decreased in flow, although two years earlier the groups were equivalent on these dimensions.

One aspect of inner experience that did not discriminate between the two groups was happiness. As discussed previously, self-reported happiness tends to decrease as challenges increase, although if skills are increasing as well, the counteracting effect on happiness may result in a net relationship of zero between the flow condition and happiness. Of course, at the same time that people report no change in happiness due to flow, they are also reporting greater enjoyment, interest, motivation, concentration, self-esteem, and engagement. "Happiness" may be so laden with cultural meanings and expectations that for many people it is reserved for only those moments that fit the stereotype of happy moments and that are not filled with challenge.

Probably more than any other single chapter in this book, this chapter exemplifies the enormous range of research that has been undertaken using ESM. The method has proven invaluable in the study of countless facets of human experience. At the same time, this breadth is accompanied by great depth in a few specific areas. In the following chapters we highlight the areas of research in which ESM has made significant contributions.

8

The Experience of Males and Females

Exploring the differences between males and females—particularly in how members of each gender experience the world—has been an engaging parlor game for centuries and a research agenda for decades. One of the recent contributions to popular culture in this area has been the idea that men and women are so different they might as well hail from different planets (Gray, 1992). Men are silent, unemotional brutes who either insist on an active solution to problems or retreat to their caves in the face of conflict and stress. Women are talkative, emotional beings whose sense of self is defined through mutual relationships. Whether or not men are from Mars and women are from Venus, these images have become powerful stereotypes in our culture. Most stereotypes are founded on some kernel of truth and these are no exception. To drill down to that kernel, we need to take a systematic approach to comparing the subjective experiences of males and females. ESM studies have rarely had the examination of gender differences as their primary purpose, but because nearly every ESM sample has included men and women or boys and girls, an enormous amount of data relevant to this issue has been generated. These data show that there are clear gender differences in certain aspects of daily experiences, but these differences are less pervasive than one might be led to believe from the stereotypes available in popular culture.

Differences in Activities

One of the ways in which the prevalence of traditional gender roles is revealed most clearly is in how men and women allocate their time. Four different ESM studies all agree that women do more housework, including food preparation, cleaning, laundry, and child care than men do (Kubey & Csikszentmihalyi, 1990; Larson & Richards, 1994a; Lee, 2005; Zuzanek & Mannell, 1993). This is true even among a sample of full-time workers (Kubey & Csikszentmihalyi, 1990). The most recent estimate of the difference in time spent on housework by dual-career mothers and fathers is 9.4 hours per week, when housework is counted whether it is the primary or secondary activity and when "mental household labor" (time spent thinking and planning about housework) is included (Lee, 2005). Women tend to do more multitasking at home than men, listing housework as a secondary activity, and they do more thinking about housework. The gender gap in household labor has of course been documented before in non-ESM studies, the most current of which give a slightly lower estimate of the difference because they do not include time spent planning and thinking. A review published in 2000 of three decades of diary and survey data estimated the gap at seven hours but also showed how women have decreased their time invested in housework dramatically over those decades and men have increased (Bianchi, Milkie, Sayer, & Robinson, 2000). Part of the imbalance reflects the fact that women are much more likely than men to work part time or stay home to take care of children. When these women are aggregated with those employed full time, ESM studies report that the average amount of time women spend working on a job is 50–75 percent as much as men. Conversely, the average amount of time men spend on housework is 40–60 percent as much as women. Larson and Richards (1994a), whose sample includes mothers working full time, part time, or not at all, estimate that mothers spend 22 percent of their time doing housework, whereas fathers spend only 9 percent. Fathers whose wives work full time spend slightly more time doing housework, but the workload is still not divided equally.

Mothers also spend about twice as much time talking with family members as fathers do (Larson & Richards, 1994a), and they socialize with friends and others more than fathers do (Hoogstra, personal communication, 2003). Women spend more time engaged in personal care, but women and men spend roughly equal amounts of time immersed in leisure activities, whether active or passive. The specific leisure activities they engage in may differ, however. Two sources report that men watch more television than women, particularly on weekends when sports are on (Larson & Richards, 1994a; Zuzanek & Mannell, 1993). A more recent study, however, showed no difference in TV time between upper-middle-class spouses (Dempsey, 2005).

Gender differences in time use naturally have their origins earlier in development. Kirshnit, Ham, and Richards (1989) found that early adolescent boys spent nearly 8 percent of their time engaged in sporting activities, whereas girls spent 4 percent. Boys and girls spend equal amounts of time in gym class and organized sports, but boys spend much more time in informal sports than girls. This gender gap was echoed in the older teen sample studied by Csikszentmihalyi and Larson (1984). The amount of time these teens spent engaged in sports and games was six hours for boys and half that for girls. On the other hand, boys spent only half as much time as girls engaged in making art or music.

Similar to the adult members of their gender, girls as young as fifth grade already report doing more housework than boys do (Duckett, Raffaelli, & Richards, 1989). However, by ninth grade, boys increase their participation in household chores so that they spend an equal amount of time on them as girls do, but the kind of chores they do differs. Girls do more kitchen work, laundry, dusting, and vacuuming, whereas boys do more outdoor work such as lawn mowing and car washing. Besides the indoor/outdoor distinction, girls' work is more often done in the presence of other family members, while boys are more apt to work alone. Among older teens, girls and boys show no differences in the number of hours they spend working at a job (Csikszentmihalyi & Schneider, 2000). When they are not working at home or at work, girls spend more of their time maintaining themselves; personal grooming occupies twice as much of their time as it does for boys (Duckett et al., 1989). As they age through the middle school years, girls spend increasing amounts of time grooming, but the amount of time boys spend grooming does not change.

Another gender gap that widens with age is the amount of time teens spend talking with others (Raffaelli & Duckett, 1989; Wong & Csikszentmihalyi, 1991). From fifth to ninth grade, the amount of time girls spend in conversation doubles to 16 hours per week. Ninth grade boys spend only 8 hours a week talking. The conversation partner and mode of communication don't matter. Girls spend more time talking with friends and with parents, and nearly twice as much time talking on the phone as boys do (Csikszentmihalyi & Larson, 1984; Raffaelli & Duckett, 1989). The topics of these conversations also split along gender lines. Compared to girls, boys tend to discuss more sports and talk less about their peers. The gender difference in topics discussed with friends widens with age but the difference in topics discussed with family members remains stable over time.

Differences in Companionship

If girls spend more time talking with others, do they also spend more time in the presence of others? The findings here do not all agree, but the weight of the evidence appears to point to an affirmative answer. Csikszentmihalyi and Larson (1984) found no gender differences in the amount of time high school students spent alone or with others. On the other hand, Wong and Csikszentmihalyi (1991) found that talented freshmen and sophomore girls spent less time alone and more time with friends than talented boys. All sources agree that time spent with family declines with age for members of both genders. Larson and Richards (1991b) reported that both boys and girls replace this family time with more time alone, but only girls also make room for more time to spend with friends. As teens mature, their friendships increasingly include members of the opposite gender, but the pattern here is not symmetrical. In the high school years, girls and boys spend the same amount of time with same-gender peers, but girls spend twice as much time as boys do with members of the opposite gender (Richards, Crowe, Larson, & Swarr, 1998). Given a roughly even gender ratio in the population, the logistics of this uneven arrangement are not clear, but it may be that girls are spending time with older boys (who were not in the study) or with a small subset of same-age boys. Contrary to popular wisdom, adolescent girls also spend more time thinking about the opposite gender than boys do. Actually, girls spend more time thinking about any of their peers, whereas boys tend to think about their peers only when they are with them.

These ESM findings are echoed by results from a questionnaire measure of the affiliation motive. Besides finding that girls have stronger motivation to affiliate with others than boys do, Wong and Csikszentmihalyi (1991) also found that the relationship of this motive to actual experience when with companions differs by gender. Their ESM results showed that girls with high affiliation motivation feel better than girls with low affiliation motivation, whether they are with friends or alone. Figure 8.1 illustrates this comparison. For girls, strong affiliation motivation is associated with feeling better about oneself and more in control, alert, involved, and happy. For boys, however, having a strong motivation to affiliate is not such a boon. While alone, highly affiliative boys feel lower motivation and less control compared to other boys. Even while with other people, highly affiliative boys do not feel better than other boys and actually report lower motivation than other boys. On questionnaires, highly affiliative boys portrayed themselves as having more feminine characteristics, such as dependence, nurturance, and not adjusting as well to their environment as other boys. Highly affiliative girls saw themselves as dominant, influential, and well-adjusted. Clearly, a strong affiliation motive is a characteristic traditionally ascribed more to the female gender role than to the male, and there are negative experiential consequences for boys who find themselves with "too much" of this characteristic.

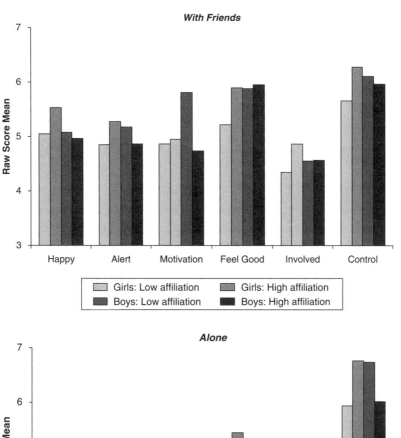

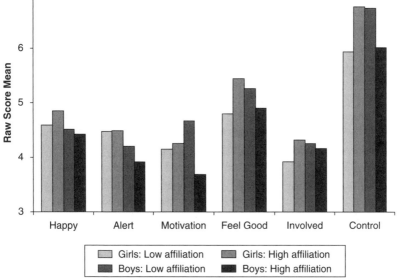

Figure 8.1   Affect of High- and Low-Affiliation Girls and Boys With Friends and While Alone

SOURCE: Adapted from Wong and Csikszentmihalyi, *Journal of Personality and Social Psychology, 60,* 1991. Copyright © 1991 by the American Psychological Association. Reprinted with permission.

Gender differences in the importance and meaning of affiliation persist in adulthood. While spending time with friends and coworkers, women report feeling much more positive affect than men do (Koh, 2005; Larson & Richards, 1994a). Compared to men, women feel more calm, interested, and kind when in the presence of friends. Women also indicate that the content of their conversations with friends is more deeply meaningful to them.

Similarities and Differences in Emotional Experience

Overall Emotional Experience

The stereotype in our culture persists that women are more emotional than men, except for anger. If one were to focus only on expressed emotion, research shows this stereotype to be accurate. Women are usually found to be more emotionally expressive than men, except for expressions of anger. Emotional expressiveness, however, may be a poor indicator of a person's actual experience of emotion (Berscheid, 1990). Perhaps men and women have similar inner experiences of emotion but simply differ in the way they express emotion. No research method could naturalistically observe and measure the inner experience of emotion to test this assertion, but ESM comes close.

Larson and Pleck (1998), reviewing several ESM studies, concluded that men and women are remarkably alike in rates of positive and negative affect. There were no differences in mean levels of affect, standard deviations, or frequency of choosing the extremes versus the middle of the response scales. In addition to overall affect, this similarity extended across the individual emotions of anger, anxiety, worry, nervousness, and guilt. More recent studies echo these findings. Adult workers showed no differences in reports of negative mood (Flory, Räikkönen, Mathews, & Owens, 2000; Koh, 2005), and adolescents did not differ by gender in their overall levels of happiness (Csikszentmihalyi & Hunter, 2003; Patton, 1998). A comparison of these results to those from non-ESM methods is revealing. Global self-descriptions of emotional characteristics collected in one study did show traditional gender differences, but when the same participants completed the ESM, their momentary ratings of emotion averaged across the week showed no gender differences (Feldman Barrett, Robin, Pietromonaco, & Eyssell, 1998). In another non-ESM study, Kring and Gordon (1998) had undergraduates view emotional films. The women were more emotionally expressive, but did not differ from men in reports of their inner experience of emotion.

On the other hand, at least three ESM studies have found that adult women report feeling more anxiety, worry, and distress than men (Almeida & Kessler, 1998; Hoogstra, 2005; Zuzanek & Mannell, 1993). The reason for the discrepancy between these findings and the lack of differences found in other studies can only be speculated. In two of the studies showing differences, women were particularly more distressed over home and family demands than men, and in the third study all of the women in the sample were mothers of school-age children. Clearly, more research needs to be conducted to determine whether the demands of motherhood and career are leading women to feel more distress than men. Consistent gender differences do emerge, according to Larson and Pleck (1998), in aspects of experience that are on the outskirts of the domain of basic emotions. Men feel more competitive, strong, awkward, and self-conscious, whereas women more often feel tired, weak, and in love.

Among adolescents, there are also some conflicting findings on gender differences in emotional experience. Comparisons of overall mean levels of affect ratings have shown no differences (Csikszentmihalyi & Hunter, 2003; Csikszentmihalyi & Larson, 1984; Patton, 1998). Larson and Pleck (1998), who conducted a more fine-grained analysis, report no differences in negative affect or mild positive affect. They did see differences, however, in rates of neutral and extreme positive affect, with boys showing neutral affect 6 percent more often and extreme positive affect 8 percent less often than girls. This pattern was replicated several years later among a sample of seventh graders (Barber, Jacobson, Miller, & Petersen, 1998). Interestingly, these gender differences do not appear in a similar ESM study of Korean adolescents, suggesting that the different emotional experiences of American young men and women are less rooted in the biology of gender than in the daily interactions of individuals and culture (Larson & Pleck, 1998).

Emotional Experience in Specific Contexts

Perhaps one of the reasons for the murky picture of overall gender differences and similarities in emotional experience that ESM studies have provided to date is that we are not asking the best question. A better question that would make fuller use of the capabilities of ESM would ask how males and females differ in their internal experiences of specific contexts. On this question, results of several different studies across many different contexts are more convergent.

Although not a context in itself, but rather a contextual parameter, time is one of the dimensions along which gender differences emerge. Across the day, week, and month, men and women have different emotional rhythms. Some of these rhythms may have a biological component. In a sample of six couples, LeFevre and colleagues (1992) found that the women were happiest in the days surrounding the ovulation phase of their monthly cycle and in the early menstrual phase. Their male partners' happiness was not associated with cycle timing, but the men did report greater levels of activation (active, alert, strong, outgoing) when their partners were premenstrual, during which the women felt their lowest levels of activation. Cyclical hormonal variations are clearly at work here, but the authors also pointed out that changes in the social environment accounted for more variation in the psychological states of these couples than did the women's menstrual cycle.

Other gender differences in the timing of emotional experiences underlie differences in the commitments and obligations members of each gender feel. For example, women in Zuzanek and Mannell's (1993) study felt the lowest affect and highest anxiety on Thursdays. This is also the day on which they worked the most number of hours for pay and spent the least amount of time on housework and family care. The gap between men and women in affect and anxiety was widest on Thursdays and was even greater while they were engaged in housework and family care on that day. Across the week, women felt the least amount of personal choice in performing these duties on Thursdays, whereas men felt a much higher degree of choice.

Emotional variations over the course of each day are also revealing. Figure 8.2 shows the emotional trajectory over a typical workday for employed mothers and fathers, as reported by Larson and Richards (1994a). Men and women start and end the day similarly, with near neutral emotions. For both, the high point of the workday is over the lunch hour and a low point occurs in late afternoon. But there are also stark contrasts. Women are happy all morning and then gradually descend to their lowest point of the day during the dinner hour, which is precisely the time when men are the happiest. For men, this is the time of day when they can relax in the comfort of home after a hard day at work. For many women, this is the time of day when they must come home and begin the "Second Shift" (Hochschild, 1989), putting dinner on the table and attending to children's needs.

These gender differences in the temporal patterns of emotion could not have been documented so clearly without ESM, but the results of other methods have shown that they could have been predicted given the highly scheduled nature of women's primary household tasks. Using interviews, Barnett and Shen (1997) found that women have a low level of control over the timing of their household tasks, meal preparation being a perfect example. Men's household chores, such as car maintenance, home repairs, and yard work, tend to allow them much more control over scheduling. When men or women have more control over the scheduling of their household tasks, they have less distress. In this study, distress was unrelated to total time spent doing household tasks, but it was related to time spent doing tasks involving little schedule control. Because these are the tasks women usually do, they experience more distress. These findings are echoed in

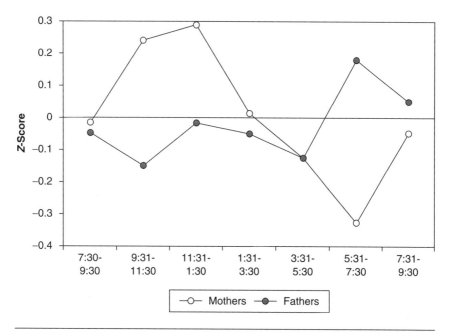

Figure 8.2   Employed Mothers' and Fathers' Emotions Across the Day

SOURCE: From *Divergent Realities* by Reed Larson. Copyright © 1994 by Reed Larson and Maryse Richards. Reprinted by permission of Basic Books, a member of Perseus Books, L.L.C.

NOTES: Based on weekdays only. Shows only mothers and fathers who were employed full time.

Dempsey's (2001) interviews with Australian adults. Men experience housework as more enjoyable and intrinsically rewarding than women do, in part because the tasks they do are more conducive to these experiences. Women's housework is more often seen as a burdensome daily responsibility. This may explain why ESM studies have shown women to experience more anxiety over home and family demands than men (Almeida & Kessler, 1998; Zuzanek & Mannell, 1993).

Differences in standards and expectations may be another factor in women's more negative emotions related to housework. A study of daily logs kept by couples over ten weeks showed that husbands were more satisfied than wives both with their own performance of housework and with their spouse's performance (Pittman, Teng, Kerpelman, & Solheim, 1999). Wives tend to have higher standards than their husbands and some even redo tasks their husbands have done that are not up to those standards (Hawkins, Marshall, & Meiners, 1995).

The greater dissatisfaction and distress of women in relation to taking care of the home and family is part of a broader division in how members of each gender respond emotionally to the major contexts of life. Several studies converge on the conclusion that women feel better at work and in public than their husbands do, whereas the husbands feel better at home and with family than their wives do, as illustrated in Figure 8.3. Men feel more negative moods than women while at their jobs, including more anger, boredom, nervousness, and loneliness (Larson, Richards, & Perry-Jenkins, 1994; see also Koh, 2005). Women feel more enjoyment than men at their jobs and more positive affect generally while away from home. By contrast, men are more frequently happy, cheerful, and friendly at home than at their jobs. These differences in the source of emotional distress may reflect perceived demands stemming from the different priorities and obligations experienced by men and women. To explain why women enjoy being in public outside of their jobs more than men, Koh (2005) suggested that women and men may do different things while in public. Women spend more time in public than men and may be more likely to socialize with friends during that time.

This conclusion leads to another possible reason behind women's greater happiness away from home. ESM studies have shown that women place a lot of emotional weight on social interactions. Recall the finding of Larson and Richards (1994a) that women derive much more satisfaction from friendships than men do. Koh (2005) also found that women enjoy the presence of nonfamily others much more than men. In another study of 100 workers, negative social interactions were related to lower positive moods for women but not for men (Flory et al., 2000). Women starting a new job in Germany placed more importance on social affiliation and experienced more stress than men over issues of social influence. More so than men, these women attributed their mood to the satisfaction or frustration of the affiliation motive (Brandstätter & Gaubatz, 1997). Given that positive social interactions are so important for women's emotional well-being, it follows that they would feel better in places where they experience many of those interactions—the workplace and in public. To be sure, positive interactions also occur at home, but much of women's time at home is occupied by housework and childcare demands. It appears that women escape from these demands by going out with their friends or going to work, whereas men escape from the demands of work by coming home to relax.

The greater emotional sensitivity of females to social interaction has also been documented among adolescents (Larson & Pleck, 1998). When teens are in the company of others, gender differences in emotional experience are magnified, boys showing more neutral affect and girls more extreme positive affect. While they are alone, the gender differences disappear. These findings

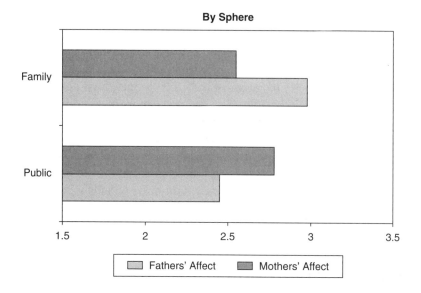

Figure 8.3   Mean Affect of Mothers and Fathers by Sphere and Mothers'
Employment Status

SOURCE: Larson, Richards, and Perry-Jenkins, *Journal of Personality and Social Psychology*,
67, 1994. Copyright © 1994 by the American Psychological Association. Reprinted with
permission.

complement those discussed previously on the affiliation patterns of girls and boys. Girls spend more time with friends than boys and feel better when with them (e.g., Larson & Richards, 1991b; Wong & Csikszentmihalyi, 1991).

Wong (2000) conducted a study of talented adolescents that also reveals the deeper commitments of girls toward other people. First she identified teens who experienced the initiation and regulation of their behavior as highly controlled, rather than autonomous. Both girls and boys with high control orientations organized their behavior with respect to controls in the environment or internal pressure. But while high-control boys were more self-focused and assertive, high-control girls spent more time doing things important to others and not for themselves. In order to satisfy their inclination to please others, these girls were more likely to forgo things important to themselves, such as taking more advanced courses.

Other Gender Differences in Adolescence

Anger Toward Single Mother

One of the other gender differences ESM studies have uncovered among adolescents is the trajectory of anger toward their single mother. Girls in early and middle adolescence from families headed by a single mom had more intense anger toward her than late adolescent girls. For boys, the developmental course of anger toward their mother is reversed, peaking in middle and late adolescence from a low in early adolescence. Thus middle adolescence (age 14–15) is a time of heightened anger for both boys and girls, but the genders show opposite patterns in early adolescence (when girls are angrier) and late adolescence (when boys are angrier). The mothers in this study did not show any age-related pattern in their reported anger toward their child (Dworkin & Larson, 2001). Reasons for the gender difference among the adolescents have not been well established, but may have something to do with the earlier maturation of girls than boys.

Experiences Associated With Puberty

In a study of more than 450 girls and boys aged 9 to 15, Richards and Larson (1993) found several changes in daily emotional experience associated with puberty for boys, but few strong changes for girls. Boys with greater pubertal development had higher ratings than their less-developed peers on scales of tension, positive affect, attention, strength, and feeling in love. For girls, pubertal development was weakly associated with more variability in affect, less frustration, and greater feelings of being in love.

Weight and Eating Concerns

Unsurprisingly, adolescent girls have more weight and eating concerns than their male peers. After finding this difference via a questionnaire, Richards, Casper, and Larson (1990) then turned to ESM to explore the links between these concerns and daily experience. Girls who had stronger weight and eating concerns also had lower self-esteem, affect, activation, and attention in their daily lives. They also had higher levels of depression and spent more time alone and less time with friends or in social activities. These links were found primarily among eighth and ninth grade girls and to a lesser degree among fifth and sixth grade girls. For boys, only one finding emerged: boys with more weight and eating concerns spent less time in sports.

Experiences of School and Sports

Playing sports is one of the most positive experiences in the daily life of many boys. Kirshnit and colleagues (1989) found that boys had higher motivation across all contexts of sports (gym class, extracurricular, informal) than girls did. Boys also felt more freedom of choice during sports participation than girls did, particularly in gym class. There is some evidence to suggest that boys take play in general more seriously than girls do. Adolescents in one study were asked to check whether the moment they were beeped was more like work, play, both, or neither. Boys "played" 3 percent more often than girls. During those moments of play, boys reported higher levels of concentration, challenge, and competitiveness than girls did (Csikszentmihalyi & Schneider, 2000). During the school day as a whole, however, girls appear to be the ones experiencing more positive moments. They achieve higher levels of flow during classroom activities than boys and report more enjoyment and concentration, particularly during group work, individual work, and videos (Csikszentmihalyi & Schneider, 2000). Compared to boys, girls also rate classroom activities as being more important to their future goals.

Relations Between Challenge and Negative Experiences

In his dissertation, John Patton (1998) uncovered some intriguing gender differences in the relations between challenge and negative experiences during low-skill situations. As in many ESM studies of flow, Patton divided moments into one of four quadrants based on levels of perceived challenge and skill (see Chapter 7). The amount of time adolescents spent in the flow condition (high challenges and skills) was not related to pain or anger, but was positively related to self-esteem and motivation two years later. The more time they spent in the relaxation condition (low challenges with high skill), the less pain or anger they felt. These relationships held for both young men and women. The genders diverged on the two low-skill conditions. For boys, time spent in the apathy condition (low skills with low challenges) was related to more frequent moments of pain and drops in self-esteem and motivation. For girls, pain, self-esteem, and motivation were related not to apathy but to the amount of time spent in the anxiety condition (low skills with high challenges). Overall, anxiety proved to be a better predictor of negative experiences for girls, whereas apathy was the better predictor of these experiences for boys. One of the reasons for this split may be that girls and boys experience anxiety during different activities. Boys tend to experience their anxiety during sports, which to them may provide a better experience than doing nothing. Girls experience more anxiety during maintenance activities, which include grooming and eating, two activities both associated with their appearance. It is also important to note that these relationships are longitudinal; within any given time point, both anxiety and apathy are associated with negative outcomes for both girls and boys. The difference occurs in the longer-term effects of these conditions. Lack of challenge may be more of a developmental risk factor for boys, while feeling insufficiently skilled is a greater developmental obstacle for girls.

These and the other gender findings reviewed in this chapter are good examples of the insights that can be gained from using ESM studies to examine questions that have already been extensively studied using more traditional means. Rather than confirming global generalizations about each gender, ESM has provided us with a more nuanced picture of the similarities and differences between males and females and the contexts in which differences are more likely to appear. This picture is less about opposites than it is about different areas of emphasis. Given a finite amount of energy and attention, men and women gravitate toward different experiences that appear to be more complementary rather than at odds. In the end, when men and women collaborate, the combination has the potential to enrich the lives of all.

9

The Experience of Family Life

The family has long been a challenging field of study for social scientists because of its nature as a system of individuals and relationships. Much family research has been plagued by reliance on retrospective reports from one member of the family or on contrived experiments that provide poor simulations of natural family interaction patterns. Often, family research treats "the family" as a single unit to be compared with other families. This approach has some value, but it also ignores the likely possibility that the husband/father, despite sharing the same household, actually "lives" in a different family than his adolescent daughter. By using ESM, family researchers have documented how each member of a family experiences family life—and how much each of these "versions" of the same family diverge. To emphasize this point, Larson and Richards (1994a) titled their landmark ESM study of families *Divergent Realities*.

As any good ESM study should, their book answers the basic descriptive questions: what families do together, at what time, for how long, and how they feel when together and apart. But by signaling family members simultaneously and analyzing sequences of experience, Larson and Richards (1994a) were also able to advance our state of knowledge on more complex aspects of family dynamics, such as the transmission of emotions between family members. Is anger contagious? Do a husband and wife have equal and reciprocal influence on each other's emotional state or do emotions tend to flow in one direction? These and other related questions were addressed in a collection of articles appearing in a special section of *Journal of Marriage and the Family* (Feb. 1999). Each of the articles used ESM or daily diaries to study the transmission of emotions within families. In an introduction to that section, Larson and Almeida (1999) cite this ability to assess differences in emotional experiences within families rather than just between families as one of the key advantages of ESM. By using Z-scores standardized to the individual, ESM researchers can also control for individual differences in response tendencies when comparing the experiences of family members. Before we continue describing the findings from this exciting research area, we will first lay some groundwork by discussing some methodological concerns and reviewing studies of the couple relationship, the arrival of the first child, and the resulting juggling of work and family roles.

Methodological Concerns and Variations

One of the first concerns of a family ESM researcher will be how to recruit families to participate. Larson and Richards (1994a) started with a larger adolescent sample that was already being recruited for an ESM study. After an adolescent agreed to participate, the researchers then asked if they could approach his or her parents about also participating. Larson and Richards found that fathers and adolescents refused participation much more than mothers. In the more recent 500 Family Study, a number of different recruitment methods were used (Hoogstra, 2005). Schools provided address lists for mailings to families and/or printed announcements about the study in the school newsletter. Some families responded to ads placed in the local newspaper. Still others were found via snowball sampling, when they were contacted by phone after a referral by a current study participant. Crucial to the success of a family ESM study is that all family members feel they are important to the study. Thus all members participating in the study should be present at the orientation session when they start their ESM recording.

The second major methodological issue to consider is the sampling schedule. In some studies (e.g., Larson & Richards, 1994a), moments in the late afternoon and evening when the family is more likely to spend time together are oversampled so that an adequate number of "family" reports are obtained. That is, family members are signaled on average every 90 minutes in the evening but every 2 hours during the day. If comparisons to other time budget studies are desired, a simple weighting procedure can adjust for the oversampling. Other family studies have kept the signal interval consistent across the day. All of the family ESM studies we are aware of used simultaneous signaling of each family member. The one benefit to be gained from signaling each member on a different random schedule would be a greater coverage of different moments in the family's overall experience. However, researchers apparently believe that giving up the ability to simultaneously collect the experiences of all family members is too great a cost for this benefit. Only through simultaneous signaling could researchers discover how different family members experience the same moment.

The Couple Relationship

One of the first ESM findings of asymmetry in a relationship was provided by Erich Kirchler (1988), who studied 21 young couples—some married, most just living together—in Austria over 4 weeks. Men felt happier, stronger, and freer when their partners were present than at other times, but women did not enjoy a corresponding boost when with their men. This difference may be partly attributable to the fact that when both partners are home, the men are more likely to be engaging in leisure while the women work. Kirchler also found that the benefits of a happy relationship extend beyond the immediate experience of the relationship. Happy couples, as assessed by a questionnaire, felt stronger and freer across situations, even when not together. They also spent more time together, more time talking about personal issues, and less time in conflict. To begin to understand what makes happy couples happy, Kirchler asked his participants at every signal occurring in the partner's presence to estimate the partner's needs. Partners in happy relationships were more accurate in knowing each other's immediate needs.

After years of marriage and the addition of children to the family, a couple's relationship is not the same as when they were newlyweds, but there is also evidence of some consistency. Couples in Larson and Richards' (1994a) study were married an average of 16 years and had at least 1 adolescent child. They spent less time together than the young Austrian couples did (21% vs. 39%), but they still enjoyed each other's company. Both wives and husbands had slightly better moods when together than when apart, a finding replicated in the 500 Family Study (Koh, 2005). For wives, the reason could be attributed to their emotional uplift whenever they had any companionship; for husbands, the reason centers on the relaxation and release from stress they felt at home. Similar to the young Austrian couples, those who were in warm, satisfying marriages spent more time together and had fewer negative emotions when together than those in cold marriages. These ESM results converge with the central finding from John Gottman's lab studies of marital interaction that the emotional tone of couple interactions is a powerful predictor of the success or failure of the marriage (e.g., Gottman, 1994; Gottman, Croan, Carrere, & Swanson, 1998; Gottman & Levenson, 1992).

Happy marriages are also characterized by fewer moments of "unmutual togetherness," those moments when one partner reports being together while the other does not (Larson & Richards, 1994a). Yet, even for happy couples, the demands of working, maintaining a household, and caring for children do take their toll on togetherness. Breaking down the 21 percent of together time, Larson and Richards found that couples reported doing the same thing together 10 percent of the time. Of that, they are in conversation or active recreation together 2.5 percent of the time, and of that, they are alone in conversation or active recreation together just 0.9 percent of the time, or about 7 minutes per day. Of course, some "alone together" moments late at night, after signaling had ceased for the day, may have been missed. Still, couples with children clearly do not share much quality time alone together.

The Arrival of the First Child

Judging from at least one study, the price that children extract from a couple's time alone together is more than worth the positive experience couples report when they become parents for the first time. In that study, 5 Italian couples completed 8 sampling periods, each 7–12 days long. Four of the periods were during the wife's first pregnancy and four were after the birth of the child, the last occurring when the child was six months old (Delle Fave & Massimini, 2000b; 2004). Table 9.1 displays how the mothers and fathers spent their time both during the pregnancy and after the birth. Before the birth, the future parents spent less than 5 percent of their time directly preparing for the child by doing things such as buying baby clothes, doing delivery exercises, and going to medical checkups. After the birth and over the subsequent six months, child-related activities consumed nearly one-third of the mothers' time. In order to create this time, mothers decreased their time spent at work and their involvement in media and maintenance activities. Italian law provides for mothers to receive two months paid leave from employment before a birth and three months after. The fathers, in contrast, typically took brief vacations from work at the time of the birth, resulting in a much smaller overall decrease in their work time. There were no significant changes in the fathers' time allocation, though small decreases in media, maintenance, and other activities can be noted in the table to compensate for the fathers' increased time in child-care activities.

Although childcare takes time away from other activities, a new parent's overall quality of experience may be just as or more positive than it was before parenthood. For the new Italian parents, childcare produced that quintessential combination of challenge and enjoyment; they rated their

Table 9.1   Mean Percentage Distribution of Daily Activities Reported by the Parents Before and After Childbirth

| | Mothers (S = 5)[a] | | | | Fathers (S = 5)[a] | | | |
| | Pregnancy (N = 1026)[b] | | After birth (N = 953)[b] | | Pregnancy (N = 1029)[b] | | After birth (N = 1021)[b] | |
Activities	Mean	SD	Mean	SD	Mean	SD	Mean	SD
Child	3.2	1.48	30.1	3.78	1.2	0.68	11.9	8.98
Work	14.1	6.24	7.2	3.04	26.3	5.67	22.4	8.08
Chores	18.2	3.84	20.5	2.58	8.6	5.18	8.9	2.97
Interaction	20.3	9.67	15.7	3.41	14.5	5.31	15.3	1.87
Leisure	3.7	1.78	3.2	0.65	4.7	2.76	4.7	3.03
Media	10.3	6.5	5.2	1.75	13.0	4.63	9.9	2.93
Maintenance	17.2	5.15	12.4	3.31	13.6	3.72	12.3	2.01
Other	13.0	3.26	8.7	3.86	18.1	3.45	14.7	4.31

SOURCE: Copyright © 2004. Reprinted with kind permission of Springer Science and Business Media. Delle Fave, A., and Massimini, F. (2004). Parenthood and the quality of experience in daily life: A longitudinal study. *Social Indicators Research, 67,* 75–106, Table 1.

NOTE: Data in each cell represent mean percentages calculated from each participant's percentage of self-reports in the activities.

a. S = number of participants, b. N = number of self-reports.

child-care activities as more challenging than their jobs and more mood lifting than leisure. During those moments in the flow condition, when challenges and skills were high and in balance, childcare was the only major activity category (the others being work, leisure, and media use) to produce significantly positive ratings on each of four dimensions of experience: mood, engagement, confidence, and intrinsic motivation. Even when the parents felt their skills being overmatched by their challenges in what we've called the anxiety condition, child-care activities continued to lead to positive moods, unlike all other major activities. Across all conditions, fathers generally experienced higher moods and greater intrinsic rewards during childcare than mothers, while mothers rated their skills and confidence somewhat lower than fathers. Fathers may have more of a choice as to when they engage in childcare, and Larson and Richards (1994a) present evidence that fathers tend to do childcare only when they are in a good mood already. The lower confidence level of mothers caring for their infants may be due to the tendency of fathers to defer to the mother for leadership during the most challenging child-care situations and to the cultural expectation that mothers should naturally know how to care for children.

After the infancy stage, when many mothers go back to work, both the challenge and enjoyment previously associated with childcare appear to wane. Mothers tend to experience less positive affect and intrinsic motivation when alone with their child than their husbands do (Koh, 2005). Wells (1988) found that working mothers in the United States with at least two children from age 2 to 14 rated child-care activities as providing few challenges. In particular, mothers with a toddler in the home spent less time in the flow condition than other mothers. The self-esteem of these mothers was negatively related to the amount of time they spent working. Those who worked less than half time had higher self-esteem than those who worked full time.

Juggling Work and Family Roles

This last finding hints at the struggle many mothers feel when trying to balance their work and family roles. For working fathers, there doesn't appear to be the same struggle. As we saw in the last chapter, fathers with full-time employed wives do participate more in housework and childcare than fathers with unemployed wives. But even when both are employed full time, fathers do less childcare and housework than mothers, and they tend to experience these activities as discretionary—things they can do to help their wives, if they are in a good mood (Larson & Richards, 1994a; Larson, Richards, & Perry-Jenkins, 1994; Lee, 2005).

Table 9.2 shows how mothers and fathers allocate their time, but the averages in the table hide wide variations across different families. For example, in families where the mother stays home, she does about 71 hours per week of child-related and household maintenance tasks, according to a Canadian study that used a "TimeCorder" device (Ellwood, 2002). Unlike ESM, participants were not signaled but recorded what they were doing each time they changed activities. The device kept track of the duration and frequency of activities. That study also found that mothers employed full time spend about half as much time as stay-home moms—36 hours—doing child-related and household tasks. The employed mothers cut back the most on preparing, serving, and cleaning up after family meals, and they spend less time in direct childcare (bathing, dressing, diapering, etc.) because their children tend to be older. They also get about five fewer hours of sleep each week than stay-home mothers. Yet there are no differences between these groups on the time they spend reading to their children or being alone with their spouses.

Table 9.2   How Family Members Spend Their Time

	Mothers	Fathers	Young Adolescents
Household Sphere			
Childcare	4.1	2.5	0.3
Housework	21.9	8.6	3.9
Family transport	4.4	3.4	3.3
Homework[a]	—	—	3.8
Personal care	6.1	3.2	5.6
Eating	4.9	4.8	4.5
Resting, idling	5.4	2.9	4.5
Family talk	12.1	5.8	5.9
Media	11.6	13.2	15.0
Active recreation	3.2	2.9	7.0
Household Total	73.8	47.4	53.8
Public Sphere			
Working at job/school	14.8	30.6	21.9
Other activities at job/school	3.8	8.9	14.0
Personal transport	2.9	5.5	1.4
Public, personal	4.7	7.6	8.9
Public Total	26.2	52.6	46.2

SOURCE: From *Divergent Realities* by Reed Larson. Copyright © 1994 by Reed Larson and Maryse Richards. Reprinted by permission of Basic Books, a member of Perseus Books, L.L.C.

NOTES: Table gives the average percentage of time people reported being in each activity.

a. This category was used only with the adolescents.

Besides the father, one might expect older children to pitch in with the housework and childcare. Typically, though, American adolescents do not contribute much to maintaining the household or caring for younger siblings. Thus working mothers experience the "six o'clock crash," that low point of the day when they come home from work not to relax, as their husbands often do, but to tend to dinner and the children (Larson & Richards, 1994a). Whether working mothers are more efficient or their houses are just messier, they do spend less time on housework than unemployed mothers. Still, given their workload, it is not surprising that mothers feel just as hurried when they are with their family as when they are not, but fathers and teens feel less hurried when they are with the family.

One study provides us with a direct estimate of how much time working mothers spend juggling two tasks at once from their different roles. Williams, Suls, Alliger, Learner, and Wan (1991) asked 20 mothers who were employed full time to report on each signal whether they were juggling 2 or more tasks at once. Mothers reported "interrole juggling," combining tasks for family with tasks for work or for other roles, 17 percent of the time. Compared to other times, these moments were characterized by less enjoyment, more negative affect, less effort, and less satisfaction with their ability. Despite the current trend toward multitasking, this finding, along with the lower self-esteem of full-time working mothers, suggests that mothers who try to do it all often end up feeling as if they are doing nothing really well. This is not to suggest that mothers should not work full time, but rather to point out the unrealistic expectations and unbalanced workloads our culture places on this one family role. As we've reported before, mothers derive much enjoyment from their work outside the home and tend to feel just as happy at work as at home.

When mothers are full-time homemakers, their well-being may be influenced by their husband's commuting schedule. Stay-home mothers in a study by Rodler and Kirchler (2001) provided ESM responses 6 times daily for 30 days. Some of their husbands worked so far from home that they commuted weekly to their job location. Some commuted between 90 and 150 minutes each way on a daily basis, and some husbands ("noncommuters") worked within 20 minutes of their home. Surprisingly, there was little difference among the three groups of wives in the amount of time they spent with their husbands. Apparently, those whose husbands were only home on weekends "made up for lost time." For all of these women, housework and childcare consumed nearly 7 hours per day but were accompanied by the lowest levels of well-being. Among the three groups, those whose husbands commuted daily were the ones who experienced the lowest overall well-being and the most negative moods during housework and childcare. Mothers with non-commuting or weekly commuting husbands felt better when their husband was present during child-care activities than when he was not there. For those whose husbands commuted daily, however, the husband's presence during child-care activities actually made them feel worse. In these families, the husbands presumably felt entitled to relax after a long day away from home and were not willing or able to help their wives with the children. Husbands commuting weekly were able to get more rest during the week and thus were more supportive when they returned home on weekends.

When mothers do work outside the home, it affects the whole family, but whether the children experience any negative impact is a question that has been debated for decades. Applying ESM to this issue, Richards and Duckett (1994) studied a group of 295 fifth through eighth graders from working- and middle-class families. Their most striking finding was actually a non-finding: in comparisons of adolescents whose mothers worked full time, part time, or not at all, there were no differences in time spent with at least one parent, with peers, or alone. Families with working mothers squeeze in more shared time in the evenings to compensate for a lack of such time in the after-noons. The father also pitches in, spending more time with the kids if his wife works full time than if she's unemployed, though he still spends less time than she does. Yet while the amount of time parents and children spend together does not vary with maternal employment, the content of that time does. Adolescents whose mothers work full time do more homework with their parents and share less leisure time with them compared to those with stay-home mothers. Despite this orientation toward less fun activities, these adolescents also perceive time with their moms as friendlier. Moreover, seventh and eighth graders whose mothers work part time have higher self-esteem and more positive affect than their peers whose mothers do not work. One potentially negative effect of full-time maternal employment is that sons, but not daughters, spend more time watching TV and less time playing sports than their peers. This may be due to the lack of transportation available for these boys to get to afternoon sports activities.

The Adolescent's Experience of Family

Because of the demands of ESM participation, there are no ESM data from younger children to address the maternal employment issue. We can, how-ever, flesh out the family experiences of preadolescents and adolescents, largely because of the work of Reed Larson and Maryse Richards and their colleagues. For example, a look at who reports being together with whom indicates that adolescents see themselves as more independent from their parents than their parents perceive them to be. Mothers report being with their adolescents 36 percent of the time, but adolescents report being with their mothers only 27 percent of the time (Larson & Richards, 1994a). Out of the 43 percent of times that at least one of them says they are together, they agree on only 20 percent. A similar, but less extreme pattern of unbalanced perceptions of togetherness occurs between adolescents and their fathers. Fathers and adolescents agree they are together 16 percent of the time and disagree another 17 percent of the time, with the adolescent being the one most likely not to regard the other as present. Those moments when both mothers and teens report being together amount to 20 percent of waking time. When together, teens do different things with each parent. They tend to spend more leisure time, particularly watching TV, with their fathers and more time talking with their mothers.

The movement of adolescents toward independent living can also be seen across the teen years in the decline in the amount of time they spend with their families. Fifth graders spend 35 percent of their waking hours with their families; by twelfth grade this figure drops to 14 percent, a 60 percent decrease (Larson, Richards, Moneta, Holmbeck, & Duckett, 1996). The process of separation starts within the home, as fifth through ninth graders gradually spend more time alone. Time spent away from home remains stable during these years, but from tenth through twelfth grade, the freedom of driving and the lure of working for pay pull teens increasingly out of the home. Sunday evenings are the most frequent time for family interaction.

Does increasing time apart mean that adolescents and their families are also growing emotionally distant? Not necessarily. The amount of time teens spend alone with their mothers or fathers does not decline over the teen years and neither does the amount of time they spend talking to family members (Larson et al., 1996). As they mature, girls actually spend more time talking to their mothers about interpersonal issues. Older teens also begin to see themselves as the leader more often when they are with their younger siblings. On the other hand, the path to a mature adult relationship between parents and their children is not straight and smooth. As Figure 9.1 shows, both girls and boys go through years of experiencing negative emotions when with their families before recovering by twelfth grade to more positive levels. During the drop in emotions in early adolescence, teens also perceive other family members to be less friendly. Considering these developmental trends, what we see happening in adolescence is a gradual disengagement from the family, coupled with a transformation in the relationship between the adolescent and the family that ultimately maintains their connectedness (Larson et al., 1996).

One of the reasons for the drop in emotions in the middle adolescent years may be that teens spend very little time doing things at home that bring them happiness. Table 9.3 shows that while at home, adolescents in the early high school years spend the largest proportion of their time at home engaged with media (TV, radio, or print), doing homework, or grooming themselves (Rathunde & Csikszentmihalyi, 1991). Yet these are precisely the activities that are accompanied by below-average levels of happiness. The activities that bring them the most happiness at home, such as games, hobbies, talking, and socializing, are the ones they do least often. There is a near-perfect negative correlation (–.93) between the rankings of activities based on frequency versus based on happiness. The presence of parents does not do

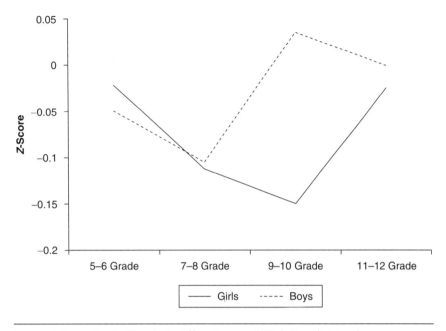

Figure 9.1   Grade Trends in Affect Reported With Family Members

SOURCE: Larson, Richards, Moneta, Holmbeck, & Duckett, *Developmental Psychology,* *32,* 1996. Copyright © 1996 by the American Psychological Association. Reprinted with permission.

much to change the happiness associated with activities. Teens are significantly happier doing homework with parents present, but talking (presumably with friends or siblings) is a more enjoyable activity when parents are not around. However, the time teens spend doing homework decreases when parents are present whereas time spent talking increases.

Even in single-mother families, the way adolescents allocate their time appears to depend on the relationship and interaction between both parents. Larson, Dworkin, and Gillman (2001) found that the frequency of conversations between the mother and the teen's father correlates positively with the amount of time the adolescent spends doing constructive activities such as hobbies, sports, and reading. Teens whose parents report greater cooperation in coparenting also spend more time playing sports. Adolescents' use of time is also affected by how their single mothers spend time. The more TV that moms watch, the more their adolescents do also, and the less they engage in constructive activities. Mothers who spend time reading or doing religious activities also have adolescents who do these things. Finally, when mothers maintain family routines and firm discipline, their adolescents spend more time doing constructive activities.

Table 9.3   Percent of Time Spent and Average Happiness in Various Home
Activities for the Overall Week and Just With Parents

	Overall		With Parents	
Activity	% of Time	Happiness	% of Time	Happiness
Media	27.9	−0.03	32.2	0.04
Homework	16.7	−0.19	9.8	0.08
Maintenance	13.0	−0.12	7.2	0.10
Miscellaneous	11.3	0.04	9.9	0.27
Housework	6.7	0.07	6.6	0.01
Eating	6.4	0.11	13.1	0.05
Games/Hobbies	6.2	0.30	4.3	0.31
Talking	6.0	0.27	13.2	0.01
Telephone	4.9	0.20	1.5	0.45
Socializing	0.9	0.35	2.1	0.31

SOURCE: Copyright © Rathunde, K., and Csikszentmihalyi, M. (1991). Adolescent happiness
and family interaction. In K. Pillemer and K. McCartney (Eds.), *Parent-child relations
throughout life* (pp. 143–162). Hillsdale, NJ: Erlbaum.

NOTES: The number of ESM signals for the overall week = 2,410, with parents = 515.
Happiness scores are Z-scores (0.0 = average happiness at home).

Transmission of Emotions Between Family Members

Single mothers influence more than just their adolescents' use of time. They
also play a role in their adolescents' emotional states. By examining two con-
secutive ESM reports from single mothers and their teenage children when
they were both at home or otherwise together, Larson and Gillman (1999)
were able to determine whether the emotions of one influence the other.
Anger and anxiety are transmitted from mothers to adolescents, but not in
the reverse direction. That is, when a mother is angry or anxious at one time
point, an hour or two later her son or daughter is more likely to be angry
or anxious. Adolescents' anger is actually better predicted by their mothers'
prior anger than by their own prior anger. Positive emotions are not contagious in this way. Mothers under a lot of stress are more likely to transmit
anxiety to their adolescents than other mothers, and when these mothers are
angry, the adolescents are likely to feel anxiety more than anger. Thus what

gets "sent" is not always the same as what gets "received." Solitude may be one way for moms to break this negative transmission cycle. Single moms who spend more time alone do not transmit anger or anxiety, but those who are controlling, according to their children, transmit their negative emotions even more strongly.

Among two-parent families, the evidence on transmission of emotions between parents and their children is less clear-cut. Using a once-daily diary, Downey, Purdie, and Schaffer-Neitz (1999) found the teenager's anger to be predicted by the mother's anger, but the same path was not found for anxiety. Similarly, Matjasko and Feldman (2005) reported in the 500 Family Study that mothers' happiness and anger, but not their anxiety, was transmitted to their adolescents when the mothers came home from work. No similar transmission was found from fathers to their adolescents. Larson and Richards (1994a, 1994b) concluded that fathers transmit their emotions to their sons and daughters but are also influenced by their daughters' prior emotions. Both sons and daughters, but especially daughters, transmit their emotions to their mothers. Unlike in other studies, transmission in the reverse direction, from mothers to their teenage children, was not found. More generally, Almeida, Wethington, and Chandler (1999) showed that marital tension on one day often spills over to parent-child relations the next day. It must be noted here that emotions spread through the family in other more subtle ways besides direct transmission over an hour or two. There are significant correlations between the emotions of parents and children, suggesting that all family members are to some degree affected by each other. Though the strength of these correlations is modest, the correlations are persistent, occurring even when parents and children are not together. Fathers, perhaps because of the less time they spend with their children, seem to be more buoyed by their presence. They have above average emotions when with either sons or daughters, but feel much more positively when with sons than daughters. Sons feel neutral emotions when with their fathers, along with more choice and intrinsic motivation than girls. Daughters have negative emotions while with their fathers.

In contrast to the findings for parents and children, the emotions of husbands and wives do not correlate when the two are not together (Larson & Richards, 1994b). There is a clear transmission effect, however, once the two are reunited, and it runs from the husband to the wife. As Figure 9.2 shows, the wife generally does not influence the husband's emotional state, but she is influenced by his prior emotional state, especially if he has just returned home from work. A more recent study using daily diaries and lab measures of physiological responses replicated this finding for male police officers and their wives. When the officer returned from a stressful shift, both he and his

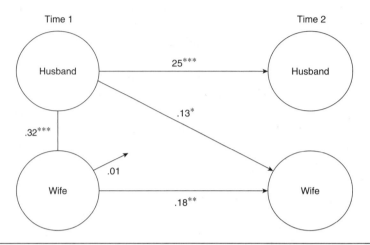

a. All Times

NOTES: Figure displays beta weights for predicting Time 2 emotions, based on times that both say they are together at Time 1 or Time 2; $N = 253$. Regressions were computed on values of emotion with activity controlled. Only occasions when reports occurred within four hours of each other are included (median time difference = 1.67 hours).

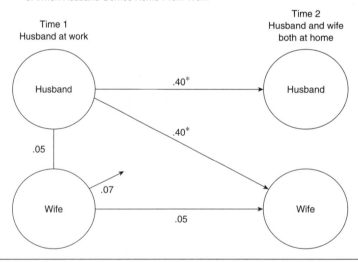

b. When Husband Comes Home From Work

NOTES: Figure displays beta weights for regressions predicting Time 2 emotions ($N = 33$). Similar analyses examining occasions when employed women came home did not yield strong or significant paths.

Figure 9.2   Emotional Transmission Between Husband and Wife

SOURCE: From *Divergent Realities* by Reed Larson. Copyright © 1994 by Reed Larson and Maryse Richards. Reprinted by permission of Basic Books, a member of Perseus Books, L.L.C.

wife showed higher levels of autonomic arousal, the body's response to stress (Roberts & Levenson, 2001). Overall, then, the mother/wife is the primary receiver of emotions in the family. She is most affected emotionally by the lives of the other family members. The father/husband is the most powerful sender of emotions. The source of those emotions is frequently his job.

These ESM and diary studies on emotion transmission within families complement earlier lab studies conducted by Levenson and Gottman (1983, 1985; Gottman & Levenson, 1988). They found that both positive and negative emotions are frequently transmitted from the husband to the wife, but in unhappy marriages, the wife's positive emotions do not get reciprocated by the husband. Further, when the wife has negative emotions, the husband, although physiologically aroused, is more likely to be nonresponsive rather than share in those negative emotions.

Comparisons Between Families: Optimal Conditions for Adolescent Development

The family research we have reviewed so far has primarily concerned itself with comparing the experiences of members within the family. Another approach, taken by Kevin Rathunde and his colleagues (Rathunde, 1996, 2001; Rathunde & Csikszentmihalyi, 1991), is to compare the experiences of adolescents from families that offer different psychosocial environments. Rathunde reasoned that, in order for adolescents to accumulate optimal experiences doing productive activities (and thus to develop into their full potential), they would need an environment that provided both support and challenge. These two dimensions are similar to the key ingredients in Baumrind's (1968) authoritative parenting style, warmth/responsiveness and structure/discipline. Rathunde emphasizes, however, that support and challenge are aspects of the dynamics of the whole family system, not just parenting practices. Families that provide support through warm relationships give their adolescents the security they need in order to take the risks associated with engaging in new challenges. Families that provide challenges encourage their adolescents to develop into unique, autonomous individuals who do not shy from pursuing new and difficult endeavors. These two family characteristics, fostering attachment and autonomy, may seem at odds, but they are actually complementary. Together, support and challenge constitute a complex family environment that leads family members to develop personalities that are both more differentiated and integrated. Compared to families that provide only support, only challenge, or neither, families in which both dimensions are strong should have adolescents who are on the most optimal developmental pathway.

Evidence from several studies seems to confirm these theoretical expectations. In these studies, a questionnaire is used to measure the degree of support and challenge adolescents perceive in their families. Support includes items related to comfort, consistency, and harmony in the family; challenge consists of items such as high expectations from the family and tolerance of individual differences. Families can then be categorized based on whether they are high in both support and challenge, low in both, or high in one but not the other. Adolescents from these four types of families have reliably different patterns of experience. For instance, those whose families provide high levels of support and challenge spend two to three more hours per week with their parents than those whose families are low in these dimensions (Rathunde & Csikszentmihalyi, 1991). The amount of time adolescents spend doing different activities also varies by family type. In a sample of talented teenagers, those from high support/high challenge families spent the most time of any group doing homework and the least time doing home routines such as chores, grooming, and eating (Csikszentmihalyi, Rathunde, & Whalen, 1993). Those from low support/low challenge families spent the most time in these routines, the least time doing homework, and the least time in interaction compared to the other three groups. Families that provided high levels of support without any challenge had adolescents who spent the most time engaged in leisure pursuits. Findings from a more recent study with a larger and more diverse sample converged with these results in that adolescents in high challenge families did two to three more hours of homework per week than those in low challenge families (Csikszentmihalyi & Schneider, 2000).

An important complement to these findings on the productive use of time is an examination of how these teens feel while they are being productive. In order to develop their talents to the fullest and to experience the best quality of life, they will need to enjoy the challenges of productive work. Results from the talented teen sample clearly show that teens from high challenge/high support families experience higher levels than other teens of enjoyment and happiness not only while at home, but also while doing any productive activities anywhere (Csikszentmihalyi et al., 1993; Rathunde & Csikszentmihalyi, 1991). This difference could not simply be attributed to a tendency by these adolescents to rate all aspects of their lives as better; during leisure time there was no difference in happiness among teens from different types of families. Tellingly, in high challenge/high support families, the presence of the parents usually improves the happiness of the teen, whereas parental presence in low challenge/low support families lowers the happiness of the teen.

Further research has shown that the challenge and support dimensions of the family environment each contribute something different to the adolescent's experience. As Figure 9.3 illustrates, teens who have supportive

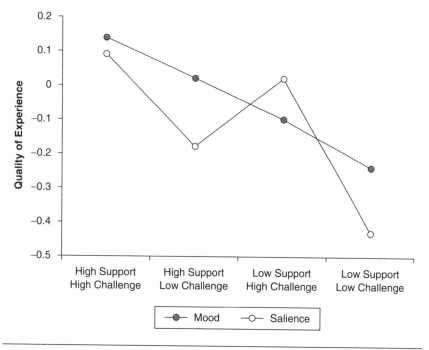

Figure 9.3   Adolescents' Mood and Salience in School-Related Tasks as a Function of Family Context

SOURCE: From *Becoming Adult* by Mihaly Csikszentmihalyi. Copyright © 2000 by Mihaly Csikszentmihalyi and Barbara Schneider. Reprinted by permission of Basic Books, a member of Perseus Books, L.L.C.

NOTE: Mood and salience scores adjusted for age, gender, ethnic background, and parental education.

families have higher moods during school-related tasks, and teens who are challenged by their families perceive these tasks to have greater importance to their present and future goals (Csikszentmihalyi & Schneider, 2000). When mood and importance coincide, Rathunde (1996, 2001) suggests that adolescents have undivided interest, that crucial combination of spontaneous interest and goal-directed interest. When adolescents have high moods but do not feel their activity is important, they can be said to be "fooling," satisfying their spontaneous interests without regard to future goals. When they have low moods but do feel their activity is important to their future goals, drudgery is the result. Rathunde found that teens from families providing more support engaged in more fooling and less drudgery two years later. Teens from high challenge families endured more drudgery two years later. Low support/high challenge families produced teens who experienced the most drudgery and least fooling. Adolescents with the most undivided interest came from families that offered high levels of both support and challenge. Moreover, families that increased in their level of support and challenge over two years had adolescents who added three hours a week to their total experience of undivided interest. By experiencing more of the joys of engaging their skills in challenging pursuits, these adolescents are surely well on their way toward optimal development.

Another characteristic of families that appears to influence how adolescents experience challenge is the occupation of the parents. Maier (2005) found that adolescents whose mothers had substantial math or science training and used those skills in a career had higher grades, better moods, and higher self-esteem in school compared to other adolescents. Unlike other mothers in professional occupations, math/science mothers treated their sons and daughters equally in providing challenge and support.

If the family is a key context for adolescent development, is it also a context in which adults develop as parents and spouses? To answer this question would require a long-term longitudinal ESM study of the sort that has not to date been attempted. Yet there is no reason not to believe that the family environment could be toxic or nourishing to the development of all of the members of the family. Only an ESM study—by examining the concurrence and sequences of interactions, activities, and emotions among the members of the family—could begin to address this issue. For now, we must be content to move on to the ESM studies that examine another major context in adults' lives, their careers.

10

The Experience of Work

The subject of paid employment is a traditional topic of study for social scientists. One reason work is such a frequently studied topic is because, in most industrialized nations at least, adults spend so much time engaged in productive activities outside the home for pay. Many adults spend close to half their waking hours working. ESM has been used extensively to study individuals' experiences in the workplace. The method has been used to better understand how workers spend their time on the job and to document how workers feel when doing various tasks on the job. Additionally, ESM has been used to compare how workers in different types of occupations (e.g., managers vs. blue-collar workers) experience their time at work in terms of levels of concentration, enjoyment, or flow. Because ESM samples experience across the range of a person's daily activities, the method is particularly suited to the study of the daily transitions parents make from work to family life and the emotional and affective changes that accompany these transitions. Researchers have also used ESM to study adolescents at work, examining their perceptions as they come to develop understandings of the world of adult work.

Methodological Concerns and Variations

In an article in the journal *Personnel Psychology,* Alliger and Williams (1993) provide a fairly comprehensive discussion of the advantages and challenges of using ESM to study psychological variables in the workplace. They argue that the traditional one-time assessments of individuals' work experience cannot possibly capture the psychological experience of work. Because one-time assessments are the norm, work researchers know surprisingly little about workers' immediate affective or emotional reactions to specific working conditions or about how these reactions may influence subsequent work. ESM allows researchers to monitor variation across the day and is particularly effective at capturing the temporal and dynamic nature of the work experience. As such, ESM enables the study of both global and specific aspects of work.

Of course, the considerable advantages of using ESM to study work come at a price. There are a number of challenges to using ESM in the workplace that must be taken into consideration when conducting studies and interpreting the data. The apparent intrusiveness of the method is of particular concern in workplace studies, as it may create real or perceived challenges to productivity in the work environment. While the questionnaires themselves take little time to complete, participants are interrupted several times during the workday, thus diverting attention from the task at hand. This apparent intrusiveness could create compliance problems among the workers themselves or among supervisors who may have to grant permission for the research to be done in the workplace. In our experience these interruptions are not nearly as intrusive as they might sound at first description, and often a thorough description of the study's importance may be enough to ease workers' and supervisors' concerns about the intrusiveness of the procedure. In some circumstances, however, the intrusiveness and unpredictability of ESM will present real challenges to participants' ability to satisfactorily complete his or her job. Consider, for example, the cardiac surgeon or the concert pianist, both of whom simply would not be able to pause from their work to complete the ESM questionnaire. Likewise, the factory-line worker who takes time to answer a questionnaire during her shift may cause serious slowdowns in production down the line. While the vast majority of workers can probably afford to sustain the minor interruptions caused by ESM with little or no impact on productivity, there are certain occupations for which ESM studies may not be suitable without minor or serious methodological variation. Alliger and Williams (1993) also point out that ESM offers the greatest advantages in studies of occupations in which there is a great deal of task variation. As such, they argue that "certain routine jobs may not be appropriate for assessment with ESM" (p. 531).

An additional concern regarding research compliance in ESM studies of the workplace has to do with establishing the "research alliance" discussed in previous chapters of this book. In order to establish trust, it may be necessary for researchers to distance themselves from management in order to obtain participation from the employees. If workers perceive the study as coming from management, they may be concerned about the impact that their responses would have on their job. They may feel that if they don't participate and/or provide positive assessments of their work experiences, their job might be in jeopardy. In a similar vein, they may believe that the study will be used to provide information about their productivity to managers and as a result may not honestly report their activities while on the job. In either of these cases, the quality of the data will be compromised by the researchers' real or perceived connection to the management structure of an organization. In order to obtain the most accurate data and to ease workers' anxieties about the potential consequences of their participation, it is important for researchers to stress the confidentiality of the research relationship and to make efforts to distance themselves as much as possible from company management. This is an admittedly delicate situation, as researchers must often obtain consent from management to collect data in the workplace prior to the recruitment of individual participants.

As it is traditionally used, ESM is designed to signal participants throughout their waking hours, with the result that data are gathered from the work, home, public, and other spheres of life. Some researchers who are interested only in participants' work experience modify the ESM schedule so that participants are only signaled during work hours. In a study of accountants, for example, Teuchmann, Totterdell, and Parker (1999) signaled subjects only during work hours over a period of four weeks. The researchers were specifically interested in the accountants' emotional states at work before, during, and after a particularly busy work period, so the signaling period was extended over several weeks but was restricted to work hours only. While such modifications might be a worthwhile tradeoff in studies designed to sample time frames longer than one week, researchers must recognize that restricting responses only to work hours limits one's ability to discuss results in the context of respondents' general experience. For example, if a particular person reports high levels of happiness at work it is impossible to determine whether her happiness is associated with working or whether she is simply a happy person most of the time. Similarly, without sampling all waking hours, making accurate estimates of time use becomes a bit more complicated.

In a detailed review of methodological concerns for those using experience sampling in organizations, Beal and Weiss (2003) discuss the potential benefits of using event-contingent sampling designs in studies of the workplace. Researchers studying organizations are often interested in examining particular interactions, activities, or experiences that occur during the workday. Sampling randomly may not provide researchers with enough data points representing those experiences they are most interested in (particularly if those experiences are rare). While studies employing this methodological variation deviate substantially from traditional ESM procedures as we have discussed them throughout this book, we summarize a few such studies (Côté and Moskowitz, 1998; Moskowitz & Côté, 1995) later in this chapter.

Time and Work

The question of how many hours Americans actually spend working, and whether this has changed over time, has been a hotly debated topic. In her 1991 book *The Overworked American,* Juliet Schor suggested that men and women's total annual work hours had increased by the equivalent of one whole month since 1969. Others (Robinson & Godbey, 1997) argue that work hours have not risen, but that the pace of life has increased with the net effect that Americans feel more overworked than they used to. The differing conclusions of researchers are often the result of differences in data collection methods. ESM is one of the more recent methods used to inform the debate about work hours. Beyond answering questions about how much time workers spend at work, ESM allows researchers to investigate more subtle differences in time use, such as distinguishing between how much time is spent engaged in work-related tasks relative to time spent socializing or taking care of personal business while at work. Several ESM studies provide estimates of the number of hours workers spend on the job. In their study of American families, Larson and Richards (1994a) report that the men in their study spend approximately 46 hours per week on the job, including transportation to and from work. They found women's work patterns to be much more variable than men's, with about only a third of women working hours comparable to men's, one-third working part-time hours, and another third not working for pay. In a more recent study involving a sample of full-time working parents, Sexton (2005) reported that men worked an average of 49 hours per week, while women worked an average of 44 hours per week. These ESM estimates may be compared to time diary estimates of adults working full time: National studies using time diaries estimate that men work about 46.5 hours per week while women work about 41.5 hours per week (Robinson & Bostrom, 1994; Robinson & Godbey, 1997).

Jeong, Mulligan, and Schneider (2004) present a rare comparison of time estimates using time diary and ESM data collected from a small sample of individuals who completed both instruments during the same period. Their detailed analysis reveals strengths and weaknesses of each method. They found ESM response rates to be higher when participants were in work settings than when they were at home or in public. Their analyses suggest that time diaries may provide more accurate time estimates than ESM for general activities that are long in duration, like total hours spent in the workplace. Time diaries are less reliable in their estimates of more specific activities, or activities that are short in duration (e.g., specific work tasks such as using computers, talking on the phone, or meeting with clients). They find ESM to be the superior instrument for estimates of these more specific activities.

Because of its ability to document specific daily activities, one advantage of using ESM in time use studies of work settings is that the method can more accurately reveal the number of hours spent on the job that participants are actually working. In standard surveys, respondents typically estimate their hours worked by considering when they typically arrive at work, and when they typically leave work. They are not often asked to take into consideration how often between their start and end times they are shopping on the Internet, talking to their spouse or children on the phone, or chatting with coworkers about things other than work. In a review of work-time concepts, Mata-Greenwood (1992) identified several distinct work-time concepts, such as "time worked," "contractual time," and "time paid," but such distinctions are often not made in research on work hours. Because ESM asks participants to report specific details of their activity at particular moments, researchers can get a sense of how often workers are engaged in nonwork activity while on the job. For example, in the Larson and Richards study cited previously, of the total time adults spent at work, only about 76 percent was spent in actual labor. In their study of five large companies in the Chicago area, Csikszentmihalyi and LeFevre (1989) found a good deal of variation in the amount of time different types of workers actually spent working. Looking across workers' entire day—not just hours in the workplace—they found that management and blue-collar workers spent about 30 percent of their total waking time working—about 33.5 hours per week. Clerical workers spent an average of 23 percent of their entire day working—totaling just under 26 hours per week. Looking only at those hours when these workers were in the workplace, the researchers found that clerical workers spent about one-third of their time on the job socializing. Managers and blue-collar workers, on the other hand, spent only about one-fifth of their total time on the job socializing. As was first suggested in Chapter 7 of this volume, ESM may provide a much more accurate and nuanced picture of workers' actual work time than standard survey questions that ask respondents to report how much time they usually spend working or how many hours they worked last week. While ESM may provide less accurate estimates than surveys or time diaries of the time workers physically spend in the workplace, its strength is that it can provide relatively accurate indication of the number of hours employees actually spend engaged in work activity.

The Quality of Experience at Work: General Trends

Another strength of ESM in the study of work lies in its ability to assess workers' subjective experiences while on the job. Studies employing ESM have revealed substantial variation in individuals' perceptions of particular jobs and in the different situations that a given worker encounters in his or her workday. Understanding how people feel at work may have important implications for well-being in general. Momentary enjoyment at work, as measured by ESM, is positively correlated with overall happiness, total life satisfaction, and psychological well-being (Haworth & Hill, 1992). Compared to leisure activities, workers report that their jobs produce less enjoyment and fewer feelings of control, though they also tend to be as interested or more interested in their work activities as their leisure ones (Haworth, 1996; Haworth, Jarman, & Lee, 1997).

Several studies have suggested that adults are more likely to experience optimal states of engagement, or flow, in work situations rather than in leisure activities or at home (Csikszentmihalyi, 1990; Csikszentmihalyi & LeFevre, 1989; Haworth & Hill, 1992; Larson & LeFevre, 1988; Richards, 1994a). When using a measure of the *flow conditions* (defined as high challenges and high skills), even assembly-line workers report more flow at work than in leisure. Csikszentmihalyi (1990; Csikszentmihalyi & LeFevre, 1989) reports that flow conditions occur three times more often at work than in free-time leisure activities. Flow conditions are present for close to half of the time adults spend actually working (which excludes nonwork-related tasks done on the job like chatting with coworkers or taking care of personal business). By comparison, only about 18 percent of the time adults spend in leisure activities have the high challenges and high skills characteristic of flow.

An interesting caveat to this research involves differences in the phenomenology of flow that occurs in work compared to flow that occurs in leisure activities. LeFevre (1988) compared those moments where challenges and skills were high (the flow condition) at work to similar moments that occurred in leisure activities. When participants experienced the flow condition while working, they felt high levels of motivation, activation, concentration, creativity, and satisfaction, but their affective evaluations of the activity were slightly negative. In contrast, in leisure activities the flow conditions were accompanied by high affect but low motivation. Thus while the conditions for flow seem to be present in both work and leisure activities, there may be some subtle variation in the affective and motivational profiles of flow in each of these contexts.

Taken as a whole, the data reveal an interesting paradox between workers' reports of their job experiences and their stated work preferences. Even though workers report experiencing the conditions for flow more often at work than in other contexts in their lives, when they are at work they often wish to be doing something other than working. In spite of the fact that workers tend to feel happy, strong, and satisfied at work, most wish that they could work less, citing that they would prefer doing activities that by their own accounts are less enjoyable and less engaging. It appears then, that in thinking about their activity preferences, people may not attend to the evidence of their own experience when it comes to work (Csikszentmihalyi, 1990). Rather than recognizing the positive emotional states that they experience at work, many workers may focus on the fact that work is something that they have to do, rather than something they choose to do, and this fact in itself may cause workers to dream about more freely chosen activities.

The most rigorous attempt to solve this apparent paradox has been carried out at the University of Zurich by Professor Urs Schallberger and his associates. They have studied Swiss workers with ESM and arrived at the conclusion that while flow *conditions* (i.e., high challenge, high skill) indeed correspond to flow *experiences* (i.e., elevated mood, self-esteem, cognitive efficiency, motivation) when the person is engaged in nonwork activities, not all the positive dimensions of experience are present when the person is in a flow condition at work (Pfister, 2002; Schallberger, 1995, Schallberger & Pfister, 2001). The researchers recombined the ESM variables according to the circumplex model of emotion (Feldman Barrett & Russell, 1998; Russell, 1980; Russell & Feldman Barrett, 1999). Thus they divided the variables into those reflecting "Positive Activation" (energetic, motivated), "Negative Activation" (nervous, stressed), and "Valence" (happy, cheerful). They found that when people find themselves in a high challenge, high skill situation, positive activation level increases, but so does negative activation—especially at work. At work, high flow conditions can actually result in lowered valence, that is, people reporting less happiness. While these results seem to contradict those obtained by the Chicago and Milan groups, they suggest that more research is needed to ascertain whether the flow conditions always result in the flow experience, or whether in some situations, like work, they also produce too much stress to be experienced as enjoyable.

Another approach is that of Haworth and Hill (1992), who studied the degree of consistency between what workers have to do on the job and what they would really like to be doing when they are working. They examined workers' perceptions of their own extrinsic and intrinsic motives for working and found that those who perceived the extrinsic nature of work in a positive light were much better off in terms of psychological well-being. In other words, workers who simultaneously reported that they have to do work activities and also that they wouldn't rather be doing something else (e.g., that if given the choice they would prefer to continue doing what they are currently doing) scored higher on several measures of well-being. The authors conclude that this consistency, which they call "positive motivational change," is good for mental health.

One of the more commonly studied outcomes in workplace studies is job satisfaction. A decade ago, Cranny, Smith, and Stone (1992) estimated that there had been more than 5,000 published articles and dissertations on this topic, and this list has grown considerably in the intervening years. For several decades, researchers studying organizations argued that retrospective accounts of mood and emotion over recent days or weeks were associated with more general evaluations of job satisfaction (Brief & Roberson, 1989; Weiss & Cropanzano, 1996; Weiss, Nicholas, & Daus, 1999). Because these accounts are often summative and retrospective, little is known about how mood or emotion at work may be linked to specific activities or circumstances. Recently, several researchers have used ESM to examine the relationship between workers' momentary states and overall job satisfaction. Weiss, Nicholas, and Daus (1999) examined the relationship between pleasant mood at work and job satisfaction, while controlling for a variety of job-related beliefs and dispositional factors. They found that positive mood predicted job satisfaction, over and above the contribution of both dispositional happiness and job-related beliefs about the potential for achieving various types of occupational success in one's current position. In an interesting application of ESM data, these authors used spectral analysis to look for daily cycles of mood among a sample of office managers. Sampling only the hours when participants were at work, the researchers found evidence of oscillating cycles in both mood and activation, with peaks and valleys falling at predictable times of the day. For example, they identified a cycle for mood that starts low in the morning, with a steady increase until about midday, at which time there is decline, followed by another increase. A cycle they identified for activation, on the other hand, starts out low, peaks around lunchtime, and then steadily declines for the rest of the day. These analyses are exploratory, and further research is needed to verify the existence of such cyclical patterns and to explain the causes of such patterns.

In another examination of the link between momentary levels of affect and overall job satisfaction, Fisher (2000) found that positive and negative emotions each make unique contributions to predicting overall job satisfaction, though they are only weakly correlated with one another ($r = -.20$). What is interesting is that she found the *frequency* of net positive emotion (as indicated by feelings of being pleased, proud, enthusiastic, and happy) to be a better predictor of job satisfaction than the *intensity* of this positive emotion. The most satisfied employees were not those who reported the greatest levels of happiness at work. Rather, the most satisfied employees tended to be those who most often felt at least a little happier or more enthusiastic than usual. This research suggests that for workers to feel satisfied on the job it is more important that they feel moderately happy a lot of the time than feeling extremely happy some of the time. As this study indicates, research on job satisfaction stands to benefit greatly from the use of ESM, as the method reveals distinctions between affective reactions, cognitions, and overall evaluations on the job.

ESM has also enabled researchers to better understand workers' physiological reactions to work situations. In a study where participants provided saliva samples after filling out their ESFs, Adam (2005) was able to track fluctuations in the stress hormone cortisol and relate these shifts to particular activities and emotional responses. Surprisingly, Adam found cortisol levels to be lower than expected when men and women were at work. Further analyses revealed that adults feel most productive and involved in work settings, and these emotional states are partly responsible for the reduction in physiological stress. Adam argues that her research supports the notion that the daily challenges that work often provides are not necessarily physiologically stressful and may actually contribute to physical health and psychological well-being. She speculates that work may provide a measure of "good stress," allowing one to stretch one's abilities without becoming completely overwhelmed. This research provides some preliminary physiological results that are consistent with research discussed earlier in this chapter about the experience flow in the workplace.

The Quality of Experience Across Workers

Beneath general trends in how people experience work there is a great deal of variation across workers and across activities. We begin with a discussion of variation across workers. The research in this area has largely included comparative analyses by gender or occupation. In their book *Divergent Realities,* Reed Larson and Maryse Richards discuss the similarities and differences they observed in the quality of men's and women's work experiences. The ESM data they collected from working women and men led them to conclude that for men more so than women, work "ruled their daily emotional metabolism." While the general distribution of emotional "highs" and "lows" was just as wide for women as it was for men, the men in this study tended to experience more extreme emotional states on the job, as opposed to when they were with their families. Men felt their strongest, most in control, and most absorbed and attentive when at work. The emotional extremes experienced by men at work were not all positive. The men in this study also experienced more frequent distress and frustration at work in comparison to the employed women. Men also felt highly competitive at work, while women tended to feel more cooperative. These observed gender differences were not attributable to differences in occupations. While there were gender differences in the types of occupations held by participants, with men holding more managerial and supervisory positions than women, the gender differences observed in the quality of work experiences were not due to the type of job a person had or the types of activities they had to do on the job. Larson and Richards propose that men and women may simply have different cognitive styles at work that result in differences in subjective experience. They speculate that these differences in men's and women's approaches to work may be a reflection of the fact that as "breadwinners" of the family, men may have more at stake on the job than women. In another study of married couples, Koh (2005) found somewhat similar patterns of emotional experience of men and women at work. Koh reports that among the men in her sample, affect was decidedly more negative at work than at home. Women on the other hand, report comparable levels of affect at home and in the workplace, but tend to experience much higher levels of affect when they are in public. These and other differences between the quality of men's and women's experiences are discussed in greater detail in Chapter 8 of this volume.

Côté and Moskowitz (1998; Moskowitz & Côté, 1995) have used a variation of ESM procedures in the workplace that provides insights into more general aspects of traditional personality research. They examined how "big five" personality traits predict the relationship between interpersonal behaviors and affect among adults. To study these complex relationships, their study employed an event-contingent sampling design (rather than signal-contingent sampling, as is typically the case with ESM research). Rather than respond to random signals, participants were instructed to complete a brief questionnaire following each interpersonal interaction they had during the day (due to the nature of the sample, most of these interactions took place at work). Participants were signaled with beepers to remind them to keep up with the study, but their actual responses were contingent upon their interactions with others, not the signals they received. The researchers found that some of the big five traits predict not only one's behavior and one's level of affect, but also the covariation between behavior and affect over time. For example, individuals with high scores on the agreeableness trait experienced higher levels of positive affect when engaging in agreeable behavior compared to low-agreeable individuals when engaging in similar behavior. Similarly, high-agreeable individuals experienced more unpleasant affect than low-agreeable individuals when engaging in quarrelsome behavior.

In a more traditional (signal-contingent) ESM study, Sexton (2005) examined the relationship between one's general orientation toward work and their emotional experiences during work tasks. She concluded that one's general orientation toward work was predictive of workers' quality of experience at work. Individuals who had a self-directed work orientation had higher levels of positive affect, engagement, and self-esteem while working, regardless of the type of work they were performing. Conversely, individuals characterized as conforming had greater levels of negative affect at work, regardless of work task.

While individual characteristics such as gender, personality traits, and general work orientation are likely to impact work experience, several studies have revealed that one's occupation affects the daily quality of experience during work as well. In a study of five companies in Chicago, LeFevre (1988) found that managers and engineers reported significantly higher motivation, concentration, and creativity when working, in comparison to clerical and assembly-line workers. Managers and engineers more often experienced the conditions for flow at work, and their flow experiences were characterized by higher levels of concentration, activation, and creativity than was observed among other workers. In a related study, Csikszentmihalyi and LeFevre (1989) report that managers felt strongest in their work flow experiences. In contrast, clerical and blue-collar workers felt strongest during flow that occurred during leisure activities. The types of work activities that produced flow for individuals varied by occupational type. This finding is likely a reflection of differences in the types of activities required of managers, clerical workers, and blue-collar workers. Csikszentmihalyi and LeFevre (1989) examined how frequently flow occurred in specific activities related to these occupations. These analyses are presented in Table 10.1. Managers experienced flow most often when they were "talking about problems" or "doing paperwork." Clerical workers experienced the most flow while typing, and blue-collar workers experienced flow most often when "fixing equipment."

The Quality of Experience Across Work Activities

As is suggested by the work of Csikszentmihalyi and LeFevre just discussed, ESM can provide information about specific work activities. ESM affords researchers the opportunity to compare how people feel in one work activity to how they feel in another. Much of the research on work surveys employees about their overall work satisfaction or mood while working, but is not able to capture subtle or even dramatic fluctuations in subjective experience over the course of a workday. Larson and Richards (1994a) have documented vast shifts in emotion as workers move from one activity to the

Table 10.1   Flow and Nonflow at Work:
Most Frequent Activities by Occupation

	Flow time at work accounted by activity (%)	Time not in flow at work accounted for by activity (%)	Difference
Manager (N = 28, reports = 418)			
Talking about problems	9.8	5.2	4.6
Doing paperwork	9.5	20.1	−10.6
Fixing equipment	8.7	7.8	0.9
Preparing assembly work	8.0	5.2	2.8
Writing reports	7.2	3.9	3.3
Other	44.8	57.8	−13.0
Total	100.0	100.0	
Clerical (N = 32, reports = 492)			
Typing	15.2	7.7	7.5
Sorting, filing	11.7	20.4	−8.7
Writing, keypunch	7.8	7.2	0.6
Phone	8.6	9.8	−1.2
Research, checking	5.1	8.1	−3.0
Other	51.6	46.8	4.8
Total	100.0	100.0	
Blue Collar (N = 18, reports = 347)			
Assembly work	39.4	63.2	−23.8
Fixing equipment	20.6	5.5	15.1
Computer	11.5	3.8	7.7
Moving things	5.5	4.9	0.6
Stacking, shelving	4.8	3.8	1.0
Other	18.2	18.8	−0.6
Total	100.0	100.0	

SOURCE: Csikszentmihalyi and LeFevre, *Journal of Personality and Social Psychology, 56,* 1989. Copyright © 1989 by the American Psychological Association. Reprinted with permission.

next. Figure 10.1 illustrates the average emotion reported by working fathers and mothers when involved in various work tasks. As shown in the figure, there is a great deal of variation in emotion from task to task and the patterns are very different for mothers and fathers. Mothers in the study experienced their most positive emotions while doing computer work or sales work, while fathers reported relatively negative emotions during these same activities. In contrast, fathers experienced more positive emotions while driving for work and while instructing employees, while these were not positive emotional experiences for mothers.

Haworth and colleagues (1997) examined intrinsic motivation, enjoyment, interest, and control in a sample of working women. Though not a focus of their research, they report mean levels of these variables for work-related tasks (e.g., writing a report, typing) and for productive interaction at work (e.g., when a person is discussing work issues on the phone or in a meeting). Their data suggest that the working women in the study were more intrinsically motivated to engage in productive interaction than they were to perform work tasks. Enjoyment and interest were also higher in productive interaction, though women felt greater control in work tasks than in productive interaction.

In a study of men and women who were working full time in a variety of occupations, Sexton (2005) examined the relationship between the degree of job-relevancy of work tasks and quality of experience at work. Based on census information and respondents' detailed descriptions of their work duties, Sexton classified the work tasks reported in ESM as either "primary work," "related work tasks," "preparation work," or "personal care and social interaction." She found that across a broad range of occupations workers generally feel the greatest levels of positive affect, highest engagement, and highest self-esteem when they are engaged in primary work tasks, as compared to tasks that are more peripherally related to their main duties.

Teuchmann and colleagues (1999) approached the notion of work activities from a different angle and conducted a study of accountants in which they examined the relationship between high- versus normal-demand periods at work and perceived control and mood. Using ESM data collected from accountants during work hours over a four-week period, they modeled the relationship between high-demand, perceptions of control, time pressure, mood, and emotional exhaustion. Path analysis showed that periods of high-sustained workload (which occur very predictably at month-end) result in decreased perception of control and increased feelings of time pressure. Interestingly, these increased demand periods had no direct effects on mood or emotional exhaustion, but rather had indirect effects operating through perceived control and time pressure (see Figure 10.2). The results suggest

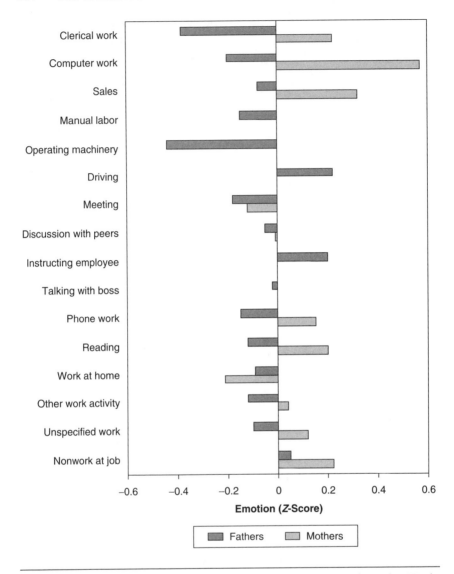

Figure 10.1   Fathers' and Mothers' Emotion During Activities Performed at Work

SOURCE: From *Divergent Realities* by Reed Larson. Copyright © 1994 by Reed Larson and Maryse Richards. Reprinted by permission of Basic Books, a member of Perseus Books, L.L.C.

that taking steps to enhance workers' perceived control may reduce some of the negative effects of time pressure. The results also suggest that a moderate level of time pressure produces the least emotional exhaustion among workers:

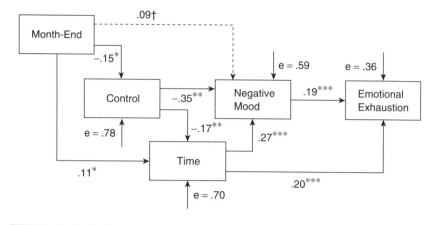

Figure 10.2   Path Analysis of Overall Model Showing the Significant Relations Between Month-End, Perceived Control, Time Pressure, Negative Mood, and Emotional Exhaustion

SOURCE: From Katja Teuchmann, Peter Totterdell, and Sharon K. Parker. Rushed, unhappy, and drained: An experience sampling study of relationships between time pressure, perceived control, mood, and emotional exhaustion of a group of accountants. *Journal of Occupational Health Psychology, 4,* 37–54. Copyright © 1999 by the Educational Publishing Foundation.

NOTES: e = error term; curv = curvilinear relationship. * $p < .05$. ** $p < .01$. *** $p < .001$. † $p < .06$. Broken line is nonsignificant.

the researchers found a curvilinear relationship between time pressure and exhaustion such that very low or very high time pressures were associated with higher levels of emotional exhaustion.

While in most ESM research the term "context" is often used to refer to a person's location, activities, or companions at the time of the signal, studies using other methods have assessed context in slightly different ways. An interesting alternative to understanding the impact of situational factors on workers' well-being is research employing Warr's (1987) principal environmental influences (PEIs). Warr identified nine PEIs that, together with personal factors, either enhance or constrain psychological well-being or mental health. These environmental factors include opportunity for control, opportunity for skill use, externally generated goals, variety, environmental clarity, availability of money, physical security, opportunity for physical contact, and valued social position. PEIs are thought to be determinants of mental health in a variety of environments but have been studied relatively extensively in the work context. While some of the PEIs clearly overlap with factors assessed by ESM (e.g., opportunity for control, opportunity for skill use), others are clearly not viable candidates for study using ESM (e.g., environmental clarity, valued social position). Each PEI is typically measured by a series of four or more questions asked in a traditional paper-and-pencil survey. Examples of questionnaire items include "much of the day I can choose the way in which I can carry out my tasks" (measuring control) and "in the things I do, I usually know the kind of results I will get" (measuring environmental clarity).

Research by Haworth and Patterson (1995) has shown that among managers, the "valued social position" and "opportunity for skill use" factors were particularly influential in predicting well-being in a sample of managers. These two factors in the workplace appear to play an important role in a person's overall mental health. Research on these environmental aspects of work complement studies that provide more momentary assessments of workers' experiences, together providing a richer picture of the work experience. In a study of working women, Haworth and colleagues (1997) found that both environmental influences (as measured by surveys) and momentary ratings of enjoyment, interest, and control (as measured by ESM) independently contributed to workers' overall well-being.

The Intersection of Work and Family

ESM is an ideal tool to study the effects that the daily demands of work and family place on one another. With the increased number of mothers in the American workforce and the resulting demands this places on mothers and fathers for fulfilling family responsibilities, there has been great concern over the psychological implications of occupying multiple family and work roles simultaneously (Eckenrode & Gore, 1990; Repetti, Mathews, & Waldron, 1989). Williams, Suls, Alliger, Learner, and Wan (1991) used ESM to track the daily activities of working mothers in order to examine the effects of role juggling on daily mood states and on shifts in these mood states from day to day. They examined both intrarole juggling (juggling multiple tasks from a single role, i.e., multiple work tasks or multiple family tasks) and interrole juggling (juggling tasks from multiple roles, i.e., work and family tasks). Using hierarchical regression analyses, they found that interrole juggling, or juggling tasks from different roles, resulted in significantly less task enjoyment and more negative mood than either juggling different tasks from the same role or not juggling tasks at all. These findings regarding role juggling are discussed in greater detail in Chapter 9.

Williams and colleagues also examined spillover of positive and negative affect to subsequent activities and to end-of-day ratings of satisfaction with one's job, one's home, and one's social life. They found that while feelings of positive or negative affect persisted from one measurement occasion to the next (e.g., from home to work or work to home), no spillover effects were found for end-of-day satisfaction ratings. In other words, affect at work was not associated with end-of-day home satisfaction ratings and affect at home was not associated with end-of-day job satisfaction ratings.

Larson and Richards (1994a) used ESM to document the different patterns in working mothers' and fathers' emotions as they transition from work to home. As was discussed in Chapter 8 of this volume (see Figure 8.2), men's emotional state rose considerably at around 6:00 p.m. when they came home from work. Dads saw this time as a chance to unwind from the stress of the workday. Mothers also ended their workday feeling rather fatigued, but their fatigue was only exacerbated upon their return home, as evidenced by the substantial drop in mothers' emotion around 6:00. For working men, coming home is a relief, while the data suggest that working women may view this time as the beginning of their second job. This explanation was validated by ESM data on the time use of the working parents in this study: Estimates of time spent doing housework showed that after a long day on the job, working mothers still did the bulk of the housework.

Some researchers have used ESM to study the impact of parental employment on children. Richards and Duckett (1994) conducted a study in which the early adolescent children of mothers who worked full time, part time, or not at all completed the ESM. The authors found that adolescent children of employed mothers spent no less time with their parents than children whose mothers didn't work. The researchers also found that very little of the variation in early adolescents' daily experience was due to maternal employment patterns, though a few appreciable differences were observed in the types of activities children did with their parents and in their daily mood. Findings from this study are also discussed in Chapter 9 of this volume.

While Richards and Duckett found no employment status differences in the time early adolescents spent with their parents, in a more recent study of older adolescents Schmidt (2005) found that mothers who worked full time spent significantly less time with their children compared to nonemployed moms. ESM time estimates indicate that mothers who do not work outside the home spend about seven more hours per week with their adolescent children compared to those working full time. These contradictory findings may be due to sampling and other methodological differences between the two studies. The adolescents in Schmidt's study were older than the participants in Richards and Duckett's research. The families in Richards and Duckett's study can be considered working and middle class, while Schmidt's sample is predominantly middle and upper-middle class. Further, Richards and Duckett used adolescents' ESM reports of companionship to estimate the time parents and children spent together, while Schmidt relied on parents' ESM reports.

The effects of maternal employment on children is one of the most widely studied topics in the area of work and family. Other research examining the intersection of work and family has examined the effects of occupational conditions on parenting, work-family spillover, and how individuals balance their multiple roles as worker, parent, and spouse. Obviously, the majority of this research has employed methods other than ESM, but there is a growing body of work in which ESM has been used to add depth to researchers' understanding of the complexities of work and family life. We have briefly mentioned a few studies in this chapter, but a more comprehensive review of ESM research on the intersection of work and family can be found in Chapter 9 of this volume.

The Experience of Unemployment

While there is a relatively large body of research examining the experience of working, only a few have focused specifically on what it feels like not to work. Kirchler (1985) used ESM to chart the well-being of unemployed people during the six months following the loss of their job. Results indicated that in the first month following the loss of employment participants' moods were substantially lower than they had been when they were employed. The second and third months following job loss were marked by a slight rebound in mood, even among persons who had not yet found a new job. However, six months following the job loss, those who remained unemployed had the lowest levels of mood reported in the study, while those who were reemployed reported the highest levels of mood reported by anyone over the course of the study. These findings suggest a cycle of psychological adjustment to unemployment characterized by initial shock, followed by a period of optimism, and then depression.

In a study of unemployed young adults, Haworth and Ducker (1991) argue that the experience of unemployment can vary greatly depending on how one spends the time that is freed up by the loss of a job. They found that even though they lacked formal employment, some unemployed people tended to engage in more active and worklike leisure activities, while others spent time in more passive endeavors. Among the unemployed, those who engaged in more worklike leisure activities had significantly higher self-esteem, life satisfaction, and enjoyment.

Adolescent Work

We have reviewed at some length many of the ways ESM has been used to examine the impact of work (and the absence of work) on the experience of adult workers and their families. We must not overlook the fact that children work too. The number of adolescents who work for pay has risen substantially in recent decades to the point where most teenagers are employed at some point during high school (Schmidt, Rich, & Makris, 2000; U.S. Department of Labor, 2000). Given that paid employment has become the norm for adolescents in the United States, researchers have recognized the need to understand adolescents' work and its effects on development. Much of the research in recent decades has focused on the structural, social, or psychological aspects of teenagers' experience of paid employment (cf. Greenberger & Steinberg, 1981, 1986; Mortimer & Borman, 1988; Mortimer, Finch, Owens, & Shannahan, 1990; National Research Council, 1998; Steinberg, Fegley, & Dornbusch, 1993). Researchers have presented strong arguments for both the costs and benefits of adolescent employment with respect to its effects on academic achievement, physical and psychological well-being, and long-term earnings and career attainment. The effects of adolescent employment on such outcomes are complex and not yet fully understood. Rather than taking a position on whether adolescent employment is good or bad, much of the ESM research on adolescent work to date has been more descriptive, focusing on how adolescents feel when working at a paid job, and how they feel about work more generally. Using data from the largest ESM study to date involving adolescents (Csikszentmihalyi & Schneider, 2000), Schmidt and colleagues (2000) report that most teens work fewer than 20 hours a week. Although the time spent working is not excessive, it appears that work schedules inevitably impinge on other domains of life. Schneider and Stevenson's (1999) analysis of the same data set indicates that when teenagers work, they spend less time at school, less time at home, less time doing homework, and more time commuting than adolescents who are not employed.

ESM reports of adolescents' quality of experience in paid work appears to be somewhat mixed (Schmidt, Rich, & Makris, 2000). Paid work is generally regarded as an activity that is engaging, important, and promotes feelings of positive self-regard. Reports of concentration, self-esteem, and salience are all above average (see Table 10.2). However, adolescents' affective experience in work appears to be neutral or even slightly negative, as indicated by average levels of affect and below-average levels of enjoyment and happiness. When experience in paid work is compared to other activities such as schoolwork, socializing, watching television, and engaging in maintenance activities such as personal care, vast differences emerge. Concentration appears to be equally high in paid work and schoolwork and considerably lower when teenagers are watching television or performing maintenance activities. Perceived salience—a measure of importance—is higher in work activities than in social activities, maintenance activities, or watching television, but salience levels are by far the highest in activities related to school. Thus adolescents tend to perceive school activities as being substantially more important to themselves personally and to their futures than work experiences. Paid work is a relatively unenjoyable and unhappy experience, at least when compared to socializing or watching TV, though it appears to be slightly more enjoyable than schoolwork.

Table 10.2   Mean Quality of Experience Scores in Paid Work Versus Other Activity Types for Teens Who Have Jobs

	Job	School	Social	TV	Maintenance
Self-esteem	0.37	0.01	0.02	−0.25	−0.07
Salience	0.34	0.59	−0.08	−0.78	−0.37
Positive affect	0.03	−0.15	0.32	−0.09	−0.04
Enjoyment	−0.17	−0.32	0.27	0.30	−0.02
Happiness	−0.10	−0.17	0.28	0.01	−0.01
Concentration	0.36	0.37	−0.09	−0.30	−0.38

SOURCE: From *Becoming Adult* by Mihaly Csikszentmihalyi. Copyright © 2000 by Mihaly Csikszentmihalyi and Barbara Schneider. Reprinted by permission of Basic Books, a member of Perseus Books, L.L.C.

NOTES: Quality of experience values are calculated as Z-scores. N = 159.

These results are consistent with those of Haworth and Evans (1995), who used ESM to examine quality of experience among participants in a youth job training program in the United Kingdom. Haworth and Evans found that only 17 percent of adolescents' very happy experiences occurred while they were working, while passive leisure activities produced a much larger proportion of very happy experiences. Similarly, only about a third of adolescents' most enjoyable moments happened at work, while close to half of all high enjoyment experiences took place at home.

These results suggest that adolescents' subjective experiences in paid work are no better and in fact might be worse than adults' experiences on the job. A paradox similar to that described for adults emerges when one considers the degree to which adolescents experience flow on the job. Similar to previously reported results of adults' flow on the job (Csikszentmihalyi, 1990; Csikszentmihalyi & LeFevre, 1989; Haworth & Hill, 1992; Larson & Richards, 1994a; LeFevre, 1988), Hektner and colleagues (2000) report that in spite of their seemingly negative affective reactions to work, adolescents too report above-average levels of flow on the job. Haworth and Evans (1995) found evidence that adolescents' flow in work is more enjoyable than the flow they experience in other activities. For adolescents as well as adults, it appears that although work is engaging, it is generally perceived as something to be avoided. This may be due to the fact that like adults, adolescents appear to be affected by the stress often associated with work, as evidenced by above-average levels of anxiety while working (Csikszentmihalyi & Schneider, 2000). Adolescents and adults alike appear to fluctuate between states of deep engagement and anxiety while working, and evaluations of the affective components of work seem to indicate that the moments of anxiety may be more salient.

The study of adolescent work is important not only because it provides additional descriptive information about teenagers' daily lives but also because it has the potential to open a window into socialization into adult work roles. Paid work during adolescence is presumed by some to provide valuable training and experience for the transition to adult work roles. Other researchers, however, have argued that most adolescent employment is an "encapsulated experience"—a series of activities that are generally unrelated to career goals, do not teach adolescents many skills that will help them as adults, and are perceived as relatively unimportant to future goals (Schneider & Stevenson, 1999). Further, career aspirations at this age are known to be relatively unstable (Csikszentmihalyi & Schneider, 2000) and may not be very good indicators of the careers adolescents will ultimately choose as adults. Further, recent decades have shown that radical career shifts are increasingly frequent (Havighurst, 1982; Jepsen, 1984; Osipow, 1986), making it highly likely that an adolescent aspiring to a particular job will likely not find himself in that job as an adult, or at least won't be in that job for very long. Given that neither actual employment nor aspirations appear to be very reliable indicators of adolescents' future as adult workers, Schmidt and colleagues (2000) used ESM to examine adolescent work from a more phenomenological perspective. They examined general attitudes toward work in an attempt to learn more about how fundamental attitudes toward work are learned in childhood and adolescence. In a study of students in sixth, eighth, tenth, and twelfth grades, they asked participants to indicate on their ESF the specific activity in which they were engaged and to mark on the sheet whether they felt that what they were doing at that moment was "more like work," "more like play," "like both work and play," or "like neither work nor play." This approach allowed the researchers to better understand how children develop conceptions of what work is and how they develop attitudes toward these worklike experiences. Schmidt and colleagues found that adolescents spend about equal amounts of time in activities they perceive to be worklike (29%) and playlike (28%). Only about 9 percent of the activities adolescents engaged in were perceived as being like both work and play, and a substantially greater percentage of daily activity (34%) was perceived as being like neither work nor play. When they looked at the specific activities that students perceived as worklike and playlike, they found that even by the sixth grade, young people have highly stereotyped understandings of what is meant by work. School and jobs are almost always perceived as being like work, whereas leisure activities are rarely perceived as worklike.

An examination of adolescents' quality of experience in worklike and playlike activities suggests that adolescents not only define work in a very stereotyped way but also experience work according to societal norms. They view work as a relatively unenjoyable experience that nonetheless is important to one's future. Playlike activities, on the other hand, are highly enjoyable but relatively unimportant (see Figure 10.3). It is when an activity is perceived as like both work and play that experience seems to be positive on all accounts. These rare activities are characterized by high levels of enjoyment, importance, and self-esteem.

In the Schmidt and colleagues study, the ESM data indicated that there were vast differences in the degree to which adolescents saw their lives as worklike or playlike. While some adolescents consistently saw what they were doing as work, others rarely did so. They examined two groups of students whom they refer to as "workers" and "players." Workers are those adolescents who spend unusually large amounts of time in worklike activities, while players are those who spend unusually large amounts of time in playlike activities. They compared how workers and players perceived their work and play activities. While workers and players found work to be equally (and highly) challenging, when engaged in worklike activity the workers reported significantly higher levels of enjoyment, strength, importance to self, and importance to the future compared to the players. Workers also reported more often than players that they were working because they wanted to rather than because they had to. Players, for some reason, seemed unable to translate the challenge of work experience into something that was meaningful or enjoyable to them. It may not be particularly surprising that workers have more positive experience in work than players do. However, the researchers also found that workers tended to be happier than players when playing. Not only do they enjoy a more meaningful work experience, they appear to enjoy play more as well.

These findings about one's general orientation toward work are consistent with research by Haworth and Ducker (1991), who used ESM to examine

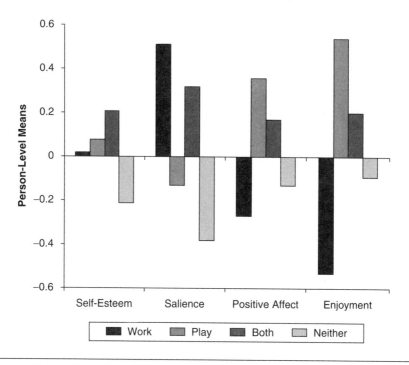

Figure 10.3   Overall Quality of Experience in Work and Play

SOURCE: From *Becoming Adult* by Mihaly Csikszentmihalyi. Copyright © 2000 by Mihaly Csikszentmihalyi and Barbara Schneider. Reprinted by permission of Basic Books, a member of Perseus Books, L.L.C.

NOTE: The raw scores for Work, Play, Both, and Neither were transformed into standardized scores at the person level (with each student's mean score being set to 0, with a standard deviation of 1) so as to compensate for individual differences in scale use and response style.

worklike activities among unemployed young people. They found that those who engaged in more worklike activities (as compared to passive leisure activities) had higher self-esteem, greater life satisfaction, and reported higher levels of enjoyment across all daily activities.

   Taken together, many of the ESM studies designed to examine work experience converge on a central paradox. For men and women, adolescents and adults alike, work provides a context for engagement, deep absorption, and the high levels of challenge and skill that tend to produce optimal experience. In spite of these positive features of work experience, however, most people view work as a relatively unenjoyable set of tasks that they would avoid if given the choice. In many respects, workers appear to ignore the messages of their own senses. There is some preliminary evidence to suggest that this apparent paradox might be explained in that the condition of high challenges and high skills may produce different experiences at work than in other activities (Pfister, 2002; Schallberger, 1995; Schallberger & Pfister, 2001). Further research is needed to clarify patterns in workers' subjective experience in situations where challenges and skills are high.

11

Examining Cross-Cultural Differences

While much of the research described to this point involves samples of *American* participants, ESM has been used widely in countries outside the United States; from the Netherlands and Italy, to Korea, Japan, and India. Just as many of the U.S. studies are not focused on the impact of culture per se, very often the data collected in countries outside of the United States are not viewed through the lens of culture, but rather the research is focused on topics such as clinical applications (deVries, 1992; Massimini, Csikszentmihalyi, & Carli, 1987), flow (Massimini & Carli, 1988), or work experiences (Schallberger & Pfister, 2001). Such studies are described in detail in the appropriate chapters of this book. In this chapter we focus on a number of ESM studies that make explicit comparisons of the phenomenology of everyday life across cultures. These studies begin to address questions such as: (1) Do people in different cultures spend their time in different ways and in different social contexts? (2) Do cultures differ with respect to dimensions of affective experience? (3) Do people across cultures experience the same activities in different ways? (4) Is *flow* experienced cross-culturally, and if so, are there cultural differences in terms of how often individuals experience *flow*, what precipitates *flow*, or how *flow* is described?

Before proceeding further, it is necessary to remind the reader that *culture* can be defined in many ways. It is not our intent in this chapter to provide you with a definitive description of what is encompassed by the term *culture*.

Rather, we leave this task to the various researchers who choose to address culture in their research. On a more practical level, however, a majority of existing ESM studies that deal with culture have drawn the lines of definition largely around issues of nationality, or racial, ethnic, or religious background. The research described in this chapter largely compares individuals' daily experience based upon where they live or upon what racial, ethnic, or religious category they use to describe themselves. We present research focusing exclusively on these cultural contexts not because we believe these are the only ways culture can be defined, but rather because these are the only ways culture has been defined in ESM research to date. We see culture as an area that researchers have only begun to address with ESM, and we believe this area has enormous potential for future research.

Methodological Concerns and Variations

The most pressing concerns when conducting cross-cultural ESM research are not unique to ESM, but rather deal with issues that should be taken into consideration when conducting any type of cross-cultural study. These concerns deal with the comparability of terms, meanings, constructs, and populations from one culture to another. This concern exists at many levels. At the simple, most practical level, this is merely a matter of translation when dealing with populations that speak different languages. Often a word or phrase that exists in one culture does not have a simple translation that will capture the same meaning in another society. One example of a translation problem encountered in ESM research concerns the word *challenge*—a central concept to the measurement of flow. There is no simple Italian translation of the English word *challenge*. In studies comparing flow in Italy and the United States, a rather lengthy description of challenge was used to obtain comparability of meaning between Italian and American responses. The question in English "How challenging did you find the activity?" was worded in Italian "Did the situation allow you to be involved, to act, or to express yourself?" In this circumstance, a verbal description in Italian was sufficient to characterize the sentiment implied by the English word *challenge*. In other situations it might not be as easy to find appropriate translations for words or concepts that do not exist in other languages.

A second concern deals with variations in the cultural context underlying many of the constructs researchers want to compare cross-culturally. For example, some cultures value and encourage emotional expressivity, while others encourage the maintenance of a more reserved emotional tone (Wierzbicka, 1986). Comparisons of individuals' emotions in two such cultures are likely to be heavily influenced by the acceptability of expressing such emotion in each cultural context. Likewise, cultures place differential value on particular personality traits or ways of being. For example, Kitayama and Markus (1994) argue that in Asian societies connection, conformity, and interdependence are highly idealized personal traits, while Americans place far greater value on qualities such as independence, individuality, and self-assertion. When making comparisons of Asians and Americans on dimensions of social interaction, it is essential to take into consideration the variation in cultural ideals that likely account for many differences that are observed. A detailed discussion of these types of issues is beyond the scope of this chapter, but is discussed in depth in Stigler, Shweder, and Herdt (1990).

Cultural and societal differences across the world may also present researchers with some difficulties in selecting appropriate groups for comparison. For example, middle-class families in the United States have very different lives than middle-class families in India—thus a comparison of middle-class families does not necessarily ensure any degree of comparability in terms of social or economic resources. Likewise, the structure of formal education varies from country to country, so it is often difficult when comparing children's school experiences to identify comparable groups from different cultures.

Having offered these cautionary words about the methodological concerns involved in defining and conducting research on cultures, we now turn to a description of the studies that have endeavored to make such examinations. Despite the many differences in language, cultural context, and cultural practices just described, what is often most interesting about findings from the cross-cultural research to date are the similarities in many key dimensions of individuals' experiences throughout the world. In the pages that follow we describe the remarkable similarity and variation in daily experience that has been described or explained using ESM.

Culture and Time Use

ESM has been used to describe the structure of daily life for individuals from different cultures. Larson, Verma, and Dworkin (2001) used ESM to examine time use in men's work and family lives in India and compared these patterns to those observed in studies of other cultures. They found that Indian fathers spent substantially more time in the workplace and in public than their wives did. In turn, Indian men spent far less time at home and far less time with their children than their wives did. When fathers were with their children, they were most likely to be engaged in some sort of leisure activity like watching television. Perhaps the greatest discrepancy observed in the family sphere was the proportion of time men and women spent on "family work" like shopping, cleaning, running errands, and helping children with homework. Larson and colleagues report that Indian men spend one-sixth the amount of time their wives spend attending to family work, a figure that is consistent with estimates of other studies of men in non-Western countries employing different methodologies (Evenson, Popkin, & Quizon, 1980; Minge-Klevana, 1980). By contrast, similar studies conducted in Western countries estimate that men invest one-third to one-half as much time as their wives do in family work (Haas, 1999; Thompson & Walker, 1989).

Among the Indian fathers studied by Larson and colleagues, their jobs claimed the highest proportion of their time and attention. These findings are consistent with results of studies employing one-time questionnaire assessments of time use among Indian mothers and fathers (Ramu, 1987, 1989). While these patterns are certainly true of men in other countries, Larson and his colleagues found that the Indian men in their sample tended to work fewer hours than men in developed and other developing countries. While many of the Indian men in their sample worked as many as 6 days a week, on average they worked a total of only 35 hours a week—substantially less than figures reported in other countries (Minge-Klevana, 1980). In their explanation of this discrepancy, Larson and colleagues cite scholars of white-collar Indian work culture who report that it is relatively commonplace for Indian employees to arrive late, leave early, and engage in nonproductive activities at work such as having tea with friends (Khare, 1999; Sinha & Sinha, 1990). These observed differences may be due to cultural differences in definitions of acceptable workplace behavior.

Time use of adolescents from around the world has been studied widely using ESM. The method has been used to study time spent in household labor, paid work, school-related activities, and leisure. For a comprehensive review of these studies as well as many others that use different methodologies for measuring adolescent time use around the world, see Larson and Verma (1999). In their review of research conducted in over 20 countries, they examine the work and leisure activities of adolescents around the world and discuss the cultural and developmental implications of the population differences they identify. They observe that adolescents in industrialized nations where schooling is a priority spend far less time engaged in household and wage labor compared to teens in other nations. ESM estimates of time use suggest that teenagers in the United States spend about 40 minutes each day engaged in household labor (Csikszentmihalyi, Rathunde, & Whalen, 1993; Duckett, Raffaelli, & Richards, 1989; Larson, Kubey, & Colletti, 1989), a figure that is consistent with ESM estimates involving adolescents in postindustrial societies in Italy (Massimini, Inghilleri, & Delle Fave, 1986) and India (Verma, 1998). ESM studies conducted in East Asia suggest that teenagers in these regions (specifically Korea and Japan) spend the least amount of time on housework—averaging approximately 6–12 minutes per day (Lee, 1994; Nishino, 1997).

Much of the data on adolescent time use in nonindustrialized societies were collected using observational and interview methods rather than ESM because of the literacy requirements imposed by ESM. Observational and interview data on time use collected from unschooled adolescents in nonindustrialized societies such as those found in rural India and Nepal indicate that teenagers in these societies spend as many as eight hours a day on household labor (Nag, White, & Peet, 1980; Saraswathi & Dutta, 1998; cross-study comparisons made in Larson & Verma, 1999). One consistent finding across nearly all these studies was that, regardless of the average amount of time teenagers in a given culture spent on housework and regardless of the method used to estimate time use, the adolescent girls in that culture generally spent more time on housework than adolescent boys, and the types of chores done by girls and boys tended to differ.

Adolescents in postindustrialized, schooled societies spent relatively little time engaged in wage labor—ESM estimates indicate that time in paid work is about 30–60 minutes per day for North American adolescents (Csikszentmihalyi & Larson, 1984; Csikszentmihalyi et al., 1993) and is almost nonexistent in Japan (Nishino, 1997) and Korea (Lee, 1994; cross-study comparisons made in Larson & Verma, 1999). These figures compare estimates produced using observational and interview methodologies of adolescents in nonindustrialized unschooled nations working as many as six hours a day (Nag et al., 1980; Saraswathi & Dutta, 1998).

Among children in postindustrial societies, there are considerable cross-cultural differences in how the time freed up by reduced housework and wage labor is spent. Obviously, a large portion of this time is spent on schoolwork. ESM studies conducted in the United States (Csikszentmihalyi & Larson, 1984; Csikszentmihalyi et al., 1993; Larson et al., 1989; Lee, 1994; Leone & Richards, 1989), Italy (Delle Fave, Massimini, & Gaspardin, 1993; Massimini et al., 1986), India (Verma, 1998), Korea (Lee, 1994; Won, 1989), and Japan (Nishino, 1997) show considerable differences, however, in the time spent on schoolwork (see Table 11.1). Looking across all of these studies, it appears that Korean adolescents spend nearly half of all their waking hours engaged in schoolwork, while Japanese adolescents and Italian adolescents attending an elite high school spend about one-third of their waking hours engaged in study. U.S. adolescents, on the other hand, spend only about a quarter of all waking hours on schoolwork, with one study of urban, African American youth (Larson et al., 1989) reporting only 19 percent of waking time on such activities (Larson & Verma, 1999). While adolescents in

East Asian postindustrialized nations clearly use the time freed up by reduced housework and wage labor to engage in study, North American teenagers spend more of this free time engaged in leisure activities such as television viewing and more active activities like sports (Larson & Verma, 1999). Findings across these studies reported by Larson and Verma are consistent with a study by Won (1989) who, in a comparison of time use of U.S. and Korean adolescents, also found that Korean adolescents spend more time doing class work while U.S teens spend more time engaged in leisure activities.

ESM estimates of the time adolescents spend with various companions—family and friends—predictably overlap with the findings we have already reviewed regarding activities. As housework is most often done in the company of family members, adolescents who tend to do more housework report

Table 11.1   Total Time in Schoolwork in Postindustrial Populations (ESM Studies Only)

Population & Study	School Grade	Percentage of Self-Reports	Estimated Hrs./Day
U.S. (Csikszentmihalyi & Larson, 1984)	High school	25	3.7
U.S. (Leone & Richards, 1989)	5th–9th grades	22	3.1
U.S. talented youth (Csikszentmihalyi, Rathunde, & Whalen, 1993)	9th–10th grades	29	4.3
U.S. urban African American (Larson, Richards, Sims, & Dworkin, 2001)	5th–8th grades	19	2.7
Italy (Massimini, Inghilleri, & Delle Fave, 1986)	High school	31	4.6
Italy (Delle Fave, Massimini, & Gaspardin, 1993)	High school	34	4.8
India, middle class (Verma, 1998)	8th grade	32	4.6
Korea [9 a.m.–9 p.m.] (Won, 1989)	8th & 11th grades	47	5.6
Japan (Nishino, 1997)	11th grade	34	5.4
Cross-cultural (Lee, 1994)			
U.S.	12th grade	19	2.9
Korea	12th grade	44	7.8

SOURCE: Larson and Verma, *Psychological Bulletin, 25,* 1999. Copyright © 1999 by the American Psychological Association. Reprinted with permission.

more time with family. Conversely, teenagers who spend more time in school are more often with peers. Looking across the studies we have already mentioned, Larson and Verma (1999) report more cultural similarity than difference in the time adolescents in these studies spend alone. Most studies, regardless of the methodology used, estimate that teenagers are alone for about 25 percent of all waking hours, with slightly lower estimates among younger adolescents and slightly higher estimates among older teens.

Cross-Cultural Variation in General Affective Experience

A central question in cross-cultural psychology is whether there is cultural variation in the frequency or intensity of particular emotions and whether the set of emotions typically examined in Western research is of value when studying non-Western populations. In a series of related papers, Scollon and colleagues (2004, 2005; Oishi, Diener, Scollon, & Biswas-Diener, 2004) used ESM to explore emotions, including pleasant and unpleasant affect in five distinct cultural groups. ESM data were collected from college students in India, Japan, and the United States (the U.S. sample included European Americans, Asian Americans, and Hispanics). Their results suggest both universality and diversity in emotional experience. They compared reports of emotion from ESM with more global self-report measures and with participants' recollection of their emotions during the ESM week (Scollon, Diener, Oishi, & Biswas-Diener, 2004). They found much more cultural variability in positive emotions than in negative emotions. Generally speaking, Hispanics and European Americans reported more pleasant affect and less unpleasant affect than their peers from the three Asian cultures studied. Examining three measures of emotion, they found that for every cultural group studied, global reports of emotion predicted retrospective recall of their ESM week, even after controlling for their ESM reports. Thus they provided strong evidence of a memory bias in recall of emotion across several cultural groups. There were, however, cultural differences in the degree to which one's memories of their emotion during the ESM week were related to their actual ESM reports, with European Americans having the strongest association between their ESM reports and their recall of emotions.

This group of researchers also examined the within-person and between-person associations between pleasant and unpleasant affect in general (Scollon, Diener, Oishi, & Biswas-Diener, 2005) and across situations (Oishi et al., 2004). At the within-person level, the researchers were interested in knowing what affective states go together at the same time (e.g., do people feel joyful and irritated simultaneously?). At the between-person level, they looked at the "long-term structure of affect" (Scollon et al., 2005, p. 29), asking, for example, if individuals who experience a lot of pleasant affect also experience a lot of negative affect. They found that global affective traits existed in all of the samples they studied, but that the degree to which situations impacted these global traits varied across cultures. For example, the association between being with friends and positive affect was larger for Hispanics and Japanese participants than it was for the other American subsamples (Oishi et al., 2004).

Looking at affect more generally, across all the samples studied, analyses suggested that pleasant and unpleasant affect tend not to co-occur: In every culture, within-person correlations for various indicators of pleasant affect were all positive, while the correlation between indicators of pleasant and unpleasantness were all negative. Looking at these momentary reports, they found little evidence of "mixed feelings" for any of the cultural groups studied. They did, however, find culturally distinct patterns of affect in the between-person analysis. In the European and Hispanic samples, there are no significant correlations between one's frequency or intensity of pleasant and unpleasant affect. These more global indicators of pleasant and unpleasant affect were positively and significantly correlated with one another in the Asian American, Japanese, and Indian samples. For example, affection and pride tended to correlate with a number of unpleasant emotions, such as guilt, irritation, sadness, and worry.

Their within-person analyses suggest that the reported affective experiences across cultures appear more similar than not: pleasant emotions tend to be experienced together, unpleasant experiences tend to be experienced together, and pleasant and unpleasant emotions tend not to co-occur. Not only does this finding suggest some degree of universality in emotional experience, but it also provides some evidence that emotional experience can be meaningfully assessed cross-culturally using the methods and measures employed by these researchers. The between-person analysis suggests very consistent cultural differences in longer-term emotional experience. Over time, pleasant and unpleasant affect were positively related to one another in the three Asian samples studied, while there were no such relationships observed among European Americans or Hispanics. The authors offer several possible explanations for these differences, pointing to differences in cultural orientation, goal structure, and interpersonal relationships (Scollon et al., 2005). Collectively, this body of research underscores the importance of examining both within-person and between-person affective experience when attempting to compare different groups.

Culture and Subjective Experience in Various Activities

Much of the cross-cultural research on affect and other dimensions of subjective experience has compared cultural groups in the way they feel when engaged in similar activities. Larson, Verma, and Dworkin (2001) studied Indian fathers' subjective experience at home and at work and compared it to similar data gathered from fathers in the United States (U.S. comparison group originally reported in Larson & Richards, 1994a). In both the Indian and the U.S. samples, it was observed that father's experience at work is characterized by very high levels of attention and generally negative emotion. At home, however, fathers' attentional levels tended to be lower, but the affective and emotional components of this experience were generally positive. An interesting pattern observed across U.S. and Indian samples is that there appeared to be differences in the degree to which subjective experience at work and at home are linked. In a U.S. sample (originally reported in Larson & Almeida, 1999), fathers' emotion at work tended to spill over into their first few hours at home. Fathers' ESM reports of their emotion at the end of their work days were highly predictive of the emotions they reported when they first arrived home, and when fathers came home from work in a bad mood, they had lower rates of involvement at home. Beyond this, Larson and Almeida found evidence to suggest that U.S. fathers' emotions at the end of the workday were often transmitted to their families. As U.S. fathers would arrive home and interact with other family members, their negative moods would "rub off" on their spouses and children. Examining those ESM responses where U.S. fathers were with their spouses or children shortly after arriving home from work, the researchers found that fathers' negative emotions at work were not only predictive of fathers' subsequent emotions at home, but also their *spouse's* and *children's* negative emotions as well. These same patterns were not observed in the Indian sample studied by Larson, Verma, and Dworkin (2001). Indian fathers did evidence some spillover of emotion from work to home, but unlike U.S. fathers, their negative emotions at work were not at all predictive of their level of involvement when they returned home and had no measurable impact on their spouses' or their children's emotions. Larson and his colleagues suggest that these findings are indicative of independence between work and home spheres that exists more strongly in white-collar Indian families than in the United States.

In another analysis of their data collected from Indian families, Verma and Larson (2001) examined women's experience of housework. Even though women in middle-class Indian families spend substantially more time than their husbands on household labor, there was very little evidence to suggest that women (whether employed or not) viewed housework as oppressive. Indian women did not experience household labor as being outside of their control, in contrast to American women who felt substantially less control over their household tasks. Similarly, while American women reported being very unhappy while doing household work, Indian women reported average levels of happiness. The authors speculate that these cross-cultural differences in reported happiness may be due in part to the previously reported differences in the perception of control, but also to differences in companionship during housework. For Indian women, housework is a social task, and they usually do housework in the company of others, while most American women's household labor is done alone.

In another study, Verma and Larson (1999) studied the daily emotions of middle-class Indian adolescents and compared these results to what is known about emotionality in adolescents from other cultures. They sought to evaluate the notion, commonly held across a number of cultures (including Indian cultures), that adolescence is a time of increased emotionality. Very limited empirical evidence exists to support this view of adolescence, and what little evidence has been generated is based exclusively on data collected from adolescents in the United States. Evidence gathered within the United States has been based on surveys (cf. Bradburn, 1969; Campbell, 1981; Diener, Sandvik, & Larsen, 1985) and ESM. In ESM studies involving parents and children, Larson and colleagues learned that adolescents reported more extreme positive and negative emotional states than did adults (Larson, Csikszentmihalyi, & Graef, 1980; Larson & Richards, 1994a). Csikszentmihalyi and Larson (1984) also found that adolescents' extreme negative and positive moods tend to dissipate much more quickly than do adults', suggesting much less emotional stability from moment to moment. Arguing that both emotions and the concept of adolescence are partly products of culture, Verma and Larson examined whether commonly held descriptions of adolescent emotionality were valid for Indian teenagers. To do this, they examined daily patterns of emotion among middle-class Indian eighth graders and their parents. Looking at averages across all ESM responses, they found that Indian adolescents' average emotional states did not differ significantly from their parents': averaging across the week, Indian teens were not happier or sadder or more or less relaxed than their parents. Indian adolescents did differ substantially from their parents, though, in the *variability* of their emotional states throughout the week. While parents' emotions tended to hover pretty close to their weekly average, adolescents' emotions were much more variable. In fact, the adolescents had significantly higher weekly standard deviations than the adults on every emotion item examined (see Table 11.2). The authors suggest, as has been suggested in

Table 11.2 Emotional States Reported by Adolescents, Mothers, and Fathers

	Average State			Standard Deviation		
	Adolescents	Mothers	Fathers	Adolescents	Mothers	Fathers
Affect items						
Happy (unhappy)	5.14	5.12	5.12	1.32	1.05***	1.02***
Friendly (angry)	4.67	4.61	4.62	1.28	1.03***	0.88***
Cheerful (irritable)	4.99	4.97	5.04	1.33	1.15***	1.06***
Activation items						
Relaxed (stressed)	4.23	4.37	4.41+	1.33	1.19**	1.12***
Excited (bored)	4.20	4.18	4.21	1.36	0.84***	0.75***
Strong (weak)	4.39	4.33	4.55+	1.02	0.86**	0.75***
Wide awake (tired)	4.82	4.94	5.15***	1.57	1.38***	1.20***
Overall emotion	**4.64**	**4.73**	**4.65**	**0.86**	**0.61*****	**0.67*****

SOURCE: Verma, S., & Larson, R. W. (1999). Are adolescents more emotional? A study of daily emotions of middle class Indian adolescents. *Psychology and Developing Societies*, 11, 179–194. Copyright © 1999. Reprinted with the permission of Sage Publications.

NOTES: The table displays the mean average and the mean standard deviation for each family member for each item. Two-tailed significance tests evaluate whether the values for mothers and fathers differ from those for adolescents: $+ p < .10$; $* p < .05$; $** p < .01$; $*** p < .001$.

215

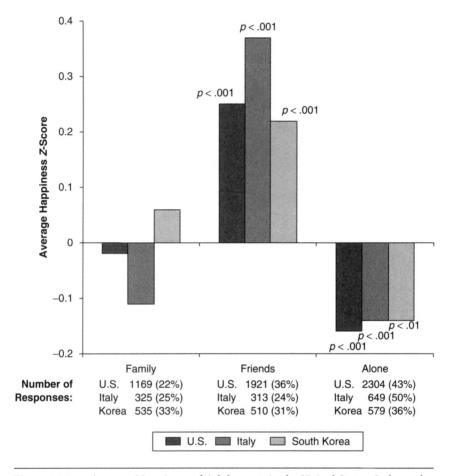

Figure 11.1   Average Happiness of Adolescents in the United States, Italy, and South Korea in Three Different Social Contexts

SOURCE: Csikszentmihalyi, 1995.

U.S. populations, that Indian adolescents' extreme moods might be a result of interactions with parents and peers or they might be a reaction to the stressful events that often accompany entry into adolescence. These results suggest some cross-cultural similarities in adolescents' emotional variability in India and the United States.

Looking across studies conducted in the United States, Korea, and Italy, Csikszentmihalyi (1995) compared adolescents' positive affect (measured as happy, cheerful, and sociable) across 14 different activities, such as class work, personal care, sports, and television (see Figure 11.1). There was little difference in the way adolescents from the three cultures perceived class work—affect in class activities was about average for the week. Interestingly, Korean and U.S. teens reported fairly high positive affect while eating, but eating did not appear to be as positive an experience for Italian teens. While playing sports was perceived positively by all teens, Italian teens appeared to have a considerably more positive experience playing sports relative to U.S. or Korean adolescents. Another striking difference involved art and hobbies: while such activities were accompanied by roughly average affect for U.S. teens, they were experienced very positively by adolescents from Italy and Korea. For Korean adolescents, reading books, newspapers, and the like was a very positive experience, while for teenagers from Italy and the United States such activities were slightly below average with respect to affect.

Cross-Cultural Examinations of Flow

A number of cross-cultural studies have been conducted to verify the existence of optimal experience or flow in other cultures and to examine cultural variation in dimensions of flow. A large body of research employing surveys, interviews, and ESM confirms that adolescents and adults in countries across the globe recognize and identify the basic features of the flow experience, suggesting that the phenomenology of optimal experience is fairly universal (Csikszentmihalyi, 1990; Massimini, Inghilleri, & Delle Fave, 1996). These studies indicate that flow occurs in a wide variety of activities, ranging from work to sports to art to social interaction. The common theme that cuts across all of these flow-producing activities is that the activity at hand provides opportunities for action, engagement, and the investment of personal skills. Tasks that are repetitive and require little skill seldom produce flow. While we have discussed these aspects of flow in detail in Chapter 7, it is important to raise this topic again because of the potential importance of optimal experience from a cultural perspective. Optimal experience promotes individual development. Because subjective experience in flow is generally positive, individuals in all cultures and in all walks of life are drawn to seek increasingly complex challenges, which in turn increase their skills. As a result, development occurs (Csikszentmihalyi, 1990; Csikszentmihalyi & Massimini, 1985). This process has been referred to as *cultivation* (Csikszentmihalyi & Rochberg-Halton, 1981). Over the course of a lifetime, the process of cultivation results in the preferential replication of activities that produce the flow experience and serves as the basis for a kind of *psychological selection*, in which certain pursuits become central in a person's life (Csikszentmihalyi & Beattie, 1979). This psychological selection does not occur in a vacuum, however. Selection at the individual level influences, and is influenced by, culture. As a result of the selections made by individuals, different cultures come to value certain artifacts (e.g., art, musical instruments, sporting equipment) because they are vehicles that provide optimal experiences. On the other hand, in order to survive and adapt to their social context, individuals must reproduce culturally adaptive behaviors. A central component to psychological selection involves achieving harmony between individuals' preferential replication of flow-producing activities and cultural opportunities for action. In order for this harmonization to be adaptive, the activities selected must at the same time satisfy the individual and contribute to the replication of the culture's basic social values (Csikszentmihalyi & Massimini, 1985; Massimini & Delle Fave, 2000).

ESM provides researchers with some basic information relevant to the process of psychological selection and allows for the comparison of this information across cultures. It describes how attention is used, records the perceived ratio of challenges and skills, and documents how often individuals experience the state of order in consciousness that we call flow. Studies involving ESM have made cross-cultural comparisons of the frequency with which individuals experience flow, the conditions under which flow is most likely to occur, and the affective qualities that accompany flow. In a study examining comparable samples of U.S. and Italian high school students, Carli and colleagues (1988) found that the distributions of responses in each of the flow channels for Italian and U.S. students were very similar. The flow channels refer to particular relationships of challenges and skills characterized as flow, anxiety, boredom, apathy, and the like (see Chapter 7 for further description). For both Italian and U.S. adolescents, the greatest number of responses fell into the flow and apathy channels—each of them accounting for approximately 20 percent of adolescents' total responses, with no significant differences between the two groups.

While Carli and his colleagues found few cross-cultural differences in the distribution of responses in each of the flow channels, they did identify differences in the quality of U.S. and Italian adolescents' experience when in these channels. They examined a variety of affective and motivational states like happiness, alertness, excitement, and concentration in each of these channels and found that for Italian adolescents nearly all variables peaked in the flow channel: when challenges and skills were high and in balance, Italian adolescents reported the highest levels of affect (happy, cheerful, friendly, sociable), motivation (free, wish to be doing activity, satisfied), and activation or potency (alert, strong, active, involved, excited, open) (see Table 11.3). Among the U.S. adolescents studied, the activation variables peaked in the flow channel, but variables indicating affect and motivation peaked in the channel labeled "control," where one's skills are slightly higher than is necessary to deal with the challenges at hand (see Table 11.4). From the affective, motivational, and activational perspectives, Italian adolescents feel most positively when in flow, as is predicted by flow theory. U.S. teens, though, prefer more control and feel best when their skills are more than adequate for the challenges that face them. For Italian adolescents, the most negative subjective experience occurs in the apathy channel, when both challenges and skills are low. U.S. teens on the other hand, feel worst in the anxiety channel, where skills are low but challenges are high (see also Massimini, Csikszentmihalyi, & Carli, 1992).

Carli and colleagues also identified differences in the types of activities that are likely to produce flow among U.S. and Italian adolescents. For U.S. teens, studying is perceived as providing greater challenges than it is for Italians, and U.S. teens are much more likely to experience flow while studying than their Italian counterparts. When Italian adolescents study, they are more likely than U.S. teens to report a sense of control or boredom, rather than flow. These findings about the experience and contexts for flow present an interesting irony with regard to high school experiences in these two countries. It appears that the American high school has potential advantages in that it presents greater opportunities for flow, but that this potential advantage may not be realized because the flow conditions are perceived relatively less positively by adolescents in the United States. The Italian adolescents, who appear to experience flow conditions more positively, are not presented with as many opportunities for such positive experiences in their educational environment.

Studies of American Subcultures

While the research discussed thus far has involved cross-national comparisons of adolescents and adults, a number of comparative studies involve individuals with different racial, ethnic, or religious backgrounds who reside in the same country. In a comparative study of the phenomenology of work experiences of Hispanic and non-Hispanic White adolescents in the United States, Schmidt (1995) examined how "work" was defined and experienced by individuals in sixth, eighth, tenth, and twelfth grade who did not yet have much experience with the adult world of work. On the ESF, each time respondents reported the activity in which they were engaged, they were asked to indicate whether the activity they were doing was "more like work," "more like play," "like both work and play," or "like neither work nor play." Examining respondents' "work/play" responses in conjunction with the actual activities they reported provides a sense of how youth view work at this early age. Comparisons of Hispanic and non-Hispanic White

(Text continues on page 224)

Table 11.3 Average Z-Scores of Italian Adolescents in Each Channel

Channels	1	2	3	4	5	6	7	8	ANOVA	
Number of Subjects	45	47	41	45	44	46	45	42	F	p
Concentration	0.60***	0.56***	0.01	−0.36*	−0.44**	−0.46**	−0.02	0.41*	23.32	<.001
Ease of concentration	0.04	0.16	−0.13	0.23	0.15	−0.31*	−0.48**	−0.36*	7.65	<.001
Unselfconsciousness	0.01	0.20	0.23	0.25	−0.07	−0.07	−0.35*	−0.65***	9.33	<.001
Control of situation	0.19	0.44**	0.41*	0.30*	−0.05	−0.55***	−0.71***	−0.58****	29.03	<.001
Alert–drowsy	0.15	0.28	0.09	−0.01	−0.26	−0.38*	−0.05	0.07	5.98	<.001
Happy–sad	0.19	0.38*	0.26	0.10	0.00	−0.37*	−0.43**	−0.16	10.37	<.001
Cheerful–irritable	0.08	0.27	0.27	0.18	−0.08	−0.24	−0.28	−0.19	6.42	<.001
Strong–weak	0.15	0.35*	0.17	0.08	−0.25	−0.41**	−0.35*	−0.14	8.43	<.001
Friendly–angry	0.13	0.26	0.36*	0.10	−0.05	−0.23	−0.37*	−0.17	9.71	<.001
Active–passive	0.40**	0.45**	0.17	−0.12	−0.41**	−0.54***	−0.34*	0.21	17.04	<.001
Sociable–lonely	0.10	0.12	0.03	0.16	−0.18	−0.18	−0.26	0.06	2.67	<.001
Involved–detached	0.40**	0.42**	0.00	−0.14	−0.21	−0.42**	−0.23	0.45**	13.29	<.001
Creative–apathetic	0.27	0.52***	0.14	0.00	−0.37*	−0.45**	−0.30*	0.22	18.97	<.001
Free–constrained	0.14	0.45**	0.15	0.12	−0.11	−0.33*	−0.61***	−0.30	16.68	<.001
Excited–bored	0.36*	0.49**	−0.05	−0.09	−0.29	−0.47**	−0.25	0.19	14.68	<.001
Open–closed	0.25	0.32*	0.19	0.06	−0.28	−0.40**	−0.35*	−0.07	10.00	<.001

Channels	1	2	3	4	5	6	7	8	ANOVA	
									F	p
Number of Subjects	45	47	41	45	44	46	45	42		
Clear–confused	0.20	0.53***	0.24	0.13	−0.15	−0.37*	−0.57***	−0.30	17.12	<.001
Relaxed–anxious	0.04	0.25	0.34*	0.28	0.08	−0.23	−0.33*	−0.44**	12.19	<.001
Wish doing the activity	0.36*	0.53***	0.02	0.02	−0.27	−0.47**	−0.42**	−0.10	15.98	<.001
Something at stake in activity	0.79***	0.47**	−0.01	−0.67***	−0.46**	−0.55***	0.29	0.56***	43.45	<.001
Time speed[a]	−0.31*	−0.26	0.08	0.03	0.29	0.28	0.09	−0.43**	9.54	<.001
Satisfaction	0.39*	0.73***	0.30	0.07	−0.31*	−0.63***	−0.50***	−0.25	36.97	<.001
W.B.S.E.[b]	−0.31*	−0.33*	−0.02	0.02	0.22	0.30*	0.23	0.05	7.50	<.001
Number of reports	200	354	112	279	152	330	133	122		

SOURCE: Csikszentmihalyi and Csikszentmihalyi, *Optimal experience: Psychological studies of flow in consciousness*, 1988. Copyright © 1988. Reprinted with the permission of Cambridge University Press.

NOTES: * $p < .05$; ** $p < .01$; *** $p < .001$.

1 = Arousal. 2 = Flow. 3 = Control. 4 = Relaxation. 5 = Boredom. 6 = Apathy. 7 = Worry. 8 = Anxiety.

a. Time speed: negative values mean that time is perceived to go faster.

b. W.B.S.E.: wish to be somewhere else, negative values mean the absence of the wish to be somewhere else.

Table 11.4   Average Z-Scores of American Adolescents in Each Channel

Channels	1	2	3	4	5	6	7	8	ANOVA	
Number of Subjects	76	77	61	73	60	78	63	63	F	p
Concentration	0.55***	0.43***	0.16	-0.23*	-0.39*	-0.45***	-0.17	-0.22	33.78	<.001
Ease of concentration	-0.30**	-0.18	0.09	0.19	0.03	0.20	-0.17	-0.49***	9.85	<.001
Unselfconsciousness	-0.20	-0.18	0.04	0.13	0.08	0.14	0.008	-0.22	4.13	<.001
Control of situation	-0.08	0.14	0.24	0.08	-0.02	-0.13	-0.20	-0.09	3.76	<.001
Alert–drowsy	0.29*	0.29*	0.18	-0.26*	-0.18	-0.19	-0.05	0.01	12.07	<.001
Happy–sad	-0.06	0.12	0.31*	0.07	0.02	-0.03	-0.11	-0.14	4.01	<.001
Cheerful–irritable	-0.14	0.11	0.29*	0.01	-0.01	0.02	-0.06	-0.14	3.67	<.001
Strong–weak	0.15*	0.17	0.14	-0.07	-0.00	-0.08	-0.05	-0.08	2.51	0.015
Friendly–angry	-0.14	0.04	0.26*	0.11	-0.02	0.04	-0.12	-0.09	2.65	0.011
Active–passive	0.28*	0.31**	0.14	-0.11	-0.10	-0.18	0.01	0.03	6.29	<.001
Sociable–lonely	0.02	0.03	0.13	-0.04	0.01	-0.06	-0.009	-0.007	0.56	0.781
Involved–detached	0.25*	0.33	0.25*	-0.16	-0.19	-0.26*	-0.06	0.01	8.62	<.001

Channels	1	2	3	4	5	6	7	8	ANOVA	
									F	p
Number of Subjects	76	77	61	73	60	78	63	63		
Free–constrained	−0.25*	0.06	0.27*	0.25*	−0.001	0.06	−0.04	−0.30*	8.20	<.001
Excited–bored	0.01	0.20	0.13	0.03	−0.09	−0.05	−0.26*	−0.23	4.22	<.001
Open–closed	−0.08	0.15	0.15	−0.01	−0.15	−0.04	−0.07	−0.26*	2.85	0.006
Clear–confused	−0.32**	0.16	0.39**	0.11	0.04	0.02	−0.06	−0.50***	9.60	<.001
Wish doing the activity	−0.13	0.12	0.25	0.18	0.03	−0.01	−0.32*	−0.40**	9.59	<.001
Something at stake in activity	0.70***	0.53***	−0.06	−0.36**	−0.42**	−0.53***	0.03	0.52***	55.48	<.001
Time speed[a]	−0.008	−0.25	0.01	−0.03	−0.09	0.08	0.07	0.14	2.54	0.014
Satisfaction	−0.18	0.16	0.48**	0.14	−0.09	−0.03	−0.12	−0.37**	9.92	<.001

SOURCE: Csikszentmihalyi, M., & Csikszentmihalyi, I. S. (Eds.). (1988). *Optimal experience: Psychological studies of flow in consciousness.* Copyright © 1988. Reprinted with the permission of Cambridge University Press.

NOTES: * $p < .05$; ** $p < .01$; *** $p < .001$.

1 = Arousal. 2 = Flow. 3 = Control. 4 = Relaxation. 5 = Boredom. 6 = Apathy. 7 = Worry. 8 = Anxiety.

a. Time speed: negative values mean that time is perceived to go faster.

adolescents by grade revealed essentially no differences in the way Hispanic and non-Hispanic White adolescents define work and play. Further, it was clear that youth of both ethnicities had a relatively stable view of what constituted these types of activities as early as the sixth grade. Activities commonly defined by adolescents from both groups as "worklike" included schoolwork, chores and household tasks, and paid work, while "playlike" activities included leisure activities like playing games and listening to the radio. Focusing on those activities defined as "worklike," Schmidt examined the amount of time adolescents spent doing these activities and the way students felt while doing them. There was no significant difference in the amount of time Hispanic and non-Hispanic White adolescents invested in worklike activities: 28 percent of Hispanics' total responses were categorized as like work, while 29 percent of non-Hispanic Whites responses were similarly categorized. Despite the cross-ethnic similarities in the way work was defined and the amount of time invested in work, there were striking differences in the way Hispanics and non-Hispanic Whites felt when engaged in these worklike activities. When doing work, Hispanic adolescents felt greater levels of enjoyment, motivation, importance to them personally, and importance to their future compared to their non-Hispanic White peers. It appears that, at least at this early age, there is no evidence to support claims that low motivation or negative experiences in school or other early work environments are responsible for the historically low levels of educational and occupational attainment among Hispanics in the United States. Instead, this research suggests that cultural and socioeconomic differences in access to information about the adult world of work may be to blame. A job knowledge test administered to participants indicated that the Hispanic youth in this study were far less knowledgeable about the adult world of work in the United States compared to non-Hispanic Whites in the study.

In a series of articles, Kiyoshi Asakawa examined academic experiences, feelings of connectedness, and family socialization practices of Asian American and Caucasian American adolescents. In a comparative study of educational experiences and academic achievement behaviors, Asakawa and Csikszentmihalyi (1998) found that the Asian American and Caucasian American adolescents in the sample did not differ from one another with respect to the amount of time they spent studying (as measured by ESM) or with respect to their parents' or their own educational aspirations (indicated by responses to a questionnaire). However, when the quality of experience during those moments when adolescents were studying was examined, consistent differences between the two groups emerged. The analysis revealed that when studying, Asian American adolescents reported much more positive experiences than their Caucasian peers. When studying, Asian American students felt happier, enjoyed themselves more, felt better about themselves, and felt more in control than Caucasian students. What's more, Asian American students were much more likely than Caucasians to perceive studying as being simultaneously enjoyable and highly important to their future goals. The simultaneous perception of enjoyment and importance is thought to be a highly motivational state (see Csikszentmihalyi et al., 1993), and the authors argue that these factors might play an important role in promoting the educational success that is widely observed among Asian Americans.

This analysis is exemplary of the type of information provided by ESM that is simply not attainable using other methods. Because of the difficulty in obtaining the necessary data, few studies have examined differences in achievement as a function of one's subjective experience while doing academic work. Instead, the considerable body of research aimed at explaining Asian Americans' high academic attainment focuses on factors such as genetics (Lynn, 1977, 1982; Lynn & Dziobon, 1980), selective immigration (Hirschman & Wong, 1986), and most notably the social context of the family and peers (Chen & Stevenson, 1995; Dornbusch, Ritter, Leiderman, Roberts, & Fraleigh, 1987; Kitano, 1984; Steinberg, Dornbusch, & Brown, 1992; Sue & Okazaki, 1990; Vernon, 1982). By enabling researchers to assess students' cognitive, affective, and emotional states while engaged in academic work, ESM adds a new dimension to our understanding of academic attainment among students of different races and ethnicities.

ESM has also contributed to our understanding of the ways socialization practices may be linked to academic achievement. In a related examination of feelings of connectedness and internalization of values, Asakawa and Csikszentmihalyi (2000a) found that among Asian American adolescents, future importance was not only correlated with enjoyment, but also with other positive dimensions of experience such as happiness, positive feelings about self, and activation. Such was not the case for Caucasian adolescents. In other words, Asian American students' levels of happiness were more likely to increase if activities were perceived to be important to future goals, while Caucasian American students' happiness did not appear to be linked in any way to the future importance of the activity they were engaging in. The authors conclude that these cultural differences in experiential covariation suggest that Asian American adolescents have more strongly internalized cultural values of hard work and high expectations for achievement.

Feelings of connectedness were examined by comparing how adolescents from the two groups felt when they were alone and with others. Although both Asian American and Caucasian American adolescents clearly preferred being with other people to being alone, the difference between these two experiential states was far more dramatic for the Asian American adolescents than the Caucasian American teens. Asian American students felt much sadder than Caucasian American students when they were alone and felt much happier than Caucasian American students when they were with others. An interesting pattern emerged when self-consciousness in the "alone" and "not alone" conditions was examined. While Caucasian Americans felt more self-conscious in the presence of others than when they were alone, the reverse was true for Asian American students: Asian Americans felt more self-conscious when alone than when with others. A closer examination of the types of activities Asian and Caucasian American adolescents engaged in while alone reveals that Asian Americans' increased self-consciousness when alone persisted regardless of the activity they were engaged in at the time. These patterns in the data suggest that Asian American adolescents may have a greater sense of connectedness to others, as their quality of experience appears to be more strongly and more positively affected by the physical presence of others. In general, this study found greater feelings of connectedness and greater internalization of values of hard work among Asian American adolescents relative to their Caucasian peers.

Following up on this research, Asakawa (2001) more closely examined the family socialization practices that might account for the differences in internalization just described. He used ESM data in combination with survey data to examine the degree of support for autonomy parents gave their children, the degree of structure parents provided for their children, and the degree of competence adolescents felt when engaged in important tasks like schoolwork. Support for autonomy and provision of structure were measured using a variety of survey items asking about family decision making, discussion, and parental assistance regarding their students' academics. Perceived competence was measured by the ESM item indicating how "in control of the situation" students felt at any given moment. The analyses revealed that Asian American parents tended to provide their children with more autonomy when it came to their actual academic activities like doing homework and making decisions about courses. At the same time, compared to Caucasian parents, Asian American parents provided an environment that may be more structured for academic success by placing greater limitations on their children's activities and decision making in certain areas. Perhaps as a result of these practices, Asian American adolescents felt much greater levels of competence than their Caucasian American peers when studying, when engaged in activities they perceived to be worklike, and in activities they perceived as important to their future goals. Asakawa tested for the impact of these three factors (autonomy, structure, and competence) on Asian American and Caucasian American adolescents' grades (see Table 11.5). The

Table 11.5   Standardized Regression Coefficients From Multiple Regressions of
Adolescents' Self-Reported Grades on Background, Parent, and
Student Variables

Independent Variables	Asian Grades	White Grades
Background		
SCC	−0.045	−0.001
Intact family[a]	0.185	0.088*
Grade (age)	−0.081	−0.032
Gender[b]	−0.052	0.081*
Parent Variables		
Educational expectations	0.405**	−0.076
Involvement in school	0.550**	0.133*
Activities[c]		
Provision of autonomy[d]	0.774****	0.058
Provision of structure[d]	0.191	0.060
Student Variables		
Educational aspirations	0.345**	0.341****
Locus of control[e]	0.080	0.156****
Perceived competence[d]	0.270**	0.003
Adjusted R^2	0.498***	0.170****

SOURCE: Copyright © Asakawa, K. (2001). Family socialization practices and their effects on
the internalization of educational values for Asian and white American students, *Applied
Developmental Science, 5*, 184–194. Reprinted by permission of Lawrence Erlbaum
Associates.

NOTES: SCC = social class of community.

a. Intact family: Used as a dummy variable, where intact family (mother and father) equals 1,
otherwise equals 0.

b. Gender: Used as a dummy variable, where boys equal 1 and girls equal 2.

c. Involvement in school activities: attending school meetings, attending school events, and
volunteering at school.

d. Internalization factors.

e. Locus of control: The higher the score, the more control students feel they have.

* $p < 0.10$; ** $p < 0.05$; *** $p < 0.01$; **** $p < 0.001$.

provision of structure in the home was not predictive of grades for either the Asian American or the Caucasian American sample. For Asian American adolescents, both perceived competence while studying and parental provision of autonomy were positively associated with grades. Neither of these factors was significantly associated with grades among Caucasian American students. While parental support for autonomy and adolescents' perceived competence favorably impact Asian Americans' academic achievement, they have no effect on the achievement of Caucasian Americans. Further, as can be seen in Table 11.5, Caucasian American adolescents' academic aspirations had a positive impact on their grades, but the expectations of their parents showed no significant net effect. For Asian American students, both their own and their parents' expectations were positively associated with grades, suggesting that Asian American students are more greatly affected by their parents' attitudes. All of these findings serve as evidence of an underlying cultural framework among Asian Americans in which parental provision of autonomy, along with adolescents' deeper internalization of values of hard work and competence, work together to promote adolescents' school performance.

While one's racial and ethnic background can exert a significant influence on individuals' attitudes and behaviors, religion is another dimension of culture whose impact can be examined with ESM. In a study of two-parent families with adolescent children, Schmidt (2005) examined associations between several dimensions of religiosity on the one hand, and parents' and children's daily emotional well-being and time use on the other. She found no association between one's denominational affiliation (Jewish, Catholic, Protestant, or other) and emotional well-being or time use. There was no evidence to suggest that the particular set of religious beliefs one ascribes to had any impact on these factors. Regardless of denomination, however, the analyses revealed consistent associations between one's *level* of personal faith and the outcomes of interest. For example, mothers who considered themselves to be "somewhat" or "very religious" reported significantly higher levels of happiness, self-esteem, and caring toward others compared to mothers who were not religious. Similar results were found for teenagers, though the associations were not as robust. Turning to time use, the data revealed that mothers who were somewhat or very religious tended to spend greater amounts of time with their children than nonreligious mothers. Thus while differences in the practices and beliefs of various religious denominations do not seem to measurably impact emotional well-being or time spent together as family, it appears that the degree to which individuals have internalized these practices and beliefs into their self-identification as a "religious person" might. ESM provides some preliminary description of the ways that deeply held religious beliefs might impact individuals' daily lives.

12

Educational Applications

A good portion of ESM research to date has involved children and adolescents. Because school looms so large in the lives of youth, substantial research has been done exploring both the structure of classrooms as well as students' and teachers' subjective experience in them. How students feel when they are in the classroom has been compared with how they feel on the job or at home, and the quality of experience in classrooms while involved in different instructional practices (such as lecture vs. group activity) has also been documented. An advantage of using ESM to study classrooms is that the researcher is able to link variation in attention, interest, or challenge to specific instructional practices or conditions while avoiding the problems of having students attempt to recall their experiences over the course of an entire day or an entire class period.

ESM can be an even more powerful educational research tool when it is used in conjunction with other information about student performance, school characteristics, or the format of particular classes. One may examine, for instance, whether there are systematic differences in how academically successful students and those who are less successful feel while in the classroom. Some ESM studies also involve an observational component where researchers have the opportunity to assess in greater detail particular teaching styles or classroom characteristics and then link these observations to students' subjective reports. In this chapter we review the variety of ways ESM research has been used to better understand students' educational experiences.

Methodological Concerns and Variations

Because of the types of demands placed on individuals who participate in ESM studies, the method is not particularly suited to studying the educational experiences of very young students. In order to fully participate, a person must be able to read and write quickly and with little effort and must be responsible enough to keep track of a signaling device and, if necessary, a diary containing the ESFs and a pen or pencil for an entire week. If participants are still learning how to read or write, participation could be too burdensome and in the end yield data of questionable quality. Looking across the many studies of children and adolescents, the youngest children studied using ESM have typically been in the fifth or sixth grade. Our experience has been that children younger than this are overburdened by standard ESM procedures and would require drastic modifications to produce meaningful data. Mulligan and colleagues (2000) examined ESM data from a national sample of students to compare response rates of students in grades 6, 8, 10, and 12. They found few systematic relationships between age and response rate. They did find, however, that twelfth graders tended to respond to fewer signals compared to sixth, eighth, or tenth graders. Overall though, they concluded that the age of students did not introduce significant selection bias into the sample.

In order to obtain the best response rates possible, we have stressed in previous chapters the importance of forming a research alliance with participants—this is no less important in studies of middle or high school students. Students are often flattered that an adult is interested in hearing what they have to say, and potential participants are often enticed by the thought that what they tell us could make things "better" for students in the future. With research conducted in schools, we have found it very effective for researchers to be a presence in the schools during the week of ESM. Whenever a school allows it, we recommend that researchers make an effort to be in the school every day, and that they make themselves unobtrusively visible to students by walking through the halls during passing periods or visiting the cafeteria during lunchtime. Often the sight of a researcher who appears genuinely interested in the school environment is enough to encourage a student to continue participating in the study. Moreover, if staff make themselves available during the school day, students are much more likely to contact them if a technical problem arises with their signaling device or if they have questions about the study. If at all possible, it is advisable to identify a "home base" in the school (e.g., a counselor's office or a conference room) where students know they can drop by to find someone if they have any questions or concerns.

Educational studies have employed a number of variations on ESM procedures in order to best answer relevant questions. In a study of motivation in mathematics classes, Turner and colleagues (1998) employed ESM-type methodology to elicit students' evaluations of their experience of a single class. In this study, which involved fifth and sixth graders in seven different mathematics classes, participants were asked to fill out an ESF during the last five minutes of the class. Rather than indicating how they felt at the moment, they were asked to rate the cognitive, affective, and motivational dimensions of their experiences over the entire class period. This procedure was repeated in each classroom for a period of 4 to 5 days. Though this study did not use any signaling device and did not gather reports at random time periods, as is typical in ESM studies, it did employ a fairly standard ESF and gathered data from the same students on multiple occasions.

A second variation to the procedures in this study was that on the days that the ESFs were gathered, the mathematics classes were audiotaped and observed by trained researchers who provided detailed descriptions of instructional activities. In this way, the students' subjective experiences in the classroom could be linked to features of instruction of interest to the researchers. Adding this observational component could be particularly valuable to educational research where investigators want to understand students' experiences as they relate to specific activities, pedagogies, or other properties of classrooms that might not be easily identifiable by the students themselves.

Using a variation of Turner's method, Uekawa, Borman, and Lee (2005) conducted a study of high school students in which students in mathematics and science classes were signaled every 10 minutes over the course of a 40-minute class period. Within a given class period, participating students were divided into two groups: one group responded only to the first and third signals and the other group responded only to the second and fourth signals. This method allowed for frequent signaling during the period of interest while attempting to minimize the disruption of students. Each student responded to two signals per class period each day for one week, producing a total of ten responses. This study also included classroom observation during the signaling period as well as focus groups with students at the end of the study.

Another variant of experience sampling has been used by Crocker and colleagues in studies of college students (Crocker, Karpinski, Quinn, & Chase, 2003; Crocker, Sommers, & Luhtanen, 2002). These studies combined interval- and event-contingent sampling methods. Participants were asked to complete Internet questionnaires at regular intervals several times a week and whenever an event of interest occurred. For example, in one study, participants were asked to log on to the survey Web site and complete a questionnaire three times a week and on days when they received a grade in one of their courses for a period of three weeks (Crocker et al., 2003).

When conducting ESM research in schools, it is important to be aware of how often participants are likely to be in the same place at the same time. For example, in a study involving 25 students randomly selected from a large urban high school, it is unlikely that many participants will be in the same classroom at the time of a signal. On the other hand, another study may involve all (or almost all) students in a sixth-grade classroom. The likely locations of students at the time of the signals is important: While one or two students receiving a signal during class may go unnoticed by the teacher and other students, 15 or 20 signaling devices sounding simultaneously can be downright annoying. In situations where large groups of participants are likely to be together, several steps can be taken to minimize the annoyance of the method. First and foremost, teachers and other relevant school personnel should be warned ahead of time of the possibility of intrusion. In situations where the majority of a class will be signaled, it is advisable to seek the teachers' cooperation in pausing for a moment if possible to allow students to respond to the signal. To make sure that a "mass signaling" passes as quickly as possible, it is crucial for all signaling devices to be synchronized to *exactly* the same time. If the display time on watches, pagers, or PDAs are set even 15 seconds apart and several students are in the same room at the time of the signal, there could be relatively constant beeping in a classroom for several minutes. Further, it may be necessary to gently remind students to turn their watches or pagers off as soon as the first signal is heard. In one study we conducted involving 33 schools across the United States, the *only* complaint from school personnel we received about the intrusiveness of the beeping came from a sixth-grade teacher who charged that her students were not properly instructed to turn their signaling devices off, which resulted in long interruptions, rather than the brief ones she had agreed to. Most of the students in her class were participating in our study, so even though all watches were synchronized to beep at the same time, the result was a cacophony of electronic sounds that lasted, according to her, nearly a minute. Worried that we had neglected some important piece of ESM training with her students, we looked into the matter further. We discovered that this teacher was particularly unpopular among her students, and students conveniently "forgot" how to turn their watches off only during those times when they were in her class, leaving the watches to beep for the full 20 seconds before they shut themselves off automatically. Once we addressed this problem with the students, they attended to their watches immediately and the disturbance was minimized.

Time Use and the Structure of Classrooms

As we have discussed in previous chapters, in most ESM studies the signaling schedule is carefully designed to provide a random sample of participants' waking hours. When multiple participants report on their experiences at these random moments over the period of a week, the resulting data yields rough but fairly reliable estimates of the amount of time participants spend doing various activities. Because the volume of data thus produced is substantial and coding schemes for activities can be very detailed, it is possible to get both general and specific descriptions of time use. For example, Leone and Richards (1989) examined classwork and homework among early adolescents and estimated that students spent about 15.5 hours per week engaged in schoolwork and only 6 hours per week doing homework outside of class. Not surprisingly, they found that students who spent more time doing homework had higher achievement than students who studied less. The researchers also found that while most students did homework alone, those who tended to study with their parents had higher achievement as well.

Csikszentmihalyi and Larson (1984) examined adolescents' reports of their activities every time they were signaled in a school class. They found that during class, students were doing some form of academic activity about 78 percent of the time (see Figure 12.1). The remaining 22 percent of classroom reports were comprised of activities such as socializing, resting, or daydreaming. The most common activity in classes was individual seatwork or studying, which accounted for approximately one-quarter of all classroom activity. The second most common activity was listening to the teacher lecture, which accounted for approximately 18 percent of all class time. In this particular study, cooperative activities such as group work and discussion were relatively rare, together accounting for only about 10 percent of all class reports. In a study of adolescents conducted nearly two decades later, Csikszentmihalyi and colleagues found nearly identical results (Shernoff, Csikszentmihalyi, Schneider, & Steele-Shernoff, 2003; Shernoff, Knauth, & Makris, 2000). The similarity in the structure of classroom time between these studies is remarkable, particularly given the push in education over the past few decades to include more constructivist, collaborative activities in classrooms. The consistency over time in the structure of classroom activities suggests that while the rhetoric about how class should be conducted has changed, what happens in classrooms (at least in middle and high school classrooms) has not.

A similar resistance to change in educational practice is also evident in research by DiBianca (2000). In a unique study of high school mathematics and science classes, each time students were signaled they recorded on a checklist whether or not they were using various tools and materials at that moment. In spite of the recent push in education to promote "hands-on" learning in these subject areas, DiBianca found that in math classes students most often reported using only textbooks (44.6%), while in science classes

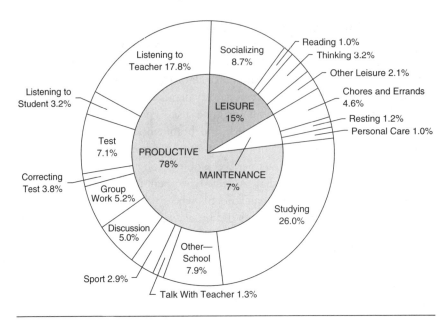

Figure 12.1   What Teenagers Do in Class

SOURCE: From *Being Adolescent: Conflict and Growth in the Teenage Years* by Mihaly Csikszentmihalyi. Copyright © 1984 by Basic Books, Inc. Reprinted by permission of Basic Books, a member of Perseus Books, L.L.C.

NOTE: *N* = 1,785 unweighted.

students most often reported using no materials at all (52.2%). The frequency and types of materials used in each subject area is reported in Table 12.1.

While lecture and individual seatwork still appear to dominate the American high school classroom, Shernoff and colleagues (2000) did find considerable variation in the types of instructional strategies used in different subject areas. They found, for example, that lecture is used far more often in history classes than it is in mathematics, science, or foreign language classes. Though lecture is still the dominant practice even in science classes, Shernoff and his colleagues found that group activities are used more frequently in science classes than any other classes (though still accounting for less than 10 percent of all class time). In contrast, only about 1 percent of students' time in history classes involves group work.

ESM has also been used to explore how participation in nonschool activities impacts the amount of time students spend on school-related activities. Schneider and Stevenson (1999) found that when students have paying jobs, their hours at the workplace appear to cut into the time they spend at school

Table 12.1   Percentage of Student Responses Indicating Use of Certain Tools and Materials[a]

Tool/Material	Math	Science
Textbook	44.6	21.3
Calculator	11.3	7.1
Other instruments/equipment	9.1	14.6
Computer	7.5	1.9
Manipulative	5.7	7.4
Measuring tool	2.9	6.3
Other tools	1.2	0.7
Materials used (total)[b]	60.3	47.8
No materials used	30.7	52.2
Total lessons	100.0	100.0

SOURCE: Copyright © 2000 by Richard P. DiBianca, *Teaching adolescents*. Reprinted with permission.

a. N = 5,238

b. Indicates the percentage of all lessons in which materials were used. It is not a sum of the percentages of lessons in which individual materials were used because some lessons featured the use of multiple tools and materials.

and doing homework. Among a national sample of high schoolers, they found that those who held jobs during the school year spent considerably less time at school than students who were not employed—averaging about an hour less per day. Teens who worked spent more time commuting than their nonemployed peers (about an hour and a half more per week) and spent about 15 minutes less per day doing homework. Thus ESM makes it possible to study whether participation in paid work or extracurricular activities takes away from school-related pursuits or whether they diminish the amount of time teenagers spend with family or friends.

The Quality of Students' Classroom Experiences

Beyond simply describing how students spend their time in classrooms, ESM can be used to understand how students feel across the various activities that make up their school days. Analyses involving person-level Z-scores make it possible to compare subjective experience in school to other contexts. Csikszentmihalyi and Larson (1984) found that compared to the other contexts in adolescents' lives, when they were in class they reported lower-than-average states on nearly every self-report dimension on the ESF (see Figure 12.2). They reported feeling generally sad, irritable, and bored. They found it difficult to concentrate, felt very constrained, and strongly wished to be doing something else. The single encouraging pattern in this profile of classroom experience was that adolescents reported relatively high levels of concentration compared to the other contexts of their lives. Thus it appears that in spite of all of the negative feelings students report from their classes, they are concentrating at least some of the time.

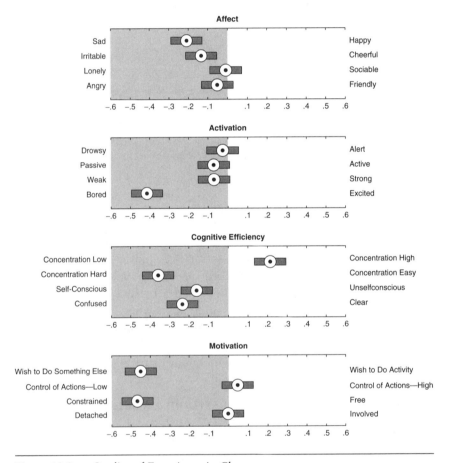

Figure 12.2   Quality of Experience in Class

SOURCE: From *Being Adolescent: Conflict and Growth in the Teenage Years* by Mihaly Csikszentmihalyi. Copyright © 1984 by Basic Books, Inc. Reprinted by permission of Basic Books, a member of Perseus Books, L.L.C.

In a study of middle school students, Larson and Richards (1991a) provide evidence that the boredom students report in school may be as much a function of their personality as a result of the tasks they are asked to complete in school. They conclude that while schools could certainly be structured to minimize students' boredom, a significant portion of students' boredom in school is attributable to dispositional traits rather than one's state. They explored boredom in and out of school and found that those who reported boredom in school were most likely to report boredom outside of school as well.

Of course, ESM is not the only method used to make the relatively unsurprising discovery that many students are bored in school. Studies using a variety of other methods have come to similar conclusions. In a study of student engagement, Steinberg, Brown, and Dornbusch (1996) reported that half of the students in their sample found their classes to be boring and a substantial proportion of students resorted to "goofing off" with their friends as a means of surviving the monotony each day. Boredom with school is not only apparent in academically unsuccessful students but in students of all achievement levels (Goodlad, 1984; Larson & Richards, 1991a). In recent years, however, a connection has been made between student engagement in school and learning and achievement (Christensen, Sinclair, Lahr, & Godber, 2001; Newmann, 1992; Steinberg, Dornbusch, & Brown, 1992).

Rather than comparing classroom experience to all other nonclassroom experiences, some researchers have made comparisons between school and other specific contexts. For example, Schneider and Stevenson (1999) compared the way high school students felt in class to they way they felt working in part-time jobs. They found that employed students reported greater levels of enjoyment at work than at school. They hypothesized that at work teenagers may feel more in control and less threatened than at school. School on the other hand may present more pressure to live up to parents' and others' high expectations. Because job-related expectations are often easier to meet, students may enjoy work more. When at school, however, students reported that their activities were far more important to their futures than what they did at work. Schneider and Stevenson argue that students feel school is more important than work because most teenagers plan to attend college (thus making high school important to their future) and because work available to teenagers seldom leads to meaningful adult employment.

Because of its repeated measures design, ESM is an ideal tool for understanding differences in student experiences as they relate to different subject matter, learning activities, or instructional formats. For the past several decades at least, researchers have recognized that student engagement and learning vary by activity and subject. In her book *The Subject Matters*, Susan

Stodolsky (1988) argues that what teachers are teaching and how they are teaching it will have profound effects on students' learning. One way that classroom activities have commonly been characterized is in terms of the degree of control students or teachers have over the activity. Whole-group instruction tends to be perceived by students as an activity where the teacher is primarily in control, whereas individual or small group instruction as advocated by constructivist approaches is perceived as being more student controlled (Marks, 2000). Research using a variety of methods suggests that students are often more engaged in student-controlled versus teacher-controlled learning activities (Grannis, 1978; Stodolsky, 1988). ESM has been used by a number of researchers to examine the way students feel when engaged in different learning activities and in different subject areas.

In a comparison of student experience in specific subject areas, Shernoff and his colleagues (2003) report that high school students generally feel more engaged in nonacademic subjects (i.e., computer science, art, and vocational education) than in academic subjects (i.e., English, science, mathematics). Overall, students reported that mathematics was the most challenging of all their courses, although it is the class where they reported the lowest levels of engagement. In fact, computer science is the only subject in which students reported both high levels of challenge and enjoyment. In a study in which only academic classes were considered, Yair (2000) found that students reported the highest rates of engagement in mathematics and natural science courses and the lowest rates of engagement in English, social sciences, reading, and foreign language courses. These findings contradict those of Shernoff, and this contradiction is particularly intriguing because both studies employ the same data set. The difference in findings between the Shernoff and Yair studies (that in math class Shernoff finds low engagement and Yair finds high engagement) is due to the way engagement was measured in the two studies. Shernoff and colleagues measured engagement using reports of concentration, interest, and enjoyment. In Yair's study, on the other hand, students were said to be engaged if their thoughts at a given moment were consistent with their reports of their physical location (e.g., a student reporting that he was thinking about simultaneous equations in math class was considered "engaged," while one who was thinking about last night's ball game was not). Shernoff, Schmidt, and Rushi (2006) examined the relationship between these two distinct measures of engagement using the same data set. They refer to Yair's measure as *attention* and find that momentary attentional focus is positively associated with their measure of engagement, though the two measures represent two distinct constructs. Measuring engagement is a complex task whether one is using ESM or any other instrument. In a recent review of the many ways engagement has been measured, Fredricks,

Blumenfeld, and Paris (2004) call for measures of engagement that are multidimensional and context dependent. ESM is an ideal tool for addressing these concerns in the field of research on engagement.

ESM has been used to assess subjective experience as a function of specific instructional methods, such as lecture, group activities, class discussion, or watching a video. Shernoff and his colleagues (2000) compared five of the most common in-class activities (TV/video, Lecture, Group work, Individual work, and Test/quiz) in terms of students' ratings of challenge, importance to future goals, concentration, and enjoyment (see Figure 12.3). The pattern revealed by these analyses suggests that students perceive their classroom activities as either enjoyable but easy and meaningless or as important but not enjoyable. Watching videos in class was rated as most enjoyable, but it was also rated as least challenging, least important to future goals, and requiring the lowest levels of concentration. Taking tests and quizzes, on the other hand, was rated as least enjoyable but most challenging, most important to future goals, and requiring the highest levels of concentration. Yair (2000) examined adolescents' engagement (defined as consistency of thoughts and physical location) when various instructional methods were used in classrooms. The highest rates of engagement were reported during laboratory work, group work, individual or group presentation, and discussions. Students were least likely to be engaged when listening to teachers' lectures and when watching television or video presentations. One of the more troubling findings to emerge from both of these studies concerns the relatively poor quality of students' experience when listening to teachers lecture. Listening to lecture—which accounts for a considerable proportion of all classroom time—is perceived to be unenjoyable, lacking in engagement, and requiring only minimal concentration.

In the research just described, the activity taking place in the classroom is reported by the students themselves, and one must rely on these subjective reports in order to categorize classroom activities. In most situations this is desirable—the whole purpose of the method is to understand those elements of daily life that are salient to the participant. Only the participant can accurately report whether her primary focus is "listening to lecture" or "daydreaming," or whether she is principally engaged in "taking notes" or "doodling." These are not distinctions that could be easily made by an outside observer. The strength of ESM is that all reports of the external dimensions of one's experience—one's activities, locations, and even companions—are filtered through the perceptual lens of the participant. This makes it possible to detect important differences in the quality of classroom experience as a function of whether or not particular students were truly focused on the activity at hand or whether they were daydreaming or making plans for the weekend.

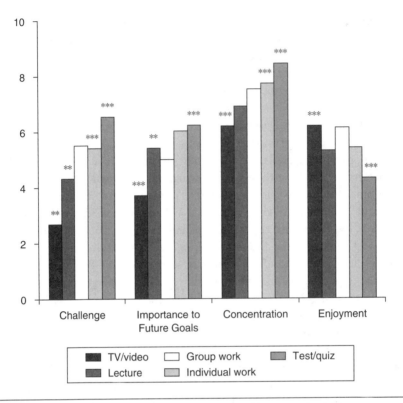

Figure 12.3   Quality of Experience in Common Classroom Activities

SOURCE: From *Becoming Adult* by Mihaly Csikszentmihalyi. Copyright © 2000 by Mihaly Csikszentmihalyi and Barbara Schneider. Reprinted by permission of Basic Books, a member of Perseus Books, L.L.C.

NOTES: * $p < .01$; *** $p < .001$. (Indicates contrast to the other activities combined.) An analysis of variance comparing mean ESM scores in the five selected classroom activities yielded the following results: for Challenge, $F = 84.77$, $p < .001$; for Importance to Future Goals, $F = 37.37$, $p < .001$; for Concentration, $F = 36.99$, $p < .001$; for Enjoyment, $F = 19.73$, $p < .001$.

In certain circumstances, however, a more "objective" description of what is going on in a classroom may be indicated in order to assess students' reactions to a given activity or instructional practice. In a study of fifth- and sixth-grade mathematics classrooms, Turner and colleagues (1998; Schweinle & Turner, 2006) sat in on multiple meetings of a given class and used a classroom observation instrument to record teachers' and students' demeanors, classroom activities, and features of classroom discourse. In addition, the researchers administered an ESM-type form during the last five minutes of each observed class to assess students' subjective experiences. This series of studies attempts to link students' lived experience to instructional patterns in their classrooms that would not typically be discernable from student reports of what they were doing. Turner and colleagues (1998) found that in certain classrooms involvement tended to be consistently higher than in others (indicated here by student ratings of challenges and skills being relatively high and in balance). The practices of teachers in these "high involvement classes" were then compared to practices of "low involvement teachers." Drawing upon the qualitative data gathered from observation, the researchers identified several differences in the instructional patterns of high- and low-involvement teachers. In those classes where students reported the highest levels of involvement, teachers were observed to provide more scaffolded instruction and more often used instructional practices that fostered intrinsic motivation. Teachers in the low-involvement classrooms tended to emphasize procedures (such as formatting assignments properly) more than content and used extrinsic motivation strategies such as the promise of rewards or punishment. This study demonstrates how student involvement and motivation may be linked to specific instructional practices in mathematics.

In a related study, Schweinle and Turner (2006) identified teacher practices that were related to students' reports of affect, efficacy, and challenge/importance. In mathematics classrooms where teachers provided extensive feedback, students' reports were higher on all three of these factors. They found teachers' use of humor and social support to be positively related to student affect, but not to efficacy or challenge/importance. This study in particular suggests that it is important to understand how certain practices operate in conjunction with one another to impact different dimensions of students' experiences.

Uekawa, Borman, and Lee (2005) combined ESM with observational data about a wide variety of features and practices in high school science and mathematics classes. Among other things, they explored how the structure of classrooms impacts student engagement (assessed using a combination of eight items on the ESF). Much to their surprise, they found that the physical seating arrangement in classrooms exerted the largest effect on engagement. In classrooms where students were seated in individual seats, engagement levels were substantially higher compared to classrooms where students were sitting with peers in clusters or around a table. Results also suggest that how seating arrangements were determined may impact engagement. In classrooms where students chose their seats, engagement was considerably lower than in classrooms where seating was assigned by the teacher. These results are important to teachers who often struggle with questions about how to best arrange classrooms to promote learning. An interesting caveat to these findings involves cultural differences in engagement as a function of seating arrangements. The data suggest that even though Hispanic students generally tended to have the lowest engagement levels and group seating generally produced lower engagement, when Hispanic students were placed in the more collaborative learning environments facilitated by group seating their engagement level soared. These results add to a growing body of research suggesting interactions between specific cultural approaches to learning and the pedagogical practices of teachers.

Up to this point, most of the research reviewed in this chapter has explored variation in students' feelings as they relate to external dimensions such as physical location or activity. Among the many contexts that have been studied are type of work (e.g., school work vs. paid work), course subject (e.g., math vs. English), instructional method (e.g., lecture vs. group discussion), and seating arrangement (e.g., individual vs. group). Another approach is to observe how ratings of affective states change with variations in *internal*, rather than external, dimensions. For example, Shernoff and colleagues (2003) examined engagement in high school classrooms from the perspective of flow theory. They defined engagement as high concentration, interest, and enjoyment, and sought to identify the conditions in which engagement in classrooms tended to be highest. They found classroom engagement to be highest when perceived challenges and skills were high and in balance, when instruction was personally relevant, and when students felt they were in control of the learning environment.

Schweinle and Turner (2006) studied the affective experience of students from the perspective of flow theory as well. Their study differs from that of Shernoff and colleagues in several important respects. First, the population was much younger—students were in the fifth and sixth grade, while Shernoff's sample was comprised of tenth and twelfth graders. Second, Schweinle's research focuses only on experience in mathematics classes while Shernoff's research examined student experience in multiple classes. Similar to Shernoff and colleagues and consistent with flow theory, Schweinle and Turner found that task relevance (called *task importance* or *value* in their research) is correlated with motivation. In contrast to flow theory however, they conclude that, at least among fifth and sixth graders in mathematics classes, challenge is perceived as a threat to students' self-efficacy and is not typically viewed as an opportunity to develop new skills. The authors speculate that children in fifth and sixth grade may have a different and more negative conception of "challenge" than older students. Perhaps to a fifth or sixth grader, "challenging" is equated with "difficult" because children at this age have not yet experienced the opportunities that optimal challenges can provide.

Comparing Students' Classroom Experiences

Until this point we have described the way different educational contexts can be compared to one another. Using the distinction made by Larson and Delespaul (1992) described in Chapter 3, these studies generally answer *questions about situations,* rather than about persons. Questions about situations are focused on comparisons made within individuals that examine different moments in time or different situations, such as how math class compares to history class, how lecture compares to class discussion, or how moments of engagement or involvement compare to less involving times. ESM can also be used to answer *questions about persons,* which involves making comparisons between groups of people who have different traits, who come from different backgrounds, or who spend their time in dramatically different ways. In educational research, questions about persons often involve comparisons of academically successful students with those who are less successful. For example, in their study of talented teenagers, Csikszentmihalyi, Rathunde, and Whalen (1993) were interested in identifying traits that distinguish talented students from their peers. They compared the daily patterns of activity and time use of talented and "average" teenagers in an attempt to "identify those daily habits that underlie the complex attentional structures that should lead to the cultivation of talent over time" (pp. 16–17). They obtained a sample of 208 ninth and tenth graders who were identified by their teachers or coaches as being particularly talented in mathematics, science, music, athletics, or art. Data from this sample were compared to data obtained from "average" students from a previous study involving students from the same school who were of the same age and approximate socioeconomic background.

In terms of time use, Csikszentmihalyi and colleagues found that talented students spent significantly more time engaged in classwork when they were in school but did not spend any more time studying outside of school than their average peers. It appears then, that the talented teens were able to work more efficiently both in and out of class. Talented teenagers spent less time working at paid jobs and less time socializing than average teenagers. In their free time, they spent more time involved in various structured activities related to art and hobbies compared to average students. Key differences in time use among talented and average teenagers are presented in Table 12.2. Talented and average teens also differed in their patterns of companionship. The talented adolescents spent more time alone and more time alone with their parents (without siblings present) than average teens. The two groups did not differ with respect to the amount of time spent with friends, though they did differ in the types of activities they did with their friends. Talented teenagers tended to study more, do more art and hobbies, do less socializing, and play fewer sports and games when in the company of their friends.

Not only did the talented and average groups differ in the way they spent their time, they also diverged with respect to how they experienced different

Table 12.2   Percentage of Time Teens Spent in Different Activities

Activity	Talented (N = 208)	Average (N = 41)
Productive		
Classwork	16.32	10.38***
Studying	12.19	10.90
Job	1.60	4.94**
Leisure		
Socializing	13.43	18.08**
Sports & games	2.70	3.96
Television	11.67	6.17***
Listening to music	1.70	1.76
Art & hobbies	4.25	1.22***
Reading	3.43	3.22
Thinking	3.51	2.52
Other	1.11	3.08***
Maintenance		
Eating	5.05	5.88
Personal care	7.06	7.18
Chores & errands	4.73	11.86***
Rest & napping	3.23	3.05
Others	3.15	2.19

SOURCE: Csikszentmihalyi, Rathunde, & Whalen, 1993. *Talented teenagers.* Copyright 1993. Reprinted with the permission of Cambridge University Press.

NOTES: These percentages are based on approximately 7,000 self-reports for the talented group and 1,500 for the average group. Significance of *t*-tests between the two groups: ** $p < .01$; *** $p < .001$.

aspects of daily life. Across all activities, talented teenagers had significantly lower moods than average students on a number of measures (e.g., happy, cheerful, alert, strong). This might be an indication that average students are simply less self-critical or that the pressure talented students feel may cause a generally more depressed mood. When Z-scores were used to examine the relative quality of experience in specific activities, the talented and average students' reports were more similar than different, but there were a few notable exceptions. First, the talented teenagers felt relatively happier and more cheerful in productive activities like classwork and studying. Their experience in these activities was not often positive, but was usually less negative than that of average students. In such productive activities, talented teens also reported much higher levels of concentration. They reported feeling significantly less unhappy and more motivated than average teenagers when they were alone, presumably because they were able to be more engaged in solitude than average students. While the experience of solitude is negative for most adolescents, the ability to make good use of time in solitude is an important asset, as it can be a time to develop skills and identify challenges. This research suggests that how one uses solitary time is an important factor in the development of talent.

To understand more fully how talent is developed and sustained, Csikszentmihalyi and his colleagues followed up on their talented sample two years after the original data collection. At this time they assessed students' commitment to their talent: Students who reported daily engagement in some activity related to their talent were categorized as committed. The researchers then examined the ESM reports of committed and uncommitted students obtained in the first data collection, two years prior. Such analyses are designed to identify the experiential predictors of commitment to a talent area. They found that compared to uncommitted students, committed students in math, science, music, and art felt more positive affect, greater potency, and greater intrinsic motivation while they were engaged in their talent. Committed students also more often described their talent-related activities as being simultaneously highly involving and highly important to their future goals. The uncommitted students in the arts reported that they were often highly involved in their talent-related activities, but these activities were perceived as unimportant to future goals. Students uncommitted in science and math showed the opposite pattern: two years earlier, when doing science or math they thought what they were doing was important but not enjoyable or involving.

Committed and uncommitted students were also compared in the relationship between perceived challenges and skills when they were doing activities related to their talent. According to flow theory, perceiving high skills and challenges are psychological preconditions for flow experiences. The researchers wanted to see whether committed and uncommitted students differed in the frequency with which the potential for a flow experience occurred in their area of talent. They found that committed students reported more often than uncommitted students that they felt high challenges and high skills in their talent activities (see Figure 12.4). Compared to committed students, uncommitted students felt more often that their talent-related activities were characterized by high levels of challenge but low levels of skill. The comparisons of committed and uncommitted students just described all point toward the same conclusion—in order for students to continue in a particular interest, it is important that activities related to that interest be engaging and personally relevant and that they provide opportunities to exercise skills in a challenging context.

There are, of course, characteristics other than academic success to define and compare groups of students in educational research. Most of the studies

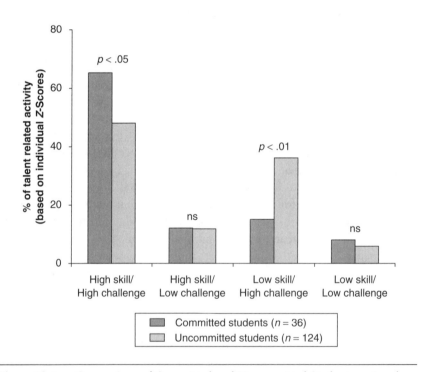

Figure 12.4   Comparison of Committed and Uncommitted Students on Levels of Skills and Challenges in Talent Work

SOURCE: Csikszentmihalyi, Rathunde, and Whalen, 1993. *Talented teenagers*. Copyright 1993. Reprinted with the permission of Cambridge University Press.

reviewed in this chapter explore how the findings vary by gender, race, ethnicity, or socioeconomic background. In some cases these factors are simply treated as statistical controls, while in other cases issues of gender, race, or socioeconomic resources are central to the research question. Looking across these studies, the findings regarding gender, race, ethnicity, and SES are too varied and complex to be adequately described, but some are taken up in the chapters regarding gender (Chapter 8) and culture (Chapter 11). As a method, ESM is capable of illuminating very subtle variations in the classroom experiences of students from different cultural backgrounds or with different resources available to them. To illustrate this, we present results from two studies of adolescent engagement. The first is Yair's (2000) study of adolescent engagement in which he identified "social differentials" in the effects of instruction on student engagement. While instructional strategies had independent effects on engagement (discussed earlier in this chapter), results indicated that Hispanic students were highly sensitive to variation in instructional strategies. Hispanic students reported extremely low rates of engagement when instruction was of low quality but became highly engaged when the quality of instruction was high (defined as challenging, academically demanding, and relevant). African American students, on the other hand, were least likely to respond to instructional variation: their rates of engagement were generally low regardless of whether the instruction was of high or low quality. Using a different measure of engagement, Shernoff and colleagues (2005) report ethnic variation in engagement that is contradictory to Yair's findings. Their research indicates that African American high school students experience high levels of school engagement relative to their peers, and that their engagement increases dramatically as their in-school activities become more focused on academic content.

ESM has also been used to illuminate subtle variations in the self-talk of students and their classroom behavior. In a study conducted by Manning (1990), a variation of ESM was used to analyze and relate teacher ratings of student behavior and the self-talk of children in grades two through five. The results of this study suggest that students rated "excellent" in classroom behavior by their classroom teachers used significantly less negative self-talk than did average and poorly rated students when working on independent assignments. Success in academics (IQ scores and academic achievement) was in fact more positively correlated with neutral, task relevant self-talk. Correlations were also found between students rated as poor in classroom behavior, low in IQ scores and academic achievement, and negative self-talk, which may negatively affect learner progress. Further research in this area may result in the development of new instructional strategies that lend themselves to more success-oriented learning environments.

Lisa Johnson (2004) used ESM to study engagement in the context of two very different American high schools. She compared the classroom experiences of students in an alternative public high school to a sample of comparable students in a traditional public high school. The alternative high school was structured to implement a democratic and egalitarian school philosophy that is presumed to facilitate student engagement in education. Students in the two samples differed substantially in both their time use in the classroom and their levels of engagement in academic activities. Students in the alternative school spent much more time involved in academic activities outside of the school's campus, and their classroom time was dominated by interactive instructional formats like discussion and debate. Students in the traditional school spent much more time in passive activities like lecture. While students in the two samples did not differ from one another in their average levels of engagement outside of school, the traditional school students generally reported lower academic engagement than students in the alternative school. Interestingly, students in the alternative school reported high levels of engagement even during those relatively rare occasions when they were being lectured to, suggesting that if used in the right context, lecture can be engaging for students.

Rathunde and Csikszentmihalyi conducted an ESM study in which they compared the experience of students in traditional public middle schools to students in a Montessori school. While students in each type of school did not differ from one another in their subjective experience of nonschool activities, several differences emerged in their experiences of school. Montessori students had greater affect, energy, intrinsic motivation, flow, and undivided interest (the combination of intrinsic motivation and importance) when participating in academic work at school. Relative to Montessori students, students in the traditional middle school reported that their schoolwork was of greater future importance, but these reports were also accompanied by low levels of intrinsic motivation. The authors argue that these differences are at least partly attributable to systematic differences in educational practices (Rathunde & Csikszenthmihalyi, 2005a). In an examination of the social environment in each of these school types, they found that Montessori students had more positive perceptions of their school environment, their teachers, and their classmates. These results might be reflective of different school organizational structures: Montessori students were more often engaged in collaborative work, individual work, and school-related tasks, while traditional students spent more school time on social and leisure activities and in more passive instructional formats like lecture (Rathunde & Csikszentmihalyi, 2005b).

After-School Programs

A small amount of ESM research has focused on the internal experience of students in after-school programs. Rather than signaling students across all activities, the research reviewed here only sampled activities that occurred after school. This line of inquiry focuses on student engagement in after-school programs and makes comparisons between the internal experience of students in these programs and their internal experience while engaged in other out-of-school activities, such as homework. Results indicate that early adolescents involved in school-based after-school programs reported higher levels of intrinsic motivation, positive affect, and concentrated effort during participation (Vandell, Shernoff, Pierce, Bolt, Dadisman, & Brown, 2005). When not participating in after-school programs, early adolescents who were enrolled in programs were more likely to report socializing with peers, while subjects who were not enrolled in after-school programs were more likely to spend time watching TV or eating in the afternoons. Students in the same study reported that unsupervised time doing homework and socializing with peers was characterized by low levels of intrinsic motivation and intensity when compared to organized activities with adults or when supervised with peers. These findings suggest that adult-supervised activities may better support positive youth development and contradict claims that programs emphasizing homework serve to promote higher academic achievement.

Studies of Adult Learners

The majority of ESM studies with educational implications have involved samples of children and adolescents. There are, however, a few in which the experience of adult learners was examined. In a follow-up to the Sloan Study of Youth and Social Development, Schneider (personal communication, 2003) recruited approximately 60 of the original participants (college age at the time of the follow-up) to again participate in the ESM. This study provides a rare look into the daily experiences of college students. Clearly, the pattern of habits laid down in middle and high school are still evident in young adulthood. Those who liked to study at age 14 are still the ones who devote much of their time to study. Such dimensions of experience as self-esteem, happiness, concentration, and so on are remarkably stable nine years later.

Jennifer Crocker and colleagues (2002, 2003) have studied contingencies of self-worth among college students using a variant of ESM in which participants answer daily questionnaires on the World Wide Web. In one study the researchers found self-worth to be contingent upon academic achievement among samples of engineering and psychology majors. More specifically, they found that self-esteem, affect, and one's identification with their major increased on days students received high grades and decreased on days students received low grades (Crocker, Karpinski, Quinn, & Chase, 2003). In another study, Crocker and colleagues (2002) studied college seniors applying to graduate school and charted students' self-worth as it fluctuated with acceptance and rejection from graduate programs. They found that some students' self-esteem was heavily based on academic competence while others' was not. Compared to students whose self-esteem was less contingent on academic competence, students whose self-esteem was more heavily based on academic competence had greater increases in self-esteem on days when they were accepted into graduate programs and had greater decreases in self-esteem on days when they received rejection letters.

In another study of adults, Hermanson (1996) studied self-directed learning among adult students. She found that adults typically define "learning" as those everyday experiences from which they get to better understand the personalities and motivations of other people or of themselves. Thus defined, a great deal of such learning is reported to take place every day and is one of the most enjoyable moments in people's lives.

ESM has great potential as a tool for understanding the experiences of adult learners. Very few ESM studies have examined the educational experiences of adult learners, and we view this as another area ripe for future research using the method.

The Experience of Teachers

While it is important for students to be involved in their own learning processes, the responsibility for learning does not fall entirely on the student. Teachers are important figures in a child's development and play a crucial role not only in what a child learns, but in how she feels about learning, how she approaches learning, and what types of goals she sets for herself in the future. To truly understand the educational process, it is just as important to consider the experience of teachers as that of learners. While there have been many ESM studies focused on students' experiences, only a few have focused on the experiences of teachers. In a unique study of high school mathematics and science classrooms, DiBianca (2000) signaled both students and teachers in classrooms. He found that teachers more often chose instructional formats in which they determined the pace of the class (e.g., lecture, demonstration, review of homework problems) over more interactive, student-paced instructional formats like computer work, lab activities, and student presentations. Moreover, teachers reported significantly higher levels of engagement when using instructional formats in which they determined the pace of class.

By contrast, students reported higher levels of engagement in more inter-active, challenging, student-paced instructional formats. Overall, DiBianca found that teacher engagement showed little impact in determining student engagement. While it appears logical that teachers might be more engaged when they are wholly responsible for creating and delivering a lesson, one might question teachers' choice of instructional format because what is engaging to teachers does not appear to be engaging to students. This research illuminates an all too frequent disjunction in classroom perceptions, where a teacher's comments indicate that "things were going well," while student comments reveal overwhelming boredom and disinterest.

In addition to studies conducted with teachers, some ESM research also recognizes the important role of the principal in school settings. Prior studies of the effective instructional leadership of principals have primarily been descriptive in nature and limited in generalizability. ESM has been used to refine the approach to this study of effective instructional leadership. In a study of 81 Chicago area principals, Scott, Ahadi, and Krug (1990) hypothe-sized that expert principals would be more likely to perceive their actions as global strategies rather than low level descriptive activities. Principals were beeped 25 times over the course of a typical week between the hours of 7:00 a.m. and 9:00 p.m. Rather than filling out the typical ESF, a Principal Activity Sampling Form (PASF) was designed that included questions about the prin-cipal's interpretation of their activities in terms of five empirically defined domains of instructional leadership. These domains include defining mission, managing curriculum, supervising teaching, monitoring student progress, and promoting school climate. This modified ESF was used in conjunction with an Instructional Leadership Inventory, which consists of 48 items that measure the aforementioned domains of instructional leadership. The findings of this study indicate that principals consistently participate in similar activities regardless of their levels of leadership effectiveness. How these individuals dif-fer lies in the way they ascribe meaning to these activities. For example, an effective principal is more likely to view a task such as monitoring the lunch-room as an opportunity to promote instructional climate. An ineffective prin-cipal may simply view this activity as "monitoring the lunchroom" or as a distraction from more important activities. Therefore, it appears that more effective instructional leaders use these activities to implement global strategies or higher-level goals such as "creating excitement about teaching or learning." This research illustrates the power of ESM to detect how global approaches rather than concrete behaviors define effective instructional leadership.

13

Clinical Applications

A s demonstrated throughout the contents of this book, ESM research has been particularly useful in providing rich information on normal developmental processes and stages, everyday life, and optimal experiences such as flow. Thus it might come as some surprise that the method has also been employed in an increasingly diverse array of studies attempting to describe, prevent, and treat pain and psychopathology. Disorders as diverse as heroin abuse, schizophrenia, eating disorders, arthritis, depression, and panic attacks have been illuminated with ESM research. In contrast to standard clinical interviews or one-time rating scales, ESM offers a number of advantages, not the least of which is that it can function as both an assessment tool and an integral component of therapy. What makes ESM data so valuable to the clinician is their ability to show the particular contexts and conditions under which a client's symptoms wax and wane. Often, patterns arise relating to time of day or social context or activities, and these patterns give clues both to the function of the disorder in the client's life and potential strategies to alleviate the problems. Clinical applications of ESM take the client's subjective experience, whether of pain or sadness or disordered thinking, as the bottom-line outcome, regardless of whether biological, neurochemical, or environmental factors play major causal roles. As in all ESM applications, the assessment of this experience is nearly instantaneous and is less susceptible to the pitfalls of recall and memory reconstruction, which may be particularly problematic in clinical populations. The studies reviewed here all illustrate one or more of these advantages of ESM for describing the lives of those with clinical disorders, designing treatments for them, and evaluating their progress.

Methodological Concerns and Variations

An obvious first concern to anyone familiar with standard ESM protocols is how the demands of the method will be met by the participants. Even in normative samples of adults and adolescents there are always some who are reluctant or unable to report repeatedly on their momentary experiences. It would only be reasonable to expect that individuals experiencing a debilitating problem would have an even greater rate of noncompliance or refusal to participate. Yet unacceptably low or erratic response rates have been the exception rather than the rule in ESM research using clinical samples, largely because of the great care that clinical ESM researchers have taken in forming a strong research alliance with the participants. An example of the problems that can arise when that alliance is not strong and when ongoing monitoring and support of participants is inadequate was provided by Litt, Cooney, and Morse (1998), who studied 27 alcoholics just released from inpatient treatment. They found that of the 11 participants who admitted to drinking during the 3-week study period, 5 of them stopped responding to their ESM signals for 1 to 3 days after a drinking episode, perhaps due to inability to respond or to shame or embarrassment. Additionally, 14 admitted noting the correct time upon hearing a signal but then delaying the rest of their ESM responses by anywhere from 5 minutes to several hours. Kaplan (1992), who studied heroin addicts, also reported that ESM responses were lost in some cases for a whole day due to participants landing in jail or bartering the signal watches to drug dealers. Nevertheless, a signal response rate of 63 percent was achieved among the 20 participants in that study. Working with depressed or physically ill elderly patients, Wilson, Hopkins, deVries, and Copeland (1992) found the participants to be receptive and enthusiastic to ESM, but hindered mainly by their physical or cognitive limitations. The levels of compliance in these studies and the ones reviewed next are comparable to those obtained in studies of normative populations. By building a strong alliance with participants, which includes careful briefing and monitoring, researchers have collected valid ESM data from individuals with diminished motivation (from depression), grasp of reality (from schizophrenia), attention span (from ADHD), or willingness to divulge behavioral details (from any stigmatized disorder).

Another concern unique to clinical studies is the measurement of physiological parameters that may be associated with the particular disorder under study. Researchers have addressed this issue by combining a typical ESM protocol with ambulatory assessment of applicable physiological processes, usually by using a portable medical device or by having participants collect samples of body fluids. For example, readings on heart rate, blood pressure, and level of cortisol (a stress hormone) in saliva have been collected in conjunction with each ESM signal. More information on ambulatory assessment of physiological parameters can be found in the volumes on this topic edited by Fahrenberg and Myrtek (1996, 2001). Because the addition of these types of measures stretches ESM beyond the measurement of subjective experience, Stone and Shiffman (1994) introduced a new term, Ecological Momentary Assessment (EMA), to apply to any method that captures momentary phenomena occurring in an individual's life processes. EMA studies often make use of palmtop computers that allow the automatic time-stamping of each response but severely limit the use of open-ended questions (Shiffman, 2000). Many recent clinical studies now refer to any repeated sampling method as EMA rather than as ESM, and the term "EMA" has been used to label methods that do not employ any ambulatory physiological assessment (i.e., traditional ESM). To avoid confusion, we will continue using "ESM" throughout this chapter, although the authors of many of the studies reviewed here had originally referred to their method as "EMA."

Taking what could be construed as an opposite approach from the quantitative focus of EMA, Hurlburt (1990, 1993) has used a "descriptive experience sampling" (DES) method to describe with great detail the inner experience of persons suffering from schizophrenia, bulimia, depression, and anxiety disorders. In this method, participants are signaled at roughly 30-minute intervals and respond to each signal simply by writing in a notebook a description of their inner experience. There are no questions to be answered, other than the general instruction to record inner experience. After completing six to eight descriptions over three to four hours, participants take a break from sampling but meet with a clinical interviewer the next day. During the conversation, the details of each moment are reconstructed. Upon completing four to eight such cycles of sampling and interviewing, the interviewer writes a comprehensive account of the participant's experience, identifying salient characteristics that seem to cohere. Finally, the participant's reactions to this account—comments, criticisms, suggestions—are integrated into the final case study.

Use of ESM for Describing and Contextualizing Experiences of Disorder

The first step toward prevention and treatment of a problem is to thoroughly understand the problem and the contexts in which it occurs. The studies summarized here all exemplify the unique contribution of ESM to clinical research in that variations in symptoms are able to be linked to particular social and physical contexts. Further, the subjective, first-person experience of those afflicted by disorder is captured, rather than only observable behaviors. An invaluable resource for those interested in clinical applications of ESM (and a common source for several of the studies mentioned next) is the book edited by Marten deVries (1992), *The Experience of Psychopathology.*

Stress and Coping

ESM studies have been useful in documenting the antecedents, physiological correlates, and the consequences of stress, as well as the effectiveness of different coping styles. Developmental change in the sources of stress was documented by Larson and Asmussen (1991), who found that the focus of emotional trauma shifted from concrete, immediate activities in late childhood to the more abstract social realm in early adolescence. Adolescent concerns centered more on the feelings of others, especially others of the opposite sex, and anticipated future social events.

Among a sample of middle-aged, white-collar, male workers, van Eck and Nicolson (1994) reported that more stressful events occurred on workdays than on weekends, and highly stressed participants were disproportionately more negatively aroused on workdays. Participants also collected salivary cortisol samples at each signal (ten times a day). Highly stressed workers showed consistently elevated cortisol levels throughout the workday. Smyth and colleagues (1998) also found a link between cortisol and stress; the cortisol levels of their participants increased both during the experience of stress and in anticipation of stress. Negative affect was associated with higher cortisol levels. Adam (2005) replicated the link between elevated cortisol and negative emotion, adding the finding that higher levels of positive-social emotions and hardworking-productive experiences are linked to lower levels of cortisol. Parents in her study had higher levels of cortisol at home than at work.

Daily stress is linked to health consequences that are much more serious than negative moods. Sorbi, Honkoop, and Godaert (1996) signaled migraine sufferers six times a day for ten weeks. Daily hassles were reported twice as often during the two days prior to a migraine as during other days. In addition, the participants rated the stressfulness of each hassle significantly higher during premigraine days than during other days. Two days prior to an attack, participants experienced increased vigilance and arousal, followed on the day preceding the attack by a loss of alertness and energy. The discovery of this sequence of events beautifully illustrates the value of ESM in providing data not obtainable through any other means.

ESM research has also contributed unique insights into the prevalence and effectiveness of different coping styles. Stone and colleagues (1998) reported that compared to ESM data, short-term retrospective recall questionnaires result in the underreporting of cognitive coping strategies and the overreporting of behavioral approaches. Other ESM research has shown some consistency within individuals in preferred coping styles, but dispositions to cope in a certain style are not measured well by one-time self-report assessments, which show very poor correlations with momentary coping (Schwartz, Neale, Marco, Shiffman, & Stone, 1999). The difference that more sophisticated coping styles can make is exemplified in a study comparing beginning and advanced Buddhist meditators. Easterlin and Cardena (1998–1999) concluded that although stress lowered affect and feelings of acceptance in both groups, the magnitude of this effect was considerably lower in the advanced group, who also showed greater self-awareness and positive moods. Similarly, Brown and Ryan (2003) showed that the trait of mindfulness ("being attentive to and aware of what is taking place in the present," p. 822) predicted ESM reports of greater autonomy and lower levels of unpleasant emotions. The state of mindfulness (measured in the moment), but not the trait, was related to greater positive emotions.

Nicolson's (1992) study of university students, medical students, and candidates for a driver's license yielded more specific conclusions on coping. All of the participants underwent an examination during their signaling period, and all three groups showed elevated stress and cortisol levels before the exam. Participants who saw the impending exam as a threat had higher pre-exam cortisol levels than those who were confident or who saw the exam as a challenge. Those using a problem-oriented coping style experienced a faster postexam reduction in cortisol than those using distraction or emotion-focused styles.

Eating Disorders

Although ESM research on eating disorders began as early as 1981, there seems to have been a long lull until new studies began to appear in the late 1990s. By now, ESM research in this area shows no sign of abating; an article in a 2001 issue of the *International Journal of Eating Disorders* enthusiastically endorsed the use of ESM for the study of eating disorders and called on more researchers to adopt the method (Smyth, Ockenfels, Porter, Kirschbaum, Hellhammer, & Stone, 2001). To date, the most valuable information obtained about eating disorders through ESM research has been the link between disordered eating patterns and social context. Larson and Johnson (1981) found in a case study of two anorexic women that they were more often alone than other women. These women were also more preoccupied with food, and their moods were tied to their sense of control. The connection between healthy social relationships and healthy eating patterns may begin in the family. In a study of 240 fifth- through ninth-grade girls, Swarr and Richards (1996) noted that those who spent more time with their parents and had more positive interactions with them had healthier eating behaviors and fewer eating concerns.

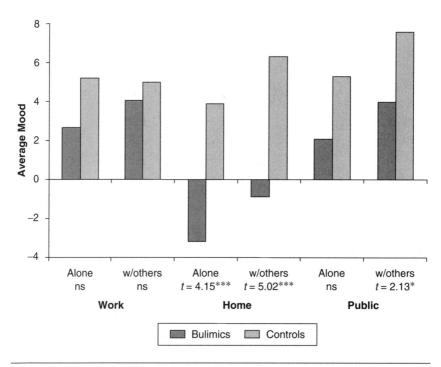

Figure 13.1   Comparison of Average Mood States Between Bulimics and
Controls in Different Contexts

SOURCE: deVries, *The experience of psychopathology,* 1992. Copyright © 1992. Reprinted
with the permission of Cambridge University Press.

NOTES: Raw mood scores are displayed. Positive values indicate positive moods; negative
values indicate negative moods.

The value of positive relationships with other people and the danger
of social isolation can be seen in virtually every ESM eating disorder study,
regardless of the specific disorder. Le Grange, Garin, Catley, and Stone (2001)
compared overweight women with binge eating disorder (BED) to other overweight women and found that the BED women were less likely to report
spending time with friends. Stress was a significant antecedent to binge eating
in the BED group but not in the comparison group. Unfortunately, however,
binge eating does not relieve these individuals of their negative moods, which
remain just as negative or worse after a binge as before (Wegner, Smyth,
Crosby, Wittrock, Wonderlick, & Mitchell, 2002).

Similar results pertaining to social context were found for women with
bulimia (Johnson & Larson, 1982; Larson & Asmussen, 1992; Larson &
Johnson, 1985). Bulimic women were alone 49 percent of the time versus 32

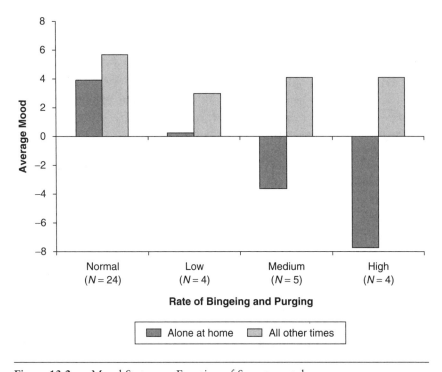

Figure 13.2   Mood State as a Function of Symptomatology

SOURCE: deVries, *The experience of psychopathology*, 1992. Copyright © 1992. Reprinted with the permission of Cambridge University Press.

percent for a normal comparison sample. Moreover, they experienced both their most negative moods and the highest number of binge-purge episodes while they were alone at home. These women reported feeling more guilt, shame, ugliness, and confusion while alone at home than while in any other context. Figure 13.1 illustrates how these negative moods were concentrated almost exclusively in the "home alone" context. In Figure 13.2 we see that the severity of bulimia is strongly correlated with how one feels in this single context but is not related to how one feels in all the other contexts of life. As Larson and Asmussen (1992) conclude, it appears that the fundamental problem of persons afflicted with bulimia is an inability to self-regulate when alone. This would also explain why bulimia is often a hidden disorder—when with others, people with bulimia behave and feel as other people do. It is worth noting once again that these conclusions could not have been reached without ESM and its ability to capture an individual's experience across the multiple contexts of daily life.

Alcohol, Tobacco, and Other Drug Use

The first conclusion to note regarding ESM research on the use and abuse of substances is simply that participants are willing to report on their experiences with alcohol, tobacco, and other drugs. As with any other self-report method on sensitive or illegal activities, some people will fail to comply. However, as previously noted, researchers have still been able to collect useful data despite the difficult subject matter. In one recent study, participants used cell phones provided by the researchers to call in to a computer system using the phone keypad to respond to multiple-choice questions about their alcohol consumption (Collins, Kashdan, & Gollnisch, 2003). This method showed no differences from a paper-and-pencil method in participant compliance, but compliance was more easily verified in the phone method.

Most ESM studies in this area have concentrated on cataloging the contexts of substance-use episodes, and a few have also focused on the internal experience of being under the influence of substances. In one study that covered both bases, Larson, Csikszentmihalyi, and Freeman (1992) reported that adolescent alcohol use occurred almost exclusively on weekends during the evening, whereas marijuana use occurred with similar frequency across all parts of the week and times of the day. When these teens smoked marijuana, they were usually alone or with just one other companion, and they were usually at home, in a car, or outdoors. By contrast, alcohol use was greatest when the adolescents were at a friend's house and with a large group of peers. As shown in Table 13.1, alcohol use was accompanied by relatively positive moods; participants reported being especially excited, free, open, and sociable, and significantly above average in several other positive dimensions. Negative effects of alcohol were seen in the below average ratings of control and concentration. Marijuana use was not accompanied by such extreme deviations in emotional state from the average. Like alcohol, marijuana was related to feelings of being free and open, but otherwise it was neutral with respect to emotional state. Motivation to smoke pot was high, however, as indicated by the significantly negative score on wishing to be doing something else.

Studies of adults have replicated the adolescent findings on the social nature of alcohol consumption. Adults drink more on weekends, after 8:00 p.m. on any days, and in the company of family and/or friends (Collins, Morsheimer, Shiffman, Paty, Gnys, & Papandonatos, 1998; Shiffman, Fischer, Paty, Gnys, Hickcox, & Kassel, 1994). Because of the convivial atmosphere surrounding alcohol consumption, ESM participants report greater arousal while drinking. The alcohol per se does not cause this experience, for alcohol is a sedative. Rather, Shiffman and colleagues (1994) showed that the

Table 13.1   Alcohol and Marijuana Use:
Reported State When Drug Use Was Reported[a]

| | Mean Z-Score | | |
| | Alcohol | Marijuana | Both |
Self-Report Item	(N = 25)	(N = 19)	(N = 4)
Mood items			
Affect	0.61***	0.37	1.09
happy (vs. sad)	0.52**	0.19	1.22**
cheerful (vs. irritable)	0.56**	0.09	1.13**
friendly (vs. lonely)	0.76**	0.29	1.30**
Activation			
alert (vs. drowsy)	0.01	−0.38	0.08
strong (vs. weak)	0.22	−0.27	0.40
active (vs. passive)	0.42*	−0.20	0.05
Other			
involved (vs. detached)	0.56**	0.20	0.52
excited (vs. bored)	0.91***	0.57*	1.46**
free (vs. constrained)	0.71**	0.55**	0.73
open (vs. closed)	0.70**	0.27	0.57
clear (vs. confused)	−0.06	−0.40	0.21
Cognitive and motivational states			
Cognitive			
concentration	−0.45*	0.34	0.15
ease of concentration	0.03	−0.29	−0.75
self-consciousness	−0.26	−0.16	0.43
Motivational			
control of actions	−0.87**	−0.76**	−1.61*
Do you wish you were doing something else?	−0.40*	−0.64**	−0.96
Social interaction			
Is talking/joking (vs. serious)?	0.79**	0.27	−0.49

(Continued)

Table 13.1 (Continued)

| | Mean Z-Score | | |
| | Alcohol | Marijuana | Both |
Self-Report Item	(N = 25)	(N = 19)	(N = 4)
Are the goals of others the same as yours (vs. different)?	0.18	0.47*	0.32
Do you expect to receive positive feedback (vs. negative feedback)?	0.44**	0.32	0.50

SOURCE: deVries, *The experience of psychopathology*, 1992. Copyright © 1992. Reprinted with the permission of Cambridge University Press.

a. Significance tests of deviation from zero: * $p < 0.05$; ** $p < 0.01$; *** $p < 0.001$.

arousal is entirely accounted for by situational factors. Alcohol and moods appear to be reciprocally related in a complex way. Moderate to heavy drinkers have a greater tendency to drink to excess when they are in a positive mood before they start drinking, but heavier drinking is related to a decline in positive moods by the end of the drinking episode (Collins et al., 1998). Adults also tend to drink when they are nervous, and they feel less nervous after drinking (Swendsen, Tennen, Carney, Affleck, Willard, & Hromi, 2000). This finding supports the idea that people use alcohol to self-medicate when they experience anxiety. The consumption of alcohol is also frequently accompanied by smoking cigarettes, and the association between smoking and drinking is even stronger among heavy drinkers (Shiffman et al., 1994).

In adolescence it appears that both smoking and drinking are associated with attention deficit hyperactivity disorder (ADHD). Whalen, Jamner, Henker, Delfino, and Lozano (2002) found that ninth graders with many ADHD symptoms were 10 times more likely to have smoked and 4 times more likely to have drunk alcohol than their peers with few or no symptoms. Teens with more ADHD symptoms also drank more soda and less water, juice, or milk. They spent less time reading and writing and more time talking or engaged in entertaining activities. They reported being with friends more often and with their family less often. Compared to those with few or no ADHD symptoms, these 14-year-olds with ADHD were 1.5 to 2 times more likely to indicate feeling anxious, sad, angry, and stressed, and half as likely to report happiness or positive well-being. Given this emotional profile, it is plausible that ADHD youth are self-medicating with alcohol and tobacco.

An association between low moods and craving a drug was found in Kaplan's (1992) study of heroin addicts. When addicts' moods were below average, they felt restless and less in control of themselves, and they thought more about obtaining heroin and the money to buy it. Craving was most intense when they were alone or with two or more others; it was weakest when they were with one other companion. The home setting appeared to offer some respite from craving. Participants felt more in control and thought less about acquiring drugs or money while they were at home than while in other more public settings. It is interesting to note the similarities and differences between these findings and those pertaining to bulimia. In both cases, being alone is related to negative outcomes, but the consequences of being at home are negative for bulimic women and positive for heroin addicts. Perhaps heroin abuse is rooted more in anxiety, which increases while out in public, whereas bulimia is linked more to depressed moods, which surface more while at home.

ESM techniques have also been used to study the process of coping with withdrawal from substance use. O'Connell and colleagues (1998) studied smokers enrolled in a smoking cessation program. In a unique methodological combination, each participant entered closed-ended responses into a palmtop computer and used a tape recorder to provide oral answers to open-ended questions about their coping strategies. The open-ended questions were used to avoid cueing the participants with a list of possible coping strategies. Participants were asked to respond both to random signals generated by the computer and after each incidence of successful coping and failed coping (i.e., smoking). Results showed that behavioral coping strategies such as distraction and breathing exercises were more frequently used than cognitive strategies. But there were also context-specific patterns for each strategy. Food and drink were more often used as substitutes for cigarettes while participants were at work. When they were outdoors, they more often avoided cigarettes by thinking of the negative health effects.

Depression and Anxiety

The common thread that is emerging in the clinical ESM research reviewed so far—that the who, what, and where of daily experience play a critical role in exacerbating, maintaining, or relieving symptoms—continues to weave through the ESM findings on clinical depression and anxiety. Merrick (1992) compared depressed, previously depressed, and normal control adolescents. As one would expect, the clinically depressed group experienced more moments of sadness, loneliness, and boredom, and fewer of pleasure. Not only did dysphoric moods occur with greater frequency in this group, they were also more intense, as indicated by higher mean ratings.

These group differences in moods persisted across all social settings, but there were also differences in the amount of time spent in each setting. The depressed group spent more time at home, alone, and watching TV, and less time engaged in productive activities, socializing, and in contact with peers of the opposite sex. Whereas the nondepressed teens spent much less time watching TV, reading, or thinking than they did socializing with peers, the depressed teens spent over twice as much time doing these three nonsocial activities as they did socializing with peers. Interestingly, mood variation across settings showed the same pattern across all three groups: all were least dysphoric when with friends and most dysphoric while alone. This finding clearly differentiates clinical depression, which is characterized by negative moods across all contexts, from bulimia, in which depressed moods occur exclusively while home alone.

Other researchers have used ESM to examine diurnal patterns of mood and the relationship of depression to how an individual attributes the cause of negative events. Swendsen (1997) showed the power of attributions to affect mood, even among college students with low scores on depression and anxiety inventories. When these students saw a negative event as due to a stable, global cause, they were more likely to feel depressed afterward. Rusting and Larsen (1998) found that as the day progressed, college students focused increasingly on causes for negative events that were more external, uncontrollable, stable, and global. These types of attributions were associated with more negative moods, but only in the evenings. Those students whose negative moods tended to peak in the evening also scored higher on global measures of neuroticism, anxiety, and mild depressive symptoms. It is possible that the more unstructured nature of evenings allows for more rumination about the cumulative hassles of the day.

Anxiety shares some similarities in contextual profile with depression and indeed sometimes occurs in conjunction with depression, but it also appears to have some unique features. A study of 11 highly anxious outpatients, all with some level of depression, revealed that they experienced more thought disorganization when they were with people than when they were alone (deVries, Delespaul, & Dijkman-Caes, 1992). While alone they were better able to align their thoughts with their current activities. The greater control they experience while alone may explain why anxiety sufferers tend to avoid social situations. Dijkman-Caes and deVries (1992) found that their sample of outpatients with various types of anxiety disorders were at home during 80 percent of their signals, which occurred 10 times a day from early morning to late evening for 6 days. However, only those with panic disorders spent most of this time alone. Patients with agoraphobia or other anxiety disorders spent more time with family than alone and virtually no time with friends or strangers. Depression appears to intensify some of the problems associated with anxiety disorders. Compared to anxiety patients with moderate depression, those with high levels of depression experienced more idle, unfocused thoughts, spent less time involved with others, and spent more time at home (deVries et al., 1992). After an anxiety-provoking event, depressed individuals took three times longer to return to their emotional baseline than nondepressed individuals.

Schizophrenia and Other Psychotic Disorders

In the study of psychotic disorders, ESM has been used to compare groups of people and situations within persons. Across several different studies, both types of analyses point to an unequivocal conclusion. Delusional thoughts are most likely when people are alone with nothing to do. By comparing delusional and nondelusional moments of a schizophrenic sample, Myin-Germeys, Nicolson, and Delespaul (2001) found that the presence of family or acquaintances decreased the likelihood of delusion, whereas a lack of engagement in any activities increased the likelihood. Compared to normal controls, the psychotic patients studied by Delespaul and deVries (1992) were more often home alone and doing nothing. While at home and while doing nothing, they showed less congruence between their current thoughts and activities, and their daydreaming increased compared to other situations. DeVries and Delespaul (1992) echoed the finding that the mental state of schizophrenic patients worsens when they are alone, but added that it is also fragile when they are in a crowd. The optimal mental state for these participants occurred when they were accompanied by one to three other persons. The problem is that the outpatients spent much more time alone than other people, while those who were institutionalized spent hardly any time alone but much more time in crowds.

The social environment appears to exert a greater effect on persons suffering from psychotic illnesses than on mentally healthy people. Delespaul and deVries (1992) first standardized ESM scores within persons, and then subtracted each person's mean scores while with others from their mean scores while alone. They take the absolute value of the resulting difference as an indication of reactivity to the social environment. These mean difference scores are shown in Table 13.2 for both a sample of chronic mental patients and age-matched normal controls. The first feature to note about this table is that most of the mean differences are meaningfully different from zero. This means that even in the general population, people have substantially different internal experiences while alone versus while not alone, a robust finding that Larson (1990) has explored in some depth. The table

Table 13.2   Daily Life of Chronic Mental Patients:
Group Differences in Reactivity to the Social Environment
(Absolute Differences Between Alone/Not Alone)

Variable	Chronics			Controls			Test
Description	x	SD	n	x	SD	n	
Thoughts	0.46	0.13	9	0.30	0.24	11	$t(18) = 1.74$ $p < 0.05$
Mood	0.53	0.44	9	0.09	0.07	11	$t(18) = 3.31$ $p < 0.005$
Psychopathology	0.37	0.34	9	0.15	0.27	9	$t(16) = 1.49$ n.s.
Activity-motivation	0.54	0.37	9	0.23	0.16	11	$t(18) = 2.30$ $p < 0.025$
Psychological complaint	0.46	0.46	9	0.24	0.24	11	$t(18) = 1.19$ n.s.
Somatic complaint	0.52	0.43	10	0.29	0.29	8	$t(16) = 1.35$ n.s.
Hunger	0.69	0.66	8	0.37	0.32	11	$t(17) = 1.41$ n.s.
Tired	0.75	0.78	10	0.47	0.32	11	$t(19) = 1.06$ n.s.
Not feeling well	0.35	0.46	9	0.42	0.54	8	$t(15) = -0.29$ n.s.

SOURCE: deVries, *The experience of psychopathology*, 1992. Copyright © 1992. Reprinted with the permission of Cambridge University Press.

NOTES: x = Mean; SD = Standard deviation.

also shows that on three variables, quality of thoughts (i.e., clear, pleasant), mood, and motivation, those with mental illness have a significantly stronger reaction to solitude than the comparison group.

Multiple personality disorder has also been the subject of an ESM study. A case study of 1 woman with 21 alternates showed that the differences in response patterns between alternates were as different as between separate persons (Loewenstein, Hamilton, Alagna, Reid, & deVries, 1992). Only seven alternates responded to the ESM signals, and three of those were the most frequent responders. Each alternate showed a characteristic response pattern of mood and motivation and an idiosyncratic style of marking the ESF.

Anger and Violence

Hillbrand and Waite (1992) used ESM to explore the experience of anger among psychiatric inpatients who had committed murder or other violent crimes. The participants indicated some degree of anger on 30 percent of the responses. Anger was more frequent during treatment and therapy activities, occurring 42 percent of the time during these sessions, but it was also markedly less severe during these sessions than during maintenance or leisure activities. The researchers concluded that treatment of these individuals involved mild anger arousal for the purpose of teaching anger management skills. Social context (whether with staff, alone, or other patients) and time of day showed no relationship to anger arousal. Interestingly, anger was just as likely to occur following a positive incident as after a neutral or negative incident, but when it followed a positive incident, it was much less severe.

Anger was also a common theme in the responses of a single violent hospitalized sex offender studied by Hillbrand and Waite (1994). The man completed 47 out of 48 ESFs, 17 percent of which indicated thoughts of a sexual nature and 38 percent of which included thoughts about a female. Many of the responses involving females also included an expression of anger and many of the other responses included indications of personal inadequacy and distress over interpersonal relations. His most positive ratings of inner experience came while looking at a female staff member and thinking "how gorgeous she is." His most negative ratings occurred while thinking "how much I hate therapy."

Blood Pressure

Although blood pressure is a key parameter of cardiovascular health, its measurement is often confounded by the "white coat effect," a tendency in many people to experience elevated blood pressure while in the doctor's office (Pickering, Coats, Mallion, Mancia, & Verdecchia, 1999). Besides the low ecological validity of the artificial clinical setting, the one-time measurement of blood pressure also does not capture its variability or its association with particular physical activities and emotional states. To address these shortcomings, several researchers have now combined ambulatory monitoring of blood pressure with ESM-style self-reports. Participants in these studies are fitted with a device that allows them to conduct their normal daily routine while measuring their blood pressure every 15 to 20 minutes throughout the course of one day. In conjunction with each measurement, participants are asked to complete an ESF. Using this design with 32 university employees, Van Egeren and Madarasmi (1992) found that the highest levels of blood pressure occurred during walking, driving, and drinking caffeinated beverages, and when participants reported feeling rushed, tense, or angry. The lowest levels occurred while participants were relaxing, sleeping, reading, or watching TV, and when they felt unrushed, relaxed, or tired.

Steptoe (2001) investigated the role of social support and stress in blood pressure. On the basis of a questionnaire, 62 schoolteachers were classified into low and high social support groups. Social support was defined as perceived availability of others to provide practical assistance, company, advice, and emotional support. Upon every blood pressure reading, participants rated their level of stress, and a triaxial accelerometer assessed their movements in three planes to estimate their energy expenditure. Factoring out the effects of concurrent energy expenditure and body mass, Figure 13.3 shows the systolic and diastolic blood pressure readings for the two groups under conditions of low and high stress. The buffering effect of social support during moments of high stress is clear from the figure. There is no main effect for social support—on the whole, those with strong social support don't necessarily have lower blood pressure—but there is an interaction effect such that high stress elevates the blood pressure of those with little social support but has no effect on those with strong support.

Rheumatoid Arthritis and Chronic Physical Pain

One of the methodological concerns of researchers interested in measuring pain intensity is reactivity, the possibility that focusing attention on pain may change a participant's experience of it. If that change were to occur in the direction of feeling less pain, then repeated measurement itself might be a therapeutic technique. Although results may be different in the treatment of psychological problems (as we will see in following sections), two studies found no change over sampling periods up to four weeks in the pain ratings of people with rheumatoid arthritis or other chronic pain (Cruise, Broderick, Porter, Kaell, & Stone, 1996; Peters, Sorbi, Kruise, Kerssens, Verhaak, & Bensing, 2000). Attending to and recording their pain many times a day did not appear to increase or decrease that pain. The intensity of pain does have some variability across the day, however, for many people. About 40 percent of the arthritis sufferers experienced a consistent daily pattern of variation in which pain was greatest in the morning (Stone, Broderick, Porter, & Kaell, 1997). The experience of stress and poor sleep also elevated pain levels. Another study of people living with chronic pain from a broad variety of sources found the same proportion, 40 percent, experienced a consistent daily pattern of higher morning pain (Vendrig & Lousberg, 1997). Pain intensity for this group, but not for the group with no daily pattern, was also correlated with negative moods and was more common in the evening as well as in the morning. Overall, those with no daily pattern had significantly less intense pain and more positive moods. Contrasting with these studies is a

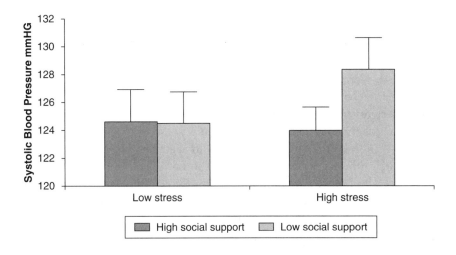

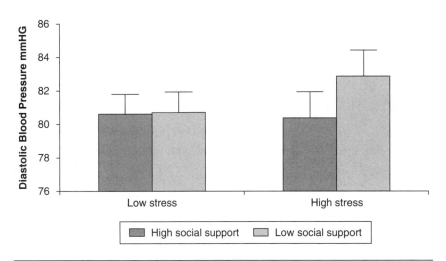

Figure 13.3   Mean Systolic Blood Pressure and Diastolic Pressure, Adjusted for Concurrent Energy Expenditure and Body Mass, During Periods of High Stress and Low Stress Over the Working Day

SOURCE: Steptoe, A. (2001). Ambulatory monitoring of blood pressure in daily life: A tool for investigating psychosocial processes. In J. Fahrenberg and M. Myrtek (Eds.), *Progress in ambulatory assessment* (pp. 257–269). Reprinted with permission of the author.

NOTE: Error bars indicate standard error of the mean.

four-week study of Dutch individuals living with chronic pain in which nearly half of the sample experienced increasing pain intensity throughout the day (Peters et al., 2000). An equal number showed no diurnal pattern, and only two individuals had worse pain in the mornings than in the evenings.

Exercise Withdrawal

In a counterpoint to studies of chronic pain, Gauvin, Rejeski, and Norris (1996) studied the effects of physical exercise on healthy women. After exercising, these women felt more positive engagement, revitalization, and positive emotions than before exercising, and they also experienced more tranquility. Given these psychological benefits, what happens when healthy, active individuals are deprived of exercise? Gauvin and Szabo (1992) recruited a sample of 21 college students who engaged in vigorous physical exercise an average of 7.5 hours per week to respond to ESM signals 4 times a day for 5 weeks. Half of them were randomly assigned to continue their normal routine throughout the signaling period, while the other half stopped exercising during week three, resuming their normal routine in weeks four and five. According to their ESM reports, members of these two groups did not differ in their psychological well-being and affect throughout the signaling period, and the no-exercise group did not report any significant changes in affect and well-being across weeks. However, during their week without exercise and the subsequent week, this group reported twice as many physical symptoms as the control group. Exercise deprivation led participants to experience more frequent bouts of one or more of the following ailments: headache, stomachache, chest pain, dizziness, acne, lack of breath, stiff or sore muscles, and cold symptoms. The researchers noted that there is little empirical evidence that one week of exercise deprivation has any significant physiological effects, and thus the reported symptoms are likely the result of psychosomatic distress. The lack of self-reported psychological changes may be because the participants attributed their cessation of exercise to their voluntary compliance with the research protocol and anticipated resuming their routine after the one-week break.

Use of ESM in Therapy and in Treatment Evaluation

Just as ESM provides invaluable information on the nature of disorders, the method can also be an effective tool for evaluating the course of treatment. For example, Ravenna and her colleagues (2001, 2002) studied the transition process of long-time heroin addicts who were adjusting to life in a residential community treatment center. ESM samples taken at intake and 6 and 12 months later revealed that participants increased in feelings of strength, freedom, and self-esteem, and sensed an increasing degree of respect from other people. Their attitudes became less fatalistic in that they attributed their moods less often to external factors. Another approach to treatment of heroin addicts is methadone maintenance therapy. By using

ESM, deVos and colleagues (1996) showed that, contrary to conventional medical wisdom, higher methadone dosage was related to more intense craving, with a peak in craving just before the patients received their daily dose of methadone. This timing may indicate that patients have been conditioned to anticipate receiving the drug at the same time every day.

In another example, ESM was used to assess the effects of a recent innovation in children's hospitals. A computer network allows pediatric patients to learn more about their condition, find other children around the United States with similar interests or illnesses, and communicate with them via chatrooms, bulletin boards, e-mail, and videoconferencing. Besides social support, the computer system also features games and opportunities for creative expression. Using ESM, researchers compared children's experience while they were using the computer system to their experience during other free time spent playing, watching TV, visiting with family or friends, reading, eating, or doing art activities (Holden, Bearison, Rode, Kapiloff, & Rosenberg, 2000). During computer time, the children expressed lower levels of anxiety, pain intensity, and pain aversiveness.

ESM has also been used to detail the changes that take place in the lives of depressed individuals when they start taking medication. In one study, participants completed ESM for one week before and six weeks after beginning treatment with antidepressants (Barge-Schaapveld, Nicolson, van der Hoop, & deVries, 1995). Although nearly all participants improved to some degree, those who responded most positively to treatment, as determined by a score on a standard clinical rating scale, also showed the most significant changes in their ESM responses. Responders began to spend less time engaged in passive leisure activities and more time on household chores. They also experienced more moments of positive affect and fewer of negative affect. In a similar study, depressed participants on antidepressant medication experienced less emotional variability and fewer moments of doing nothing than participants on placebo (Barge-Schaapveld & Nicolson, 2002). These results show how ESM can be used not only to cross-validate information from other clinical instruments but also to provide much more detail than those instruments can.

Van der Poel and Delespaul (1992) used ESM in this way to supplement the information they were obtaining from standard clinical interviews of a schizophrenic man. Over the course of a year following his discharge from a psychiatric hospital, the patient completed three separate weeks of ESM, each separated by three to six months. Results from the ESM were used both to tailor treatment to the patient's particular situation and to evaluate the effects of that treatment. For example, it was determined that the menial industrial therapy job he was given at the hospital was beneath his skills, and he was subsequently assigned to drive a hospital shuttle bus. ESM reports after this switch indicated a gradual improvement in mental health. Lack of social contact was also a problem, so opportunities for social interaction were expanded. The researchers noted that in some cases, reliance on clinical interviews alone would have led to different, perhaps less effective, treatment decisions. The patient indicated in interviews feeling more dependency, loneliness, and lack of meaning than was evident in his daily experience. This discrepancy does not prove that one method is inaccurate, but that both methods used together provide a more complete set of information than either one could alone.

In a similar case study of a woman with panic disorder and agoraphobia, Delle Fave and Massimini (1992) extended the use of ESM one step further by integrating it into ongoing psychotherapy. The client completed a week of ESM every 6 to 8 weeks, for a total of 9 separate ESM samplings over a 16-month period. Her therapist would read her reports as a diary of her life between sessions and tailor the therapeutic approach to address specific strengths and needs that were apparent. In addition, after the fifth and ninth ESM weeks, the data were analyzed to provide a more systematic picture of the client's progress. This analysis was instrumental in identifying goals for future therapeutic sessions. One of the overall goals of therapy was to help the client increase engagement in self-rewarding activities. Figure 13.4 documents the dramatic changes that occurred in this regard over the nine ESM samplings. The amount of time she spent watching TV decreased from 45 percent to 14 percent in the eighth ESM week, with no TV watching reported in the ninth sampling. At the same time, new, more engaging activities gradually replaced TV watching. These activities included volunteering, reading, and socializing. Not depicted in this graph is the considerable amount of time she spent at work or commuting—13 hours per day—that remained constant across all nine samplings. Another indication of her clinical improvement was the gradual increase in the time she was able to spend alone, from 19 percent to 44 percent, and in the time she spent outside of the home. Finally, Figure 13.5 depicts how this woman's internal experience also improved dramatically from the first to the final sampling. The variables plotted in the graph include affective, motivational, and cognitive dimensions of experience, and in every case, her experience switched from negative to positive. This change was also observed in her experience of flow, which increased from 15 percent to 51 percent, and apathy, which decreased from 61 percent to 35 percent.

Another approach to the use of ESM in the treatment of panic disorder was tested by Newman, Kenardy, Herman, and Taylor (1997). Their patients carried palmtop computers throughout 12 weeks of therapy, using them to complete a daily diary of anxiety and panic attacks. Half of the patients in

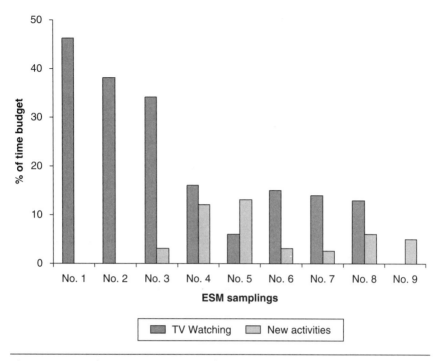

Figure 13.4   Changes in Percentage of Time Devoted to TV Watching and New Activities During the Nine ESM Samplings

SOURCE: deVries, *The experience of psychopathology*, 1992. Copyright © 1992. Reprinted with the permission of Cambridge University Press.

NOTE: *N* = 428.

this study received 12 sessions of standard cognitive-behavioral therapy (CBT). The other half received only four sessions of CBT with a therapist, but then received computer-assisted therapy via the palmtop computer for the remaining eight weeks. This group, in addition to completing the daily diary, also responded to four additional signals throughout each day and any other time they felt panicky. At each of these moments, the computer would prompt them with self-statements, coping suggestions, and instructions to practice breathing techniques they had learned. The effectiveness of treatment was measured immediately following the completion of therapy and again six months later. According to results at both time points, participants in both groups experienced significant improvement, with two-thirds experiencing no more panic attacks. There were no differences in outcome between the two groups. Given this equivalence, the computer-assisted approach might be

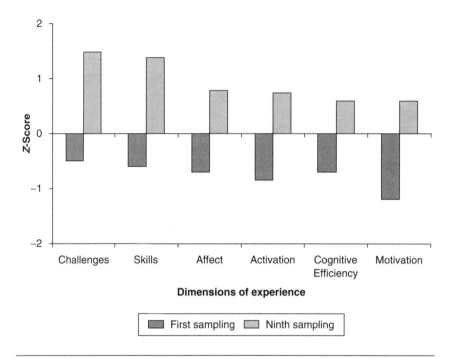

Figure 13.5   Mean Z-Scores for Six Dimensions of Experience in the First and Ninth ESM Samplings

SOURCE: deVries, *The experience of psychopathology*, 1992. Copyright © 1992. Reprinted with the permission of Cambridge University Press.

NOTES: Number of calls in first sampling = 33; number of calls in the ninth sampling = 55.

preferable due to its greater cost effectiveness. Of course, the function of human therapists can never be replaced by computers, but the researchers note that even when individual therapy is necessary, ESM-style self-reporting can be a valuable therapeutic tool. Apparently, other researchers agree; the use of ESM for therapeutic ends is spreading. Recently, Norton and colleagues (2003) extended therapy into the daily lives of their bulimic patients by using therapeutic modules programmed into palmtop computers.

We believe the value of ESM for the treatment and prevention of clinical disorders is best exemplified in the following case, which is excerpted from deVries and Delespaul (1992, pp. 106–107).

Alfred is a 28-year-old man, first diagnosed at the age of 22 with undifferentiated schizophrenia. His other DSM-III diagnoses were passive dependent personality disorder and hypertensive illness. He had been employed as a dishwasher and store clerk, and had lived alone or with his parents in a relatively unstressful environment over the last eight years. Since he was diagnosed the patient was treated steadily on 20 to 30 mg of Stelazine which allowed him to function socially at a marginal level. The patient was referred for two reasons: the exacerbation of his schizophrenia as well as a hypertensive crisis which had required intensive medical intervention. On ESM assessment it was found that, rather than being present throughout the day, the patient experienced anxiety and increased blood pressure primarily at 11:00 a.m. each day while at work. At this time, as a dishwasher, he had to sort silverware—spoons from forks—on an automated conveyor belt system during the pre-lunch rush. In this anxious state his blood pressure increased markedly often to 180/120. In the clinical setting, the agitated patient with rampant high blood pressure appeared puzzling. The time assessment, however, linked the problem to a specific environment that the patient experienced as socially and cognitively distressful and pointed to a clinical intervention. The circumstances were explained to his employer with the suggestion to change the patient's work tasks. The employer cooperated and over the next three weeks the patient's blood pressure returned to near normal, a quite remarkable change since his extremely high blood pressure over the previous two months had lead to intensive treatment with Aldomet, Propranodol, and Valium in addition to Stelazine. After three weeks, the patient was again assessed with the ESM and an increase in the patient's agitation between 10:00–11:00 a.m. was again noted. At this time, the lunch-work shift, made up primarily of female workers, came to prepare the noon meal. This brought up a host of fearful, sexual, and aggressive feelings in the patient which he experienced as psychological disorganizing. This situation uncovered new psychotherapeutically useful information about the nature of the patient's relationship with women and particularly his mother, relationships which he was previously unable to discuss. A focused psychotherapy approach was thus possible and resulted in a relatively symptom-free year. While this information could have been derived from careful clinical interviewing, other medical workers missed the importance of the environmental influence. The ESM assessment method brought it to the fore. In this case, it proved doubly powerful since it provided a capacity for both a medical and a social intervention as well as guiding a psychotherapeutic approach. It is important to remember that the patient during interview had been unable to communicate the linkage of these events.*

---

* Copyright © 1992. Reprinted with the permission of Cambridge University Press.

Concluding Thoughts

Perhaps by now the chapters of this book have convinced the reader that to measure how one person, or a group, differs from another—how they spend their time, how they feel about what they do, how their subjective experience changes as a result of external events—the serious application of ESM is the best choice. It is difficult to imagine that in the foreseeable future a more precise method will emerge, unless by a natural evolution of what we now know as ESM.

Shortcuts in the measurement of experience can be dangerous. For instance, the December 3, 2004, issue of *Science* carried an article by Daniel Kahneman and others presenting studies based on the Day Reconstruction Method (DRM). In that article they argue that DRM is a good way to assess activities and moods in everyday life and support its validity by saying that it provides substantially the same information as ESM, which they claim is the "gold standard" in the field. Yet DRM is just a more intense form of the diary method, subject to all of its biases. Nevertheless the authors advocate the use of DRM over ESM because the former is cheaper and easier to administer.

The problem with a measure that is cheaper and easier to use is that it might provide information that distorts reality. A very apt illustration of this danger was provided by the Kahneman article itself. On the same day the article appeared in *Science*, and for days afterwards, the media gloated over some of its findings: "TV time ranks high in mood study," headlined the *New York Times*; "Feeling of good cheer? Maybe it was the TV," suggested the headline of the *International Herald Tribune*. The fact that the diaries on which the study was based were only kept during workdays and the respondents were Texas women employed mainly in unskilled service work did not register with the media. They reported what the findings were, unaware that working women who have little time to do anything very memorable during working days might rate, *retrospectively*, TV watching as better than almost any other part of their day. Unfortunately the message conveyed to the reading audience was that, "Hey, TV watching is not so bad after all—it does improve your moods!" This is despite tons of evidence that if you measure moods as they occur and sample them so as to represent the full gamut of a person's week, TV watching looks like the choice of last resort. A misleading conclusion of this magnitude is not just an issue involving academic accuracy; potentially it can have serious deleterious effects for society as a whole.

Price and convenience are certainly not the only considerations in how to conduct basic research. They are not even the ultimate factors in consumer purchasing choices. If you had to decide whether to buy a high-resolution TV and one cheaper but providing a much less clear picture, which one would you choose? If you were worried about having caught a bad virus, you would not want the cheapest diagnostic system to identify the state of your health. Nor would you want an airline to use the cheapest directional device on the plane you fly—unless it is as accurate as the more expensive ones. The quality of people's subjective lives is more important than anything else one can find out about them. So if one claims to be a research psychologist who studies subjective experience, one should use the best tools for that particular task.

But no matter how exquisite a tool is, its worth ultimately depends on the value it adds to those who use it. So, is ESM worth the trouble? After working for more than 30 years with the data this method generates, I must confess to be even more taken with it than I was back when the results of our first study appeared on the computer screen. There are few things more exciting than looking for the first time at a spreadsheet or a statistical table containing ESM data. The array of numbers is like a fascinating novel; it stimulates a series of mental images, like the inner movie one plays in imagination when reading a story by Dickens or Dostoyevsky. One might see, for instance, a group of high school students listless in a lecture class revive when the period ends and lunch begins; or a stressed worker begin relaxing when he gets home (if he is a man), or feeling even more beleaguered (if she is a woman). One can read the state of mind before an attempted suicide or that following being buried by an avalanche.

But these might seem trivial, idiosyncratic reasons. Science depends on objective, cumulative evidence, and the value it adds to objective understanding. How does ESM fare by this criterion? Again, I will try to express the worth of this method in terms of what I have found most interesting about the findings it generates, but this time highlighting what these findings add to an understanding of human psychology. In doing so, I will focus on ten main issues. This means that I will not comment here on the great majority of ESM studies and their findings, but restrict myself, in no particular order, only to a few topics that in my personal opinion are uniquely illuminated by the method.

Ten Major Issues ESM Illuminates

The Unaided Mind Returns to Chaos

The usual view people have of the mind is that when free from external pressures and demands, a person is liberated to use it in any way he or she wishes. One can relish beautiful thoughts, plan great ventures, and indulge in happy memories and comfortable feelings. The cumulative evidence from ESM studies suggests that almost the opposite is the case. When left to itself, the mind turns to bad thoughts, trivial plans, sad memories, and worries about the future. Entropy—disorder, confusion, decay—is the default option of consciousness.

The mind escapes this entropic state under two conditions. The first is when a goal provides order to our psychic energy and we strive to reach it. The goal can be as simple and transient as getting into a conversation with another person, balancing the checkbook, even watching TV—or as momentous as working on a multimillion dollar contract. The second way to escape from mental chaos is to develop an internal discipline that allows one to follow an ordered chain of thought, a directed stream of consciousness. People who learn to meditate, who have trained their imagination, or who have learned to manipulate symbolic content such as poetry or mathematics are much more likely to be free to use their minds, just as we all should be, at least ideally.

But relatively few individuals seem to become emancipated from external controls on their minds. As Jerome Singer (1966, 1973) has found, a great number of children never even learn to daydream or to fantasize. Their attention is too much under the control of outside stimuli to be able to focus inward on a story or on a sequence of imaginary events, no matter how trite. And the ability to sit and think about real plans or creative solutions to problems is an even more rare ability.

It is surprising how the science of psychology has ignored this essential trait of the mind. ESM has revealed the chaos descending on people's consciousness when left without external stimuli or internal guidance. This conclusion emerged unexpectedly and in small, apparently unrelated bits. If no other contribution were to ensue beyond the realization of how much the mind needs structure to function well, ESM would have added enough value to be taken seriously. One can imagine hundreds of studies pursuing the implications of this one conclusion. And what about the practical applications for childrearing, formal education, and adult lifestyles? This is not the place to follow up all these leads, but it is likely that they will enrich psychology for years to come.

Loneliness Sucks

The fact that we are social animals has been known at least since Aristotle. But the extent to which we depend on the company of other people in order to lift our spirits had not been documented systematically before ESM. Young or old, rich or poor, American, Asian, or European, people prefer to do almost anything more when they are with others than when they are alone. This feature of subjective experience is in part related to the earlier point, namely, that the presence of people helps to structure consciousness. But it is more than that: as social animals, we are attracted to other humans more than to most other stimuli in the environment. In their company we tend to feel more alive than when we are alone.

The amount of time people spend by themselves varies with personality—extraverts are more keen on companionship than introverts—and with a person's occupation—for instance some lumberjacks in the Northwoods spend months working alone in the forests, which in part may explain their high suicide rate. In general, close to a fourth of a person's waking hours are spent in solitude. If an adolescent spends much more or much less than this amount alone, he or she tends to have behavioral problems.

Learning adult skills in the "knowledge economy" means that young people need to spend many hours alone, studying, programming, rehearsing, and practicing. Teenagers who are unable to tolerate solitude tend to spend as much time as possible with their peers and as a consequence may be handicapped in acquiring complex symbolic skills. Talented adolescents spend about five more hours a week alone than their less talented peers, and even when they are with peers they are more likely to study, think, and be involved in arts and hobbies, instead of just "hanging out" (Csikszentmihalyi, Rathunde, & Whalen, 1993, pp. 90–93).

Excessive reliance on the company of others might also have important political consequences. In her compendium of studies entitled *The Spiral of Silence,* the political scientist Elizabeth Noelle-Neumann (1984) has documented huge effects on political behavior and voting patterns attributable to citizen's desire to avoid ostracism by being part of the winning side. The connection between her findings covering almost half a century and our ESM results suggests the power for good or ill that the desire to belong to a group can have on our behavior (Csikszentmihalyi, 1992). If it is true, as some critics contend, that children who have access to all sorts of entertainment technologies and whose daily schedules are filled with adult-supervised activities are losing the ability to structure their own time and develop their own interests, this would not be a minor lifestyle change, but one with potentially momentous social consequences.

Familiar Power Struggles

ESM has brought to light many new facets of the dynamics of family life, some previously invisible to researchers. One of the "Aha!" moments in this respect occurred almost 20 years ago when I was leafing through a teenager's booklet of ESF sheets (Csikszentmihalyi & Larson, 1984). I was surprised to see that the worst experience of the week for this young man was reported when the family was driving to church on a Sunday morning. In reading the page, it became clear that the event was the culmination of a series of confrontations between the boy and his parents, all of which he lost. In brief, (a) he didn't want get up "early" on a Sunday morning; (b) He didn't want to go to church; (c) He did not want to sit in the car between his sisters; (d) He did not want to listen to opera on the car radio. None of the three dozen or so responses during the week showed this boy so powerless as in that one situation. Even the information that was coming through his ears was dictated by the parents, and this was happening on a holy day of respite from school!

Ever since that time, it has become clearer and clearer that ESM does not show just what happens inside a person's mind, but it also describes the lines of tension, conflict, or alignment in groups of interacting individuals. Some of these facets of family dynamics have been beautifully illustrated in the works of Reed Larson and Maryse Richards (1994a), Kevin Rathunde (1996), Barbara Schneider and Linda Waite (2005), and the highlights reported in Chapter 9 of this book. It is quite sad to see, for instance, how the moods of teenagers when they are with their parents decline year by year, while that of their parents declines relatively much less.

These and many other findings of this kind are the result of the unflinching way ESM cuts through the niceties of social facades to expose lines of tension and conflict. It shows how the parental role, no matter how loving and close, also involves a great deal of effort directed at socializing children to habits and behaviors that the parents hope will serve them well, but the children resent—at least at the moment. In 20 years, the now-grown children may be grateful to their parents for having disciplined them; but few of them take kindly to the incursion on their experience that parental control represents. Of course this built-in conflict has been observed for thousands of years; yet with the help of ESM it is possible, for the first time, to have a record of how it plays out in real time and to analyze its antecedents and consequences.

But these examples open up an entirely unexpected perspective on human psychology. They alert us to the fact that human interactions can be seen as reciprocal attempts to influence each other's attention by controlling the information participants attend to and therefore affect their subjective experience. Parents expect their children to attend to where they put their clothes, to household chores, to doing homework; children on the other hand want to preserve control over their attention so they can invest it in what provides them with positive experiences—watching television, listening to music, hanging out with friends. And this is just the beginning; later in life teachers will expect students to invest their attention in the academic subjects mandated by the school authorities, and employers will expect workers to pay attention to the tasks that the job requires. We may call this the psychic economy of experience or perhaps more accurately the *politics of experience,* because much of the control over attention is based on power rather than on free exchange.

On a societal scale, when a large segment of the population feels that what they are doing is not what they want to do, this leads to what sociologists may call *alienation;* when the experiences of their everyday lives are meaningless, it leads to *anomie* (Mitchell, 1988). One might argue about whom to blame for such conditions—the opportunity structures of society or the individual's lack of initiative. In either case, pressures are built up as people resent wasting their psychic energy in tasks that do not provide positive experiences. It could well be that revolutions and other changes in regime are due at least as much to the frustration of people's desire to control their own experiences as they are to the frustration of material wants.

The Paradox of Work

One of the earliest puzzles that ESM results presented had to do with people's experiences on the job. On the one hand, workers—including service workers and those on the assembly line—reported some of their best experiences at work. Generally they felt more alert, skilled, and creative at work than they felt in free time at home. They also reported to be in the high-challenge, high skills "flow condition" when working on the job. At the same time, when paged at work they typically said they would have liked to do something else, whereas at home they had no desire to do something else, even when they felt passive and bored (see Chapter 10 of this volume; Csikszentmihalyi & Le Fevre, 1989).

For over a decade this anomaly presented a nagging paradox. Apparently our belief that people were motivated to do whatever they were doing by the quality of experience was in need of qualification: there were reasons that motivated people in free time besides the quality of experience, which was not nearly as influential as it was supposed to be. The best explanation we could find was that at work people tended to disregard their own experiences, and even though they should have enjoyed them, they told themselves: "No, this could not be right—how could I feel good at work, when everybody knows work is stressful and depressing?" In other words, the cultural stigma attached to most jobs overrode the actual experience.

Recently two other possible explanations have emerged. One is based on the work of the Swiss psychologists Schallberger and Pfister (2001), who found among their subjects that the experience at work, while in many ways positive, is often also accompanied by more negative dimensions that in our earlier research we had failed to pick up. Even flow, they find, is different at work than in leisure: the positive elements are qualified by a sense of stress and anxiety that is lacking when the flow conditions are present in free time. While the verdict is still out on this question, another possible explanation is worth mentioning; one that has even wider implications.

The paradox of work is part of a larger issue; namely, that we find two quite different types of situations rewarding. One includes situations where we can relax, indulge, and be comfortable. The other includes an almost opposite set of conditions: risk, hardship, and excitement. The first is *homeostatic* and often provides pleasure or the satisfaction of genetically programmed needs. The second is *heterostatic,* pushing the organism to new states. To use a shorthand notation, we could call the first kind of reward *pleasure* and the second *enjoyment* or *flow*. Pleasure is conservative; it offers the advantage of conserving energy and making us feel good at a biological level. Enjoyment is destabilizing, pushing the organism into uncharted waters—it is the motivation that keeps us struggling ahead. It is the mechanism responsible for cultural evolution (Csikszentmihalyi, 1996; Inghilleri, 1999).

If human beings had been crafted like clocks, with all parts working together for the same purpose, the conservative and the evolutionary motives would nicely support each other. But unfortunately our psychic makeup was made on the run, so to speak, shaped by survival requirements that were often conflicting. For instance a person who can make friends and alliances easily may do better than one who lives alone and shuns the company of others; however, the friendly person runs the risk of being exploited and betrayed, so a dose of suspicion also comes in handy. In giving advice to men in positions of secular authority, Martin Luther wrote: "no man is to be trusted, no matter how wise, holy, or great he may be." It is not easy to reconcile empathy, cooperation, and charity to all on the one hand, with prudent suspicion on the other; yet both confer special advantages. So do many other apparently contrary impulses such as humility and ambition, left- and right-brain thinking, or pleasure and enjoyment. The paradox revealed by ESM findings might actually represent a fact we often forget: the human brain is not a unified machine but a multipurpose organ that often defeats itself by pursuing contradictory ends.

We Learn What We Like

All through the book we have reported results showing that learning can be either enjoyable or boring or stressful, depending on how the material is taught and on other situational conditions. This finding is different from the educational message of behaviorism, which consisted in providing rewards for learning—gold stars, candy, or other external incentives. These were better than the ancient inducement, the cane and the strap, but they were just as irrelevant to the content of learning. Except for innovators who by and large failed to convert mainline schools, such as Froebel or Maria Montessori, educators rarely took seriously the possibility that learning itself could be its own reward.

One of the first doctoral dissertations that used ESM, by Pat Mayers (1978), showed that course grades in high school could be better predicted by how much students enjoyed the class than by prior grades and test scores. A smart child who was bored in a class would perform below par, while one with a much less promising record would do well if he or she enjoyed it. Almost 20 years later Carl Heine (1996) replicated these findings with mathematically gifted children. Chapter 12 deals extensively with the various ESM studies that have been done in academic settings in the past 27 years.

But isn't the goal of making learning enjoyable naive? After all, at least since Cicero it has been repeated that "The roots of knowledge are bitter, but its fruits are sweet"—the intellectual equivalent of the athlete's mantra: "No pain, no gain." Unfortunately, this perspective applies to education quite often. But it does not describe learning. What we often miss is that learning and education don't necessarily go together. Children are continuously learning and generally enjoy the process. Formal education, which is supposed to facilitate learning, all too often inhibits it. Learning is part of human nature, and we are at our best when we learn. Education is a cultural institution, which at its best enhances and refines our nature; but which all too often only frustrates it. Thus there is no reason to assume that education cannot be enjoyable, as long as it takes into account the learner's needs and desires.

The present educational arrangements—obligatory schooling that consists of having children sit and process abstract information transmitted mainly by lectures—grotesquely ignores the nature of young persons. For many thousands of generations, young people had to take responsibilities early, be active, help with adult tasks. It was not particularly strange for John Quincy Adams, the future sixth president of the United States, to leave his family for three years at age 14 to go on an American mission to Paris and Russia and act as personal secretary to the Ambassador. That was approximately the age Alexander the Great took charge of the armies of Macedonia, and Lorenzo de Medici left Florence to negotiate a loan of worth billions today between his family's bank and the King of France. Now children at that age are considered capable of little more than sitting passively in a classroom.

But the need to be active and responsible has been bred in our bones for too long to be easily shed at the school door. In much of the Third World the application of standard educational practices has effortlessly driven young men to form machine-gun-toting gangs that devastate the countryside. Our schools are mercifully still standing thanks to thousands of selfless teachers and to reasonably healthy communities, but the amount of human capital being wasted in most schools is frightening.

Does ESM data suggest any improvement on the current state of affairs? We know how much more alive and motivated teenagers are when they are with friends, when they are involved in active learning, when they have challenges appropriate to their skills, when they have clear goals, and receive quick feedback. And we know that when we feel alive and motivated we learn better. On these few principles a new educational system could be built—one similar in some respects to the Montessori pedagogy, which has anticipated these ideas by almost a century (Rathunde & Csikszentmihalyi, 2005). Of course helping children to learn, rather than "educating" them, is more time consuming and therefore more expensive than our current methods of schooling are. But a cheap education is a foolish economy; sooner or later, the habits of boredom and the years of passivity and frustration will exact a much higher price.

Illness and the Mind

One of the most surprising facts revealed by ESM is that psychic illness and chronic physical pain are not constant states of the organism but vary in intensity depending on how much free attention we have left. The psychiatrist Marten deVries (1992) was the first to notice that ESFs filled out by patients diagnosed as chronic schizophrenics showed evidence of disturbed thoughts only at certain times of day and only when the patient was involved in some activities. Otherwise they could express their subjective states just as well as people considered to be normal.

Similarly, as Chapter 13 reports, it has been found that patients suffering from chronic depression, eating disorders, or chronic pain—even breast cancer patients—show little psychological effects from their condition as long as they are working or interacting with people. But when attention is not focused it turns to the pain or to the psychic trauma. Then patients become fully aware of their condition and suffering invades their consciousness. Alone, with nothing to do, on weekends and evenings is when the reality of the illness emerges in full force.

Thus the dismissive phrase, "It's all in your head," turns out to have some truth to it but in a very different sense than usually meant. It is true that in order for pain to be felt, it has to be experienced—that is, attended to. To the extent that our attention is taken up with other tasks, pain has less chance of registering. This is an important example of the connection between objective and subjective realities. The former may be the cause of pain, but how much we attend to it will modify its impact on consciousness and thus its psychic reality. Objective and subjective reality are usually quite closely connected, but even a little space for maneuvering between them is an essential feature of what we mean by being human.

Another interesting relationship between pain and experience is the longitudinal finding from John Patton's (1998) dissertation mentioned in Chapter 8. It may be remembered that teenagers who reported using their skills to a lesser extent in the first year of the Sloan Study (Csikszentmihalyi & Schneider, 2000) tended to report worse outcomes five years later—including significantly more physical pain, such as headaches, muscle pain, and so on. There was also a potentially important gender difference: the worst outcomes for boys followed when both challenges *and* skills were lacking in early adolescence—the condition of *apathy;* but the worst prognosis for girls, including more pain, was reported when low skills were combined with high challenges earlier in life—the condition we call *anxiety.* These findings might suggest that certain attentional habits formed in adolescence predispose a child to spend more attention monitoring internal states, thus to be more aware of discomfort, and therefore report more pain. In addition it suggests that prevention of future subjective health might require different conditions for boys and girls: while both need to feel they are using their skills, for boys more challenges are important, for girls challenges have a positive effect only when accompanied by skills.

Flow in Everyday Life

ESM was originally designed to study flow in everyday life. The initial studies of the optimal experience of flow involved interviews with artists, scientists, musicians, and athletes who described retrospectively how it felt when their work was going well. These accounts were invaluable in developing a typology and then a theory of what some of the best moments in life feel like. But then the question presented itself: to what extent is it possible to approximate these intense moments in everyday life—at work, in the family, or in leisure time? To answer this question with more precision than interviews could yield, we started experimenting with ESM to identify those moments when people approximate flow in their mundane activities.

The results provided an unexpectedly complex pattern that described when and how much people enjoyed the various aspects of their day. Television, and passive mass entertainment in general, turns out to be less exhilarating than one might have imagined, whereas driving a car—unless the traffic is horrible—shows up as better than one would have thought. We have already commented on loneliness and the paradox of work. So where do flowlike experiences happen? They often happen in public places and more often at work than at home during hobbies, sports, and active leisure in general. People often ask, so how often are people in flow? To answer that question with ESM one must first agree on what constitutes flow and on how it is operationalized.

For instance, if we say that a flow condition exists every time a person indicates that both challenges and skills are above average, then one would expect people to experience flow about a quarter of the time. Yet even so, individuals differ from each other a great deal: some are only in the flow quadrant 5 percent during a week, others as often as 50 percent. But if one defines a flow condition as one where challenge and skills are above average and within one scale point from each other, then the frequency of flow—as measured by this convention—dwindles considerably.

The same holds true of the flow experience. If one operationalizes it as any moment when a person is above average on enjoyment, interest, and concentration, flowlike moments are relatively frequent; but if one also adds the requirement that they should be one standard deviation above the average, then many fewer events would be counted as flow. Like a microscope that reveals a very different map of a cell depending on what magnification the lenses are set to, ESM will give a different reading on the frequency of flow depending on whether flow is defined broadly or narrowly. The important thing is not to attach a numerical value to this frequency, but to use the results comparatively, both within individuals and within groups, to assess where flowlike experiences are most likely to exist.

One of the great advantages of science is that it proceeds in a dialectic fashion, with theory pointing the way and empirical results correcting the direction. This happened, for instance, when ESM began to show that contrary to the earlier models of flow, it was not enough for challenges and skills to be in balance to usher in optimal experience: The two also had to be above the person's average, and the farther above the average they were, the more intense the flow experience reported. When challenge and skills were both very low, instead of flow people reported a state of listlessness that we ended up calling *apathy* or psychic entropy. The first investigators to take this pattern seriously and to document it were Fausto Massimini and Massimo Carli at the University of Milan, Italy. The definition of what to count as a flow condition has been following their insight ever since.

The psychologist Kurt Lewin is credited with the saying: "There is nothing more practical than a good theory." If this is true, flow theory is good indeed; for while it developed purely as a result of intellectual curiosity, as basic research its applications have spread far and wide. Starting with sports and leisure, then education, and lately business, ideas from flow have been adopted to a great variety of practical issues. A detailed article in the August 2005 issue of *Fast Company* gives some idea of the many uses people have made from the results that were hatched and confirmed in the ivory towers (Marsh, 2005). One of my favorite examples is that of a Swedish government-owned company that had been losing money for 120 years. When Stefan Falk, who had studied flow and applied it previously in other firms, started a new management program based on flow, the company made its first profit, and he was credited with the turnaround. Saving taxpayers' money is not the premier goal of science, but there is no need to be ashamed when it happens.

Experience and Time

There is a polite debate among scientists who study happiness and subjective well-being (SWB) as to whether momentary experiences of SWB add up over time to a happy life or whether enduring happiness is something relatively independent of how one feels moment by moment. Daniel Kahneman (1999) supports the first position when he writes that happiness is the sum total of momentary experiences through life. Edward Diener (2000), on the other hand, argues that a great deal of what we call happiness is retrospective reconstruction—at any moment our happiness depends more of how we evaluate the past and the future than on what actually happened. And some philosophers, like Hannah Arendt (1958), claim that one moment of ecstasy can compensate for an otherwise humdrum life, a conclusion directly at odds with the works of Diener and others that suggest that profound moments of happiness actually reduce SWB as a whole because we keep yearning for them after they pass instead of enjoying what we actually have.

ESM suggests that there is some truth to all of these apparently contradictory claims. The first position, that experience is cumulative, seems to be supported by the few (and short-term) longitudinal studies done to date.

Children who are happy at 10 are more likely to be happy at 17 years of age; people who experience self-esteem and optimism time after time will also have high scores on these variables when tested with a one-time measure. Of course this does not mean, necessarily, that it is the previous experiences that cause the latter ones. To the extent that behavioral geneticists are right, it could also mean that we have a "set point" for happiness as well as for other traits, and continuity over time is due to this genetically set thermostat, not to the additive effect of momentary experiences. However the estimates for the genetic component of such experiences as happiness hovers around 50 percent, leaving quite a bit of room for the effect of good or bad momentary feelings to affect one's overall well-being.

But ESM also alerts us to the fact that sometimes a series of negative experiences end up improving the quality of our lives. I poignantly became aware of this when I personally experimented with using the method in the early 1970s. After a week of filling out ESFs, I sat down to look for patterns in my own responses. One pattern that caught my attention concerned the times I spent in the company of my sons, then in their teens. It should be said that if you had asked about my relationship with them I would have said truthfully that I loved them, was proud of them, and that I enjoyed their company. Yet flipping through the ESF pages a drastically different picture seemed to emerge. When thinking of or being with my sons, more often than not, I was worried, angry, or irritable. The reason was not hard to find: much of our interaction focused on whether they were studying enough, whether they were home on time, and whether they were keeping their rooms within the semblance of neatness.

Then it dawned on me what should have been obvious in the first place: both pictures were accurate. To feel good about one's children, one has to worry and get irritated along the way. Looking back now that they are in their 40s, both they and I feel that the early confrontations were worth it because they led to later well-being. Of course if the parent's discipline is too harsh and unleavened by genuine love and liking, then such confrontations don't change sign with time—they remain negative experiences that add up to a negative quality of life.

What Does ESM Contribute to Our View of Human Nature?

It might seem too ambitious to expect that a method only one generation old might change anything about the way we understand ourselves. Yet if taken seriously, many of the points already mentioned bring new light on that old chestnut, human nature. It could be argued that none of these points are really new, that some philosopher or scientist had already intuited it long ago. The claim made here is not that of absolute novelty but of some further steps forward in the march of understanding.

Perhaps the most far-reaching conclusion I personally drew from the ESM findings is to realize how fragmented the architecture of our brain really is. Jacques Monod (1972), in writing about how chance and necessity shape the development of species by favoring carriers of certain genes that make the organism adapt better to one environment or another, used the French term *bricolage,* or "unplanned construction," to describe the results. ESM clearly shows the results, at the subjective level, of such *bricolage.* The Cartesian view of a mind designed to apprehend reality in its pure form, or even the Freudian or Skinnerian views, give far too great credit to the organization of the mind. Certainly some genetic programs are quite universal, and the "hierarchy of needs" (Maslow, 1970) is reasonably constant: most of the time most people care more about survival than safety, more about safety than belonging to a group, and so on. Nevertheless each of us has programs for behaviors and feelings that don't match each other: the desires to be brave and cautious, to be outgoing and reserved, to compete and cooperate, survive side by side in our brains because—who knows why? Sooner or later one of these opposites might come in handier than the other.

The second conclusion might appear at first sight to contradict the first one. This conclusion based on ESM seems to point in the direction of the unity of humankind. Ever since the great anthropologist Franz Boaz began to document the enormous differences between cultures—in language, beliefs, values, and practices—even when the cultures were small and lived next to each other since time immemorial, "cultural relativism" has become one of the most widely accepted beliefs in the social sciences. In its vulgar form—and most beliefs accepted too quickly and too widely quickly become vulgar—cultural relativists claim that a belief held to be valid within any given group cannot be evaluated by members of any other group. Eating a defeated enemy's brain should not be judged less tasteful than eating *foie gras.* If a widow is burned to death on her husband's pyre, who are we to criticize it?

Of course cultural relativism is a good corrective to ethnocentrism up to a certain point, but beyond it becomes silly. Clearly many cultural practices are self-destructive and make the people who live by them miserable. Given a chance, people living under oppressive political systems will try to escape to a freer society; those living in poverty or in a rigid culture will try to move to where the conditions are more favorable. It is useful to remember that the United States, from its beginning to the present, was largely populated by individuals fleeing their native culture. In other words, despite the enormous superficial variations from one culture to the next, there seem to be shared universal parameters to what constitutes a good life.

ESM supports the view that the inner life of individuals is in many important respects the same across the globe. A good example is the similarity in the *experience* of flow, regardless of culture, despite the difference in the *activities* that produce it. Navajo shepherds experience flow while riding their horses, Korean seniors as they read sacred texts—and they both describe how they feel when doing so in very similar ways. Swiss engineers may feel it when designing watches, Japanese teenagers when racing motorcycles, and Thai mountain people while planting rice. All of them report the concentrated focus of attention when goals are clear, challenges match their abilities, and feedback is unambiguous. Thus flow appears to be a universal survival adaptation for our species, just as the pleasure we all take in food, sex, and also, unfortunately, in power and possessions has evolved in similar ways everywhere.

Finally, ESM suggests a view of how our minds work that is quite different from the highly individualistic, autonomous, self-sufficient image we tend to have of it in the Western world. It is not "natural" for humans to be alone; we feel lonely, and it is difficult for us to think well or act with purpose when alone. Of course people learn to do so, but often under duress, and often paying a high psychic price for it. It is not a picture that someone like Ayn Rand would find congenial, but there it is: human nature.

There is much more one could say, but sometimes it is better to focus on the larger issues and let the lesser ones fade into the background temporarily. But the chapters in this volume contain hundreds of insights into how people live and feel, and some of them might be more important, for any particular reader, than the three highlighted in this section.

What Value Does ESM Add to Psychology?

Psychology as a scientific discipline emerged in the late nineteenth century in an intellectual climate where rigorous experimental studies based on mechanistic models were considered the most fruitful means for understanding reality. Ever since, psychology has suffered from what has been called "physics envy"—the ambition to live up to the objective precision that nineteenth century physicists believed was attainable. But whereas all the other sciences, from biology to chemistry to physics, had been based on centuries of careful observation and recording, psychology took the short cut of becoming "scientific" with very little prior systematic accumulation of knowledge. As a result, much of what this new discipline started measuring was not what mattered most but what was most easily measurable—reaction times, response frequencies, and visual discriminations—often in a decontextualized, atheoretical manner. Modeling itself on the already established sciences, psychology relegated subjective experience to the periphery because of its ephemeral nature.

One way to think about ESM is that it tries to provide psychology with a method and a theoretical perspective that makes it possible to study whole individuals functioning in their everyday environments, both as *behaving* organisms and as *acting*, conscious beings. While this approach is unlikely to constitute more than a small fraction of what the field of psychology encompasses, it is an essential fraction. Without it, psychology loses its central purpose, which is to understand the inner experiences of people in order to improve their lives. The emerging field of positive psychology recognizes this connection between experience and mental well-being and has generated renewed interest in the types of questions ESM is most suited to addressing (Seligman & Csikszentmihalyi, 2000).

The purpose of this book has been to share the many unprecedented insights into how life can be studied that ESM is able to provide. Another goal was to inspire young investigators to use this method themselves so they can experience the exhilaration of this process of discovery first hand and in the process contribute to the important goal of establishing a systematic phenomenology as a serious scientific theme in psychology. Even a handful of good researchers taking up this challenge can make a lasting difference in our understanding of human life and the human mind.

—Mihaly Csikszentmihalyi

Appendix A

Sample ESM Data Collection Forms (ESFs)

The first form to follow is a modification of a form used in the Sloan Study of Youth and Social Development (Csikszentmihalyi & Schneider, 2000). The second was used in the 500 Family Study (Schneider & Waite, 2005).

Date _____ Time beeped _____ a.m./p.m. Time you answered _____ a.m./p.m.

As you were beeped . . . (be specific)
Where were you?

What were you thinking about?

What was the main thing you were doing?

What else were you doing?

	Not at all				Very much
Did you enjoy what you were doing?	1	2	3	4	5
How well were you concentrating?	1	2	3	4	5
Did you feel good about yourself?	1	2	3	4	5
Were you learning anything or getting better at something?	1	2	3	4	5
Did you have some choice in picking this activity?	1	2	3	4	5

Describe your mood as you were beeped:

	very	quite	some	neither	some	quite	very	
Happy	3	2	1	0	1	2	3	Sad
Passive	3	2	1	0	1	2	3	Active
Ashamed	3	2	1	0	1	2	3	Proud
Worried	3	2	1	0	1	2	3	Relaxed
Weak	3	2	1	0	1	2	3	Strong
Lonely	3	2	1	0	1	2	3	Sociable
Excited	3	2	1	0	1	2	3	Bored
Angry	3	2	1	0	1	2	3	Friendly

Who were you with? (Check all that apply)

( ) alone

( ) mother

( ) father

( ) sister(s) or brother(s)

( ) other relatives

( ) others (who?_____)

( ) teacher(s)

( ) classmates, peers

( ) other adult (coach, etc.)

( ) friend(s) How many?

___ females ___ males

Indicate how you felt about the main activity:

	Not at all			Very much	
How challenging was it?	1	2	3	4	5
Was it important to you?	1	2	3	4	5
How skilled are you at it?	1	2	3	4	5
Did you wish you had been doing something else?	1	2	3	4	5
Was this activity interesting?	1	2	3	4	5
How important was it to your future goals?	1	2	3	4	5

Since you were last beeped, estimate how much time you spent:

Hanging out with friends	0	¼	½	¾	1	1¼	1½	1¾	2 Hours
Chores, errands	0	¼	½	¾	1	1¼	1½	1¾	2 Hours
Playing/practicing sports	0	¼	½	¾	1	1¼	1½	1¾	2 Hours
After-school program or club/religious activity	0	¼	½	¾	1	1¼	1½	1¾	2 Hours
Doing homework	0	¼	½	¾	1	1¼	1½	1¾	2 Hours

If you were feeling a lot of something, why did you feel that way?

If you turned the watch off or didn't carry it with you since the last time you responded, what were you doing during that time?

Date _____ Time you were beeped _____ a.m./p.m. Time you responded ___ a.m./p.m.

As you were beeped . . .

Where were you?_____

_____

What was the **main thing** you were **doing?** _____

_____

What else were you doing at the same time? _____

_____

What was **on your mind?** _____

_____

Were you alone . . .   Yes _____   No _____   . . . or were you with . . .
(please check all that apply)

Your Spouse _____   Your Boss _____   Co-workers _____   Friend(s) _____   Girl/Boyfriend _____

Your Mother _____   Your Father _____   Teacher _____   Classmates/peers _____   Other(s) _____

Your child(ren) _____ (please indicate who) _____

Your sibling(s) _____ (please indicate who) _____

Think back on how you got into this activity . . .

Were you doing this **main activity** because you . . . (check all that apply)
(1) wanted to _____   (2) had to _____   (3) had nothing else to do _____

Indicate how you felt about the main activity.   (please circle one number for each question)

	Not at all	A little	Somewhat	Very much
Did you **enjoy** what you were doing?	0	1	2	3
Was this activity **interesting?**	0	1	2	3
How well were you **concentrating?**	0	1	2	3
Were you living up to **your own expectations?**	0	1	2	3
Did you feel **in control of the situation?**	0	1	2	3
Did the situation allow you to be **involved** or **to act?**	0	1	2	3
Did you have the **abilities to deal** with the situation?	0	1	2	3
Was the activity **important to you?**	0	1	2	3
Were others **expecting** a lot from you?	0	1	2	3
Were you **succeeding** at what you were doing?	0	1	2	3
Did you wish you **were doing something else?**	0	1	2	3
Did you **feel good** about yourself?	0	1	2	3

How did you feel as you were beeped? (For every pair of opposites, please circle only one mark.)

Happy   Sad   **Weak**   **Strong**   Passive   Active   **Excited**   **Bored**

○○○○○○○   ○○○○○○○   ○○○○○○○   ○○○○○○○

As you were being beeped, were you feeling . . . ?   (circle one number for each question)

	Not at all	A little	Some-what	Very much		Not at all	A little	Some-what	Very much
Cheerful	0	1	2	3	Worried	0	1	2	3
Lonely	0	1	2	3	Caring	0	1	2	3
Nervous	0	1	2	3	Irritated	0	1	2	3
Cooperative	0	1	2	3	Relaxed	0	1	2	3
Angry	0	1	2	3	Stressed	0	1	2	3
Responsible	0	1	2	3	Proud	0	1	2	3
Frustrated	0	1	2	3	Friendly	0	1	2	3
Competitive	0	1	2	3	Hardworking	0	1	2	3
Strained	0	1	2	3	Productive	0	1	2	3

Did you feel any **physical pain** or
discomfort as you were beeped?
(Please describe) _____

	None	Slight	Bothersome	Severe
	0	1	2	3

If you were talking with people, please answer the following 3 questions:	Not at all	A little	Some-what	Very much
Were you able to **express** your opinion?	0	1	2	3
Were others really listening to what you had to say?	0	1	2	3
Did you **care** about what others were saying?	0	1	2	3

If you felt a strong emotion since the last report, what did you feel and why did you feel that way?

I felt _____ because _____

Please   be   specific

If anyone else you were with expressed a strong emotion to you since the last report, what did they feel and why?

(who) _____ felt _____ because _____

Please   be   specific

COMMENTS, ETC.

Appendix B

ESM Coding Scheme Used in the Sloan Study of Youth and Social Development*

Variable Name

ID   ID number of student

BOOK   Booklet number

BEEP   Beep number of booklet

MONTH   Month of the year

DAY   Day of the month

YEAR   Current year

TIME1   Time signaled—military time (HHMM)

TIME2   Time answered—military time (HHMM)

---

*SOURCE: Csikszentmihalyi & Schneider, 2000. The ESF to which the coding scheme corresponds can be found in this volume.

CODES for PLACE: Where the student is when signaled

10	Unspecified/Other School Class Academics	55	School Grounds Outside
11	Mathematics	56	Band/Orchestra Practice
12	English/English Composition/ Literature	57	Social Service
13	Reading	58	Sports/Playing Field
14	General Science	59	Locker Area
15	Biology	60	Study Hall
16	Chemistry	61	Restroom
17	Physics	62	Teacher Area
18	Earth Science	63	Principal/Counselor Office
19	Computer Science/ Programming	70	Unspecified/Other Home
20	Foreign Language	71	Kitchen
21	History	72	Bedroom
22	Political Science/Civics	73	Dining Room
23	Geography/World Cultures	74	Living Room/Family Room/Den
24	Business Theory/Economics	75	Bathroom
25	Psychology	76	Basement
26	Social Studies/Sociology/ Anthropology	77	Yard or Garage
27	Ethic/Multicultural Studies	80	Unspecified/Other Public Not Work
30	Physical Education	81	Automobile
31	Music	82	Bus
32	Driver Education	83	Train
33	Fine Art	84	Store
34	Photography	85	Park
35	Drafting	86	Indoor Recreation
36	Graphics/Applied Art	87	Mall
37	Drama	88	Restaurant/Cafe
38	Agriculture	89	Street
39	Shop/Vocational-Technology	90	Religious Building
40	Family Planning/Sex Education/Health	91	Sport Event Not School
41	Domestic Arts/Home Economics	92	Friend Home
42	Business Skills	93	Relative Home
43	Career Exploration/Counseling	94	Hospital
44	Religious Studies	110	Unspecified/Other at Work
50	Gym	111	Store
51	Library	112	Office
52	Cafeteria/Lunch Room	113	Restaurant
53	Halls/Foyer	114	Yard
54	Student Center/Auditorium	115	Farm
		116	Garage (Mechanics)
		117	Household
		118	Factory
		130	Others

CODES for THOUGHT, DOING1, and DOING2

THOUGHT: Thoughts when signaled, DOING1: Primary activity when signaled, DOING2: Secondary activity when signaled.

200	Unspecified/Other School	253	Fine Art
210	Unspecified/Other in class	254	Photography
211	Listening to Lecture	255	Drafting
212	Listening/Taking Notes	256	Graphics/Applied Art
213	Listening/Discussion	257	Drama
214	Participation in Discussion	258	Agriculture
215	Labwork with Group	259	Shop/Vocational-Technology
216	Labwork Alone	260	Family Planning/Sex Education/Health
217	Group Work/Activity		
218	Individual Work	261	Domestic Arts/Home Economics
219	Solo Presentation	262	Business Skills
220	Group Presentation	263	Career Exploration/Counseling
221	Watching TV/Film/Video	264	Religious Studies
222	Talking to Teacher	265	Assembly
223	Test/Quiz	270	Unspecified/Other Extra Curricular Activity Taking Place at School
230	Unspecified/Other Homework/Study		
231	Mathematics	271	Athletics
232	English/English Composition/Literature	272	Music
		273	Art
233	Reading	274	Science
234	General Science	275	Drama
235	Biology	276	Literary
236	Chemistry	277	Political
237	Physics	278	Social Service
238	Earth Science	279	Computer
239	Computer Science/ Programming	280	Math
		281	International/Language Club
240	Foreign Language	282	Field Trip
241	History	290	Unspecified/Other Job/Work
242	Political Science/Civics	291	At Work, Paid
243	Geography/World Cultures	292	At Work, Not Paid
244	Business Theory/Economics	293	Finding a Job
245	Psychology	294	Talking about Present/Future Job
246	Social Studies/Sociology/ Anthropology		
		295	Quitting a Job
247	Ethic/Multicultural Studies	296	Housework/Chores
248	Library	297	Errands, Nonpersonal
250	Physical Education	310	Unspecified/Other Life Plans
251	Music	311	Talking about Future Career/Unspecified
252	Driver Education		

312	Talking about Future Career/Specific	373	Playing/Other Games
313	Gathering Info. about Future Career/Unspecified	380	Unspecified/Other TV
		381	TV: News
314	Gathering Info. about Future Career/Specific	382	TV: Educational
		383	TV: Sports
315	College/College Application–Related Activity	384	TV: Sitcom/Cartoon/Soap/Game Show
316	Awards	385	TV: Movie or Drama
317	Future—General	390	Unspecified/Other Movie/Theater
330	Unspecified/Other Social Life	391	Movie—in Cinema
331	Talking with Family	392	Videocassette/DVD
332	Talking with Relatives	393	Live Drama (Theater)
333	Talking with Classmates	400	Unspecified/Other Radio/Stereo
334	Talking with Friends	401	Listening to Music
335	Talking with Boyfriend/Girlfriend	402	Radio News
		410	Unspecified/Other Art/Hobby Not School Related
336	Sexual Activity		
337	Preparing for Date	411	Athletic Hobby Nonschool
338	Dating (Not Talking)	412	Music Hobby Nonschool
339	Hanging Out/Partying	413	Art Hobby Nonschool
340	Going Out/Downtown/Mall	414	Science Hobby Nonschool
341	Phone—Unspecified/Other	415	Drama Hobby Nonschool
342	Phone—Family	416	Writing/Reading Lit. Nonschool
343	Phone—Friends		
344	Writing Letters	417	Fun Reading/Writing
345	Argue/Fight/Yelling	418	Politics
346	Joke/Kid/Laughing	419	Social Service
347	Religious Events	420	Computer
348	Kiss/Hug/Flirting	430	Unspecified/Other Maintenance
350	Unspecified/Other Thinking about		
		431	Eating a Meal
351	Thinking about Self	432	Snacking
352	Thinking about Immediate Family	433	Personal Care, Grooming
		434	Sleeping/Relaxing/Resting
353	Thinking about Other Relatives	435	Walking, Transit
		436	Sitting/Standing
354	Thinking about Friends	437	Being Sick
355	Thinking about Romantic Interest—Unspecified	440	Smoking Tobacco
		441	Drug Activity, Not Marijuana
356	Thinking about Romantic Interest—Specific	442	Drinking Alcohol
		443	Thinking: Dying, Death of Others
357	Vacationing/Traveling/Trip		
370	Unspecified/Other Sports/Games	444	Thinking: Meaning of Life/Religion
371	Watching Sports, Not TV (Spectator)	445	Participating in This Study (e.g., Completing Survey or Interview)
372	Video Games/Nintendo		

446	Waiting to Do Something	454	Getting into Trouble
447	Crying	455	Running Away from Home
448	Thinking: Going Home	800	Nothing
449	Using Marijuana	810	Not Telling
450	Dazing/Daydreaming	820	Missing the Beep
451	Playing with Pets	850	Others (e.g., "I forgot")
453	Skipping Class/Cutting School	851	Holiday Activity

LIKE   Was the main activity more like work or play?
       1 Work, 2 Play, 3 Both, 4 Neither

CONC   How well were you concentrating?
       0 Not at all–9 Very much

EXPO   Were you living up to others' expectations?
       0 Not at all–9 Very much

CONCEASE Was it hard to concentrate?
       0 Not at all–9 Very much

NSELF   Did you feel self-conscious or embarrassed?
       0 Not at all self-conscious–9 Very self-conscious

GOOD   Did you feel good about yourself?
       0 Not at all–9 Very much

ENJOY   Did you enjoy what you were doing?
       0 Not at all–9 Very much

EXPY   Were you living up to your expectations?
       0 Not at all–9 Very much

CONTROL Did you feel in control of the situation?
       0 Not at all–9 Very much

WHYDO   Why were you doing the main activity?

       1 You wanted to

       2 You had to

       3 You had nothing else to do

       4 You had to and wanted to

       5 You wanted to & nothing else

       6 You had to & nothing else

       7 All of the above

DESCRIBE YOUR MOOD AS YOU WERE BEEPED:

HAPPY
Felt happy
1 Very happy–7 Very sad

STRONG
Felt strong
1 Very weak–7 Very strong

ACTIVE
Felt active
1 Very passive–7 Very active

SOCIABLE
Felt sociable
1 Very lonely–7 Very sociable

PROUD
Felt proud
1 Very ashamed–7 Very proud

INVOLVED
Felt involved
1 Very involved–7 Very detached

EXCITED
Felt excited
1 Very excited–7 Very bored

CLEAR
Felt clear
1 Very clear–7 Very confused

RELAXED
Felt relaxed
1 Very worried–7 Very relaxed

COOP
Felt cooperative
1 Very competitive–7 Very cooperative

ALONE
Student was alone
0 No, 1 Yes

MOTHER
Student was with mother
0 No, 1 Yes

FATHER
Student was with father
0 No, 1 Yes

SIBLING
Student was with sibling
0 No, 1 Yes

RELATIVE
Student was with relatives
0 No, 1 Yes

OTHER	Student was with others 0 No, 1 Yes
TEACHER	Student was with teacher 0 No, 1 Yes
CLASMATE	Student was with classmates 0 No, 1 Yes
STRANGER	Student was with strangers 0 No, 1 Yes
FRIEND	Student was with friends 0 No, 1 Yes
NFRIEND	Number of friends 0 Not indicated–9 Nine or more
SFRIEND	Sex of friends 0 Not indicated 1 Male 2 Female 3 Both
CHALL	Challenges of the activity 1 Low–9 High
SKILL	Your skills in the activity 1 Low–9 High
IMPY	Was this activity important to you? 1 Low–9 High
EASY	How easy did you find this activity? 1 Low–9 High
SUCCEED	Were you succeeding at what you were doing? 1 Not at all–9 Very much
WISH	Did you wish to be doing the present activity? 1 Not at all–9 Very much
INTEREST	Was this activity interesting? 1 Not at all–9 Very much
FUIMPO	How important was it in relation to your future goals? 1 Not at all–9 Very much

WISHWITH   Who do you wish you were with?

1   Siblings
2   Parents
3   Parents and siblings (family)
4   Other relatives
5   Same-sex friend
6   Same-sex group
7   Opposite-sex friend
8   Opposite-sex group
9   Mixed-sex group
10   Friend, gender unspecified
11   Friends, gender unspecified
12   Friends & relatives
13   Alone
14   Class/teammates
15   Teachers
16   Famous person(s)
17   Actual boy/girlfriend
18   Wished boy/girlfriend
19   Pets
20   Actual child (children)
21   Religious character
22   Spouse
23   Friends of the family
24   Family relatives
80   Others

WISHSAM1   Do you wish to be with this person (or these people)?
0 different, 1 same

WISHDO   What would you rather be doing? (see above codes for DOING1, DOING2, and THOUGHT)

TV   Time spent watching TV since last report
0   None
1   15 minutes
2   30 minutes
3   45 minutes
4   1 hour
5   1 hour 15 min
6   1 hour 30 min
7   1 hour 45 min
8   2 hours

CHORE   Time doing chores and errands since last report
0   None
1   15 minutes

2	30 minutes
3	45 minutes
4	1 hour
5	1 hour 15 min
6	1 hour 30 min
7	1 hour 45 min
8	2 hours

WORK   Time doing paid work since last report
0	None
1	15 minutes
2	30 minutes
3	45 minutes
4	1 hour
5	1 hour 15 min
6	1 hour 30 min
7	1 hour 45 min
8	2 hours

HANGOUT   Time spent hanging out with friends since last report
0	None
1	15 minutes
2	30 minutes
3	45 minutes
4	1 hour
5	1 hour 15 min
6	1 hour 30 min
7	1 hour 45 min
8	2 hours

HOMEWORK   Time spent doing homework since last report
0	None
1	15 minutes
2	30 minutes
3	45 minutes
4	1 hour
5	1 hour 15 min
6	1 hour 30 min
7	1 hour 45 min
8	2 hours

HAPPEN   Has anything happened or have you done anything that could have affected how you feel?
0	Nothing or no
1	Negative event
2	Ambivalent event
3	Positive event

COMMENT   Comments

0	None
10	Negative unspecified
11	Negative school
12	Negative family
13	Negative friends
14	Negative teacher
15	Negative job
16	Negative ESM
20	Positive unspecified
21	Positive school
22	Positive family
23	Positive friends
24	Positive teacher
25	Positive job
26	Positive ESM
30	Ambivalent unspecified
31	Ambivalent school
32	Ambivalent family
33	Ambivalent friends
34	Ambivalent teacher
35	Ambivalent job
36	Ambivalent ESM

References

Adam, E. K. (2005). Momentary emotion and cortisol levels in the everyday lives of working parents. In B. Schneider & L. J. Waite (Eds.), *Being together, working apart: Dual-career families and the work-life balance* (pp. 105–133). New York: Cambridge University Press.

Adlai-Gail, W. S. (1994). *Exploring the autotelic personality.* Doctoral dissertation, University of Chicago.

Alliger, G. M., & Williams, K. J. (1993). Using signal-contingent experience sampling methodology to study work in the field: A discussion and illustration examining task perceptions and mood. *Personnel Psychology, 46,* 525–549.

Almeida, D. M., & Kessler, R. C. (1998). Everyday stressors and gender differences in daily distress. *Journal of Personality and Social Psychology, 75,* 670–680.

Almeida, D. M., Wethington, E., & Chandler, A. L. (1999). Daily transmission of tensions between marital dyads and parent-child dyads. *Journal of Marriage and the Family, 61,* 49–61.

Alwin, D. F. (1986). Religion and parental child-rearing orientations: Evidence of a Catholic-Protestant convergence. *American Journal of Sociology, 92,* 412–440.

Arendt, H. (1958). *The human condition.* Chicago: University of Chicago Press.

Asakawa, K. (2001). Family socialization practices and their effects on the internalization of educational values for Asian and White American students. *Applied Developmental Science, 5,* 184–194.

Asakawa, K., & Csikszentmihalyi, M. (1998). The quality of experience of Asian American adolescents in activities related to future goals. *Journal of Youth and Adolescence, 27,* 141–163.

Asakawa, K., & Csikszentmihalyi, M. (2000a). Feelings of connectedness and internalization of values in Asian American adolescents. *Journal of Youth and Adolescence, 29,* 121–142.

Asakawa, K., & Csikszentmihalyi, M. (2000b). The quality of experience of Asian-American adolescents in academic activities: An exploration of educational achievement. *Journal of Research on Adolescents, 8,* 241–262.

Bahr, H. M., & Martin, T. K. (1983). 'And thy neighbor as thyself': Self-esteem and faith in people as correlates of religiosity and family solidarity among Middletown High School students. *Journal for the Scientific Study of Religion, 22,* 132–144.

Barber, B. L., Jacobson, K. C., Miller, K. E., & Petersen, A. C. (1998). Ups and downs: Daily cycles of adolescent moods. In A. C. Crouter & R. Larson (Eds.), *Temporal rhythms in adolescence: Clocks, calendars, and the coordination of daily life* (pp. 23–36). San Francisco: Jossey-Bass.

Barge-Schaapveld, D. Q., & Nicolson, N. A. (2002). Effects of antidepressant treatment on the quality of daily life: An experience sampling study. *Journal of Clinical Psychiatry, 63,* 477–485.

Barge-Schaapveld, D. Q., Nicolson, N. A., van der Hoop, R. G., & deVries, M. W. (1995). Changes in daily life experience associated with clinical improvement in depression. *Journal of Affective Disorders, 34,* 139–154.

Barkow, J. H., Cosmides, L., & Tooby, J. (1992). *The adapted mind: Evolutionary psychology and the generation of culture.* New York: Oxford University Press.

Barnett, R. C., & Shen, Y. (1997). Gender, high- and low-schedule-control house-work tasks, and psychological distress: A study of dual-earner couples. *Journal of Family Issues, 18,* 403–428.

Bartkowski, J. P., & Xu, X. (2000). Distant patriarchs or expressive dads? The discourse and practice of fathering in conservative Protestant families. *The Sociological Quarterly, 41,* 465–485.

Bassi, M. (2000). *A climbing expedition in the Himalaya: Individual differences in the quality of experience.* Paper presented at the First International Positive Psychology Summit, Washington, DC.

Baumrind, D. (1968). Authoritarian vs. authoritative parental control. *Adolescence, 3,* 255–272.

Baumrind, D. (1971). Current patterns for parental authority. *Developmental Psychology Monograph, 4,* 1–103.

Baumrind, D. (1973). The development of instrumental competence through social-ization. In A. D. Pick (Ed.), *Minnesota symposium on child psychology* (pp. 3–46). Minneapolis: University of Minnesota Press.

Beal, D. J., & Weiss, H. M. (2003). Methods of ecological momentary assessment in organizational research. *Organizational Research Methods, 6,* 440–464.

Belsky, J. (1988). The effects of infant day care reconsidered. *Early Childhood Research Quarterly, 3,* 235–272.

Belsky, J. (1990). Parental and nonparental care and children's socioemotional devel-opment: A decade in review. *Journal of Marriage and the Family, 52,* 885–903.

Benson, P. L., & Donahue, M. J. (1989). Ten year trends in at-risk behaviors: A national study of black adolescents. *Journal of Adolescent Research, 4,* 125–139.

Berry J. W., Poortinga, Y. H., Pandey, J., Dasen, P. R., Saraswathi, T. S., Segall, M. H., et al. (Eds.). (1997). *Handbook of cross-cultural psychology* (Vol. 3). Boston: Allyn & Bacon.

Berscheid, E. (1990). Contemporary vocabularies of emotion. In A. M. Isen & B. S. Moore (Eds.), *Affect and social behavior* (pp. 22–38). New York: Cambridge University Press.

Bianchi, S. M., Milkie, M. A., Sayer, L. C., & Robinson, J. P. (2000). Is anyone doing the housework? Trends in the gender division of household labor. *Social Forces, 79,* 191–228.

Bolger, N., Davis, A., & Rafaeli, E. (2003). Diary methods: Capturing life as it is lived. *Annual Review of Psychology, 54,* 579–616.

Borrie, W. T., & Roggenbuck, J. W. (2001). The dynamic, emergent, and multiphasic nature of on-site wilderness experiences. *Journal of Leisure Research, 33,* 202–228.

Boyd, R., & Richerson, P. J. (1985). *Culture and the evolutionary process.* Chicago: University of Chicago Press.

Boyd, R., & Richerson, P. J. (1990). Group selection among alternative evolutionary stable strategies. *Journal of Theoretical Biology, 145,* 331–342.

Bradburn, N. M. (1969). *The structure of psychological well-being.* Chicago: Aldine.

Bradburn, N. M. (2000). Temporal representation and event dating. In A. A. Stone, J. S. Turkkan, C. A. Bachrach, J. B. Job, H. S. Kurtzman, & V. S. Cain (Eds.), *The science of self-report: Implications for research and practice* (pp. 49–61). Mahwah, NJ: Lawrence Erlbaum Associates.

Brandstätter, H. (1983). Emotional responses to other persons in everyday life situations. *Journal of Personality and Social Psychology, 45,* 871–883.

Brandstätter, H., & Gaubatz, S. (1997). Befindenstagebuch am neuen Arbeitsplatz in differentialpsychologischer Sicht. *Zeitschrift für Arbeits- und Organisationspsychologie, 41,* 18–29.

Brief, A. P., & Roberson, L. (1989). Job attitude organization: An exploratory study. *Journal of Applied Social Psychology, 19,* 717–727.

Brown, K. W., & Ryan, R. M. (2003). The benefits of being present: Mindfulness and its role in psychological well-being. *Journal of Personality and Social Psychology, 84,* 822–848.

Bryk, A. S., & Raudenbush, S. W. (1992). *Hierarchical linear models.* Newbury Park, CA: Sage.

Buss, D. (1994). *The evolution of desire: Strategies of human mating.* New York: Basic Books.

Campbell, A. (1981). *The sense of well-being in America.* New York: McGraw Hill.

Carli, M., Delle Fave, A., & Massimini, F. (1988). The quality of experience in the flow channels: Comparison of Italian and U.S. students. In M. Csikszentmihalyi & I. S. Csikszentmihalyi (Eds.), *Optimal experience: Psychological studies of flow in consciousness* (pp. 288–318). New York: Cambridge University Press.

Carstensen, L. L., Pasupathi, M., Mayr, U., & Nesselroade, J. R. (2000). Emotional experience in everyday life across the adult life span. *Journal of Personality and Social Psychology, 79,* 644–655.

Cerin, E., Szabo, A., & Williams, C. (2001). Is the Experience Sampling Method (ESM) appropriate for studying pre-competitive emotions? *Psychology of Sport and Exercise, 2,* 27–45.

Chalmers, D. J. (1995). Facing up to the problem of consciousness. *Journal of Consciousness Studies, 2,* 200–219.

Changeux, J. P., & Chavaillon, J. (1995). *Origins of the human brain.* Oxford, UK: Clarendon.

Chao, R. K. (1994). Beyond parental control and authoritarian parenting style: Understanding Chinese parenting through the cultural notion of training. *Child Development, 65,* 1111–1119.

Chen, C., & Stevenson, H. W. (1995). Motivation and mathematics achievement: A comparative study of Asian-American, Caucasian-American, and East Asian high school students. *Child Development, 66,* 1215–1234.

Chen, H., Wigand, R. T., & Nilan, M. (1999). Optimal experience of Web activities. *Computers in Human Behavior, 15*(5), 585–608.

Chen, H., Wigand, R. T., & Nilan, M. (2000). Exploring Web users' optimal flow experiences. *Information Technology & People, 13*(4), 263–281.

Christensen, S. L., Sinclair, M. F., Lahr, C. A., & Godber, Y. (2001). Promoting successful school completing: Critical conceptual and methodological guidelines. *School Psychology Quarterly, 16,* 468–484.

Cochran, J. K., & Beeghley, L. (1991). The influence of religion on attitudes toward nonmarital sexuality: A preliminary assessment of reference group theory. *Journal for the Scientific Study of Religion, 30,* 45–62.

Cohen, P., & Brook, J. (1987). Family factors related to the persistence of psychopathology in childhood and adolescence. *Psychiatry, 50,* 332–345.

Cole, M. (1996). *Cultural psychology: A once and future discipline.* Cambridge, MA: Bellknap Press.

Collins, R. L., Kashdan, T. B., & Gollnisch, G. (2003). The feasibility of using cellular phones to collect ecological momentary assessment data: Application to alcohol consumption. *Experimental and Clinical Psychopharmacology, 11,* 73–78.

Collins, R. L., Morsheimer, E. T., Shiffman, S., Paty, J. A., Gnys, M., & Papandonatos, G. D. (1998). Ecological momentary assessment in a behavioral drinking moderation training program. *Experimental and Clinical Psychopharmacology, 6,* 306–315.

Conner Christensen, T., Feldman Barrett, L., Bliss-Moreau, E., Lebo, K., & Kaschub, C. (2003). A practical guide to experience-sampling procedures. *Journal of Happiness Studies, 4*(1), 53–78.

Conti, R. (2001). Time flies: Investigating the connection between intrinsic motivation and the experience of time. *Journal of Personality, 69,* 1–26.

Côté, S., & Moskowitz, D. S. (1998). On the dynamic covariation between interpersonal behavior and affect: prediction from neuroticism, extraversion, and agreeableness. *Journal of Personality and Social Psychology, 75*(4), 1032–1046.

Cranny, C. J., Smith, P. C., & Stone, E. F. (1992). *Job satisfaction: Advances in research and applications.* New York: Free Press.

Crocker, J., Karpinski, A., Quinn, D. M., & Chase, S. K. (2003). When grades determine self-worth: Consequences of contingent self-worth for male and female engineering and psychology majors. *Journal of Personality and Social Psychology, 85,* 507–516.

Crocker, J., Sommers, S. R., & Luhtanen, R. K. (2002). Hopes dashed and dreams fulfilled: Contingencies of self-worth and graduate school admissions. *Personality and Social Psychology Bulletin, 9,* 1275–1286.

Cruise, C. E., Broderick, J., Porter, L., Kaell, A., & Stone, A. A. (1996). Reactive effects of diary self-assessment in chronic pain patients. *Pain, 67,* 253–258.

Csikszentmihalyi, M. (1975). *Beyond boredom and anxiety.* San Francisco: Jossey-Bass.

Csikszentmihalyi, M. (1978). Attention and the holistic approach to behavior. In K. S. Pope & J. L. Singer (Eds.), *The stream of consciousness* (pp. 335–358). New York: Plenum.

Csikszentmihalyi, M. (1988). The flow experience and its significance for human psychology. In M. Csikszentmihalyi & I. S. Csikszentmihalyi (Eds.), *Optimal experience: Psychological studies of flow in consciousness* (pp. 15–35). New York: Cambridge University Press.

Csikszentmihalyi, M. (1990). *Flow: The psychology of optimal experience.* New York: HarperCollins.

Csikszentmihalyi, M. (1992) Öffentliche Meinung und die Psychologie der Einsamkeit. (Public opinion and the psychology of loneliness). In J. Wilke (Ed.), *Öffentliche Meinung: Theorie, Methode, Befunde* (pp. 31–40). Freiburg: Verlag Karl Alber.

Csikszentmihalyi, M. (1995). [Average happiness in three contexts of adolescents from three cultures]. Unpublished data.

Csikszentmihalyi, M. (1997). *Creativity: Flow and the psychology of discovery and invention.* Chicago: University of Chicago Press.

Csikszentmihalyi, M. (1997). *Finding flow: The psychology of engagement with everyday life.* New York: HarperCollins.

Csikszentmihalyi, M. (2000). *Beyond boredom and anxiety* (2nd ed.). San Francisco: Jossey-Bass.

Csikszentmihalyi, M., & Beattie, O. (1979). Life themes: A theoretical and empirical exploration of their origins and effects. *Journal of Humanistic Psychology, 19,* 677–693.

Csikszentmihalyi, M., & Csikszentmihalyi, I. S. (Eds.). (1988). *Optimal experience: Psychological studies of flow in consciousness.* New York: Cambridge University Press.

Csikszentmihalyi, M., & Figurski, T. J. (1982). Self-awareness and aversive experience in everyday life. *Journal of Personality, 50,* 14–26.

Csikszentmihalyi, M., & Graef, R. (1980). The experience of freedom in everyday life. *American Journal of Community Psychology, 18,* 402–414.

Csikszentmihalyi, M., & Hunter, J. (2003). Happiness in everyday life: The uses of Experience Sampling. *Journal of Happiness Studies, 4,* 185–189.

Csikszentmihalyi, M., & Larson, R. W. (1984). *Being adolescent: Conflict and growth in the teenage years.* New York: Basic Books.

Csikszentmihalyi, M., & Larson, R. W. (1987). Validity and reliability of the experience sampling method. *Journal of Nervous and Mental Disease, 175,* 526–536.

Csikszentmihalyi, M., Larson, R. W., & Prescott, S. (1977). The ecology of adolescent activities and experiences. *Journal of Youth and Adolescence, 6,* 281–294.

Csikszentmihalyi, M., & LeFevre, J. (1989). Optimal experience in work and leisure. *Journal of Personality and Social Psychology, 56,* 815–822.

Csikszentmihalyi, M., & Massimini, F. (1985). On the psychological selection of bio-cultural information. *New Ideas Psychology, 3,* 115–138.

Csikszentmihalyi, M., Rathunde, K., & Whalen, S. (1993). *Talented teenagers: The roots of success and failure.* New York: Cambridge University Press.

Csikszentmihalyi, M., & Rochberg-Halton, E. (1981). *The meaning of things.* New York: Cambridge University Press.

Csikszentmihalyi, M., & Schneider, B. (2000). *Becoming adult: How teenagers prepare for the world of work.* New York: Basic Books.

Dawkins, R. (1976). *The selfish gene.* Oxford, UK: Oxford University Press.

Deci, E. L., Koestner, R., & Ryan, R. M. (1999). A meta-analytic review of experiments examining the effects of extrinsic rewards on intrinsic motivation. *Psychological Bulletin, 125,* 627–668.

Deci, E. L., & Ryan, R. M. (1985). *Intrinsic motivation and self-determination in human behavior.* New York: Plenum Press.

Delespaul, P. A. E. G. (1992). Technical note: Devices and time-sampling procedures. In M. W. deVries (Ed.), *The experience of psychopathology: Investigating mental disorders in their natural settings* (pp. 363–373). New York: Cambridge University Press.

Delespaul, P. A. E. G., & deVries, M. W. (1987). The daily life of ambulatory chronic mental patients. *Journal of Nervous and Mental Disease, 175,* 537–544.

Delespaul, P. A. E. G., & deVries, M. W. (1992). The daily life of ambulatory chronic mental patients. In M. W. deVries (Ed.), *The experience of psychopathology: Investigating mental disorders in their natural settings* (pp. 110–122). New York: Cambridge University Press.

Delle Fave, A., & Bassi, M. (2000). The quality of experience in adolescents' daily lives: Developmental perspectives. *Genetic, Social and General Psychology Monographs, 126,* 347–367.

Delle Fave, A., Bassi, M., & Massimini, F. (2003). Quality of experience and risk perception in high-altitude rock climbing. *Journal of Applied Sport Psychology, 1,* 1–38.

Delle Fave, A., & Massimini, F. (1992). The ESM and the measurement of clinical change: A case of anxiety disorder. In M. W. deVries (Ed.), *The experience of psychopathology: Investigating mental disorders in their natural settings* (pp. 280–289). New York: Cambridge University Press.

Delle Fave A., & Massimini F. (1999). Inter-cultural relations: A challenge for psychology. In A. Delle Fave & F. Meli (Eds.), *Modernization and cultural identity* (pp. 11–22). Milan: Edizioni Dell'Arco.

Delle Fave, A., & Massimini F. (2000a). Living at home or in institution: Adolescents' optimal experience and life theme. *Paideia. Cadernos de Psicologia e Educaçao, 19,* 55–66.

Delle Fave, A., & Massimini, F. (2000b). Subjective experience and the building of parental roles in a bio-cultural perspective. In A. L. Comunian & U. P. Gielen (Eds.), *International perspectives on human development* (pp. 159– 175). Lengerich, Germany: Pabst Science.

Delle Fave, A., & Massimini, F. (2003). Making disability into a resource: The role of optimal experience. *The Psychologist, 16,* 9–10.

Delle Fave, A., & Massimini, F. (2004). Parenthood and the quality of experience in daily life: A longitudinal study. *Social Indicators Research, 67,* 75–106.

Delle Fave, A., Massimini, F., & Gaspardin, M. B. (1993). Televisione e qualita dell'esperienza quotidiana [Television and the quality of daily experience]. *IKON-Ricerche sulla communicazione, 26,* 81–109.

Dempsey, K. C. (2001). Feelings about housework: Understanding gender differences. *Journal of Family Studies, 7,* 141–159.

Dempsey, N. P. (2005). Television use and communication within families with adolescents. In B. Schneider & L. J. Waite (Eds.), *Being together, working apart: Dual-career families and the work-life balance* (pp. 277–296). New York: Cambridge University Press.

deVos, J. W., Van Wilgenburg, H., Van den Brink, W., Kaplan, C. D., & deVries, M. W. (1996). Patterns of craving and pharmacokinetics in long-term opiate addicts in methadone maintenance therapy. *Addiction Research, 3,* 285–295.

deVries, M. W. (Ed.). (1992). *The experience of psychopathology: Investigating mental disorders in their natural settings.* New York: Cambridge University Press.

deVries, M. W., & Delespaul, P. A. E. G. (1989). Time, context and subjective experience in schizophrenia. *Schizophrenia Bulletin, 15,* 233–244.

deVries, M. W., & Delespaul, P. A. E. G. (1992). Variability of schizophrenia symptoms. In M. W. deVries (Ed.), *The experience of psychopathology: Investigating mental disorders in their natural settings* (pp. 97–109). New York: Cambridge University Press.

deVries, M. W., Delespaul, P. A. E. G., & Dijkman-Caes, C. I. M. (1992). Consequences of depression for the experience of anxiety in daily life. In M. W. deVries (Ed.), *The experience of psychopathology: Investigating mental disorders in their natural settings* (pp. 141–147). New York: Cambridge University Press.

deVries, M. W., Delespaul, P. A. E. G., & Theunissen, J. R. (1984). *Diurnal variations in the conscious experience of schizophrenics.* Symposium on the Development of Schizophrenia, WPA Congress, Helsinki.

Diamond, J. (1997). *Guns, germs, and steel: The fates of human societies.* New York: W. W. Norton.

DiBianca, R. (2000). *Teaching adolescents: Relationships between features of instruction and student engagement in high school mathematics and science classrooms.* Chicago: University of Chicago.

Diener, E. (2000). Subjective well-being: The science of happiness and a proposal for a national index. *American Psychologist, 55,* 34–43.

Diener, E., Sandvik, E., & Larsen, R. J. (1985). Age and sex effects for emotional intensity. *Developmental Psychology, 21,* 542–546.

Diener, E., Smith, H., & Fujita, F. (1995). The personality structure of affect. *Journal of Personality and Social Psychology, 69,* 130–141.

Diener, E., Suh, E., & Oishi, S. (1997). Recent findings on subjective well-being. *Indian Journal of Clinical Psychology, 24,* 25–41.

Dijkman-Caes, C. I. M., & deVries, M. W. (1992). The social ecology of anxiety: Theoretical and quantitative perspectives. In M. W. deVries (Ed.), *The experience of psychopathology: Investigating mental disorders in their natural settings* (pp. 129–140). New York: Cambridge University Press.

Donahue, M. J., & Benson, P. L. (1995). Religion and the well-being of adolescents. *Journal of Social Issues, 51,* 145–160.

Dornbusch, S. M., Ritter, P. L., Leiderman, P. H., Roberts, D. F., & Fraleigh, M. J. (1987). The relation of parenting style to adolescent school performance. *Child Development, 58,* 1244–1257.

Downey, G., Purdie, V., & Schaffer-Neitz, R. (1999). Anger transmission from mother to child: A comparison of mothers in chronic pain and well mothers. *Journal of Marriage and the Family, 61,* 62–73.

Duckett, E., Raffaelli, M., & Richards, M. H. (1989). "Taking care": Maintaining the self and the home in early adolescence. *Journal of Youth and Adolescence, 18,* 549–565.

Durham, W. H. (1991). *Coevolution: Genes, culture and human diversity.* Stanford, CA: Stanford University Press.

Dworkin, J. B., & Larson, R. (2001). Age trends in the experience of family discord in single-mother families across adolescence. *Journal of Adolescence, 24,* 529–534.

Easterlin, B. L., & Cardena, E. (1998–1999). Cognitive and emotional differences between short- and long-term Vipassana meditators. *Imagination, Cognition and Personality, 18,* 69–81.

Eckenrode, J., & Gore, S. (Eds.). (1990). *Stress between work and family.* New York: Plenum.

Eid, M., & Diener, E. (1999). Intraindividual variability in affect: Reliability, validity, and personality correlates. *Journal of Personality and Social Psychology, 76,* 662–676.

Eldredge, N., & Grene, M. (1992). *Interactions: The biological context of social systems.* New York: Columbia University Press.

Ellis, G. D., Voelkl, J. E., & Morris, C. (1994). Measurement and analysis issues with explanation of variance in daily experience using the flow model. *Journal of Leisure Research, 26,* 337–356.

Ellison, C. G. (1991). Religious involvement and subjective well-being. *Journal of Health and Social Behavior, 32,* 80–99.

Ellison, C. G., & Bartkowski, J. P. (2002). Conservative Protestantism and the division of household labor among married couples. *Journal of Family Issues, 23,* 950–985.

Ellison, C. G., & Sherkat, D. E. (1993). Conservative Protestantism and support for corporal punishment. *American Sociological Review, 58,* 131–144.

Ellwood, M. (2002). *Time trade-offs among busy mothers.* Paper presented at Time Pressure, Work-Family Interface, and Parent-Child Relationships: An International Time Use Conference, University of Waterloo, Canada.

Evenson, R. E., Popkin, B. M., & Quizon, E. K. (1980). Nutrition, work, and demographic behavior in rural Phillippine households. In H. P. Binswanger, R. E. Evenson, C. C. Florencio, & B. N. White (Eds.), *Rural household studies in Asia* (pp. 280–366). Kent Ridge, Singapore: Singapore University Press.

Fahrenberg, J., & Myrtek, M. (Eds.). (1996). *Ambulatory assessment: Computer-assisted psychological and psychophysiological methods in monitoring and field studies.* Seattle, WA: Hogrefe & Huber.

Fahrenberg, J., & Myrtek, M. (Eds.). (2001). *Progress in ambulatory assessment: Computer-assisted psychological and psychophysiological methods in monitoring and field studies.* Seattle, WA: Hogrefe & Huber.

Farnworth, L. (2000). Time use and leisure occupations of young offenders. *The American Journal of Occupational Therapy, 54,* 315–325.

Feldman Barrett, L. (1998). Discrete emotions or dimensions? The role of valence focus and arousal focus. *Cognition and Emotion, 12*(4), 579–599.

Feldman Barrett, L. (2004). Feelings or words? Understanding the content in self-report ratings of emotional experience. *Journal of Personality and Social Psychology, 87*(2), 266–281.

Feldman Barrett, L., & Barrett, D. J. (2001). An introduction to experience sampling in psychology. *Social Science Computer Review, 19,* 175–185.

Feldman Barrett, L., Gross, J., Christensen, T. C., & Benvenuto, M. (2001). Knowing what you're feeling and knowing what to do about it: Mapping the relation between emotion differentiation and emotion regulation. *Cognition and Emotion, 15,* 713–724.

Feldman Barrett, L., Robin, L., Pietromonaco, P. R., & Eyssell, K. M. (1998). Are women the "more emotional" sex? Evidence from emotional experiences in social context. *Cognition & Emotion, 12,* 555–578.

Feldman Barrett, L., & Russell, J. A. (1998). Independence and bipolarity in the structure of current affect. *Journal of Personality and Social Psychology, 74*(4), 967–984.

Fisher, C. D. (2000). Mood and emotions while working: Missing pieces of job satisfaction? *Journal of Organizational Behavior, 21,* 185–202.

Fleeson, W. (2001). Toward a structure-and process-integrated view of personality: Traits as density distributions of states. *Journal of Personality and Social Psychology, 80,* 1011–1027.

Fleeson, W., & Cantor, N. (1995). Goal relevance and the affective experience of daily life: Ruling out situational explanations. *Motivation and Emotion, 19,* 25–57.

Flory, J. D., Räikkönen, K., Matthews, K. A., & Owens, J. F. (2000). Self-focused attention and mood during everyday social interactions. *Personality and Social Psychology Bulletin, 26,* 875–883.

Fosse, R., Stickgold, R., & Hobson, J. A. (2001). Brain-mind states: Reciprocal variation in thoughts and hallucinations. *Psychological Science 12,* 30–36.

Frable, D. E. S., Platt, L., & Hoey, S. (1998). Concealable stigmas and positive self-perceptions: Feeling better around similar others. *Journal of Personality and Social Psychology, 74,* 909–922.

Frankl, V. E. (1978). *The unheard cry for meaning.* New York: Simon & Schuster.

Franzoi, S. L., & Brewer, L. C. (1984). The experience of self-awareness and its relation to level of self-consciousness: An experiential sampling study. *Journal of Research in Personality, 18,* 522–540.

Fredricks, J. A., Blumenfeld, P. C., & Paris, A. H. (2004). School engagement: Potential of the concept, state of the evidence. *Review of Educational Research, 74,* 59–109.

Fredrickson, B. L., & Kahneman, D. (1993). Duration neglect in retrospective evaluations of affective episodes. *Journal of Personality and Social Psychology, 65,* 45–55.

Freeman, M., Csikszentmihalyi, M., & Larson, R. (1986). Adolescence and its recollection: Toward an interpretive model of development. *Merrill-Palmer Quarterly, 32,* 167–185.

Gauvain, M. (1995). Thinking in niches: Sociocultural influences on cognitive development. *Human Development, 38,* 25–45.

Gauvin, L., Rejeski, W. J., & Norris, J. L. (1996). A naturalistic study of the impact of acute physical activity on feeling states and affect in women. *Health Psychology, 15,* 391–397.

Gauvin, L., & Szabo, A. (1992). Application of the experience sampling method to the study of the effects of exercise withdrawal on well-being. *Journal of Sport & Exercise Psychology, 14,* 361–374.

Giannino, S., Graef, R., & Csikszentmihalyi, M. (1979). *Well-being and the perceived balance between opportunities and capabilities.* Paper presented at the 87th Convention of the American Psychiatric Association, New York.

Gibbons, R. D., Hedeker, D., Elkin, I., Waternaux, C., Kraemer, H. C., Greenhouse, J. B., et al. (1993). Some conceptual and statistical issues in analysis of longitudinal psychiatric data: Application to the NIMH treatment of depression collaborative research program dataset. *Archives of General Psychiatry, 50,* 739–750.

Goldstein, H. (1987). *Multilevel models in educational and social research.* London: Griffin.

Goldstein, H. (1995). *Multilevel statistical models.* New York: Halsted.

Gollwitzer, P. M. (1999). Implementation intentions: Strong effects of simple plans. *American Psychologist, 54,* 493–503.

Gomes, G. (1995). Self-awareness and the mind-brain problem. *Philosophical Psychology, 8,* 155–165.

Goodlad, J. I. (1984). *A place called school: Prospects for the future.* New York: McGraw-Hill.

Gortner, D. T. (1999). *Single-focus and divided attention in the everyday lives of adolescents.* Presented at the annual meeting of the American Psychological Association, Boston.

Gortner, D. T. (2000). *Developmental, contextual, and gender-based differences in cognitive "multi-tasking."* Paper presented at the annual meeting of the American Educational Research Association, New Orleans.

Gottman, J. M. (1994). *What predicts divorce?* Hillsdale, NJ: Lawrence Erlbaum Associates.

Gottman, J. M., Croan, J., Carrere, S., & Swanson, C. (1998). Predicting marital happiness and stability from newlywed interactions. *Journal of Marriage and the Family, 60,* 5–27.

Gottman, J. M., & Levenson, R. W. (1988). The social psychophysiology of marriage. In P. Noller & M. A. Fitzpatrick (Eds.), *Perspectives on marital interaction* (pp. 182–200). Philadelphia: Multilingual Matters.

Gottman, J. M., & Levenson, R. W. (1992). Marital processes predictive of later dissolution: Behavior, physiology, and health. *Journal of Personality and Social Psychology, 63,* 221–233.

Graef, R. P. (1978). *Consistency in people's everyday mood and cognitive responses: An analysis of people's self-reports using a repeated measures design.* Doctoral dissertation, University of Chicago.

Graef, R. P., McManama, G. S., & Csikszentmihalyi, M. (1981). Energy consumption in leisure and perceived happiness. In J. D. Claxton et al. (Eds.), *Consumers and Energy Conservation* (pp. 47–55). New York: Praeger.

Grannis, J. C. (1978). Task engagement and the consistency of pedagogical controls: An ecological study of different structured classroom settings. *Curriculum Inquiry, 8,* 3–37.

Gray, J. (1992). *Men are from Mars, women are from Venus.* New York: HarperCollins.

Greenberger, E., & Steinberg, L. D. (1981). The workplace as a context for the socialization of youth. *Journal of Youth and Adolescence, 10,* 185–210.

Greenberger, E., & Steinberg, L. D. (1986). *When teenagers work: The psychological and social costs of adolescent employment.* New York: Basic Books.

Haas, L. (1999). Families and work. In M. Sussman, S. Steinmetz, & G. Peterson (Eds.), *Handbook of marriage and the family* (2nd ed., pp. 571–612). New York: Plenum.

Hamilton, J. A., Haier, R. J., & Buchsbaum, M. S. (1984). Intrinsic enjoyment and boredom coping scales: Validation with personality, evoked potential and attention measures. *Personality and Individual Differences, 5,* 183–193.

Harlow, R. E., & Cantor, N. (1994). Social pursuit of academics: Side effects and spillover of strategic reassurance seeking. *Journal of Personality and Social Psychology, 66,* 386–397.

Harvey, E. (1999). Short-term and long-term effects of early parental employment on children of the National Longitudinal Survey of Youth. *Developmental Psychology, 35,* 445–459.

Havighurst, R. J. (1982). The world of work. In B. B. Wolman (Ed.), *Handbook of developmental psychology.* Englewood Cliffs, NJ: Prentice Hall.

Hawkins, A. J., Marshall, C. M., & Meiners, K. M. (1995). Exploring wives' sense of fairness about family work: An initial test of the distributive justice framework. *Journal of Family Issues, 16,* 693–721.

Haworth, J. T. (1996). Mental health, work, and leisure. In J. T. Haworth (Ed.), *Psychological research: Innovative methods and strategies* (pp. 21–33). New York: Routledge.

Haworth, J. T., & Ducker, J. (1991). Psychological well-being and access to categories of experience in unemployed young adults. *Leisure Studies, 10,* 265–274.

Haworth, J., & Evans, S. (1995). Challenge, skill and positive subjective states in the daily life of a sample of YTS youth. *Journal of Occupational and Organizational Psychology, 68,* 109–122.

Haworth, J. T., & Hill, S. (1992). Work, leisure and psychological well-being in a sample of young adults. *Journal of Community and Applied Psychology, 2,* 147–160.

Haworth, J., Hill, S., & Paterson, F. (1995). Access to categories of experience and mental health in a sample of managers. *Journal of Applied Social Psychology, 25*(8), 712–724.

Haworth, J. T., Jarman, M., & Lee, S. (1997). Positive psychological states in the daily life of a sample of working women. *Journal of Applied Social Psychology, 27,* 345–370.

Heine, K. (1996). *Flow and achievement in mathematics.* Doctoral dissertation, University of Chicago.

Hektner, J. M. (1996). *Exploring optimal personality development: A longitudinal study of adolescents.* Doctoral dissertation, University of Chicago.

Hektner, J. M. (2001). Family, school, and community predictors of adolescent growth-conducive experiences: Global and specific approaches. *Applied Developmental Science, 5,* 172–183.

Hermanson, K. L. (1996). *Learning in everyday life: An experience sampling of urban adults.* Doctoral dissertation, University of Chicago.

Hillebrand, M., & Waite, B. M. (1992). The social context of anger among violent forensic patients. *Journal of Offender Rehabilitation, 18,* 81–89.

Hillebrand, M., & Waite, B. M. (1994). The everyday experience of an institutionalized sex offender: An idiographic application of the experience sampling method. *Archives of Sexual Behavior, 23,* 453–464.

Hirschman, C., & Wong, M. G. (1986). The extraordinary educational attainment of Asian Americans: A search for historical evidence and explanations. *Social Forces, 65,* 1–27.

Hnatiuk, S. H. (1991). Experience sampling with elderly persons: An exploration of the method. *International Journal of Aging and Human Development, 33,* 45–64.

Hochschild, A. R. (1989). *The second shift.* New York: Avon.

Hoffman, L. W. (1974). Effects of maternal employment on the child: A review of the research. *Developmental Psychology, 10,* 204–228.

Hoffman, L. W. (1989). Effects of maternal employment in the two-parent family. *American Psychologist, 44,* 283–292.

Holden, G., Bearison, D. J., Rode, D. C., Kapiloff, M. F., & Rosenberg, G. (2000). The effects of a computer network on pediatric pain and anxiety. *Journal of Technology in Human Services, 17,* 27–47.

Hoogstra, L. (2005). The design of the 500 Family Study. In B. Schneider & L. J. Waite (Eds.), *Being together, working apart: Dual-career families and the work-life balance* (pp. 18–38). New York: Cambridge University Press.

Hoover, M. D. (1983). *Individual differences in the relation of heart rate to self-reports.* Doctoral dissertation, University of Chicago.

Hormuth, S. E. (1983). *Ortswechsel als Gelegenheit zur Anderung des Selbst.* [Relocation as an opportunity for self-concept change.] Report and continuation proposal to the German Science Foundation (DFG), University of Heidelberg, Psychological Institute.

Hormuth, S. E. (1986). The sampling of experiences *in situ. Journal of Personality, 54,* 262–293.

Hoyle, R. H., Harris, M. J., & Judd, C. M. (2000). *Research methods in social relations* (7th ed.). Boston: Wadsworth.

Hufford, M. R., Shields, A. L., Shiffman, S., Paty, J., & Balabanis, M. (2002). Reactivity to ecological momentary assessment: An example using undergraduate problem drinkers. *Psychology of Addictive Behaviors, 16,* 205–211.

Hunter, J. P. (2002). Vital powers and wasted possibilities: Engaged and bored teenagers in America. *Dissertation Abstracts International, 62,* 4818.

Hunter, J. P., & Csikszentmihalyi, M. (2003). The positive psychology of interested adolescents. *Journal of Youth and Adolescence, 32,* 27–35.

Hurlburt, R. T. (1979). Random sampling of cognitions and behavior. *Journal of Research in Personality, 13,* 103–111.

Hurlburt, R. T. (1990). *Sampling normal and schizophrenic inner experience.* New York: Plenum.

Hurlburt, R. T. (1993). *Sampling inner experience in disturbed affect.* New York: Plenum.

Hurlburt, R. T. (1997). Random sampling thinking in the natural environment. *Journal of Consulting and Clinical Psychology, 65,* 941–949.

Inghilleri, P. (1999). *From subjective experience to cultural change.* New York: Cambridge University Press.

James, W. (1890). *Principles of psychology* (Vol. 1). New York: Henry Holt.

Jeong, J., Mulligan, C. B., & Schneider, B. (2004). *A systematic comparison of time use instruments: The time diary and the Experience Sampling Method.* Sloan Center on Parents, Children, and Work, Working Paper Series, University of Chicago.

Jepsen, D. (1984). The developmental perspective on vocational behavior: A review of theory and research. In S. D. Brown & R. W. Lent (Eds.), *Handbook of counseling psychology.* New York: Wiley.

Johnson, C., & Larson, R. (1982). Bulimia: An analysis of moods and behavior. *Psychosomatic Medicine, 44,* 341–351.

Johnson, L. S. (2004). *Academic engagement from the perspective of flow theory: A comparative analysis of student experience in non-traditional and traditional schools.* Doctoral dissertation, Northern Illinois University.

Juster, F. T., & Stafford, F. P. (1985). *Time, goods, and well-being.* Ann Arbor: Institute for Social Research, University of Michigan.

Kahneman, D. (1999). Objective happiness. In D. Kahneman, E. Diener, & N. Schwarz (Eds.), *Well-being: The foundations of hedonic psychology* (pp. 33–25). New York: Russell Sage Foundation.

Kahneman, D., Krueger, A. B., Schkade, D. A., Schwarz, N., & Stone, A. A. (2004). A survey method for characterizing daily life experience: The Day Reconstruction Method. *Science, 306,* 1776–1780.

Kaplan, C. D. (1992). Drug craving and drug use in the daily life of heroin addicts. In M. W. deVries (Ed.), *The experience of psychopathology: Investigating mental disorders in their natural settings* (pp. 193–218). New York: Cambridge University Press.

Kegan, R. (1994). *In over our heads.* New York: Cambridge University Press.

Kenny, D. A., Kashy, D. A., & Bolger, N. (1998). Data analysis in social psychology. In D. Gilbert, S. Fiske, & G. Lindzey (Eds.), *Handbook of social psychology* (4th ed., pp. 233–265). New York: McGraw-Hill.

Khalil, E L., & Boulding, K. E. (Eds.). (1996). *Evolution, order and complexity.* New York: Routledge.

Khare, A. (1999). Japanese and Indian work patterns: A study of contrasts. In H. S. R. Kao, D. Sinha, & B. Wilpert (Eds.), *Management and cultural values: The indigenization of organizations in Asia* (pp. 121–136). New Delhi, India: Sage.

Kim, U., & Berry, J. W. (1993). *Indigenous psychologies.* Newbury Park, CA: Sage.

King, B. J. (2000). Another frame shift: From cultural transmission to cultural co-construction. *Behavioral and Brain Sciences, 23,* 154–155.

Kirchler, E. (1985). Job loss and mood. *Journal of Economic Psychology, 6,* 9–25.

Kirchler, E. (1988). Marital happiness and interaction in everyday surroundings: A time-sampling diary approach for couples. *Journal of Social and Personal Relationships, 5,* 375–382.

Kirshnit, C. E., Ham, M., & Richards, M. H. (1989). The sporting life: Athletic activities during early adolescence. *Journal of Youth and Adolescence, 18,* 601–615.

Kitano, M. K. (1984). Early education for Asian-American children. In O. N. Saracho & B. Spodek (Eds.), *Understanding the multicultural experience in early childhood education.* Washington, DC: National Association for the Education of Young Children.

Kitayama, S., & Markus, H. R. (1994). *Emotion and culture: Empirical studies of mutual influence.* Washington, DC: American Psychological Association.

Klein, S. B. (2001). A self to remember: A cognitive neuropsychological perspective on how self creates memory and memory creates self. In C. Sedikides & M. Brewer (Eds.), *Individual self, relational self, collective self,* (pp. 25–46). Philadelphia: Psychology Press.

Klinger, E., Barta, S. G., & Maxeiner, M. E. (1980). Motivational correlates of thought content frequency and commitment. *Journal of Personality and Social Psychology, 39,* 1222–1237.

Koh, C. (2005). The everyday emotional experiences of husbands and wives. In B. Schneider & L. J. Waite (Eds.), *Being together working apart: Dual-career families and the work-life balance* (pp. 169–189). New York: Cambridge University Press.

Kraan, H., Meertens, H., Hilwig, M., Volovics, L., Dijkman-Caes, C. I. M., & Portegijs, P. (1992). Selecting measures, diagnostic validity and scaling in the study of depression. In M. W. deVries (Ed.), *The experience of psychopathology: Investigating mental disorders in their natural settings* (pp. 324–338). New York: Cambridge University Press.

Kring, A. M., & Gordon, A. H. (1998). Sex differences in emotion: Expression, experience, and physiology. *Journal of Personality and Social Psychology, 74,* 686–703.

Krosnick, J. A., & Fabrigar, L. R. (2005). Questionnaire design for attitude measurement in social and psychological research. New York: Oxford University Press.

Kubey, R., & Csikszentmihalyi, M. (1990). *Television and the quality of life: How viewing shapes everyday experience.* Hillsdale, NJ: Lawrence Erlbaum Associates.

Kubey, R., & Csikszentmihalyi, M. (2002). Television addiction is no mere metaphor. *Scientific American, 286,* 74–80.

Kubey, R., Larson, R. W., & Csikszentmihalyi, M. (1996). Experience sampling method applications to communication research questions. *Journal of Communication, 46,* 99–120.

Kunnen, E. S., & Bosma, H. A. (1996). Adolescent conflict and the development of meaning making. In L. Verhofstadt-Denève, I. Kienhorst, & C. Braet (Eds.), *Conflict and development in adolescence* (pp. 61–74). Leiden, Netherlands: DSWO Press.

Kunnen, E. S., & Bosma, H. A. (2000). Development of meaning making: A dynamic systems approach. *New Ideas in Psychology, 18,* 57–82.

Laland, K. N., Kumm, J., & Feldman, M. W. (1995). Gene-culture coevolutionary theory. A test case. *Current Anthropology, 36,* 131–156.

Laland, K. N., Odling-Smee, J., & Feldman, M. W. (2000). Niche construction, biological evolution, and cultural change. *Behavioral and Brain Sciences, 23,* 131–146.

Larson, R. W. (1977). *The significance of solitude in adolescents' lives.* Doctoral dissertation, University of Chicago.

Larson, R. W. (1990). The solitary side of life: An examination of the time people spend alone from childhood to old age. *Developmental Review, 10,* 155–183.

Larson, R. W., & Almeida, D. (1999). Emotional transmission in the daily lives of families: A new paradigm for studying family process. *Journal of Marriage and the Family, 61,* 5–20.

Larson, R. W., & Asmussen, L. (1991). Anger, worry and hurt in early adolescence: An enlarging world of negative emotions. In M. Colten & S. Gore (Eds.),

324   Experience Sampling Method

Adolescent stress: Causes and consequences (pp. 21–41). New York: Aldine De Gruyter.

Larson, R. W., & Asmussen, L. (1992). Bulimia in daily life: A context-bound syndrome. In M. W. deVries (Ed.), *The experience of psychopathology: Investigating mental disorders in their natural settings* (pp. 167–179). New York: Cambridge University Press.

Larson, R. W., Csikszentmihalyi, M., & Freeman, M. (1984). Alcohol and marijuana use in adolescents' daily lives: A random sample of experiences. *The International Journal of the Addictions, 19,* 367–381.

Larson, R. W., Csikszentmihalyi, M., & Freeman, M. (1992). Alcohol and marijuana use in adolescents' daily lives. In M. W. deVries (Ed.), *The experience of psychopathology: Investigating mental disorders in their natural settings* (pp. 180–192). New York: Cambridge University Press.

Larson, R. W., Csikszentmihalyi, M., & Graef, R. (1980). Mood variability and the psychosocial adjustment of adolescents. *Journal of Youth and Adolescence, 9,* 469–490.

Larson, R. W., & Delespaul, P. A. E. G. (1992). Analyzing experience sampling data: A guidebook for the perplexed. In M. W. deVries (Ed.), *The experience of psychopathology: Investigating mental disorders in their natural settings* (pp. 58–78). New York: Cambridge University Press.

Larson, R., Dworkin, J., & Gillman, S. (2001). Facilitating adolescents' constructive use of time in one-parent families. *Applied Developmental Science, 5,* 143–157.

Larson, R. W., & Gillman, S. (1999). Transmission of emotions in the daily interactions of single-mother families. *Journal of Marriage and the Family, 61,* 21–37.

Larson, R. W., & Ham, M. (1993). Stress and "storm and stress" in early adolescence: The relationship of negative events with dysphoric affect. *Developmental Psychology, 29,* 130–140.

Larson, R. W., & Johnson, C. (1981). Anorexia nervosa in the context of daily experience. *Journal of Youth and Adolescence, 10,* 455–471.

Larson, R. W., & Johnson, C. (1985). Bulimia: Disturbed patterns of solitude. *Addictive Behaviors, 10,* 281–290.

Larson, R. W., Kubey, R., & Colletti, J. (1989). Changing channels: Early adolescent media choices and shifting investments in family and friends [Special issue: The changing life space of early adolescence]. *Journal of Youth and Adolescence, 18,* 583–599.

Larson, R., Mannell, R., & Zuzanek, J. (1986). Daily well-being of older adults with friends and family. *Psychology and Aging, 1,* 117–126.

Larson, R. W., Moneta, G., Richards, M. H., & Wilson, S. (2002). Continuity, stability, and change in daily emotional experience across adolescence. *Child Development, 73,* 1151–1165.

Larson, R., & Pleck, J. (1998). Hidden feelings: Emotionality in boys and men. In D. Berstein (Ed.), *Nebraska Symposium on Motivation: Vol. 45. Gender and motivation* (pp. 25–74). Lincoln: University of Nebraska Press.

Larson, R. W., & Richards, M. H. (1991a). Boredom in the middle school years: Blaming schools versus blaming students. *American Journal of Education, 99,* 418–443.

Larson, R., & Richards, M. H. (1991b). Daily companionship in late childhood and early adolescence: Changing developmental contexts. *Child Development, 62,* 284–300.

Larson, R. W., & Richards, M. H. (1994a). *Divergent realities: The emotional lives of mothers, fathers, and adolescents.* New York: Basic Books.

Larson, R. W., & Richards, M. H. (1994b). Family emotions: Do young adolescents and their parents experience the same states? *Journal of Research on Adolescence, 4,* 567–583.

Larson, R. W., & Richards, M. H. (1998). Waiting for the weekend: Friday and Saturday night as the emotional climax of the week. In A. C. Crouter & R. W. Larson (Eds.), *Temporal rhythms in adolescence: Clocks, calendars and the coordination of daily life* (pp. 37–51). San Francisco: Jossey-Bass.

Larson, R. W., Richards, M. H., Moneta, G., Holmbeck, G., & Duckett, E. (1996). Changes in adolescents' daily interactions with their families from ages 10 to 18: Disengagement and transformation. *Developmental Psychology, 32,* 744–754.

Larson, R. W., Richards, M. H., & Perry-Jenkins, M. (1994). Divergent worlds: The daily emotional experience of mothers and fathers in the domestic and public spheres. *Journal of Personality and Social Psychology, 67,* 1034–1046.

Larson, R., Richards, M. H., Sims, B., & Dworkin, J. (1998). How urban African American young adolescents spend their time: Time budgets for locations, activities, and companionship. *American Journal of Community Psychology, 29*(4), 565–597.

Larson, R. W., & Verma, S. (1999). How children and adolescents spend time across the world: Work, play and developmental opportunities. *Psychological Bulletin, 25,* 701–736.

Larson, R. W., Verma, S., & Dworkin, J. (2001). Men's work and family lives in India: The daily organization of time and emotion. *Journal of Family Psychology, 15,* 206–224.

Larson, R., Zuzanek, J., & Mannell, R. (1985). Being alone versus being with people: Disengagement in the daily experience of older adults. *Journal of Gerontology, 40,* 375–381.

Laurenceau, J., Feldman Barrett, L., & Pietromonaco, P. R. (1998). Intimacy as an interpersonal process: The importance of self-disclosure, partner disclosure, and perceived partner responsiveness in interpersonal exchanges. *Journal of Personality and Social Psychology, 74,* 1238–1251.

Lawton, M. P. (1999). Methods and concepts for time-budget research on elders. In W. E. Pentland, A. S. Harvey, M. P. Lawton, & M. A. McColl (Eds.), *Time use research in the social sciences* (pp. 107–125). New York: Kluwer.

Leahey, T. H. (1997). *A history of psychology.* Upper Saddle River, NJ: Prentice Hall.

LeDoux, J. (2002). *Synaptic self: How our brains become who we are.* New York: Viking Penguin.

Lee, M. (1994). *Cultural differences in the daily manifestations of adolescent depression: A comparative study of American and Korean high school seniors.* Urbana: University of Illinois.

Lee, Y. S. (2005). Measuring the gender gap in household labor: Accurately estimating wives' and husbands' contributions. In B. Schneider & L. J. Waite (Eds.), *Being together, working apart: Dual-career families and the work-life balance* (pp. 229–247). New York: Cambridge University Press.

LeFevre, J. (1988). Flow and the quality of experience during work and leisure. In M. Csikszentmihalyi & I. S. Csikszentmihalyi (Eds.), *Optimal experience: Psychological studies of flow in consciousness* (pp. 307–318). New York: Cambridge University Press.

LeFevre, J., Hendricks, C., Church, R. B., & McClintock, M. (1992). Psychological and social behavior of couples over a menstrual cycle: "On-the-spot" sampling from everyday life. In A. J. Dan & I. L. Lewis (Eds.), *Menstrual health in women's lives* (pp. 75–82). Chicago: University of Illinois Press.

le Grange, D., Gorin, A., Catley, D., & Stone, A. A. (2001). Does momentary assessment detect binge eating in overweight women that is denied at interview? *European Eating Disorders Review, 9,* 309–324.

Leone, C. M., & Richards, M. H. (1989). Classwork and homework in early adolescence: The ecology of achievement. *Journal of Youth and Adolescence, 18,* 531–548.

Levenson, R. W., & Gottman, J. M. (1983). Marital interaction: Physiological linkage and affective exchange. *Journal of Personality and Social Psychology, 45,* 587–597.

Levenson, R. W., & Gottman, J. M. (1985). Physiological and affective predictors of change in relationship satisfaction. *Journal of Personality and Social Psychology, 49,* 85–94.

Litt, M. D., Cooney, N. L., & Morse, P. (1998). Ecological momentary assessment with treated alcoholics: Methodological problems and potential solutions. *Health Psychology, 17,* 48–52.

Loewenstein, R. J., Hamilton, J., Alagna, S., Reid, N., & deVries, M. W. (1992). Capturing alternate personalities: The use of Experience Sampling in multiple personality disorder. In M. W. deVries (Ed.), *The experience of psychopathology: Investigating mental disorders in their natural settings* (pp. 157–166). New York: Cambridge University Press.

Luthar, S. S., & Becker, B. E. (2002). Privileged but pressured: A study of affluent youth. *Child Development, 73,* 1593–1610.

Lynn, R. (1977). The intelligence of the Japanese. *Bulletin of the British Psychological Society, 30,* 69–72.

Lynn, R. (1982). IQ in Japan and the United States shows a growing disparity. *Nature, 297,* 222–223.

Lynn, R., & Dziobon, J. (1980). On the intelligence of Japanese and other Mongoloid peoples. *Personality and Individual Differences, 1,* 95–96.

Maier, K. S. (2001). A Rasch hierarchical measurement model. *Journal of Educational & Behavioral Statistics, 26,* 307–330.

Maier, K. S. (2002). Modeling incomplete scaled questionnaire data with a partial credit hierarchical measurement model. *Journal of Educational & Behavioral Statistics, 27,* 271–289.

Maier, K. S. (2005). Transmitting educational values: Parent occupation and adolescent development. In B. Schneider & L. J. Waite (Eds.), *Being together, working apart: Dual-career families and the work-life balance* (pp. 396–418). New York: Cambridge University Press.

Mannell, R. C., Zuzanek, J., & Larson, R. W. (1988). Leisure states and "flow" experiences: Testing perceived freedom and intrinsic motivation hypotheses. *Journal of Leisure Research, 20,* 289–304.

Manning, B. (1990). A categorical analysis of children's self-talk during independent school assignments. *Journal of Instructional Psychology, 17*(4), 208–217.

Marco, C. A., & Suls, J. (1993). Daily stress and the trajectory of mood: Spillover, response assimilation, contrast, and chronic negative affectivity. *Journal of Personality and Social Psychology, 64,* 1053–1063.

Marks, H. M. (2000). Student engagement in instructional activity: Patterns in the elementary, middle and high school years. *American Educational Research Journal, 37,* 153–184.

Markus, H. R., & Kitayama, S. (1994). The cultural construction of self and emotion: Implications for social behavior. In S. Kitayama & H. R. Markus (Eds.), *Emotion and culture: Empirical studies of mutual influence* (pp. 89–130). Washington, DC: American Psychological Association.

Marsh, A. (2005, August). The art of work. *Fast Company,* pp. 77–79.

Maslow, A. (1968). *Toward a psychology of being* (2nd ed.). Princeton, NJ: Van Nostrand.

Maslow, A. (1970). *Motivation and personality* (2nd ed.). New York: Harper & Row.

Massimini, F. (1982). Individuo, cultura, ambiente: i Papua Kapauku della Nuova Guinea Occidentale. [Individuals, culture and environment: The Papua Kapauku of Western New Guinea]. *Ricerche di Psicologia, 22–23,* 27–154.

Massimini, F., & Carli, M. (1988). The systematic assessment of flow in daily experience. In M. Csikszentmihalyi & I. S. Csikszentmihalyi (Eds.), *Optimal experience: Psychological studies of flow in consciousness.* New York: Cambridge University Press.

Massimini, F., Csikszentmihalyi, M., & Carli, M. (1987). Optimal experience: A tool for psychiatric rehabilitation. *Journal of Nervous and Mental Disease, 175,* 545–549.

Massimini, F., Csikszentmihalyi, M., & Carli, M. (1992). The monitoring of optimal experience: A tool for psychiatric rehabilitation. In M. W. deVries (Ed.), *The experience of psychopathology: Investigating mental disorders in their natural settings* (pp. 270–279). New York: Cambridge University Press.

Massimini, F., & Delle Fave, A. (2000). Individual development in a bio-cultural perspective. *American Psychologist, 55,* 24–33.

Massimini, F., Inghilleri, P., & Delle Fave, A. (1986). [The daily experience of Italian adolescents.] Unpublished data. L'Isituto di Psicologia, Universit degli Studi Milano.

Massimini, F., Inghilleri, P., & Delle Fave, A. (1996). *La Selezione Psicologica Umana [Human Psychological Selection]*. Milan: Cooperativa Libraria IULM.

Mata-Greenwood, A. (1992). *An integrated framework for the measurement of working time* (STAT Working Paper No. 92). Geneva: International Labor Organization.

Matjasko, J. L., & Feldman, A. F. (2005). Emotional transmission between parents and adolescents: The importance of work characteristics and relationship quality. In B. Schneider & L. J. Waite (Eds.), *Being together, working apart: Dual-career families and the work-life balance* (pp. 138–158). New York: Cambridge University Press.

Maturana, H. R. (1975). *Autopoietic systems: A characterization of the living organization*. Urbana: University of Illinois.

Maturana, H., & Varela, F. (1986). *The tree of knowledge: A new look at the biological roots of human understanding*. Boston: New Science Library.

Mayers, P. L. (1978). *Flow in adolescence and its relation to school experience*. Doctoral dissertation, University of Chicago.

McAdams, D., & Constantian, C. A. (1983). Intimacy and affiliation motives in daily living: An experience sampling analysis. *Journal of Personality and Social Psychology, 45*, 851–861.

McIntyre, N., & Roggenbuck, J. W. (1998). Nature/person transactions during an outdoor adventure experience: A multi-phasic analysis. *Journal of Leisure Research, 30*, 401–416.

Merrick, W. A. (1992). Dysphoric moods in depressed and non-depressed adolescents. In M. W. deVries (Ed.), *The experience of psychopathology: Investigating mental disorders in their natural settings* (pp. 148–156). New York: Cambridge University Press.

Minge-Klevana, W. (1980). Does labor time decrease with industrialization? A survey of time-allocation studies. *Current Anthropology 21*, 279–298.

Mitchell, R. G., Jr. (1988). Sociological implications of the flow experience. In M. Csikszentmihalyi & I. S. Csikszentmihalyi (Eds.), *Optimal Experience* (pp. 36–59). New York: Cambridge University Press.

Molenaar, P. C. M. (1985). A dynamic factor model for the analysis of multivariate time-series. *Psychometrika, 50*, 181–202.

Moneta, G. B., & Csikszentmihalyi, M. (1996). The effect of perceived challenges and skills on the quality of subjective experience. *Journal of Personality, 64*, 275–310.

Moneta, G. B., & Csikszentmihalyi, M. (1999). Models of concentration in natural environments: A comparative approach based on streams of experiential data. *Social Behavior and Personality, 27*, 603–638.

Moneta, G. B., Schneider, B., & Csikszentmihalyi, M. (2001). A longitudinal study of self-concept and experiential components of self-worth and affect across adolescence. *Applied Developmental Science, 5*, 125–157.

Monod, J. (1972). *Chance and necessity*. New York: Vintage.

Mordkowitz, E. R., & Ginsburg, H. P. (1987). Early academic socialization of successful Asian-American college students. *Quarterly Newsletter of the Laboratory of Comparative Human Cognition, 9*, 285–291.

Mortimer, J. T., & Borman, K. M. (1988). *Work experience and psychological development through the lifespan: AAS selected symposium*. Boulder, CO: Westview Press.

Mortimer, J. T., Finch, M. D., Owens, T. J., & Shannahan, M. (1990). Gender and work in adolescence. *Youth and Society, 22*, 201–224.

Moskowitz, D. S. (1994). Cross-situational generality and the interpersonal circumplex. *Journal of Personality and Social Psychology, 66*, 921–933.

Moskowitz, D. S., & Côté, S. (1995). Do interpersonal traits predict affect? A comparison of three models. *Journal of Personality and Social Psychology, 69*(5), 915–924.

Moskowitz, D. S., & Hershberger, S. L. (Eds.). (2002). *Modeling intraindividual variability with repeated measures data: Methods and applications*. Mahwah, NJ: Lawrence Erlbaum Associates.

Mulligan, C. B., Schneider, B., & Wolfe, R. (2000). *Time use and population representation in the Sloan Study of Adolescents*. Unpublished manuscript, Alfred P. Sloan/University of Chicago Center for the Study of Working Families.

Mundinger P. C. (1980). Animal cultures and a general theory of cultural evolution. *Ethology and Sociobiology, 1*, 183–223.

Myin-Germeys, I., Nicolson, N. A., & Delespaul, P. A. E. G. (2001). The context of delusional experience in the daily life of patients with schizophrenia. *Psychological Medicine, 31*, 489–498.

Nag, M., White, F. B. N., & Peet, R. C. (1980). An anthropological approach to the study of the economic value of children in Java and Nepal. In P. Binswanger, R. E. Evenson, C. A. Florencia, & F. B. N. White (Eds.), *Rural household studies in Asia* (pp. 188–217). Kent Ridge, Singapore: Singapore University Press.

Nakamura, J. (1988). Optimal experience and the uses of talent. In M. Csikszentmihalyi & I. S. Csikszentmihalyi (Eds.), *Optimal experience: Psychological studies of flow in consciousness* (pp. 319–326). New York: Cambridge University Press.

National Research Council. (1998). *Protecting youth at work: Health, safety and development of working children and adolescents in the United States*. Washington, DC: National Academy Press.

Newman, M. G., Kenardy, J., Herman, S., & Taylor, C. B. (1997). Comparison of palmtop-computer-assisted brief cognitive-behavioral treatment to cognitive-behavioral treatment for panic disorder. *Journal of Consulting and Clinical Psychology, 65*, 178–183.

Newmann, F. M. (Ed.). (1992). *Student engagement and achievement in American secondary schools*. New York: Teachers College Press.

Nicholson, N. (1997). Evolutionary psychology: Toward a new view of human nature and organizational society. *Human Relations, 50*, 1053–1078.

330   Experience Sampling Method

Nicolson, N. A. (1992). Stress, coping and cortisol dynamics in daily life. In M. W. deVries (Ed.), *The experience of psychopathology: Investigating mental disorders in their natural settings* (pp. 219–232). New York: Cambridge University Press.

Nishino, J. (1997). *Will the two-day weekend bring more leisure (Yutori) to Japanese adolescence?* Urbana: University of Illinois.

Noelle-Neumann, E. (1984). *The spiral of silence—Our social skin.* Chicago: University of Chicago Press.

Norem, J. K., & Illingworth, K. S. S. (1993). Strategy-dependent effects of reflecting on self and tasks: Some implications of optimism and defensive pessimism. *Journal of Personality and Social Psychology, 65,* 822–835.

Norton, M., Wonderlich, S. A., Myers, T., Mitchell, J. E., & Crosby, R. D. (2003). The use of palmtop computers in the treatment of bulimia nervosa. *European Eating Disorders Review, 11,* 231–242.

Nurmi, J. E. (1993). Adolescent development in an age-graded context: The role of personal belief, goals, and strategies in the tackling of developmental tasks and standards. *International Journal of Behavioral Development, 16,* 169–189.

O'Connell, K. A., Gerkovich, M. M., Cook, M. R., Shiffman, S., Hickcox, M., & Kakolewski, K. E. (1998). Coping in real time: Using ecological momentary assessment techniques to assess coping with the urge to smoke. *Research in Nursing & Health, 21,* 487–497.

O'Connor, S., & Rosenblood, L. (1996). Affiliation motivation in everyday experience: A theoretical comparison. *Journal of Personality and Social Psychology, 70,* 513–522.

Offer, D., & Sabshin, M. (1967). Research alliance versus therapeutic alliance: A comparison. *American Journal of Psychiatry, 123,* 1519–1526.

Offer, D., & Sabshin, M. (1991). Normatology: The next step. In D. Offer & M. Sabshin (Eds.), *The diversity of normal behavior: Further contributions to normatology* (pp. 405–417). Chicago: Northwestern University.

Oishi, S. (2002). The experiencing and remembering of well-being: A cross-cultural analysis. *Personality and Social Psychology Bulletin, 28,* 1398–1406.

Oishi, S., Diener, E., Scollon, C. N., & Biswas-Diener, R. (2004). Cross-situational consistency of affective experiences across cultures. *Journal of Personality and Social Psychology, 86,* 460–473.

Oleckno, W. A., & Blacconiere, M. J. (1991). Relationship of religiosity to wellness and other health-related behaviors and outcomes. *Psychological Reports, 68,* 819–826.

Oosterwegel, A., Field, N., Hart, D., & Anderson, K. (2001). The relation of self-esteem variability to emotion variability, mood, personality traits, and depressive tendencies. *Journal of Personality, 69,* 689–708.

Osipow, S. H. (1986). Career issues through the life span. In M. S. Pallak & R. O. Perloff (Eds.), *Psychology and work: Productivity, change, and employment. The Master Lectures, Vol. 5* (pp. 141–168). Washington, DC: American Psychological Association.

Patton, J. D. (1998). *Exploring the relative outcomes of interpersonal and intrapersonal factors of order and entropy in adolescence: A longitudinal study.* Doctoral dissertation, University of Chicago.

Pawlik, K., & Buse, L. (1982). Rechnergestutzt verhaltensregistrierung im Feld: Beschreibung und erst psychometrische überprüfung einer neuen erhebungsmethode. [Computer-based behavior registration in the field: Description and first psychometric evaluation of a new recording method.] *Zeitschrift für Differentielle und Diagnostiche Psychologie, 3,* 101–118.

Pearce, L. D., & Axinn, W. G. (1998). The impact of family religious life on the quality of mother-child relations. *American Sociological Review, 63,* 810–828.

Penner, L. A., Shiffman, S., Paty, J. A., & Fritzsche, B. A. (1994). Individual differences in intraperson variability in mood. *Journal of Personality and Social Psychology, 66,* 712–721.

Perrez, M., Schoebi, D., & Wilhelm, P. (2000). How to assess social regulation of stress and emotions in daily family life? A computer-assisted family self-monitoring system (FASEM-C). *Clinical Psychology and Psychotherapy, 7,* 326–339.

Peters, M. L., Sorbi, M. J., Kruise, D. A., Kerssens, J. J., Verhaak, P. F. M., & Bensing, J. M. (2000). Electronic diary assessment of pain, disability, and psychological adaptation in patients differing in duration of pain. *Pain, 84,* 181–192.

Pfister, R. (2002). *Flow in Alltag.* Bern, Switzerland: Peter Lang.

Pickering, T. G., Coats, A., Mallion, J. M., Mancia, G., & Verdecchia, P. (1999). Blood pressure monitoring. Task force V: White-coat hypertension. *Blood Pressure Monitoring, 4,* 333–341.

Pittman, J. F., Teng, W., Kerpelman, J. L., & Solheim, C. A. (1999). Satisfaction with performance of housework: The roles of time spent, quality assessment, and stress. *Journal of Family Issues, 20,* 746–770.

Poloma, M. M., & Pendleton, B. F. (1989). Exploring types of prayer and quality of life: A research note. *Review of Religious Research, 31,* 46–53.

Porac, J. F. (1987). The job satisfaction questionnaire as a cognitive event: First and second-order processes in affective commentary. *Research in Personnel and Human Resource Management, 5,* 51–102.

Pribram, K. H. (1996). Interfacing complexity at the boundary between the natural and social sciences. In E. L. Khalil & K. E. Boulding (Eds.), *Evolution, order and complexity* (pp. 40–60). New York: Routledge.

Prigogine, I. (1980). *From being to becoming.* San Francisco: W. H. Freeman.

Prigogine, I., & Stengers, I. (1984). *Order out of chaos.* New York: Bantam.

Pychyl, T. A., Lee, J. M., Thibodeau, R., & Blunt, A. (2000). Five days of emotion: An experience sampling study of undergraduate student procrastination. *Journal of Social Behavior and Personality, 15,* 239–254.

Raffaelli, M., & Duckett, E. (1989). "We were just talking . . .": Conversations in early adolescence. *Journal of Youth and Adolescence, 18,* 567–582.

Ramu, G. N. (1987). Indian husbands: Their role perceptions and performances in single- and dual-earner families. *Journal of Marriage and the Family, 49,* 903–915.

Ramu, G. N. (1989). *Women, work, and marriage in urban India.* New Delhi, India: Sage.

Rathunde, K. (1996). Family context and talented adolescents' optimal experience in school-related activities. *Journal of Research on Adolescence, 6,* 605–628.

Rathunde, K. (2001). Family context and the development of undivided interest: A longitudinal study of family support and challenge and adolescents' quality of experience. *Applied Developmental Science, 5,* 158–171.

Rathunde, K., & Csikszentmihalyi, M. (1991). Adolescent happiness and family interaction. In K. Pillemer & K. McCartney (Eds.), *Parent-child relations throughout life* (pp. 143–162). Hillsdale, NJ: Lawrence Erlbaum Associates.

Rathunde, K., & Csikszentmihalyi, M. (2005a). Middle school students' motivation and quality of experience: A comparison of Montessori and traditional school environments. *American Journal of Education, 111,* 341–371.

Rathunde, K., & Csikszentmihalyi, M. (2005b). The social context of middle school: Teachers, friends, and activities in Montessori and traditional school environments. *Elementary School Journal, 106,* 59–79.

Raudenbush, S. W., & Bryk, A. S. (2002). *Hierarchical linear models: Applications and data analysis methods* (2nd ed.). Thousand Oaks, CA: Sage.

Ravenna, M., Hölzl, E., Costarelli, S., Kirchler, E., & Palmonari, A. (2001). Diary reports on emotional experiences in the onset of a psychosocial transition: Becoming drug-free. *Journal of Community and Applied Social Psychology, 11,* 19–35.

Ravenna, M., Hölzl, E., Kirchler, E., Palmonari, A., & Costarelli, S. (2002). Drug addicts in therapy—Changes in life space in the course of one year. *Journal of Community and Applied Social Psychology, 12,* 353–368.

Reis, H. T., & Gable, S. L. (2000). Event-sampling and other methods for studying everyday experience. In H. T. Reis & C. M. Judd (Eds.), *Handbook of research methods in social and personality psychology* (pp. 190–222). New York: Cambridge University Press.

Repetti, R. L., Matthews, K. A., & Waldron, I. (1989). Employment and women's health: Effects of paid employment on women's mental and physical health. *American Psychologist, 44,* 1394–1401.

Richards, M. H., Casper, R. C., & Larson, R. (1990). Weight and eating concerns among pre- and young adolescent boys and girls. *Journal of Adolescent Health Care, 11,* 203–209.

Richards, M. H., Crowe, P. A., Larson, R., & Swarr, A. (1998). Developmental patterns and gender differences in the experience of peer companionship during adolescence. *Child Development, 69,* 154–163.

Richards, M. H., & Duckett, E. (1994). The relationship of maternal employment to early adolescent daily experience with and without parents. *Child Development, 65,* 225–236.

Richards, M. H., & Larson, R. (1993). Pubertal development and the daily subjective states of young adolescents. *Journal of Research on Adolescence, 3,* 145–169.

Richerson P. J., & Boyd, R. (1978). A dual inheritance model of the human evolutionary process I: Basic postulates and a simple model. *Journal of Social and Biological Structures, 1,* 127–154.

Roberts, N. A., & Levenson, R. W. (2001). The remains of the workday: Impact of job stress and exhaustion on marital interaction in police couples. *Journal of Marriage and Family, 63,* 1052–1067.

Robinson, J. P. (1977). *How Americans use time: A social-psychological analysis of everyday behavior.* New York: Praeger.

Robinson, J. P. (1985). The validity and reliability of diaries versus alternative time use measures. In F. T. Juster & F. P. Stafford (Eds.), *Time, goods, and well-being.* Ann Arbor: Institute for Social Research, University of Michigan.

Robinson, J. P., & Bostrom, A. (1994, August). The overestimated work week? What time diary measures suggest. *Monthly Labor Review,* pp. 11–23.

Robinson, J. P., & Godbey, G. (1997). *Time for life: The surprising ways Americans use their time.* University Park: Pennsylvania State University Press.

Robinson, M. D., & Clore, G. L. (2002). Belief and feeling: Evidence for an accessibility model of emotional self-report. *Psychological Bulletin, 128,* 934–960.

Robinson, R. E. (1986). [The experience of high school math students.] Unpublished raw data. University of Chicago.

Rodler, C., & Kirchler, E. (2001). Everyday life of commuters' wives. In H. Brandstätter & A. Eliasz (Eds.), *Persons, situations, and emotions: An ecological approach* (pp. 163–183). Oxford, UK: Oxford University Press.

Rokeach, M. (1974). *The nature of human values.* New York: Free Press.

Russell, J. A., (1980). A circumplex model of affect. *Journal of Personality and Social Psychology, 39,* 1161–1178.

Russell, J. A., & Feldman Barrett, L. (1999). Core affect, prototypical emotional episodes, and other things called emotion: Dissecting the elephant. [Special section on the structure of emotion]. *Journal of Personality and Social Psychology, 76,* 805–819.

Rusting, C. L., & Larsen, R. J. (1998). Diurnal patters of unpleasant mood: Associations with neuroticism, depression, and anxiety. *Journal of Personality, 66,* 85–103.

Ryan, R. M., & Deci, E. L. (2000). Self-determination theory and the facilitation of intrinsic motivation, social development, and well-being. *American Psychologist, 55,* 68–78.

Salmela-Aro, K., & Nurmi, J. E. (1997). Goal contents, well-being, and life context during transition to University: A longitudinal study. *International Journal of Behavioral Development, 20,* 471–491.

Saraswathi, T. S., & Dutta, R. (1988). *Invisible boundaries: Grooming for adult roles.* New York: Northern Book Centre/Advent Books.

Schaeffer, N. C., & Presser, S. (2003). The science of asking questions. *Annual Review of Sociology, 29,* 65–88.

Schallberger, U. (1995). The influence of personality characteristics on self reports of working conditions. *Zeitschrift for Experimentelle Psychologie, 42*(1), 111–131.

Schallberger, U., & Pfister, R. (2001). Flow-Erleben in Arbeit und Freizeit. Eine Untersuchung zum "Paradox der Arbeit" mit der Experience Sampling Method. [Flow experiences in work and leisure: An experience sampling study about the paradox of work]. *Zeitschrift für Arbeits und Organisationspsychologie 45*, 176–187.

Schimmack, U., Oishi, S., Diener, E., & Suh, E. (2000). Facets of affective experiences: A framework for investigations of trait affect. *Personality and Social Psychology Bulletin, 26*, 655–668.

Schmidt, J. (1995). *Preparing for the world of work: Knowledge and attitudes about work among Hispanic and Caucasian adolescents.* Paper presented at the annual meeting of the American Educational Research Association, San Francisco.

Schmidt, J. A. (2005). Religiosity, emotional well-being, and family processes in working families. In B. Schneider & L. J. Waite (Eds.), *Being together, working apart: Dual-career families and the work-life balance* (pp. 303–324). New York: Cambridge University Press.

Schmidt, J., Rich, G., & Makris, E. (2000). Images of work and play. In M. Csikszentmihalyi & Schneider B. (Eds.), *Becoming adult: How teenagers prepare for the world of work.* (pp. 67–94). New York: Basic Books.

Schmidt, J. A., Shernoff, D. J., & Csikszentmihalyi, M. (2006). Individual and situational factors related to the experience of flow in adolescence: A multilevel approach. In A. D. Ong & M. van Dulmen (Eds.), *Oxford handbook of methods in positive psychology.* New York: Oxford University Press.

Schneider, B., & Stevenson, D. (1999). *The ambitious generation: America's teenagers, motivated but directionless.* New Haven, CT: Yale University Press.

Schneider, B., & Waite, L. J. (Eds.) (2005). *Being together, working apart: Dual-career families and the work-life balance.* New York: Cambridge University Press.

Schor, J. (1991). *The overworked American.* New York: Basic Books.

Schwarz, N. (2000). Attitude measurement. In A. E. Kazdin (Ed.), *Encyclopedia of psychology* (Volume 1). New York: Oxford University Press.

Schwarz, N., Grayson, C. E., & Knauper, B. (1998). Formal features of rating scales and the interpretation of question meaning. *International Journal of Public Opinion Research, 10*, 177–183.

Schwarz, N., & Hippler, J. J. (1995). The numeric values of rating scales: A comparison of their impact in mail surveys and telephone interviews. *International Journal of Public Opinion Research, 7*, 72–74.

Schwartz, J. E., Neale, J., Marco, C., Shiffman, S. S., & Stone, A. A. (1999). Does trait coping exist? A momentary assessment approach to the evaluation of traits. *Journal of Personality and Social Psychology, 77*, 360–369.

Schwartz, S. H., & Bilsky, W. (1987). Toward a theory of the universal structure and content of values: Extensions and cross-cultural replications. *Journal of Personality and Social Psychology, 58*, 878–891.

Schweinle, A., & Turner, J. C. (2006). Striking the right balance: Students' motivational experiences and affect in upper elementary mathematics classes. *Journal of Educational Research, 99*(5), 271–293.

Scollon, C. N., Diener, E., Oishi, S., & Biswas-Diener, R. (2004). Emotions across cultures and methods. *Journal of Cross-Cultural Psychology, 35,* 304–326.

Scollon, C. N., Diener, E., Oishi, S., & Biswas-Diener, R. (2005). An experience sampling and cross-cultural investigation of the relation between pleasant and unpleasant affect. *Cognition and Emotion, 19,* 27–52.

Scollon, C. N., Kim-Prieto, C., & Diener, E. (2003). Experience sampling: Promises and pitfalls, strengths and weaknesses. *Journal of Happiness Studies, 4,* 5–34.

Scott, C., Ahadi, S. A., & Krug, S. E. (1990). *An experience sampling approach to the study of Principal Instructional Leadership II: A comparison of activities and beliefs as bases for understanding effective school leadership.* Project report. Urbana, IL: National Center for School Leadership.

Seligman, M. E. P., & Csikszentmihalyi, M. (2000). Positive psychology: An introduction. *American Psychologist, 55,* 5–14.

Sexton, H. R. (2005). Spending time at work and at home: What workers do, how they feel about it, and how these emotions affect family life. In B. Schneider & L. J. Waite (Eds.), *Being together working apart: Dual-career families and the work-life balance* (pp. 49–71). New York: Cambridge University Press.

Shaffer, J. A. (1968). *Philosophy of mind.* Englewood Cliffs, NJ: Prentice Hall.

Shapiro, Y. (1997). Consciousness according to James. *Theory and Psychology, 7,* 457–481.

Sherkat, D. E., & Ellison, C. G. (1999). Recent developments and current controversies in the sociology of religion. *American Review of Sociology, 25,* 363–394.

Shernoff, D. J. (2001). *The experience of student engagement in high school classrooms: A phenomenological perspective.* Doctoral dissertation, University of Chicago.

Shernoff, D. J., & Csikszentmihalyi, M. (2001). *The emotional and affective development of adolescents from differing socioeconomic communities.* Paper presented at the biennial meeting of the Society for Research in Child Development, Minneapolis.

Shernoff, D. J., Csikszentmihalyi, M., Schneider, B., & Steele-Shernoff, E. (2003). Student engagement in high school classrooms from the perspective of flow theory. *School Psychology Quarterly, 18,* 158–176.

Shernoff, D. J., Knauth, S., & Makris, E. (2000). The quality of classroom experiences. In M. Csikszentmihalyi & B. Schneider (Eds.), *Becoming adult: How teenagers prepare for the world of work* (pp. 142–164). New York: Basic Books.

Shernoff, D. J., Schmidt, J. A., & Rushi, P. J. (2006). Ethnicity, socioeconomic status and engagement in high school: Further evidence of an engagement-achievement paradox. Manuscript under review.

Shiffman, S. (2000). Real-time self-report of momentary states in the natural environment: Computerized ecological momentary assessment. In A. A. Stone, J. S. Turkkan, C. A. Bachrach, J. B. Jobe, H. S. Kurtzman, & V. S. Cain (Eds.),

The science of self-report: Implications for research and practice (pp. 276–293). Mahwah, NJ: Lawrence Erlbaum Associates.

Shiffman, S., Fischer, L. A., Paty, J. A., Gnys, M., Hickcox, M., & Kassel, J. D. (1994). Drinking and smoking: A field study of their association. *Annals of Behavioral Medicine, 16,* 203–209.

Shweder, R. A. (1991). *Thinking through cultures: Expeditions in cultural psychology.* Cambridge, MA: Harvard University Press.

Simonton, D. K. (1999). *Origins of genius.* Oxford, UK: Oxford University Press.

Singer, J. L. (1966). *Daydreaming: An introduction to the experimental study of inner experience.* New York: Random House.

Singer, J. L. (1973). *The child's world of make-believe.* New York: Academic Press.

Sinha, J. B. P., & Sinha, D. (1990). Role of social values in Indian organizations. *International Journal of Psychology, 25,* 705–714.

Sloboda, J. A., O'Neill, S. A., & Ivaldi, A. (2001). Functions of music in everyday life: An exploratory study using the Experience Sampling Method. *Musicae Scientiae, V,* 9–32.

Smith, J. A., Harré, R., & Van Langenhove, L. (1995). *Rethinking psychology.* London: Sage.

Smyth, J., Ockenfels, M. C., Porter, L., Kirschbaum, C., Hellhammer, D. H., & Stone, A. A. (1998). Stressors and mood measured on a momentary basis are associated with salivary cortisol secretion. *Psychoneuroendocrinology, 23,* 353–370.

Smyth, J., Wonderlich, S., Crosby, R., Miltenberger, R., Mitchell, J., & Rorty, M. (2001). The use of ecological momentary assessment approaches in eating disorder research. *International Journal of Eating Disorders, 30,* 83–95.

Snijders, T. & Bosker, R. (1999). *Multilevel analysis: An introduction to basic and advanced multilevel modeling.* London: Sage.

Snijders, T., Bosker, R., & Guldemond, H. (1999). *The Power analysis IN Two-level designs (PINT) software.* Retrieved from http://stat.gamma.rug.nl/multilevel.htm

Sorbi, M. J., Honkoop, P. C., & Godaert, G. L. (1996). A signal-contingent computer diary for the assessment of psychological precedents of the migraine attack. In J. Fahrenberg & M. Myrtek (Eds.), *Ambulatory assessment* (pp. 403–412). Seattle, WA: Hogrefe & Huber.

Steinberg, L. D., Brown, B. B., & Dornbusch, S. M. (1996). *Beyond the classroom: Why school reform has failed and what parents need to do.* New York: Simon & Schuster.

Steinberg, L., Dornbusch, S. M., & Brown, B. B. (1992). Ethnic differences in adolescent achievement: An ecological perspective. *American Psychologist, 47,* 723–729.

Steinberg, L., Fegley, S., & Dornbusch, S. M. (1993). Negative impact of part-time work on adolescent adjustment: Evidence from a longitudinal study. *Developmental Psychology, 29,* 171–180.

Steptoe, A. (2001). Ambulatory monitoring of blood pressure in daily life: A tool for investigating psychosocial processes. In J. Fahrenberg & M. Myrtek (Eds.), *Progress in ambulatory assessment: Computer-assisted psychological and psychophysiological methods in monitoring and field studies* (pp. 257–269). Seattle, WA: Hogrefe & Huber.

Stevenson, H. W., & Stigler, J. W. (1992). The learning gap: Why our schools are failing and what we can learn from Japanese and Chinese education. New York: Touchstone.

Stickgold, R., Malia, A., Fosse, J. A., & Hobson, J. A. (2000). Brain-mind states: I. longitudinal field study of sleep/wake factors influencing mentation report length. *Sleep: Journal of Sleep and Sleep Disorder Research 24*, 139–242.

Stigler, J. W., Shweder, R. A., & Herdt, G. (Eds.). (1990). *Cultural psychology: Essays on comparative human development.* New York: Cambridge University Press.

Stodolsky, S. S. (1988). *The subject matters: Classroom activity in math and social studies.* Chicago: University of Chicago Press.

Stone, A. A., Broderick, J. E., Porter, L. S., & Kaell, A. T. (1997). The experience of rheumatoid arthritis pain and fatigue: Examining momentary reports and correlates over one week. *Arthritis Care and Research, 10*, 185–193.

Stone, A. A., Schwartz, J. E., Neale, J. M., Shiffman, S., Marco, C. A., Hickcox, M., et al. (1998). A comparison of coping assessed by ecological momentary assessment and retrospective recall. *Journal of Personality and Social Psychology, 74*, 1670–1680.

Stone, A. A., & Shiffman, S. (1994). Ecological momentary assessment (EMA) in behavioral medicine. *Annals of Behavioral Medicine, 16*, 199–202.

Stone, A. A., Shiffman, S., Schwartz, J. E., Broderick, J. E., & Hufford, M. R. (2002). Patient non-compliance with paper diaries. *British Medical Journal, 324*, 1193–1194.

Sudman, S., & Bradburn, N. (1982). *Asking questions: A practical guide to questionnaire design.* San Francisco: Jossey-Bass.

Sue, S., & Okazaki, S. (1990). Asian-American education achievements: A phenomenon in search of an explanation. *American Psychologist, 45*, 913–920.

Super, C. M., & Harkness, S. (1986). The developmental niche: A conceptualization at the interface of child and culture. *International Journal of Behavioral Development, 9*, 545–569.

Swarr, A. E., & Richards, M. H. (1996). Longitudinal effects of adolescent girls' pubertal development, perceptions of pubertal timing, and parental relations on eating problems. *Developmental Psychology, 32*, 636–646.

Swendsen, J. D. (1997). Anxiety, depression, and their comorbidity: An experience sampling test of the helplessness-hopelessness theory. *Cognitive Therapy and Research, 21*, 97–114.

Swendsen, J. D. (1998). The helplessness-hopelessness theory and daily mood experience: An idiographic and cross-situational perspective. *Journal of Personality and Social Psychology, 74*, 1398–1408.

Swendsen, J. D., Tennen, H., Carney, M. A., Affleck, G., Willard, A., & Hromi, A. (2000). Mood and alcohol consumption: An experience sampling test of the self-medication hypothesis. *Journal of Abnormal Psychology, 109*, 198–204.

Taylor, S. E., & Gollwitzer, P. M. (1995). Effects of mindset on positive illusions. *Journal of Personality and Social Psychology, 69*, 213–226.

Teuchmann, K., Totterdell, P., & Parker, S. K. (1999). Rushed, unhappy, and drained: An experience sampling study of relationships between time pressure, perceived control, mood, and emotional exhaustion a group of accountants. *Journal of Occupational Health Psychology, 4,* 37–54.

Thompson, L., & Walker, A. J. (1989). Gender in families: Women and men in marriage, work, and parenthood. *Journal of Marriage and the Family, 51,* 845– 871.

Tononi, G., & Edelman, G. M. (1998). Consciousness and complexity. *Science, 282,* 1846–1851.

Tugade, M. M., & Feldman Barrett, L. (2002). *Correlates of positive emotional granularity.* Poster presented at the First International Positive Psychology Summit, Washington, DC.

Turner, J. C., Cox, K. E., DiCintio, M., Meyer, D. K., Logan, C., & Thomas, C. T. (1998). Creating contexts for involvement in mathematics. *Journal of Educational Psychology, 90,* 730–745.

Tzanetakis, R. (2002). *Flow-experience, the internet and its relationship to situation and personality.* Poster presented at the First International Positive Psychology Summit, Washington, DC.

Uekawa, K., Borman, K., & Lee, R. (2005). Student engagement in America's urban high school mathematics and science classrooms: Findings on social organization, race, and ethnicity. Unpublished manuscript.

U.S. Department of Labor. (2000). *Geographic profile of employment and unemployment, 1999.* Washington, DC: Bureau of Labor Statistics.

U.S. Department of Labor. (2003). *Geographic profile of employment and unemployment, 2001.* Bulletin 2556. Washington, DC: Bureau of Labor Statistics.

Valsiner, J., & Moelnaar, P. (2005). *International Journal of Idiographic Science.* Retrieved August 1, 2005, from http://www.valsiner.com/index.shtml

Vandell, D. L., Shernoff, D. J., Pierce, K. M., Bolt, D. M., Dadisman, K., & Brown, B. B. (2005). Activities, engagement, and emotion at after-school programs (and elsewhere). In H. Weiss, P. Little, & S. Bouffard (Eds.), *New directions for youth development: Conceptualizing participation in out-of-school time programs* (pp. 121–129). San Francisco: Jossey Bass.

Van Der Poel, E. G., & Delespaul, P. A. E. G. (1992). The applicability of ESM in personalized rehabilitation. In M. W. deVries (Ed.), *The experience of psychopathology: Investigating mental disorders in their natural settings* (pp. 290–303). New York: Cambridge University Press.

van Eck, M. M., & Nicolson, N. A. (1994). Perceived stress and salivary cortisol in daily life. *Annals of Behavioral Medicine, 16,* 221–227.

van Eck, M. M., Nicolson, N., & Berkhof, J. (1998). Effects of stressful daily events on mood states: Relationship to global perceived stress. *Journal of Personality and Social Psychology, 75,* 1572–1585.

Van Egeren, L. F., & Madarasmi, S. (1992). Blood pressure and behavior: Mood, activity and blood pressure in daily life. In M. W. deVries (Ed.), *The experience of psychopathology: Investigating mental disorders in their natural settings* (pp. 240–252). New York: Cambridge University Press.

Vendrig, A. A., & Lousberg, R. (1997). Within-person relationships among pain intensity, mood and physical activity in chronic pain: A naturalistic approach. *Pain, 73,* 71–76.

Verma, S. (1998, July). *Daily effects of academic stress on psychological states and family interactions of Indian adolescents.* Paper presented at the Meeting of the International Society for Behavioral Development, Berne, Switzerland.

Verma, S., & Larson, R. W. (1999). Are adolescents more emotional? A study of daily emotions of middle class Indian adolescents. *Psychology and Developing Societies, 11,* 179–194.

Verma, S., & Larson, R. W. (2001). Indian women's experience of household labour: Oppression or personal fulfillment. *The Indian Journal of Social Work, 62,* 46–66.

Vernon, P. E. (1982). *The abilities and achievements of Orientals in North America.* New York: Academic.

Voekl, J. E., & Ellis, G. D. (1998). Measuring flow experiences in daily life: An examination of the items used to measure challenge and skill. *Journal of Leisure Research, 30,* 380–390.

Voekl, J. E., & Mathieu, M. A. (1993). Differences between depressed and non-depressed residents of nursing homes on measures of daily activity involvement and affect. *Therapeutic Recreation Journal, 27,* 144–155.

Voekl, J. E., & Nicholson, L. A. (1992). Perceptions of daily life among residents of a long term care facility. *Activities, Adaptation & Aging, 16,* 99–114.

Waite, B. M., Claffey, R., & Hillbrand, M. (1998). Differences between volunteers and nonvolunteers in a high-demand self-recording study. *Psychological Reports, 83,* 199–210.

Walls, T. A., Jung, H., & Schwartz, J. E. (2006). Multilevel models for intensive longitudinal data. In T. A. Walls & J. L. Schafer (Eds.), *Models for intensive longitudinal data.* New York: Oxford University Press.

Walls, T. A., & Schafer, J. L. (2006). *Models for intensive longitudinal data.* New York: Oxford University Press.

Warr, P. (1987). *Work, unemployment and mental health.* Oxford, UK: Clarendon.

Wegner, K. E., Smyth, J. M., Crosby, R. D., Wittrock, D., Wonderlick, S. A., & Mitchell, J. E. (2002). An evaluation of the relationship between mood and binge eating in the natural environment using ecological momentary assessment. *International Journal of Eating Disorders, 32,* 352–361.

Weiss H. M., & Cropanzano, R. (1996). Affective events theory: A theoretical discussion of the structure, causes and consequences of affective experiences at work. *Research in Organizational Behavior, 8,* 1–74.

Weiss, H. M., Nicholas, J. P., & Daus, C. S. (1999). An examination of the joint effects of affective experiences and job beliefs on job satisfaction and variations in affective experiences over time. *Organizational Behavior and Human Decision Processes, 78,* 1–24.

Wells, A. (1985). *Variations in self-esteem in the daily life of mothers.* Doctoral dissertation, University of Chicago.

Wells, A. J. (1988). Self-esteem and optimal experience. In M. Csikszentmihalyi & I. S. Csikszentmihalyi (Eds.), *Optimal experience: Psychological studies of flow in consciousness* (pp. 327–341). New York: Cambridge University Press.

Whalen, C. K., Jamner, L. D., Henker, B., Delfino, R. J., & Lozano, J. M. (2002). The ADHD spectrum and everyday life: experience sampling of adolescent moods, activities, smoking, and drinking. *Child Development, 73,* 209–227.

Wheeler, L., & Reis, H. T. (1991). Self-recording of everyday life events: Origins, types, and uses. *Journal of Personality, 59,* 339–354.

Wierzbicka, A. (1986). Human emotions: Universal or culture specific? *American Anthropologist, 88,* 584–594.

Wierzbicka, A. (1994). Emotion, language, and cultural scripts. In S. Kitayama & H. R. Markus (Eds.), *Emotion and culture: Empirical studies of mutual influence* (pp. 133–196). Washington, DC: American Psychological Association.

Wilcox, W. B. (1998). Conservative Protestant childrearing: Authoritarian or authoritative? *American Sociological Review, 63,* 796–809.

Wilcox, W. B. (2002). Religion, convention, and paternal involvement. *Journal of Marriage and Family, 64,* 780–792.

Williams, K. J., Suls, J., Alliger, G. M., Learner, S. M., & Wan, C. K. (1991). Multiple role juggling and daily mood states in working mothers: An experience sampling study. *Journal of Applied Psychology, 76,* 664–674.

Wilson, E. O. (1975). *Sociobiology: The new synthesis.* Cambridge, MA: Bellknap.

Wilson, K. C., Hopkins, R., deVries, M. W., & Copeland, J. R. (1992). Research alliance and the limit of compliance: Experience sampling with the depressed elderly. In M. W. deVries (Ed.), *The experience of psychopathology: Investigating mental disorders in their natural settings* (pp. 339–346). New York: Cambridge University Press.

Won, H. J. (1989). *The daily experience of Korean high school adolescents.* Eugene: University of Oregon.

Wong, M. M. (2000). The relations among causality orientations, academic experience, academic performance, and academic commitment. *Personality and Social Psychology Bulletin, 26,* 315–326.

Wong, M. M., & Csikszentmihalyi, M. (1991). Affiliation motivation and daily experience: Some issues on gender differences. *Journal of Personality and Social Psychology, 60,* 154–164.

Wood, P., & Brown, D. (1994). The study of intraindividual differences by means of dynamic factor models: Rationale, implementation, and interpretation. *Psychological Bulletin, 116,* 166–186.

Yair, G. (2000). Educational battlefields in America: The tug-of-war over student's engagement with instruction. *Sociology of Education, 73,* 247–269.

Yarmey, D. (1979). *The psychology of eyewitness testimony.* New York: Free Press.

Zautra, A. J., Berkhof, J., & Nicolson, N. (2002). Changes in affect interrelations as a function of stressful events. *Cognition and Emotion, 16,* 309–318.

Zelinski, J. M., & Larsen, R. J. (2000). The distribution of basic emotions in everyday life: A state and trait perspective from experience sampling data. *Journal of Research in Personality, 34,* 178–197.

Zuzanek, J. (1999). *Experience sampling method: Current and potential research applications.* Paper presented at the Workshop on Time-use Measurement and Research, National Research Council, Washington, DC.

Zuzanek, J., & Mannell, R. (1993). Leisure behaviour and experiences as part of everyday life: The weekly rhythm. *Loisir et Sociaetae [Society and Leisure], 16,* 31–57.

Index

About the Authors

Joel M. Hektner is an associate professor in Child Development and Family Science at North Dakota State University. He holds a Ph.D. in Psychology: Human Development from the University of Chicago and an A.B. in psychology from Princeton University. Before arriving at NDSU, Hektner was a research scientist in child and adolescent psychiatry at the University of Minnesota. He has used ESM to study the developmental implications of longitudinal changes in adolescent experiences of flow. His research interests primarily involve family and peer factors that promote optimal development and evaluations of preventive interventions for antisocial behavior. He is presently working on strategies to strengthen positive peer culture among elementary and middle school children.

Jennifer A. Schmidt is Assistant Professor of Educational Psychology at Northern Illinois University. She earned her Ph.D. in Psychology: Human Development from the University of Chicago. Her current research focuses on resilience, motivation, and adolescent engagement in daily challenges. She has been conducting research involving ESM for more than 10 years. She is former Director of Research at the Alfred P. Sloan Center on Parents, Children, and Work at the University of Chicago where she directed an ESM study involving parents and children from 500 families across the United States. Her work to date has involved samples of children, adolescents, and adults. She has conducted ESM research within the context of families, elementary schools, middle schools, and high schools. She has trained national and international teams of researchers in ESM study design, administration, and analysis.

Mihaly Csikszentmihalyi is the Davidson Professor of Psychology at the Claremont Graduate University in California. He is the author of *Flow: The Psychology of Optimal Experience*, translated in 27 languages, as well as 15 other books and more than 230 scholarly articles. He is a fellow of the American Academy of Arts and Sciences, the American Academy of Education, the American Academy of Political and Social Sciences, among others; and the recipient of several honorary degrees. In 2005 he received the Gallup Prize for Research in Positive Psychology and the President's Award from the National Association for Gifted Children.